The
Compassionate
Christ

The Compassionate Christ

Reflections from the Gospel of Luke

WALTER RUSSELL BOWIE

ABINGDON PRESS • *New York* • *Nashville*

THE COMPASSIONATE CHRIST

Copyright © 1965 by Abingdon Press

Library of Congress Catalog Card Number: 65-13144

SET UP, PRINTED, AND BOUND BY THE
PARTHENON PRESS, AT NASHVILLE,
TENNESSEE, UNITED STATES OF AMERICA

To

JOHN EDMUND ROBERTS

Present-day beloved physician

Who both by his technical skill

And by his spirit brings healing

contents

introduction

This book has its source in the direct suggestion that comes from
a previous notable work. In 1940, William Temple, Archbishop
of York and afterward Archbishop of Canterbury, published his *Readings
in St. John's Gospel*. In the first paragraph of that work he wrote:

This book is not a systematic commentary or exposition; nor is it intended for
scholars or theologians—though whatever value it has for souls on pilgrimage
may be as real for them as for others. Again, it is not a series of devotional
meditations, though it contains some of these. It has no distinctive and consistent
character. But it is an attempt to share with any who read it what I find to be my
own thoughts as I read the profoundest of all writings.

For numberless Christians the Gospel of St. John has had the same supreme value which Archbishop Temple accorded to it. Among the four
Gospels it is the one which embodies the deepest and most developed reflection of the meaning of Christ. No one would question its limitless
significance. Yet no one would wish that it stood alone. Its own climactic
value rests upon the fact that the Christ whom it interprets is the Christ
whom the other three Gospels had already portrayed. They are earlier than
the Gospel of John, closer in time to the original events and to objective
recollections of them. The figure of Jesus moves in clearer outline against
the background of his world, and his transmitted words bring a more immediate echo of his voice. Therefore the so-called synoptic Gospels, Matthew
and Mark and Luke, have their imperishable value, which the particular greatness of the Fourth Gospel does not diminish. With their own
convincing power they answer the great desire which the Fourth Gospel
records as voiced by the men who came to one of the disciples and said
to him, "Sir, we would see Jesus."

And if among the three earlier Gospels—or indeed if among all four—
we had to choose one to read and dwell upon, which one would it be?
Different needs and different interests may lead to different answers, and
each would-be Christian can only give his own. The answer which this

book represents is obvious. For me the Gospel which makes Jesus, as Master and Lord and Christ and Savior, most vivid and beautiful and compelling is the Gospel of Luke. If that choice were only a personal idiosyncrasy, it would be of no account. But there may be many who are moved to that same conclusion, or if not to that conclusion categorically, yet certainly to the conviction that this Gospel—regardless of comparisons —has such richness in it that time and thought devoted to exploring it will be well spent. So as Archbishop Temple wrote his *Readings in St. John's Gospel,* here, by parallel at least in purpose, are readings and reflections from the Gospel of Luke, meant not for specialists but—to use the Archbishop's words—"for souls on pilgrimage," who look to the compassionate Christ.

As there is a pilgrimage for the soul, so too there must be a pilgrimage for the mind. The horizons of knowledge are continually expanding, and our perspectives must likewise be enlarged. Any reading of one of the Gospels must take into account the kind of questions—even if they be disturbing questions—raised by scholars such as Rudolf Bultmann with his declaration that the New Testament must be "demythologized"; or more lately by the Bishop of Woolwich, of the Church of England, in his *Honest to God.* The pilgrimage in quest of truth may not lead over smooth and easy roads, but the great trust of Christians is that it has been marked out by one who said, "I am the way."

chapter 1

WHO WROTE THIS GOSPEL, AND WHY?

Inasmuch as many have undertaken to compile a narrative of the things which have been accomplished among us, just as they were delivered to us by those who from the beginning were eyewitnesses and ministers of the word, it seemed good to me also, having followed all things closely for some time past, to write an orderly account for you, most excellent Theophilus, that you may know the truth concerning the things of which you have been informed.

(Luke 1:1-4.)

This third Gospel, written like a letter to the man called Theophilus, does not tell here at the beginning or anywhere else who wrote it. But ever since there has been a New Testament, it has been known as the Gospel of Luke. What are the reasons for that?

In the first place it is clear that the man who wrote this Gospel is the same man who wrote the book of Acts. That book also is addressed to Theophilus, and in the first sentence the author reminds Theophilus of what he had written to him before of "all that Jesus began to do and teach." So if we can name the writer of Acts, we can name the writer of this Gospel.

Now the book of Acts is mostly the story of the Apostle Paul, and parts of that story are written in the first person, as what "we" did. Therefore these sections, and inferentially the whole book, were the work of one of Paul's companions. Among his companions was a man named Luke. In his letter to Philemon, Paul adds the greeting of Luke as one of his "fellow workers." In the second letter to Timothy, which contains a message of Paul when he was a prisoner in Rome, it is written: "Luke alone is with me"; and in his letter to the Colossians Paul speaks of "Luke the beloved physician." Luke, then, may have been the particular companion of Paul who wrote Acts, and in that case was the writer of the Gospel also.

That is the most we could say if we had only the record as it stands in the printed New Testament. But the early church had knowledge of its own: knowledge which came from the word passed down from men who had lived in the time of Paul and knew what they were saying. Irenaeus, Bishop of Lyons in the second century, was reflecting that report when he wrote of the book of Acts and the Gospel as both being the work of Luke. And Clement of Alexandria and Tertullian in that same period took it as a matter of general knowledge that it was Luke who wrote the Gospel which now bears his name. Nor is there any other word from the first two centuries to contradict this confident tradition.

When one turns to the Gospel itself and reads what is written and the way in which it is written, it is plain *what sort* of man must be back of the story which is told with such sensitive compassion: a man who like Paul the evangelist realized that the mercy of Jesus reached out to Gentile as well as Jew; a man who reflected his Lord's tenderness toward all shamed and sorrowing sinners; a man concerned for the disadvantaged and the poor; a man who accorded dignity to women in a world that ordinarily gave dignity only to men. Such a man was the one whom the grateful Paul called "the beloved physician," whose name was Luke.

But when all is said and done, the fact of supreme importance is not the name of the writer of the Gospel but the nature of what is written. Other parts of the New Testament give us their portrayals of Jesus, but in this third Gospel there are reflections of him which are incomparable in their vividness and beauty. It is because of this Gospel that we can know the Jesus who looked with redeeming pity upon a sinful woman who knelt at his feet; the Jesus whose quick understanding marked the boastful Pharisee and the humbled Publican in the temple; the Jesus who told his parables of the Good Samaritan, the lost sheep, and the Prodigal Son; who went home with the despised Zacchaeus and stopped to answer the cry of blind Bartimaeus by the roadside; and who on the cross would say to the dying thief beside him, "Today you will be with me in Paradise." These are the imperishable pictures of Jesus which are due to this third Gospel. And Luke himself, if he might hear our modern discussion of whether or not it was he who wrote that Gospel, might say in substance what another great servant of the Master said. When William Carey, the heroic pioneer of foreign missions, was visited near the end of his life by Alexander Duff, and Duff was leaving, Carey called him back. "Mr. Duff," he said, "you have been speaking about Dr. Carey, Dr. Carey. When I am gone, say nothing about Dr. Carey; speak about Dr. Carey's *Saviour*." [1]

The "most excellent Theophilus" or in twentieth-century terms, "Your Excellency"—to whom Luke particularly addresses what he writes—was apparently a Roman official. One purpose which is evident throughout Luke's presentation is to show that the Christian church was not a politically subversive sect, as after the reign of Nero it was often accused of

---

[1] George Smith, *The Life of William Carey* (Philadelphia: The American Baptist Publishing Society, 1883), p. 303.

being. But Luke's purpose was wider and more affirmative than that. He wanted to make clear that in Jesus something had happened which was of crucial importance not only to the Jew but to the Roman and to all mankind. "The things which have been accomplished among us," says the Revised Standard Version more accurately and more significantly than the King James translation of "those things which are most surely believed." In Jesus something had been *done* among men and for men which had never been accomplished before. There had been prophets and teachers in earlier times who had been authentic witnesses to spiritual truth. Through them, in partial accents at least, the heavenly word had spoken. But in Jesus—as the Gospel of John would say—"the Word became flesh and dwelt among us." In the earthly life of Jesus the divine pattern for all redeemed existence was embodied, in his death the sacrificial love of God made supremely manifest, in his risen life the saving power of the Spirit set free to change the world. As Paul had said before, "If any one is in Christ, he is a new creation; the old has passed away, behold, the new has come."

How did Luke know that there was a new creation? Evidently he had not himself seen Jesus—just as we have not seen him. But he made it his business to learn from those who had known Jesus. Perhaps he had listened to some of the inner group whom everybody would reckon as the great disciples— Peter, James, and John—but he does not say so. Perhaps, instead, he had learned from little people whose names are not handed down in any history. Certainly that is the way it often is. The living Spirit of Jesus may be transmitted not only through those who are the conspicuous figures in the church, but through the unpretentious men and women who can tell in ordinary words—or not in any words at all, but just by being what they are—"This is what Jesus has meant to me."

THE HERITAGE FROM THE OLD TESTAMENT

In the days of Herod, king of Judea, there was a priest named Zechariah, of the division of Abijah; and he had a wife of the daughters of Aaron, and her name was Elizabeth. And they were both righteous before God, walking in all the commandments and ordinances of the Lord blameless. But they had no child, because Elizabeth was barren, and both were advanced in years. Now while he was serving as priest before God when his division was on duty, according to the custom of the priesthood, it fell to him by lot to enter the temple of the Lord and burn incense.

(Luke 1:5-9.)

It has been pointed out, and scholarly readers of the text will note for themselves, that beginning here at the fifth verse of the first chapter and

15

continuing through the second chapter, there is a difference in the style of the Lukan narrative. The opening four verses were in idiomatic Greek; then the form changes to one that echoes a Hebraistic manner of speech. Luke apparently is drawing on some special source, perhaps written and perhaps by way of spoken word, which had come to him from somewhere in the early church. He has said already that he had undertaken to gather together that which was "delivered" by those who had preceded him, and here was part of the tradition which a wondering devotion had handed on.

The account begins not with the story of the birth of Jesus which is presently to follow, but with the birth of John the Baptist. In him, for the first time in many centuries, a prophet had appeared in Israel. Once more, as in the great period that began with Elijah, the word of God was spoken to a generation with new, commanding power. The impression which John made upon many was immense. His disciples still clung together years after his death—as the reference to them in Acts 19:3 strikingly makes evident. It would not be surprising if there should have grown up among them what S. MacLean Gilmour in *The Interpreter's Bible* speaks of as "a collection of legends about John the Baptist that circulated independently of the Christian tradition." [2] In these legends the awesome admiration which men felt for him was reflected in the belief that divine promises heralded his coming.

Of Zechariah and Elizabeth his wife it is written that "they were both righteous before God, walking in all the commandments and ordinances of the Lord blameless," and in those words there is a reminder of the rich religious inheritance which already belonged to those to whom Jesus came. Back of what was to be the New Testament lay the long history of the Old Testament. God had not left himself without witness. Through patriarchs and prophets he had revealed his holy will, and sensitive souls in every generation had lifted their eyes to the guiding light. Moreover, their religious obedience was linked directly with actual life. True worship of God as he had been revealed to Israel could never be merely ceremonial. It was ethical through and through. And so must Christianity be, and the Christian church. The redemption which Jesus came to bring did not begin in a void. He built upon the legacy of Israel, with its moral law of the Ten Commandments as the structure of integrity in which and above which by God's grace the souls of men must grow. Therefore the Christian church, and men and women in it, will not be going beyond the Old Testament but falling short of it if religious profession ever forgets that the proof of its reality is in everyday behavior. If it could be said of Zechariah and

[2] (12 vols.; Nashville: Abingdon Press, 1952-57), VIII, 30.

Elizabeth that they were "walking in all the commandments and ordinances of the Lord blameless," who is there that can have excuse unless it is at least his heart's desire to try to do the same?

THE PROMISE CONCERNING JOHN

And the whole multitude of the people were praying outside at the hour of incense. And there appeared to him an angel of the Lord standing on the right side of the altar of incense. And Zechariah was troubled when he saw him, and fear fell upon him. But the angel said to him, "Do not be afraid, Zechariah, for your prayer is heard, and your wife Elizabeth will bear you a son, and you shall call his name John.
And you will have joy and gladness,
and many will rejoice at his birth;
for he will be great before the Lord,
and he shall drink no wine nor strong drink,
and he will be filled with the Holy Spirit,
even from his mother's womb.
And he will turn many of the sons of Israel to the Lord their God,
and he will go before him in the spirit and power of Elijah,
to turn the hearts of the fathers to the children,
and the disobedient to the wisdom of the just,
to make ready for the Lord a people prepared."
And Zechariah said to the angel, "How shall I know this? For I am an old man, and my wife is advanced in years." And the angel answered him, "I am Gabriel, who stand in the presence of God; and I was sent to speak to you, and to bring you this good news. And behold, you will be silent and unable to speak until the day that these things come to pass, because you did not believe my words, which will be fulfilled in their time." And the people were waiting for Zechariah, and they wondered at his delay in the temple. And when he came out, he could not speak to them, and they perceived that he had seen a vision in the temple; and he made signs to them and remained dumb. And when his time of service was ended, he went to his home.
After these days his wife Elizabeth conceived, and for five months she hid herself, saying, "Thus the Lord has done to me in the days when he looked on me, to take away my reproach among men." (Luke 1:10-25.)

The first promise to Zechariah concerning the son who would be given to him was that "many will rejoice at his birth" and that "he will be great before the Lord." Of course, there is always rejoicing somewhere when a child is born into the world: rejoicing for his parents and for their friends. But the sort of rejoicing which may be in the world at large is an uncertain matter. When John the son of Zechariah began his role as a prophet in the desert, there were many who were a long way from rejoicing. Would the Pharisees who came out from Jerusalem look joyful when John denounced them as a brood of vipers? They would not. Nor would Herod when he heard what John had to say about him. To these men and to others like them John was an offense and an intolerable nuisance. This uncouth disturber who had come from nowhere, with his rough figure and rude voice, this self-appointed preacher whom nobody of importance had commissioned—who was he that he should have the audacity to denounce the great ones of church and state?

But this John, the son of Zechariah, nevertheless should have a greatness beside which the tinsel importance of a Herod and the pretentious eminence of Pharisees and priests shriveled into nothing. His was the greatness of the man who had no need of human trappings, because he was clothed with the awful moral authority which belongs only to those who have yielded themselves to be the instruments of the will of God. In him men saw again the power which had been in Elijah, Amos, and Isaiah and would appear again in Athanasius and Augustine, in John Huss and Savonarola, in Martin Luther and John Wesley—the power of those who bring some flaming truth of God to kindle what otherwise might be the dry, dead fagots of a people's life. This sort of fire can be dangerous to vested interests and to jealous privileges. Consequently, there will be some in every place and time who will fear and resent the flame of the new moral challenge, and will rise in fierce antagonism against the one who brings it. But in the long run the worth of any generation will be measured by its willingness to recognize that the leader who comes with a prophetic word for church or state is the one who can make a people "great before the Lord."

There would be two influences that must unite in order for John to be made ready for his ministry: the deliberate human dedication, and the divine empowering. From far back in the history of Israel there had been the Nazarites—men vowed to sobriety and iron self-control—the shock troops, as it were, in any moral warfare. This son of Zechariah should have the inward strength which does not come by accident but is made possible through the self-discipline which can make a man despise indulgent softness, and give him mastery over circumstances because he has first been master of himself. Such a man, and only such a man, can be the adequate instrument for the Holy Spirit, and when the Holy Spirit takes possession of him, he can be irresistible.

THE ANNUNCIATION

In the sixth month the angel Gabriel was sent from God to a city of Galilee named Nazareth, to a virgin betrothed to a man whose name was Joseph, of the house of David; and the virgin's name was Mary.

(Luke 1:26-27.)

Who could ever begin to estimate all the loveliness to which the mind and imagination of the Christian centuries have been lifted by what Luke has here mirrored in his words? Before the eyes of Mary as she kneels, there floats the wide-winged glory of the angel Gabriel, bringing to earth the transfiguring atmosphere of heaven. In the art galleries of the world are the innumerable canvases on which the great artists—Fra Angelico, Perugino and the rest—have put into form and color the scene which Luke evokes. No two of these pictures are alike. Each man has painted the spiritual reality as his imagination saw it, against the background of his own time. Those who look at these portrayals are not disturbed by their differences, for the details of the pictures are only the instruments by which the artists tried to express, as best they could, that which went beyond complete expression. They were not bound by any rigid literalism. And in that fact they were repeating what had been true of the Gospel narrative itself.

For the first chapters of Luke's Gospel, as we have noted, are of a different fabric from most writings. It is as though the light of another world breaks through them, so that they become not a plodding chronicle but the reflection of an adoring wonder.

As men and women who had felt the ineffable greatness of Jesus talked to one another of him, their effort to find ways of speech that would be sufficient broke through all flat prose language and reached up—as the instinctive poetry of the soul will always do—for the shining descriptions which dramatize the truth. So the promise to Mary that she should bear a son becomes a proclamation from the lips of Gabriel descending straight from the presence of God. So the story of the birth of Jesus tells of a multitude of the heavenly host that filled the sky, of chanting heavenly voices heard by shepherds on the plains, and of a message spoken by one of the angels directly to these same astonished shepherds concerning the Savior whom they should find in Bethlehem. And within this framework of wonder in which the ways of God's supreme manifestation are seen as other than his familiar ways, Luke includes the indication that the birth of Jesus should be by unique miracle, of Mary with no husband.

Such then, in the divine mystery, may have been the fact. But it is true that in the long following chapters of Luke's Gospel Jesus appears to be thought and spoken of as Mary and Joseph's son. Certainly in the letters of Paul, written before the Gospels, and the part of the New Testament nearest in time to those who had known Jesus, there is no word that indicates a miraculous conception of him who to Paul was the saving Son of God. Neither is there any such indication or suggestion in Mark, the earliest of the Gospels, or in John, the latest. Of course, the lack of mention of something in any particular writing can never be affirmative evidence that the event in question did not occur. But this is unquestionably evident: that the message which the early church proclaimed of Jesus as Lord and Savior could be set forth in its transforming power without any reference to a miraculous conception or a virgin birth.

The recognition of Jesus as the One who supremely brought God near depended upon the impact which his living presence had upon those he touched, and not upon any speculation as to the manner of his birth.

The most precious significance of the incarnation is the faith that the nature of the unseen Father is actually revealed in the human life of him of whom the men who loved and followed him could say, "We have seen [him] with our eyes, . . . have looked upon and touched with our hands."

There were some in the first-century world whose intellectual notions rejected the belief that through the fully human there could be the complete communication of the divine. So in the early church there grew up the heresy called *Docetism*, which held that Christ was a divine being who only *seemed* to be human—a figure like the gods of Homer's *Iliad* who came down for a while from Olympus but in their real selves belonged always there and assumed human appearance only as a disguise. But the prevailing faith of the church went deeper. It believed that the love of God had answered the longing of human hearts in the one nearest way by which that love could be understood: in a man who entered fully into the lot of men, "made like his brethren in every respect" (Heb. 2:17), from birth to death. Therefore, the first emphasis in what became the creedal proclamation of the virgin birth was the remembrance that Christ was "born of woman" (Gal. 4:4). It was not the unlikeness of his birth, but its likeness to all our life, that was the first precious recognition. Then as men searched the Scriptures, they read the prophecy of Isaiah (7:14), which in the actual Hebrew reads: "Behold, a young woman shall conceive and bear a son, and shall call his name Immanuel," but which in the Septuagint translation had been rendered: "Behold, a virgin shall conceive and bear a son." It may have been from the accidental scriptural influence of the Septuagint change in wording that there rose the tradition of the virgin mother, with its corollaries of the miraculous birth.

One thing is sure: that all the lovely Gospel stories of the infancy should be dealt with not by clamorous argument, but with a reverent hush that feels the essential glory which is always there. Whether or not Jesus was born by what in biological process would be a special miracle, he himself was a miracle in that through him the reality of God did enter into the life of earth with a beauty and a power that was incomparable. Therefore, all the heavenly colors of Luke's narrative belong to its essential truth. The light in the sky above the plains of Bethlehem, the host of angels, the voice of Gabriel speaking the promise which the heart of Mary heard— all these are the symbols by which the spiritual facts are lifted in expression to the greatness which belongs to them.

THE FAVORED OF THE LORD

And he came to her and said, "Hail, O favored one, the Lord is with you!" But she was greatly troubled at the saying, and considered in her mind what sort of greeting this might be. And the angel said to her, "Do not be afraid, Mary, for you have found favor with God. And behold, you will conceive in your womb and bear a son, and you shall call his name Jesus."   (Luke I: 28-31.)

The favored of the Lord! What brighter promise for a life could there be than this? Surely the favor of God must mean that all the paths ahead will lead into sunlight. When Mary heard what was spoken to her, was not this the expectation that glowed in her heart?

But as time went on, the facts for her seemed strangely different. In a little while, when her strength was least, she would have to take a long and wearying journey from Nazareth in Galilee all the way to Bethlehem of Judea, not at her own choice but under compulsion of the Roman overlords who chose to have a census of the subject people. There in the unfamiliar town, which seemed so lonely and so far away, would come her hour of travail; and when her baby was delivered, there would be no place to lay him except in the straw of a manger where the oxen fed.

Presently she would take this little son of hers home to Nazareth and for the first years watch him with joy as he "increased in wisdom and stature, and in favor with God and man." But this would not last. As he grew up and went out on what he had seen to be his "Father's business," the greatness of his spirit would come into collision with the stubborn resistance of the world. She, his mother, would yearn to shield him from the dangers she knew he faced, but could not. She would see the neighbors and one-time friends there in their own Nazareth draw together in ugly resentment when he preached one day in the synagogue, and then rise up in mob fury to drive him out. She would go with his brothers on another day at Capernaum to try to persuade him to withdraw from public notice and come home. At last she would see him go up to Jerusalem where the danger for him would be deadliest; and following him there, she would have the final agony of standing on the stark hill outside the city and looking up at her son crucified, while the jeering crowd shouted, "He saved others; he cannot save himself."

Was that the favor of God? Was that what it meant to be blessed above all women?

Surely to the ordinary estimate it would not seem so. Yet the great truth lay deep and still beneath the seeming contradiction. To the soul of Mary there had come a divine gift which no shallow existence could ever bring. She was linked with the life of Jesus. As she had been part of all his sorrows, she would be part of his spiritual triumph too.

Not to slide through life smoothly, but to enter into it profoundly—*that* is to know the favor of God. The kind of happiness which we may instinctively desire is not the ultimate gift. Happiness may be only the glint of good weather on the surface of the stream; but joy is like the current of the river that flows on, whether under sunlight or shadows, toward its appointed junction with the sea. In every generation souls have learned that truth. They have been thankful at last for the divine compulsion which would not let them drift into the shallow pools and eddies where they might have been content to stay, but forced them instead into the rapids where the dangerous waters ran. They have known that life has been most enlarged when it has been most sorely tried by sorrows met steadfastly even when these seemed most shattering, by duties carried through even when there was most temptation to despair, by courage that was not broken when at the moment there seemed nothing but calamity. A great modern Christian, looking back on his own career, saw his whole experience as so marked by wounds and suffering that he could not bear to think of living through the years again. Even so, he could also write:

Yet year by year, aye, day by day, I felt the warrior joy of life and the conqueror's joy of getting the mastery. In my worst agony I could not pray to have it taken away, so utterly by degrees did I feel the power and light that came. And now all creation has opened out to me by living, and everything that I count happy I know to have come out of the self-mastery and training and truth which those years of anguish brought. My positive creed is an absolute, unfaltering certainty of life triumphant.[3]

He had learned, and others in every time may learn, that the noblest and most exalting prayer which can be offered for any soul is that which the Spanish philosopher Unamuno put into words: "May God deny you peace, but give you glory."

THE CALL AND THE ANSWER

And Mary said to the angel, "How can this be, since I have no husband?" And the angel said to her, . . . "With God nothing will be impossible."

[3] George R. Parkin, *Life and Letters of Edward Thring* (London: The Macmillan Company, 1910), p. 462.

And Mary said, "Behold I am the handmaid of the Lord; let it be to me according to your word." And the angel departed from her.

(Luke I: 34, 35a, 37, 38.)

When some heavenly summons comes to a human heart, there may be confused emotions. So it was with Mary; and many others in their own experience may know again what was true for her.

When the message which Luke puts upon the lips of Gabriel was brought to her, she was greatly troubled. In that first moment she was overwhelmed with awe. Nor was it strange that it should be so. When some sudden awareness of a divine command and a divine commission breaks upon any human conscience, there is an instant shrinking from its appalling greatness. The new suggestion of a responsibility that must be borne, a duty that must be done, a hard choice that leads to ends that still are in the dark—when these come, they do not bring elation. Instead they may strike us like a shock. With an unknown road ahead, the spirit stands dismayed; and like Moses, when the vision and the voice at the burning bush commanded him to carry the word of God to Pharaoh in Egypt, it stammers, "Who am I that I should go?"

To the troubled Mary came the angelic answer, "Be not afraid." That is the first reinforcement which is given to those who hesitate to respond to what may be a revelation. If it really brings a summons from on high, then we will not be left to our own resources. There will be the heavenly strength to undergird the human weakness.

Yet even then there may be hesitation. The spirit is ready to try to answer, but it may be caught in uncertainties as to what can be the way. The trembling may have passed away, but there is still the fog of wondering and doubt. "How can this be?" said Mary. The reason why many souls stop short of what might have been their experience of God is that they are halted by that "how?" But Mary made the right response which could be stronger than perplexity. "Let it be to me according to your word," she said. To trust what in our highest hour we have seen, to go forward the *next* step even when the one step is all we can discern—this is to find the way that will open out ahead. To be obedient to the best we know is to learn what at first we might not have dared believe—that with God nothing will be impossible.

THE ETERNAL KINGDOM

He will be great, and will be called the Son of the Most High;
and the Lord God will give to him the throne of his father David,

and he will reign over the house of Jacob for ever;
and of his kingdom there will be no end." (Luke 1:32-33.)

Read in the perspective of the centuries and against the background of the world that is, how incredible seem those words concerning the son of Mary, "Of his kingdom there will be no end." Where was his kingdom that day when he was crucified, with no crown except the bitter one which the mocking Roman soldiers had twisted out of thorns? And where is his kingdom now in an earth that seems forever cursed with hate and war, and possessed by the same evils that rejected Jesus once and would reject his spirit now? A kingdom that will have no end? When—the cynical might ask—did it ever have even a beginning? And who can show that the notion of it has any prevailing power?

It depends upon what we mean by power. "So you are a king!" laughed the incredulous and scornful Pilate. But Jesus answered, "My kingship is not of this world." It would not come by the world's means of violence or compulsion. It would not come, and will not come, for those who are looking only "for a king to slay their foes, and lift them high," though that is what the blind passions of many in Israel were wanting, and that is what a desire that calls itself religious may cry out for today. Why can we not expect that God will strike our adversaries down and set us up? If Christ is king, then there ought to be a smashing victory for "our Christian civilization" against "the godless Communists." So everything would be well with the world.

But the kingdom will not come by our devices. "My kingdom is not of this world," said Jesus. "For this I have come into the world, to bear witness to the truth." His kingdom therefore cannot be brought about by manipulation of our material forces. It is not something we can appropriate for our own ends. It is the kingdom of the truth that is forever above us, to judge us as individuals and as nations; and as *that* kingdom, it is sovereign and eternal. It presses in upon the conscience of mankind, and in the long run what is out of tune with it will perish, and only by its inspiration can life move on toward its fulfillment. Deep in their hearts men know that there can be no salvation for all of us or for any of us except in the measure that we are trying to learn to love God, and our neighbor as ourselves. In Christ, said the First Assembly of the World Council of Churches (in Amsterdam in 1948), "a reign of love and forgiveness has been inaugurated, molding the hearts and lives of men, calling them to find their common centre and desire in Him, and so to discover that real community for which mankind is longing." Such is the kingdom that waits to be made manifest upon the earth, and to the challenge of its moral and spiritual authority there will be no end.

ELIZABETH AND MARY

In those days Mary arose and went with haste into the hill country, to a city of Judah, and she entered the house of Zechariah and greeted Elizabeth. And when Elizabeth heard the greeting of Mary, the babe leaped in her womb; and Elizabeth was filled with the Holy Spirit and she exclaimed with a loud cry, "Blessed are you among women, and blessed is the fruit of your womb! And why is this granted me, that the mother of my Lord should come to me? For behold, when the voice of your greeting came to my ears, the babe in my womb leaped for joy. And blessed is she who believed that there would be a fulfillment of what was spoken to her from the Lord."   (Luke 1:39-45.)

In the illuminated manuscripts which have come down from the monasteries in the years before the invention of printing and the development of printed books, there are exquisite little representations, wrought in color and gold, of New Testament events as some devoted monk imagined them. In these early chapters of Luke's Gospel one may trace the reverent imaginations expressed not by the artist's brush but by the narrator's word. Back of what the Evangelist has written lie the earlier traditions as these came into being when the disciples talked together of what they heard and thought; and one of the influences which affected them was the relationship between their Christian fellowship and the still-existent group of those who had known only John the Baptist and counted themselves as belonging to him. It had come true, as the Fourth Gospel would express it, that John had decreased and Jesus had increased. So it was by way of natural process to suppose that what had become the fact must have been foreshadowed from the first. John's mother, and even the unborn child, would respond to the presence of the mother of Christ.

THE MAGNIFICAT

And Mary said, "My soul magnifies the Lord,
and my spirit rejoices in God my Savior,
for he has regarded the low estate of his handmaiden.
For behold, henceforth all generations will call me blessed;
for he who is mighty has done great things for me,
and holy is his name.
And his mercy is on those who fear him
from generation to generation.

25

> He has shown strength with his arm,
> he has scattered the proud in the imagination of their hearts,
> he has put down the mighty from their thrones,
> and exalted those of low degree;
> he has filled the hungry with good things,
> and the rich he has sent empty away.
> He has helped his servant Israel,
> in remembrance of his mercy,
> as he spoke to our fathers,
> to Abraham and to his posterity for ever."
> And Mary remained with her about three months, and returned to her
> home.   (Luke 1:46-56.)

Full of gentleness, like the spirit of Mary herself, are the words of this magnificat which Luke records as having come from Mary's lips. But through the gentleness there sounds also another note: a prophecy of the power which can come forth from that which seems to have no power. Mary, and the son who should be born of her, would have no greatness as the arrogant count greatness. Yet in what they represented, forces would be let loose that would be more formidable than all that kings and conquerors can command. The dynamic of pure goodness—like the seed which can thrust its way invincibly through hard ground and like the root of the tree which can split the rock—will prevail at last against whatever be the world's resistance. There is strength in the arm of God. "He has scattered the proud in the imagination of their hearts; he has put down the mighty from their thrones, and exalted those of low degree." Such was and is the tremendous meaning of the Christian message. It comes with joyous blessing to those whose hearts are humble. But it comes as a shattering challenge to all entrenched evil in stubborn hearts and in an unredeemed society—against the privilege of riches that has no concern for protection of the poor, against pride of social rank, against arrogance of race. In every time there are those who do not want that kind of judgment to fall on what they are and what they do. They think that the Christian church and Christian preachers may properly have something to say about the personal behavior of individuals, especially on Sundays; but for the crucial area of life and work that begins on Monday, with its economic, industrial, and political decisions, the sign is—"keep out." Let us have only "the pure gospel," they say; by which they mean a glow of disconnected piety which comes no nearer to their practical concerns than the flickering of the aurora on a far-off horizon of the earth. But to such men the real Gospel can come like fire focused through a burning glass, and then its impact upon all that is alien to it can be terrible.

Yet it does not have to be terrible. The gospel of God's saving mercy is meant to come to all life as a benediction. Thus it has come and can come in the measure in which any society responds to the goodness of God by a widening human compassion, and by a social concern which reflects God's purpose of enlargement of life for those of low estate.

A NEW NAME

> Now the time came for Elizabeth to be delivered, and she gave birth to a son. And her neighbors and kinsfolk heard that the Lord had shown great mercy to her, and they rejoiced with her. And on the eighth day they came to circumcise the child; and they would have named him Zechariah after his father, but his mother said, "Not so; he shall be called John." And they said to her, "None of your kindred is called by this name." And they made signs to his father, inquiring what he would have him called. And he asked for a writing tablet, and wrote, "His name is John." And they all marveled. And immediately his mouth was opened and his tongue loosed, and he spoke, blessing God. And fear came on all their neighbors. And all these things were talked about through all the hill country of Judea; and all who heard them laid them up in their hearts, saying, "What then will this child be?" For the hand of the Lord was with him. (Luke 1:57-66.)

The little son of Zechariah and Elizabeth is brought to the Temple for the circumcision rite which would make him a sharer in the covenant of Israel. As in our parallel of baptism the first question would be, "Name this child." His mother answered, "John." The kinsfolk and the neighbors were astonished. They had taken for granted that the child would be called Zechariah, after his father. What did Elizabeth mean by saying "John"? "None of your kindred is called by this name," they reminded her.

The idea and the words of the neighbors and kinsfolk are curiously familiar. Something has never been done, and therefore why do it now? Here is a family custom; why should anybody want to change it?

There is of course nothing to be blamed in that instinctive feeling. Instead, it is natural and understandable. Old customs and old ways, family names and family ways of speech, can have their positive value. Tradition and sentiment are woven into a sense of oneness, and affection and loyalty may be strengthened by associations which do not change.

But there may be a point where conservatism becomes too rigid. A family pattern, inflexibly imposed, can prevent the blossoming of the new possibilities beyond those which the preceding generation has embodied. The special gifts, the latent genius even, of a child may be frozen by the disapproval of elders who frown upon the unfamiliar interests as eccentric oddities. The assumption is that family names ought to be handed down,

27

and family occupations too. The son ought to want to carry on his father's business, and the daughter to take the same sort of place her mother has held in "the best society." But as for the girl who has no great taste for formal dinners, dances, bridge tables, and the rest, is tired of softness, and would like to give part of her life to real devotion where there is poverty, suffering, and pressing need; and as for the boy whose chief desire is not to increase a family fortune but to take up some poorly paid public service, or join the Peace Corps, or go to some difficult foreign mission field—"none of your kindred is called by this name."

It seemed right and expected that Zechariah's son should be called Zechariah. It might have seemed a happy thing also that he should grow up to be a priest in the unchanging ritual of the Temple, as his father was. But he was to be more than a priest in the conventional order. He was to be a prophet. He would bring to his generation the new flame of righteousness and truth which God had kindled in his soul. Therefore it was appropriate that he should have a new name, for in the great conception of Israel a name was not a mere label to mark one individual from another. It was instead the ultimate sign and symbol of what the person himself was meant to be. So in the Bible story there are the instances of names changed at some crucial moment of a man's life and destiny: Abram to Abraham, Jacob to Israel, Simon to Peter, Saul to Paul. What matters is the readiness to face and to accept enlarging facts of life, and to be the sort of person fit to meet them, even if "none of your kindred is called by this name."

THE LONG PERSPECTIVE

And his father Zechariah was filled with the Holy Spirit, and prophesied, saying,
"Blessed be the Lord God of Israel,
for he has visited and redeemed his people,
and has raised up a horn of salvation for us
in the house of his servant David,
as he spoke by the mouth of his holy prophets from of old,
that we should be saved from our enemies
and from the hand of all who hate us;
to perform the mercy promised to our fathers,
and to remember his holy covenant,
the oath which he swore to our father Abraham, to grant us
that we, being delivered from the hand of our enemies,
might serve him without fear,
in holiness and righteousness before him all the days of our life.

(Luke 1:67-75.)

In the thanksgiving which Zechariah lifts up to God, his gratitude for the son born to him is linked with a larger reference. His child's life should be not something self-concerned and unrelated, but instead a part of ongoing history, an inheritor and also an instrument of the timeless covenant. Back of him lay the past which gave significance to the present: the promise of God to Abraham, and the invincible faith in that promise and in its fulfillment which all the prophets had dared proclaim. Israel had often been in the hands of its enemies. It had been bruised and battered. But it could not be destroyed. And that same assurance surrounded every life that was caught up into the life of the whole people. God who had been sufficient for the fathers would enable the sons also to serve him without fear.

THE MESSENGER OF GOD

"And you, child, will be called the prophet of the Most High;
for you will go before the Lord to prepare his ways,
to give knowledge of salvation to his people
in the forgiveness of their sins,
through the tender mercy of our God,
when the day shall dawn upon us from on high
to give light to those who sit in darkness and in the shadow of death,
to guide our feet into the way of peace."   (Luke 1:76-79.)

Here in these beautiful final verses of the chanted prayer, which is familiar in Christian worship as the *Benedictus,* the faith of Zechariah moves from the mighty background of Israel's history to the immediate hope. This is what he trusts that John will be and do—and this is what every father may well pray that his own son in some measure at least shall become.

The prophet of the Most High! To be a spokesman for the righteousness of God: is not that what every man in his own place and way can aspire to, and thus be one of the influences which will lift up the moral standards of his time? There are too many influences which work toward what is low: in personal life, in business, in politics. A whole society may drift toward demoralization through lax ideas about gambling, liquor, sex relations. Many men and women have an uneasy, hidden consciousness that what they do when they follow the crowd will "soil and weaken the noblest energies of the spirit"—to use the words of the 1962 Encyclical, *Paenitentiam agere,* of Pope John XXIII. Those same men and women, down deep in their hearts, may be restless for the voice of someone who will call them back to their better selves. That voice will not have to come out of the wilderness, as John's voice did. It can come from someone in their own company who by the clean courage of what he stands for and what he says in the

29

conversation on the commuters' train, in the office, in the country club, or anywhere, reminds men of an integrity to which the best in them responds.

Such a person may not think of himself as being one who goes before the Lord to prepare his ways. He does not wear any startling dress, as John the Baptist did. He does not stand up and talk in public to a multitude. But nonetheless, by what the people around him get every day from the impact of his character he will be giving knowledge of salvation and waking an inward longing for the forgiveness of their sins.

Nor is it only in the area of personal morals that there is need for those who will go before the face of the Lord to prepare his ways. In these ominous times, with the dark menace of the hydrogen bomb threatening all humanity, it is only stark literalism to say that multitudes "sit in darkness" and "the shadow of death." No living person is wise enough to work out at this moment a method of international adjustment which can guide our feet into the way of peace. Immense efforts of intellect will be required to accomplish that. But back of intellect, to inspire and direct it, must be the deeper and more primal power of religious dedication. There is a kind of vision which belongs only to those who in public choice try in some real sense to be God's prophets, interpreters, and spokesmen of his long-range purposes. Only they can bring to our immense problems the ultimate wisdom of faith and hope and charity.

OUT OF THE SILENCES

> And the child grew and became strong in spirit, and he was in the wilderness till the day of his manifestation to Israel. (Luke 1:80.)

For John, the wilderness meant the solitary places where he could be alone to think the thoughts of God. Great new awarenesses are not likely to come to the man who is caught always in the clamor and confusion of the crowd. Those who are to be the prophets must be able to go apart sometimes into the silences where they can hear the inner voice that may be drowned out by the noise of tongues. That was true for Elijah and Amos, as it would be true also for John the Baptist; and when such men have come back from what seemed the empty spaces, they come as men clothed with irresistible authority because they have found God there.

What was evident in these instances remains a fact everywhere. If any life is to have the power of independently achieved conviction, it has got to have the chance somewhere, sometime, to be still and think. And we cannot be still unless there is some place of actual stillness. One of the dangers of our material development and our so-called progress is that we may actually swallow up the beauty of the earth by our cities and their sprawling suburbs. Unregulated greed for making money out of real estate may take possession more and more of all the open spaces, begrudge the cost for parks and playgrounds, and exploit and spoil even the great scenic glories of a nation. But there is an estate of the inner spirit which is more important and for our human destiny actually more real than "real estate," and *that* estate calls imperatively to be protected. Those leaders in any community who are determined that there yet shall be spaces where people can find trees, streams, and the wide sky are saving not only human bodies but also human souls. Walking in a parkland which blessedly continued to exist within less than a dozen miles from the heart of Washington, D. C., William O. Douglas, of the United States Supreme Court, stopped on some huge granite rocks that were warm in the sun. He wrote,

The din of the city, the roar of its traffic was behind me. . . . The schemes and machinations of the little men who possess the place seemed far away. I did not have to go far this winter morning to reach this wilderness of solitude and quiet. Only a few miles. "That's what the cities need," I found myself saying, "A wilderness at their back door, where a man can go and once more find harmony and peace in his inner being." [4]

[4] William O. Douglas, *My Wilderness: East to Katahdin* (Garden City: Doubleday & Company, 1961) p. 189.

31

chapter 2

THE STORY OF BETHLEHEM

It may well be believed that no other writing of equal length which has come from a human hand has meant so much to so many minds and hearts as this passage from the Gospel according to Luke. There is haunting beauty in the manner of its telling; there is astonishing dramatic contrast; and from it flows a spiritual significance which all our wondering worship cannot exhaust.

The beauty of it has stirred an instinctive poetry of response all down the Christian centuries. In Christmas carols and Christmas hymns men of many nations and in many languages, in translation or in their own new words, have repeated the immortal theme. "Good Christian Men Rejoice" comes from ancient Latin verses, sung in medieval Europe to a fourteenth-century German melody. To Isaac Watts of England are due the words, and to Handel the music, of "Joy to the World!" Charles Wesley wrote "Hark! the Herald Angels Sing," and the tune to which it is most often sung is adapted from Mendelssohn. The gift to Christian worship from the nineteenth century is that loveliest of modern Christian hymns, Phillips Brooks's "O Little Town of Bethlehem." What happened long ago in the far-off Judean town is made to seem so vivid that again it is real and near; and not only in the dark streets of little Bethlehem but also on the needy ways of our own place and time there shines again "the everlasting light."

But the beauty of its expression is of course not the most important fact in the Bethlehem story. There is, as has been noted, the drama of the immense historic contrast which is here expressed: between the power which to the world seemed imperishable and a new power which would rise and spread when the old sovereignty had crumbled into dust.

GREATER THAN THE EMPEROR'S DECREE

In those days a decree went out from Caesar Augustus that all the world should be enrolled. This was the first enrollment, when Quirinius was governor of Syria. And all went to be enrolled, each to his own city.
(Luke 2:1-3.)

A decree went out from Caesar Augustus. That is Luke's preface to the Bethlehem story. Who was Augustus? Born Gaius Octavius, he was the nephew of Julius Caesar, conqueror of new regions brought under the rule of Rome; and by Julius Caesar he was adopted to be that conqueror's son and heir. Not at once did he advance to power; for the great Julius, rousing the envy and fear of some in Rome because he seemed to "bestride the narrow world like a Colossus," was struck down by the daggers of Brutus and Cassius. After that assassination Octavius was for the instant in mortal peril. But he fought his way to mastery over enemies and rivals, Brutus, Cassius, and Mark Antony; and having gained at length unrivaled dominance, he was seated upon the imperial throne and given by the Roman senate the title of Augustus.

Under him Rome became, as no city had been before, the mistress of the Mediterranean world. The eagles which the legions carried were the symbols of an authority which extended from the island of Britain in the West, across the continent along the Rhine and Danube to Greece and on beyond the Aegean Sea into Asia, and across the Mediterranean to North Africa—a vast circle which included the richest provinces of the civilized earth.

Proconsuls and legates of the Roman rule reported to the emperor whatever events were important enough for him to notice, but it is safe to say that none reported to him that a man and woman had come from Galilee to Judea in obedience to the decree for taxing, and that in Bethlehem a baby had been born. What did it matter that there was one more among the population of a subject people?

Certainly it would appear that it would not matter for the future, any more than it mattered for that moment in Augustus' reign. Was not Rome the Eternal City and its imperial throne the symbol of a power which would last as long as time? Caesar Augustus in the world's capital; in the obscure Judean town a child named Jesus. What greater contrast could there be than that in estimating the forces which would affect the destinies of mankind?

Yet the empire of the Caesars would be invaded by barbarian tribes, its defenses broken, Rome itself possessed, its palaces and monuments reduced to ruins, and its immemorial greatness trampled into dust. The statues of Augustus set up for homage in the temples would be forgotten. And on the other hand, in Rome itself and in a world far vaster than Rome had ever known, there would arise churches and cathedrals in the name of the child born in Bethlehem. *That* is the vast reversal of what seemed to be important which emerges from the pages of Luke.

Also it is more than a drama of history. It is a revelation of what is longer than history and deeper than all material force. What Luke desired to write was not only history but gospel: the good news of an infinite reality which is greater than the shifting appearances of earth. It is the power of God and not our little pretentiousness which will speak the final word. A decree went out from Caesar Augustus; yes, but it is also written that "God sent forth his Son." (Gal. 4:4.) And the spirit which has come into the world in him is more lasting than the word and work of all the Caesars, for it brings the redeeming love that alone can get inside men's hearts and make them new. The child of Bethlehem was cradled in a stable and would die upon a cross; yet that was not the end but only the beginning. Because of Jesus faith and hope reach on to the infinite purpose which the love of God can ultimately accomplish for his human children, notwithstanding the long entail of ignorance and sin. In the diary of Anne Frank, the little Jewish girl whose family was hunted down by the Nazis in World War II, it was written, "Times will change . . . and these pitiless days will come to an end and the world will know again order, trust and peace." That better world has been and is a long time coming; but the ultimate promise of it is bound up with Jesus who is more enduring than the Caesars, and with the words in the book of Revelation: "The kingdom of the world has become the kingdom of our Lord and of his Christ."

THE HOUSE OF BREAD

> And Joseph also went up from Galilee, from the city of Nazareth, to Judea, to the city of David, which is called Bethlehem, because he was of the house and lineage of David, to be enrolled with Mary, his betrothed, who was with child. (Luke 2:4-5.)

Two different impulses in the thought of the early church linked the birth of Jesus with the city of David. There was, on the one hand, the desire which is instinctive in every people to reassert old pride and glory. David had been the king who, above all others, had brought to the kingdom of Israel glamor and at least a relative greatness among the nations of the time. Patriotism would seem to require that this sort of greatness might come again. But there was, on the other hand, at least the dawning recognition that greatness in the eyes of God must be of another kind. David was a king to whom men looked up; but more importantly, David was a man who looked up to God on high. What men remembered and attributed to him was not any boast about his power, but the psalm of contrition and of would-be consecration: "Create in me a clean heart, O God, and put a new and right spirit within me." What then would be the marks of the Christ when he should come? A clean heart and a perfect consecration: because of these he would have a kingliness beyond the kingliness of David.

There is long suggestion also in the name of Bethlehem, for that name meant the "house of bread." The origin of the name was in the simple fact that in Bethlehem people could get enough to eat. Much of Palestine was—and still is—a hard land for men who have to get their sustenance out of the ground. Jerusalem rises from its bare hills; to the south and east of it lie the stony wilderness of Tekoa, the stark slopes that fall away toward the Jordan River, the Dead Sea, and beyond, the desolate mountains of Midian. Still farther south are the hot sands of the Negeb, where any settled life could have only a precarious hold. But in the little area round Bethlehem wheat would grow, and figs and olives. And there were wells of water.

So Bethlehem, the house of bread, was linked with men's primal needs. To live at all, men must be fed; and the human struggle to win food enough is as old as the story of Adam and Eve driven out of the garden to dig the ground—with toil and sweat. For Jesus all these facts were real and near. He would not need to have someone tell him what existence meant for the great multitudes of the little people. He would grow up among them, in the small town, where no one had great possessions. He knew how much it meant just to be sure that there was food enough so that children would not go hungry. Therefore, he was never forgetful of men's physical necessities, nor did love of God ever mean to him a mystical absorption which would take him away from contact with the common human lot. He would teach his disciples to pray, "Give us this day our daily bread."

Wherever his spirit speaks in the present world it will speak again in terms that human beings can feel and understand. It will have no likeness to the smug religiosity which preaches to men as though their souls have no relation to their bodies. He knew how much of life has to be concerned with the ordinary routine things: the man sowing seed in the field, or building a house on right foundations; the woman leavening the flour or sewing a new piece on old clothes which the family might be too poor to throw away. Therefore, the Christian gospel in every time, if it is to be true to the spirit of Jesus, must have not only an individual but also a social message: challenging the injustices which put cruel handicaps on the poor and the weak, championing in economics and in politics the social responsibility which will help the disadvantaged, and making sure that all the people—and not only some of them—will live in a "house of bread."

But the suggestion in the name of Bethlehem of the richness which the love of God in Jesus can bring to men is not limited, of course, to the material bread. Life begins with its material needs, but it does not stop there. Men might have not only bread but luxuries besides and still be miserable. There is something within a man which all well-being of the body cannot satisfy. It is his awareness that he has a soul, which cries out for the spiritual food without which it is starved; for great thoughts and purposes that bring a strength which surpasses the energies of this earth. "Blessed are they who hunger and thirst for righteousness." *This* is the hunger which men need to pray that God will satisfy, and it was this hunger for which Jesus promised that he would be the bread of life.

THE CROWDED INN

> And while they were there, the time came for her to be delivered. And she gave birth to her firstborn son and wrapped him in swaddling cloths, and laid him in a manger, because there was no place for them in the inn. (Luke 2:6-7.)

In the words of Luke there is stark simplicity. There was no room for them in the inn. That is all the Gospel says. The bare fact is not elaborated or moralized upon. It is left just as it might have appeared to those whom the Evangelist imagined as having been there in Bethlehem when Mary and Joseph came: an insignificant event which made no particular difference to the miscellaneous crowd. At the end of the long, exhausting journey they needed shelter, and all the more acutely because the hour had almost come for childbirth. But who had any obligation to be concerned with that? Other people had their own interests. Since they had got to Bethlehem early, they had a right to expect the better lodging. And when they had found it, and these two from Nazareth, coming late, had found none, why should they be troubled? Let this Mary and Joseph shift as best they could.

There the whole matter might have been left, so far as the indifferent estimate of the moment regarded it. But the thought of all the Christian centuries since that time has turned back to the story of that crowded inn and has seen in it an everlasting meaning. It is more than a description of what happened once and long ago; it is a parallel of what happens again and again for human souls.

So far as the hurrying crowd that milled about the gates of Bethlehem could see, nothing was more important than pushing ahead for their own accommodations. That a child to be named Jesus might be born that night, and that his birth could have infinite significance, did not enter their imagination.

Of course it did not, we might say; and it is fantastic to suppose that actual people there in Bethlehem could have foreseen the full fact of Jesus and acted in the light of it. Yet, in relation to the story as it is told, it is not fantastic to think that some two or three might have had the human sensitiveness which could lead them closer than they knew to God. Suppose they had really looked at this gentle girl, who was so near the pangs of motherhood, and had said to one another, "Somehow we must make room for her," and had sheltered her when her travail came. Then their lives would have been linked with the life of Jesus, and all the years ahead might have been different in ways which at first they could not know.

If that is the way it might have been, so certainly that is the way it is. The heavenly opportunities come to us in visitations that have no conspicuous labels. As the people in Bethlehem had no idea that the child born unnoticed in their midst was destined to be the Christ, so we may not see that in some fact we might ignore, the spirit of Christ is seeking room within our souls. Into the midst of our hurry and preoccupation comes the wistful human need: the loneliness that cries out for understanding, the suffering that can be helped by someone standing by. But our attention is turned only toward ourselves, and so we do not see. Yet, "As you did it not to one of the least of these, you did it not to me." To lose the little chance for human compassion may be to lose the great chance of coming close to Christ.

So the scene of that first century may be reenacted in the same way. In us, as in the ancient town, there may be no room for the heavenly birth. Yet that need not be the fact. Instead of the crowded inn, full of our clamorous self-concern, there can be the open door of a more eager expectation. The warning of the past can inspire a better present.

> Far, far away is Bethlehem
> And years are long and dim,
> Since Mary held the holy Child
> And angels sang for Him.
> But still to hearts where love and faith
> Make room for Christ in them,
> He comes again, the Child from God,
> To find His Bethlehem.[1]

WHEN THE INFINITE BREAKS IN

And in that region there were shepherds out in the field, keeping watch over their flock by night. And an angel of the Lord appeared to them, and the glory of the Lord shone around them, and they were filled with

[1] "The Continuing Christ" by Walter Russell Bowie.

> fear. And the angel said to them, "Be not afraid; for behold, I bring you good news of a great joy which will come to all the people.
>
> (Luke 2:8-10.)

As one reads on in the poetry of Luke's portrayal, the unearthly happens. The dimensions of our universe expand, and over our small affairs there breaks the stupendous revelation of the infinite. At the beginning a man and woman at a painful journey's end, an undistinguished little town to which unwilling people come, anonymous shepherds tending their sheep at the close of what seemed another common day. Then comes "an angel of the Lord"—the symbol for Luke of the other world that overarches the seen and the familiar.

The glory of the Lord shone round about them. Then, the Gospel says, they were sore afraid. This is the way a sudden spiritual awareness may often result. We go about our humdrum ways preoccupied with our small concerns, forgetting that there is a world of higher fact to which we are accountable. Then in some breathless moment the unseen and the unthought-of breaks through into our stunned perception. A crisis comes in our affairs bringing demands which stagger us, but which we cannot deny. God, who has been a name off somewhere in the distance, becomes an inescapable reality. There is a voice of conscience we have to listen to, a duty that we have to do. Instead of the comfortable half-light in which we have been satisfied, we know now what life might be in the glory of the Lord. But we shrink from the awful possibilities of it, and we are afraid.

So the unexpected religious experience has often seemed. It seemed that way not only to the shepherds but to Moses at the burning bush, to Isaiah in the Temple, to Elijah, Amos, and Hosea. There can be moments when the revelation of some heavenly meaning, which a life is compelled to look at and to answer with a yes or no, becomes intolerable. It is no mere invention but the expression of a timeless fact which makes the leading character in the modern play *Susan and God,* by Rachel Crothers, cry out, "I wish I had never *heard* of God!"

But if that is the first emotion, for souls of any depth, it is not the final one. "Be not afraid," the angel said. The heavenly revelations awe, but they are not meant to overwhelm. They break through the contented surface of ourselves, but only that they may stir in us a deeper response than we had known was possible. The spiritual commands which once might have seemed only to be frightening become tidings of great joy.

THE EXALTATION OF THE HUMBLE

> For to you is born this day in the city of David a Savior, who is Christ the Lord."
>
> (Luke 2:11.)

To you is born. To whom? Not to the emperor in Rome, not to Herod in Jerusalem, not to priests and scribes, not to those who thought they knew enough and had enough already, but, in the Evangelist's conception, to shepherds in the field. He "has exalted those of low degree" was one of the realizations that Mary sang of in the Magnificat. And the beautiful fact all through the Christian centuries has been the reflection of God's light in the lives of little people. The saints have often come from the ranks of those whom the world's estimate of importance would have counted as the least.

Many a minister knows that he may learn more from his congregation, from the men, women, and little children who look up at him from the pews, than they may learn from what he says to them. In the biography of David Hummel Greer, afterwards a bishop, it is recorded that sometimes when he was trying to write a sermon and mind and spirit ran dry, he would leave his writing and go out to visit among the humblest people of his parish. When he did that, he would come back with his own spirit fortified and refreshed; for he would have seen again the uncomplaining patience of the poor, the limitless devotion of a mother to her sick child in some dark tenement room, the integrity of the shoemaker or the carpenter who seldom had the money that he needed for his family but would never try to make it by shortcuts and shoddy work.

Thus in every place, as well as on the fields of Bethlehem, it may be true that those who are to be the surest witnesses that the spirit of Christ is born into the world will be the simple-hearted, who do not have the kind of erudition that the theologians might suppose is needed. As Francis Greenwood Peabody has written in *Reminiscences of Present Day Saints*, it is well

to realize that, even within the circle of one's own experience or memory, there have been lives, some of them conspicuous and some obscure, which teach one what saintliness means. Much has been written also of late about sinners, great and small. . . . Is it not time to call attention to the dimensions and the dramatic interest of goodness, and to review the evidences, in literature or life, which justify faith in integrity and consecration?[2]

WHEN GOD COMES NEAR

> "And this will be a sign for you: you will find a babe wrapped in swaddling cloths and lying in a manger."   (Luke 2:12.)

According to the message which the shepherds heard, something immense was about to happen. God's redeeming purpose for the life of men would be fulfilled. "And this will be a sign for you."

[2] Francis Greenwood Peabody, *Reminiscences of Present Day Saints* (Boston: Houghton Mifflin Co., 1927), p. vii.

What was the sign? Some earth-shattering event? That is what the shepherds—or we, if we had been there in their place—might have supposed. A great overturn of the world's affairs would not seem to come about in silence and in some secluded corner, but rather at the world's center, with all the trumpets blowing. The crowning of a new emperor, the massing of armies, uprisings of whole peoples—any of these might seem to be a sign appropriate for a crucial change in the destinies of the earth. But it was no such proclamation that the shepherds heard. "This will be a sign for you: you will find a babe wrapped in swaddling cloths and lying in a manger."

Here one stands confronting the incredible paradox which lies at the heart of the Christian gospel. The greatest may be that which appears to be the least. The illimitable power of God may be hidden in something so little and commonplace that the world in general will ignore it as of no account. By the life that began in a stable all the life possible to men has been transfigured, because in that life of Jesus men for the first time could really see what God could mean to them.

From the beginning of human consciousness there had been some sort of awareness of God. Human beings had bowed down before the awful facts of a universe they could not control: the darkness of night, the cold of winter, wind and fire, thunderstorm and earthquake; and in their worship they groped toward the God, or gods, they thought must be somewhere there in the sky. If those gods could be made favorable, then at least existence would be more secure.

The religion of Israel of course was deeper than that. Not only in the consciousness of physical needs, but in the moral conscience that was concerned with good and evil, men longed for God, and their faith was that God had made a covenant with his people; and because he was on his throne in heaven, righteousness would at last prevail. The single individual might seem sometimes as dust and ashes before the dreadful sovereignty that spoke—as it did to Job—out of the whirlwind and humbled the human littleness that dared contend against the Almighty. But still there was the unquenchable longing of the human heart for a surer sense that the high God really cared, and a far-off hope that somehow there might be one "between us, who might lay his hand upon us both" (Job 9:33).

It was this longing that was answered in the incarnation, when "the Word became flesh and dwelt among us." Theology puts the truth into that one majestic word with its long Latin syllables, the "incarnation"; and to many it may have an abstract sound which does not speak to their instinctive understanding. But what the incarnation means is a thrilling fact to which the human mind and heart responds. God did come near in

Jesus. Jesus, growing up in the home in Nazareth, sharing the ordinary duties which men and women had to carry out, talking to fishermen by the Lake of Galilee and making them his companions, was part of their world; and yet through him their world was lifted up to touch another one. He talked of God whom they had known by name, but now through him God became an immediate reality. So this was what the divine redemption meant: not some cataclysmic happening in the imagined future, but what was happening to their own lives here and now when Jesus touched them! God's self was revealed not most in the laws of Moses, but in the man of Nazareth—in Jesus' blazing rebuke to all meanness and hypocrisy, his great encouragement to every little struggling goodness, and his outreaching and undiscouraged mercy!

In the light of the incarnation, therefore, all life must have its values measured and set right. " 'I come in the little things,' saith the Lord." So he may come to us—not in our large, pretentious projects, but through daily attempted obedience to the spirit of Christ. Even in these small beginnings of obedience there can be the heavenly power that was incarnate—even though the world's eyes could not see it—in the baby wrapped in swaddling cloths and lying in a manger.

PEACE THROUGH THE GLORY OF GOD

And suddenly there was with the angel a multitude of the heavenly host praising God and saying,
"Glory to God in the highest,
and on earth peace among men with whom he is pleased!"
(Luke 2:13-14.)

The proclamation of the angel is in the right order of importance. To lift up heart and mind to God and know his glory comes first. Well-being for our human life comes after that—not the other way round.

Yet there is always the temptation to take the other way: our own devices first, thought of God later. Our own ideas of what we need and how to get it seem so near and natural that the impulse is to follow them. "Peace" is a pleasant word to contemplate, and we can think of it in very pleasant terms. It may seem synonymous with being undisturbed: no inconvenient demands upon our conscience, no interference with our plans by other people, to do each day only what we should like to do, to take things easy everywhere, to yawn and settle down—that would make existence peaceful, wouldn't it? And what could be more desirable than that?

Actually many men and women do cast their eyes about for that kind of imagined peace. They suppose they will find it if they can get away from troublesome relationships. A misunderstanding has arisen with someone who used to be a friend; it is too much trouble and rubs our pride the wrong way to look at the full truth and see our own fault that ought to be corrected. It is simpler to let the friendship go. If there is any disturbing inner consciousness that we may be wrong, forget it. Even in relationships which are deepest, the same may happen. Members of a family quarrel, and each one thinks that peace can be made only on his or her own terms. Friction grows between a husband and a wife. "Why should I go on denying my own personality in deference to some rigid notion of marriage and what marriage ought to be?" this one and that one ask. "Divorce will settle it. Then I can live my own life again and do as I please. And what could be better than that?"

Whoever follows this line of thinking is on a dead-end road. The only open roads are the great roads which men and women follow because on them God is glorified. These are not the easy roads They lead on long distances and over mountains. But they go somewhere, and those who take them will have the disciplined strength which is never made known to the flabby self-indulgence which walks only on the low levels. It is a law of life that not until a man has done his best can he really have serenity and steadiness within. Deep in every one of us there is something indestructible which knows that only when we are in tune with the purposes of God can life fall into place and find fulfillment. "Thou hast made us for thyself, and our hearts are restless till they rest in thee." [3] To keep on facing the hard duty because at the moment that is the one right thing to do, to take care for our own faithfulness and not to be reckoning up someone else's faults, to do this because we have been mindful of the greatness of God which can come to us as glory—this is to have life centered where it is secure.

Such is true concerning our individual selves. We can have peace of mind and spirit when what we are trying to do gets past distracted impulse and finds its unity in a ruling purpose to glorify God. But what about the wider life of peoples and nations? Can a promised "peace on earth" in this vast relationship seem anything but ironic mockery in a century which has been shaken by two world wars and lies under the monstrous shadow of the atomic bomb?

Certain it is that there can be no lasting peace for men who imagine they can get peace by balance of terror and by being ready to make more hideous wars. Neither will any peace be won by the well-meant but pagan patriotism which has no loyalty more ultimate than "my country, right or wrong." If the heavenly promise is to be brought down to earth, it can

[3] St. Augustine in his *Confessions*.

come only to men whose spirit is big enough to want it and to welcome it. And by God's grace that spirit could be born: in a new type of leadership in high places and among innumerable little people who together shape public opinion and give it final power. Its mark will be concern for human beings whatever be their race or nation—just because they also belong to God—human beings with the same instinctive hungers that we have and the same instinctive hopes for themselves and for their children. That sort of goodwill can inspire and fortify the patient effort needed to find the road that leads, past all discouragements, to the glory of God in a world at peace.

THE POWER OF WONDER

> When the angels went away from them into heaven, the shepherds said to one another, "Let us go over to Bethlehem and see this thing that has happened, which the Lord has made known to us." And they went with haste, and found Mary and Joseph, and the babe lying in a manger. And when they saw it they made known the saying which had been told them concerning this child; and all who heard it wondered at what the shepherds told them.   (Luke 2:15-18.)

Let us go to Bethlehem and see. Such was the natural response of the shepherds to the revelation which had been given them. It is essentially the response which all souls must make. Any spiritual experience which comes to us may have its final moment when the light has faded out of the sky and the angels are "gone away into heaven." Then the need is not to stand looking into the empty spaces, but to remember and act upon what in the great moment we were told—to go and see whether some new gift from God is born for us, and whether we ourselves may find a Savior who is Christ the Lord.

But when the shepherds had gone to Bethlehem, what did they think then? It might have been hard for them to accept the fact that what they had been told was all there was. A little child wrapped in swaddling cloths and lying in a manger: was that enough to fulfill a promise that came in the name of God? No sign of greatness anywhere. Nothing that looked much different from the ordinary realities of their earth.

When they recited what had happened to them in the fields of Bethlehem, "all who heard it wondered." To wonder may mean one of two opposite things. It may be the voicing of a doubt, as when we say of something told to us, which seems to stretch the limits of the probable, "Now, I wonder about that." Or it may mean the great receptiveness of a reverent awe. Something has happened for our spirits which at its moment brings an overwhelming certainty. We cannot explain it clearly. We do not know how it can be reconciled with the circumstances of our familiar world. But we do know that suddenly it gives the whole meaning of life a new dimension. To stand amazed before that—but to believe in it and live in the light of it—that is creative wonder.

Existence shrivels when it loses the capacity for that kind of wondering. The shepherds of the Gospel story could not have foreseen how Mary's child could ever become more influential than all the kings of earth, and people in Bethlehem who listened to them might have thought that all they told of open skies and angel voices was only so much nonsense. Thus people in every time may think, if they grow deaf and blind to any voice or vision that lies outside the little circle of what they call practical reality. In their pride of trying to be hardheaded they become empty-hearted, with no warm expectations anymore.

Meanwhile, there is the other possibility. There comes to us a witness such as that which was expressed and symbolized in the immortal poetry of Luke's story of the shepherds and angels. Someone has made us aware that into his life or hers the inspiration from a higher world has actually broken through. Something that we have read, some chance word heard, some intuition waking in our conscience, startles us into recognition of the reality of God. "Go to Bethlehem and see," the haunting intuition says. See if in what you have allowed to be the littleness of your life a power of Christ which you have never believed in is ready to be born. Then all that once may have seemed to be only cheap and common can become illimitably wonderful.

WHEN THOUGHT IS DEEP

But Mary kept all these things, pondering them in her heart.
(Luke 2:19.)

Here in the Gospel description there is a word not very frequently heard in general conversation—and perhaps not often reflected in fact. As Mary, the mother, listened to the awed words of the shepherds as they told the promises which they said had come from heaven, she pondered them in her heart. To ponder is "to weigh in the mind; deliberate upon deeply and continuously." Who can say that his thinking is generally like that? Instead, what we call thinking may be only a fleeting succession of momentary ideas, with none of them held long enough in mind to be significant. If we stop to see what has been registered, we discover that it may have no more meaning than the film of a moving picture camera which has been pointed indiscriminately here and there. The whole result is trivial.

But to ponder is something else; and as Luke has expressed it in one lovely phrase, it is something more than is suggested by the definition in the dictionary. Mary pondered in her heart. That is to say, her profound emotions, as well as her mental understanding, were weighing what the shepherds said.

If that were true of all parents, the earth would be a better place. Every child born into the world has its potential sacredness; and somehow and sometime to every parent, even to the ignorant or the careless, there may come a glimmering consciousness of responsible parental duty. The roughest man and woman will want their child to have a decent chance. Most parents of course will want more than that. They would like to have their child amount to something when he grows up. He must be one of whom they can be proud. If they searched about for a proper pious phrase to express what they think they want, they might say that they would like for him to be in favor with God and man.

Yet the trouble is that it may be only the human favor that they are thoroughly concerned with. Oh, yes—they may tell themselves—they ought to be grateful to God, and the child ought to have some religion. But those ideas have not gone deep. What too often actually happens is that they let the child be shaped—because they are shaped themselves—by shifting impulses which fit in with everything that is most easygoing.

In 1962 the Archdeacon of Chesterfield in England issued a "handy guide" concerning the bringing up of children which hit so close to truth in the sardonic twist of its advice that it was caught up in the newspapers and spread abroad. This is part of what he said:

Begin from infancy to give the child everything he wants. In this way he will grow up to believe that the world owes him a living. . . .

Never give him any spiritual training. Wait until he is twenty-one, and then let him decide for himself.

Avoid the use of the word "wrong." It may develop a guilt complex. This will condition him to believe later when he is arrested for stealing a car that society is against him and he is being persecuted. . . .

Give the child all the spending money he wants. Never let him earn his own. Why should he have things as tough as you had them?

Satisfy his every craving for food, drink and comfort. See that every desire is gratified. Denial may lead to harmful frustration.

Take his part against the neighbors, teachers and policemen. They are all prejudiced against your child.

When he gets into real trouble, apologize for yourself by saying, "I never could do anything with him."

Prepare for a life of grief—You will have it.

The title he gave to his handy guide was "How to Turn Your Child into a Crook." That is what sometimes does happen; but actual delinquency is only the tragic fringe of a wider fact. Most children from most homes will not be delinquents. But the pity is that so many will fail to be all that they might have been, for the reason that fathers and mothers have not weighed in their minds and hearts the relative worth of what their child is getting—and might get—from the sort of life they give him. The cheap accomplishments of a shallow crowd, shortcuts to supposed popularity, irresolute standards about anything—these are what he is accepting. He will measure up to conventional expectations. But for this boy, or for this girl, life may become a thing only of shreds and patches, with no steady purpose and no sense of divine accountability running through it like a golden thread. Outwardly they may be pleasant and polite. But inwardly, where clear ideals and steady purpose might have been, there is only emptiness.

ON THE ROAD BACK

And the shepherds returned, glorifying and praising God for all they had heard and seen, as it had been told them. (Luke 2:20.)

All life has its alternations. It goes up to heights of intense experience, but then it comes down again to the common roads. So it was with the shepherds. They had had their hour of amazement when the very gates of heaven seemed to open in what had been the familiar sky. Then they had gone to the stable in Bethlehem and seen the light on Mary's face as she looked at the Holy Child. But now they had to return to ordinary living, in the old surroundings which seemed no different from what they had been before.

Did the shepherds begin to doubt then if anything extraordinary had really happened? That vision in the sky, those angelic voices—were they anything more than dreams that men see in their sleep? And what they had found in Bethlehem, now that they had a chance to think about it, might not be very wonderful after all.

So our imagination can picture what might have been the sequel to the Bethlehem story, because it would be parallel to what is sometimes true for us. We have our times when the spiritual world has suddenly seemed near. We could not describe it in such dramatic terms as Luke describes the experience of the shepherds. We have not had any vision of angels or open skies. But nevertheless we have had a new consciousness of God, a feeling surer than words with which to describe it, that there is a light which can break in upon our everyday existence and give it glory. We have known that feeling perhaps in the glow of a Christmas morning. We have known it at other moments when something melted our emotions: an unexpected word of confidence spoken to us in some crisis that made the heart leap up in gratitude, the trustfulness in the eyes of a little child. Or in the midst of circumstances which seemed mostly commonplace and mean, we have encountered some superb example of courage and devotion and seen what a human soul can rise to—and then the depths within us cry, *this* is the way life is meant to be! But tomorrow? Tomorrow we may not think so. The light has faded, and emotions have died down. We are immersed again in small preoccupations over which the dust of our materialism drifts. It is not that we want to disbelieve in God. It is simply that in the world we have to deal with he seems to disappear. There was the hour when like the shepherds we heard the heavenly message of a newness in Christ actually at hand for us. But now we are not moving toward the Bethlehem of a spiritual awareness. We are on the road back.

That might be the end, and sometimes it is the end. The pathos of many lives is that they have lost their first beliefs; the idealism they once had is left behind.

But the narrative in the Gospel has a more beautiful climax. The shepherds returned. They, like the rest of us, had to come back to the old surroundings. They could not stay indefinitely within the circle of the heavenly glow. The special experience had to come to its end. But what then? They returned, *glorifying and praising God* for all that they *had* seen and heard.

So it is meant to be for all men and women in what are bound to be the ups and downs of the spiritual life. The influence of the high moments need never come to an end. The particular emotion may seem to pass, but it can become the hidden energy of a steady faithfulness. Never mind, then, if the consciousness of God is not always at its height. Remember the times when it was. Hold on to the certainties which have come home to us when goodness, truth, and the promise of Christ have been most radiant. Then, no matter on what routine road we go, we can be praising God for all that we *have* seen and heard.

RELIGIOUS INHERITANCE

And at the end of eight days, when he was circumcised, he was called Jesus, the name given by the angel before he was conceived in the womb.
(Luke 2:21.)

At the end of eight days he was circumcised. Thus was Jesus linked with the people and the promise which had come down from Abraham. It is an irony of history that among those who call themselves Christians there should have grown up a thing so perverse as anti-semitism. Yet it has not only grown up; a pseudo scholarship has tried to justify it. Early in the twentieth century Houston Stewart Chamberlain and some other writers elaborated a double notion: that the Jews have been and are a warped and inferior breed, and that Jesus was an Aryan, not a Jew. Thus a cloak of rationalization would be thrown around an ancient evil. Anti-semitism itself, as distinguished from particular rationalizations of it, is no recent fact. Its beginnings can be traced back almost to the period of the Gospels, when the new Christian fellowship began to be separated from the jealous exclusiveness of orthodox Israel, and when Christians, especially among the Gentile converts, began to identify all Judaism with Jews like Caiaphas and other priests who for their own reasons had brought Jesus to the cross. So it could come about that ignorance and passion would presently begin to think of all Jews only as "the Christ-killers," and to stain the history of medieval Europe with cruel and relentless persecution. It might have seemed that this particular evil had reached its depths in those earlier centuries, but the tragic fact is that the world has waited until this modern time to know what anti-semitism can produce. For *this* is what it has produced: the demonic viciousness of Naziism, the gas chambers in the extermination camps of Dachau and Auschwitz and Buchenwald, the murder of six million European Jews. And although the malignity of anti-semitism reached its extreme in Nazi Germany, the infection of it was not buried in the ruins of the Third Reich. The germs of it spread, hidden at first but virulent—as the Black Death used to spread—to other lands. It broke out in England in Mosley and his Fascists. It has been exploited in the United States by demagogues who pretend to turn darkness into light when they foment anti-semitism and blasphemously call their hatemongering a "Christian crusade"!

All this is possible in Christian lands only because a great fact has been forgot or twisted into impudent denial. It is the fact that Christians have an everlasting bond of blood and brotherhood with Jews, because it was Judaism that gave us Jesus. Notwithstanding the nonsense of Houston Chamberlain and his ilk, Jesus was born of a Jewish mother. He was taken to the Temple, as the Gospel of Luke makes plain, to be circumcised. He was taught in a synagogue school. He went up to Jerusalem as a boy of twelve for his first Passover. And, as may be read in a later chapter in Luke's Gospel, when he went into the synagogue in Nazareth to the service on the sabbath day, it was "as his custom was."

No Christian disciple then, unless for him the truth has been completely outraged, can despise the inheritance he has received from Israel. It was this people that through the centuries had most passionately sought for God; this people whose soul could be expressed in the cry of the psalmist, "As a hart longs for flowing streams, so longs my soul for thee, O God"; this people that produced the prophets, with their proclamation of a Redeemer who would come to men. All this lay back of Jesus, and the immensity of his appeal was in the fact that when he spoke to human souls, he spoke to longings deep in them which the whole history of Israel had created.

Jesus went beyond Judaism. This is so obvious that it hardly needs to be put into words. He brought in himself his own incomparable revelation of the Father. But no one who knew him could forget that he had said: "Think not that I have come to abolish the law and the prophets; I have come not to abolish them but to fulfil them." All that was deep and true in the Old Testament was enduring foundation on which the new covenant should be built. If that was a fact for Jesus, it must be a fact for the church that bears his name. Instead of anti-semitism there needs to be the reverent humility which will repossess the moral and spiritual convictions of Judaism which were the heritage of Jesus.

THE RIGHTEOUS AND DEVOUT

> And when the time came for their purification according to the law of Moses, they brought him up to Jerusalem to present him to the Lord (as it is written in the law of the Lord, "Every male that opens the womb shall be called holy to the Lord") and to offer a sacrifice according to what is said in the law of the Lord, "a pair of turtledoves, or two young pigeons." Now there was a man in Jerusalem, whose name was Simeon, and this man was righteous and devout, looking for the consolation of Israel, and the Holy Spirit was upon him.
>
> (Luke 2:22-25.)

In the words which introduce and describe Simeon one may be aware again of the richness of religious devotion which belonged to the Judaic heritage. He was a man "righteous and devout," and righteous because devout. In Judaism at its best there could be no arrogant assumption of moral self-sufficiency. All human character and conduct stood in the light of the High and Holy One, and only by his grace could men be lifted up to righteousness.

It is said of Simeon also that he was looking for the consolation of Israel —an ancient phrase which meant that he was looking for the fulfillment of Jewish messianic hopes. In this fact too, as in his personal devoutness, Simeon reflected one of the qualities which had made Judaism spiritually great. It was the recognition always that the life of the individual was

49

wrapped up with the life of the whole people and that faith, hope, and prayer must have to do with a corporate redemption. If this recognition were put into modern terms, it would mean that devotion to God must enter into and be expressed in a man's relationship to his country, and that he will be continually desiring for his country not some mean success but the working out of God's redeeming purpose in its life.

THE NUNC DIMITTIS

And it had been revealed to him by the Holy Spirit that he should not see
death before he had seen the Lord's Christ. And inspired by the Spirit
he came into the temple; and when the parents brought in the child
Jesus, to do for him according to the custom of the law, he took him
up in his arms and blessed God and said,
"Lord, now lettest thou thy servant depart in peace,
according to thy word;
for mine eyes have seen thy salvation
which thou hast prepared in the presence of all peoples,
a light for revelation to the Gentiles, and for glory to thy people Israel."
And his father and his mother marveled at what was said about him.
(Luke 2:26-33.)

At the end of this passage there is an item in the text of the Gospel which might not be noticed unless one had the King James Version and the Revised Standard Version side by side. The King James Version says: "And Joseph and his mother marvelled at those things which were spoken of him"; the Revised Standard Version says not "Joseph and his mother," but "his father and his mother."

The precious actual papyrus rolls over which the hands of Luke once moved have long since vanished. No eyes can look at them again. What New Testament scholars do have available, and must depend upon, is the great number of ancient manuscripts in which the original writings of the Evangelists, copied and recopied, have been handed down. In these manuscripts, though the substance is the same, there are variations here and there. Sometimes a copyist misread a word; sometimes he wrote a marginal note to explain a word; and someone coming after him and making a further copy put into his text the marginal note of the scribe preceding him, instead of the original word. Modern scholarship, seeking with devoted faithfulness to get as surely as it can to what it would have read if it could have looked over the shoulder of Luke himself, must compare one representation with another and decide as best it can which manuscript has more authority. Various factors determine comparative valuation: the date a manuscript was written and therefore its proximity in time to the Evangelists; the character of the manuscript itself and such signs as it may give of steady carefulness—or the lack of it; the environment in which the manuscript was produced and therefore the influences, conscious or unconscious, which may have played upon each scribe in the long succession, who looked at what his predecessor had written and was not sure what some word unclearly written meant.

Three and a half centuries ago when the scholars whom King James the First of England brought together made the immortal English translation since called by King James's name, they built their work on the best foundation which their time possessed. They went back for the Old Testament to the earliest Hebrew writings and for the New Testament to the earliest Greek writings which then had been discovered. But in the twentieth century there have been thrilling finds, in ancient monasteries and elsewhere, of manuscripts which carry authority outweighing what had been known before. It is upon these that the Revised Standard Version rests; and because of these this version says "his father and his mother."

Here in the Gospel of Luke two traditions meet. On the one hand, there was the belief which had begun to spread in the early church that a life so incomparable as that of Jesus must have begun in a uniquely marvelous way, from a virgin mother whose conception was a miracle of the Holy Spirit. Therefore in that strand of the tradition Joseph is spoken of only as Joseph. But there was also the other and apparently earlier assumption, which is reflected in the Gospel of Mark and in parts of Luke, that Jesus came as the child of Joseph and Mary, and so could be in the fullest sense the Savior because he had completely shared the human lot. Thus Joseph was not only a half-related figure standing at the side of Mary; he was for Jesus what the words in oldest manuscripts of the Gospel are found specifically to say, *his father.*

When all that has been remembered, the shining fact is this: the words which Simeon spoke are true in either case—true if the virgin birth was a miraculous physical fact, or true if the tradition concerning it was the creation of the church's adoring wonder. The divineness of Jesus would be in the power of his life. The supreme reality was not a question of how he had been born, but rather the new spiritual birth which would come to all mankind through him. Because his soul foresaw the future which was dawning in this child laid in his arms, old Simeon could sing the *Nunc Dimittis* of a man whose holiest hopes were about to be fulfilled. "For mine eyes have seen thy salvation, . . . a light to lighten the Gentiles, and the glory of thy people Israel."

THE FORMIDABLENESS OF CHRIST

And Simeon blessed them and said to Mary his mother,
"Behold, this child is set for the fall and rising of many in Israel,
and for a sign that is spoken against." (Luke 2:34.)

The first words of Simeon were spontaneous thanksgiving that his deepest lifelong desire could be satisfied. The redemption of Israel was at hand, a redemption that could reach out and include all the peoples of the earth.

Only joy was in those words; and only beauty and gentleness have been thus far in the whole story of the child of Mary born in Bethlehem. But now there comes another note:

Behold this child is set for the fall and rising
of many in Israel,
And for a sign that is spoken against.

What was to follow would not be marked by serenity and peace. It would bring a sword of cleavage for the destinies of men.

This is not a welcome fact to contemplate. If only everything could be continually pleasant and all the Gospel like the Christmas story, how satisfactory that would seem to be. For Christmas, beginning with the child in Bethlehem, has been linked with the innocent happiness of all little children and with a softening spirit generally—with lighted Christmas trees, holly wreaths, the opening of presents, and the coming together of whole families for Christmas dinner. That is all beautiful and right, but it is not the full reality.

The Christmas story and the Christmas mood do stand at the beginning of the Gospel, but there is something else to follow. It is easy to feel well-disposed when we face nothing more disturbing than a little child. Most people would have looked with a smile at the baby Jesus. Few would have done him any harm. The Gospel of Matthew says that Herod, with his sinister foreboding at the rumor that someone might be born who would supplant him, did try to kill all the children in Bethlehem in order to get rid of the unknown one he feared. But hardly any others, not even a Caiaphas or a Pilate, would have been capable of that. And certainly not ourselves, we think. We find all tender sentiments quite natural at Christmas. We like to sing of how

Away in a manger,
No crib for his bed,
The little Lord Jesus
Laid down his sweet head.

But the trouble is that Jesus is not always away in a manger, and he will not always seem just sweet. The child of Bethlehem, who would bring to those whose souls were sensitive the infinite gift of the love of God, would bring also the light of truth that could be terrible. Jesus the man confronted his world with a challenge which it did not want to recognize. He would be a sign that was spoken against—a sign to men that they must begin to reckon now with God's purpose for their own lives, as that purpose was revealed in Jesus.

What would happen to them if they let themselves respond to Jesus? They sensed it well enough. Pharisees and scribes who had made themselves believe that ritual observances and a conventional religious code would get them into heaven were forced to face what they had forgotten: justice and mercy, and the weightier matters of the law. Priests of the Temple who had made the worship required of the people a thing of personal profit for themselves stood in the presence of the man of Nazareth who dared to say that they had turned the house of God into a den of thieves. Aristocrats in Israel, with their fierce pride of blood and race and religious privilege, were outraged when Jesus made a Samaritan the hero of one of his parables. If men listened to him, they would have to go through a drastic readjustment, and they did not want it. Jesus could be a friend of tax-gatherers and sinners if he chose to, but did he expect *them* to go out and associate with people beneath their class? Jesus could draw his rude picture of the man who kept on storing up possessions and then suddenly had his soul required of him, but who was Jesus that he should be making them uncomfortable about their souls? To be more interested in giving than in getting, to treat the poor and needy as though they mattered as much to God as the educated and the privileged, to find life by losing it for God's kingdom—this was what Jesus would be saying, and it was too much. They were not going to have all their ideas upset. Jesus was a constant threat to the kind of world that suited them; and there was nothing to do but to get rid of Jesus.

"A sign that will be spoken against." And not in the first century alone. In any land and time the full-grown fact of Jesus' spirit may be unwelcome; for it has again the formidableness which men felt when they were faced by the man of Nazareth. He is not the "Jesus, meek and mild" to which some sentimental hymns reduce him. He is the Christ who confronts human affairs with the measurements of God. A scholarly official of pre-Communist China, speaking once to an American visitor, said that he himself was no Christian, but that he did recognize one great fact about the spirit of Christ: it creates a more sensitive conscience. It brings old evils under judgment, no matter how deeply they have been entrenched.

And not only that. It can create the faith which believes in, and the courage which will pay the price for, the better future that fortitude and suffering may win. It is this spirit which has given strength to those in many places who have fought against social wrongs: to Alan Paton in South Africa, to F. D. Shuttlesworth, Medgar Evers and other Negro leaders in Alabama and Mississippi who have dared mob violence and the more sinister brutality of men supposed to be officials of the law to win for their people the decent opportunities which too long have been denied. What their convictions have made them champion has back of it the ultimate power of the spirit of Christ, which can put down the mighty from their seats and exalt those of low degree. As that spirit, in the words of Simeon, was set for the fall and rising again of many in Israel, so also it can bring its contemporary warning. Those influences which stand in the way of justice and human brotherhood will crumble, and only those which are in tune with God's far purpose will prevail.

SYMPATHY THROUGH SUFFERING

> And a sword will pierce through your own soul also,
> that thoughts out of many hearts may be revealed."   (Luke 2:35.)

"A sword will pierce through your own soul also." Spoken directly to Mary, those words come as a sudden interjection in the midst of what Simeon forecast as the destiny of Jesus. Jesus should be a center of conflict. Wounds would come to him and therefore were bound to come to Mary. Because she was his mother, she would suffer too.

But with her, as is always true, suffering need not be in vain. Except for the little that is told of her in the early chapters of the Gospel, there is almost nothing written concerning Mary. But this we do know: that she saw her glorious son rejected by the people he had come to bless and save, accused by the priests to Pilate, crucified on a Roman cross. According to the book of Acts, she was with the disciples in Jerusalem when they first rallied after the shock of what had happened. Perhaps by then she could bring to them a faith born out of her own affliction. If so, it is not strange that in the everlasting search of human souls for light and strength many Roman Catholics go to churches which they have named "Our Lady of Sorrows." In this name there is at least the symbol of what all human beings know: that only those who have themselves known grief and pain can bring help and consolation to others in their need.

> He cannot heal who has not suffered much,
> For only Sorrow sorrow understands;

They will not come for healing at our touch
Who have not seen the scars upon our hands.[4]

No one in distress wants some bright tinkling words of cheerfulness from persons whose emotions have never gone down into the depths. When we are there ourselves, we want someone who can say, "I have been there too." The men and women who were in the leper colony of Molokai doubtless had many well-meaning would-be comforters, but certainly no word spoken to them before made their hearts leap up as did the two words which one day came from the lips of Father Damien, the priest who had gone to live among them. "*We* lepers," he began. Then they knew that nothing they might suffer would be beyond his understanding. And as it is with the distresses of the body, so it is with the distresses of the soul. Let someone whose experience has stirred the deep chords in himself come to us, and we listen to him with grateful, complete response. The sword has pierced through his own heart also; and because he has been wounded and yet somehow has found the healing of God, he can himself bring healing.

It is possible not to desire to be that sort of person. The temptation is to want an easy and untroubled life, even though those who have lived that kind of life will have little to give to souls who are crying out for great companionship. But to grow to greatness in understanding and in helpfulness can be worth the cost. Only out of suffering can come the power to sympathize, and to have gained that power is to have achieved an inner joy which transfigures all that went before. Looking at his life in its ultimate relationships, a man can thank God for the crucial hours in his experience which when he endured them seemed only a sword-thrust in his heart.

THE INCONSPICUOUS SAINTS

And there was a prophetess, Anna, the daughter of Phanuel, of the tribe of Asher; she was of a great age, having lived with her husband seven years from her virginity, and as a widow till she was eighty-four. She did not depart from the temple, worshiping with fasting and prayer night and day. And coming up at that very hour she gave thanks to God, and spoke of him to all who were looking for the redemption of Jerusalem.
(Luke 2:36-38.)

The men and women who will make the greatest difference in a people's life are not always the conspicuous ones. Who were those referred to in

[4] Edward McNeill Poteat, "Stigmata." From *Masterpieces of Religious Verse*. Reprinted by permission of Harper & Row.

the Gospel who looked for the redemption of Jerusalem? No answer to that, for they are not named. But they were there. The general crowd might be engrossed in nothing larger than its everyday concerns, but here were at least a few who cared for something greater. Their eyes looked out to far horizons toward a new day of God's redeeming purpose that might dawn. And because they were looking for it, they were the ones who could respond to the light of it when it came.

The glory of Israel through all its long history was in its spiritual minorities. Ordinary human nature goes along in the humdrum grooves of accustomed thinking. It takes things as they are and has no great imagination of how they might be different. If the life of a people has nothing to lift it above that level, it is cheap and common. But then there may come the individuals or the little groups whose expectations are not common: an Abraham "who looked for a city which hath foundations, whose builder and maker is God"; a Moses who "endured, as seeing him who is invisible"; the prophets who dared believe that "the crooked shall be made straight, and the rough places plain: and the glory of the Lord shall be revealed" (KJV).

It was not easy in Old Testament times to keep great hopes burning. Sometimes it may be even less easy as the years go on. In this twentieth century, with its monstrous threat of Armageddon, the fainthearted may think that all they hear are the iron bells of disaster and doom. But the promise of the future can come through the undismayed minority who keep believing in "the redemption of Jerusalem": the ultimate penetration of society by the saving purposes of God which can work like leaven wherever there are courageous souls.

The ends of history are in the hands of God, but it is the men of faith who are his instruments.

THE DIVINE IN THE FAMILIAR

And when they had performed everything according to the law of the Lord, they returned into Galilee, to their own city. Nazareth.

(Luke 2:39.)

To Nazareth: that was where Mary and Joseph returned, and that was where Jesus would grow up as a boy and spend almost all the years of his manhood life. In general estimation Nazareth was a place of no consequence: an obscure village off the main highway, in the Galilean hills. In the whole Old Testament record it is never mentioned. The natural inference seemed to be that nothing identified with it was likely to be important. In the Gospel of John it is recorded that when Jesus came down to the Jordan River where John was baptizing, and Philip, in awed excitement, said to a man named Nathanael that Jesus might be the Messiah, Nathanael's incredulous answer was, "Can anything good come out of Nazareth?" But in God's creative mystery the greatness of a soul takes no limitation from littleness in its surroundings. It is the divine fire that matters, not the particular environment in which it may have come to earth.

The true lesson of Nazareth may be reflected in wide areas of human affairs. It used to be taken for granted that leadership belonged only to those who were born to privilege. There was a divine right of kings to rule the common people. Children of the aristocracy should inherit the prerogatives for which the crowd was supposed not to be fit, and government should be kept in the hands of men of wealth and rank. But in societies which have been affected most by Christianity the facts begin to change. Christianity and democracy are not the same, but in the democratic ideal at its best there is implicit the recognition that the saving influence which is God's gift to a generation may come "out of Nazareth." Not autocratic rule, but government of the people, by the people, and for the people is what the Christian spirit is most naturally attuned to. And the one who will be the most kingly servant of the people may arise in the least regarded place.

WHEN LIFE DOES NOT NEED HALOS

And the child grew and became strong, filled with wisdom; and the favor of God was upon him. Now his parents went to Jerusalem every year at the feast of the Passover. And when he was twelve years old, they went up according to custom; and when the feast was ended, as they were returning, the boy Jesus stayed behind in Jerusalem. His parents did not know it, but supposing him to be in the company they went a day's journey, and they sought him among their kinfolk and acquaintances; and when they did not find him, they returned to Jerusalem, seeking him. After three days they found him in the temple, sitting among the teachers, listening to them and asking them questions; and all who heard him were amazed at his understanding and his answers. And when they saw him they were astonished; and his mother said to him, "Son, why have you treated us so? Behold, your father and I have been looking for you anxiously." And he said to them, "How is it that you sought me? Did you not know that I must be in my Father's house?" And they did not understand the saying which he spoke to them. And he went down with them and came to Nazareth, and was obedient to them; and his mother kept all these things in her heart. (Luke 2:40-51.)

If God's saving influence is to come into the world, how will it come? By the obviously miraculous, many would reply. If one appears who is to be the Christ, would he not have a halo on? And what would he have to do with all the patient processes of life through which the rest of us have to go?

That is what some might ask, but the Gospel of Luke has its surprising answer. It sees the divine as coming not through the strange but through the familiar. It makes plain that the presence of God does not have to be identified by halos, but that all the common facts of every day are hallowed if the heavenly purpose is working there.

In the so-called apocryphal Gospels which were written later, when crude imagination had given rise to fantastic tales, Jesus is turned into a worker of marvels whose distinction was that he could astonish the gaping crowd. But the beautiful simplicity of the Lukan story is completely different. Jesus would grow up as all others grow, a child in a human family, listening to what a father and mother told him. He would be enrolled in the synagogue school at Nazareth. With all the humble neighbors of the little Galilean town he would go up to Jerusalem for the great feasts of the Jewish year. And there at the Passover what he did was not any startling or abnormal thing. It was the custom for scribes learned in the law to sit there in the Temple to answer questions which the pilgrims and worshipers might want to ask. The instinctive interest of Jesus drew him to where they were. Christian artists who have imagined the scene and tried to portray it have represented the boy Jesus as standing dominant in the midst of the humbled teachers, as though he himself were laying down the law. But what Luke says is that he was "listening to them and asking them questions." He who in his soul's devotion was supremely the Son of God had no rude self-assertion. In mind and heart he was receptive to everything that came to him from any who were trying to hear the heavenly word.

THE DOUBLE RELATIONSHIP

And Jesus increased in wisdom and in stature, and in favor with God and man. (Luke 2:52.)

Jesus increased in wisdom and in stature, and in favor with God and man. In favor with God, first. In the deep mystery of his personality there was that complete attunement of his mind and heart with the mind and heart of God which is the living meaning that breaks through the mighty phrases of the Nicene Creed: "God of God, Light of Light, Very God of very God; . . . Being of one substance with the Father."

On the other hand, there would be times and ways in which Jesus would seem certainly not to be in favor with man. The nobility of soul in him made men of the world look mean; the terrible white light of his sincerity exposed the falsehoods where hypocrisy tried to hide; and the very greatness of his spiritual challenge could rouse only resentment and hate in those who did not want to answer it. So the sort of favor that some men gave him, such as Herod, Caiaphas, and the relentless ones among the Pharisees, was to put him first among the foes they were determined to destroy. But that fact should not obscure the greater truth that the spirit of Jesus does win the love and loyalty of the best in man. He stirs the depths, and the depths respond.

chapter 3

THE PERISHABLENESS OF EARTHLY POMP

In the fifteenth year of the reign of Tiberius Caesar, Pontius Pilate being governor of Judea, and Herod being tetrarch of Galilee, and his brother Philip tetrarch of the region of Ituraea and Trachonitis, and Lysanias tetrarch of Abilene, in the high-priesthood of Annas and Caiaphas, the word of God came to John the son of Zechariah in the wilderness.

(Luke 3:1-2.)

Here for the second time in Luke's Gospel there is an association of names out of which emerges an ironic contradiction of what might have been expected to be history. At the opening of the second chapter there was the contrast between Augustus Caesar and the child born in Bethlehem. Now there is the contrast between another emperor, Tiberius, and John, the son of Zechariah. The matter-of-course opinion of the time would have had no doubt as to where importance lay. Who cared about this John in comparison with Tiberius?

There are other names which are given as being also of such consequence that they shaped the calendar: Pontius Pilate; Herod, Philip, and Lysanias, tetrarchs in their principalities; Annas and Caiaphas, the priests. Everybody knew of them and understood their power. Events that were crucial for the people of whole provinces were dated by the periods of their rule. In one way or another, they were representatives of the sovereign authority which centered in the capital of the world. And there in what seemed to be the Eternal City, the symbol of the relentless dominance of Rome, was Tiberius.

Where are they now? Gone like the figures of some far-off pageant long since vanished from the stage. Even the names of most of them—Herod, Philip, Lysanias, and Annas—would be forgotten except that they have been carried down with no more value than as incidental references in the Christian Gospels. As factors in history they are fading ghosts, and ghosts of men who when they still had substance were marked with evil omen. Even at the peak of such importance as they had, all of them but one were only underlings. And as to the emperor himself, Gibbon, in *The Decline and*

Fall of the Roman Empire, has dismissed him as "the dark, unrelenting Tiberius . . . condemned to everlasting infamy."

These men who belonged to the world they lived in had no concern for any other. Measured by what they had, they were already great, and by the same measurement this John seemed insignificant. But it is the figure of John that now stands dominant, while their specious greatness has disappeared. And the reason is in five short monosyllables: to this John *came the word of God.* Through him the world of spiritual reality which overarches this one broke through. The eternal values would judge the appearances of time.

THE GREATNESS OF JOHN THE BAPTIST

And he went into all the region about the Jordan, preaching a baptism of repentance for the forgiveness of sins. As it is written in the book of the words of Isaiah the prophet,
"The voice of one crying in the wilderness:
Prepare the way of the Lord,
make his paths straight.
Every valley shall be filled,
and every mountain and hill shall be brought low,
and the crooked shall be made straight,
and the rough ways shall be made smooth;
and all flesh shall see the salvation of God."
He said therefore to the multitudes that came out to be baptized by him, "You brood of vipers! Who warned you to flee from the wrath to come? Bear fruits that befit repentance, and do not begin to say to yourselves, 'We have Abraham as our father'; for I tell you, God is able from these stones to raise up children to Abraham. Even now the axe is laid to the root of the trees; every tree therefore that does not bear good fruit is cut down and thrown into the fire." (Luke 3:3-9.)

What were the facts about John which made him into a prophet of the word of God?

First was the fact that he had been so much alone. In the crowd a man may lose his inner self. The brazen noises of the multitude and the clatter and commotion of trivial things may so beat upon his ears that he cannot hear the higher voice. Long before John, men knew that somewhere they had to find solitude if they were to listen to what might come to them from God. This was true with Elijah and Amos. It is the truth which has led men in many generations into the contemplative religious orders where the supreme emphasis has been upon meditation and prayer. They have sought for the promise which the psalmist expressed when he wrote, "Thou holdest them safe under thy shelter from the strife of tongues." Most men of course will not go into monasteries, nor could the full life of the world go forward if they did. But there is need nevertheless that all should find for themselves little islands of quiet where they can become acquainted with their souls. The salt of any society—a sensitive conscience that revolts against familiar wrongs, a belief in spiritual possibilities not yet proved, and the will to take roads leading in the direction of those possibilities—depends upon the men and women who thus are listening for the voice of God.

Nor is that impossible even when conditions are most difficult. Nicholas Herman, of Lorraine, an humble person who had been a footman to a French aristocrat, was accepted by the Carmelite Order in Paris in 1666 as a servant and given the name of Brother Lawrence. He spent the rest of his life, it is true, in a monastery, but not as a monk off in the silence saying his prayers; instead he was a cook in the kitchen. Conversations with him and a few letters from him were gathered by one who knew him under the title of *The Practice of the Presence of God*. That little book, printed and reprinted, still brings its inspiration to innumerable readers after nearly three hundred years. For Brother Lawrence had learned that "his greatest business did not divert him from God" and that everywhere he could establish himself "in a sense of God's presence by continually conversing with Him." So he could write, "A little lifting up of the heart suffices"; and he could say of himself, "The time of business does not with me differ from the time of prayer, and in the noise and clatter of my kitchen, while several persons are at the same time calling for different things, I possess God in as great tranquility as if I were on my knees at the blessed sacrament." [1]

A second fact about John the Baptist was his courage. Courage has been defined as follows: "That quality of mind which meets danger or opposition with intrepidity, calmness, and firmness." But an adequate definition of courage must strike a deeper note. It is not enough to call it "a quality of mind." A man cannot think himself into courage. Indeed, the more he tries to muster arguments and reasons why he ought to be courageous, the more the threatening facts of the situation may press upon him and make him fearful—until, in Hamlet's words,

> . . . the native hue of resolution
> Is sicklied o'er with the pale cast of thought.

It is not from the mind but from the heart that courage comes. Thomas Chalmers, of Scotland, preached one of the greatest among remembered sermons on "The Expulsive Power of a New Affection." Let a man's heart

[1] (New York: Fleming H. Revell Company, 1895), pp. 19, 14, 40, 30.

be filled by some sovereign emotion, let him be possessed by a blazing loyalty to some exalted cause, and what might have been the barrier of his timidity is consumed like so much paper before the fire of his intense commitment.

So it was with John. He would know danger and opposition right enough! Pharisees and scribes would hate him for his terrible rebukes of their hypocrisy. Herod would be looking for a chance to seize him. But he had a mightier concern. He looked at life and saw that it was going nowhere, but it was meant to find a road, the road of repentance and of righteousness that would lead toward the promises of God. To help build that road— to break down contradictions, to straighten what was crooked, to make the rough ways smooth—was the purpose that possessed him. There were no empty spaces in his consciousness where fear could get in. This is the secret of courage always. It is not in a quality of mind, nor in strength of body either. It is in the burning heart.

THE POWER OF JOHN'S PREACHING

And the multitudes asked him, "What then shall we do?" And he answered them, "He who has two coats, let him share with him who has none; and he who has food, let him do likewise." Tax collectors also came to be baptized, and said to him, "Teacher, what shall we do?" And he said to them, "Collect no more than is appointed you." Soldiers also asked him, "And we, what shall we do?" And he said to them, "Rob no one by violence or by false accusation, and be content with your wages." (Luke 3:10-14.)

The preaching of John the Baptist had a smashing directness. Unlike too many tame modern sermons which seem to have no particular target and are like blank cartridges fired in a conventional salute to miscellaneous piety, what John said spoke straight to the people there before him. It is safe to say that nobody went up to John afterwards and said to him, "That was a nice sermon today"—or reflected blandly how fortunate it was that some other people heard it. Every man there felt his own conscience laid open to this preacher's searching. "What shall *I* do?" they responded one by one. And John told them. Those who were in official posts should stop taking graft. Roman soldiers and Herod's constabulary should quit their brutal handling of the common people and begin to treat them decently. The selfish, contented upper classes were to practice some responsibility toward the poor. Granted that this was a limited message, and that the full sweep of a gospel of salvation was not in it. All the same it had the virile power of concreteness. It *meant* something, and something inescapable. It told people how they had to begin to behave, right now, right where they were.

There is everlasting danger that the plain matter of morality may drop out of preaching and drop out of people's idea of what religion is. Large theological conceptions may become a convenient cloudland into which men and women manage to get themselves transported away from the inconvenient realities of this earth. Supposed right beliefs, proper use of the sacraments, going to church and saying the "General Confession" will somehow put them in the state of grace, even when their ordinary conduct is still shady. But against that sort of complacency come the indignant words of John: "Even now the axe is laid to the root of the trees; every tree therefore that does not bear good fruit is cut down and thrown into the fire"; and the still more devastating words of Jesus: "Woe to you, . . . hypocrites! for you are like whitewashed tombs, which outwardly appear beautiful, but within . . . are full of dead men's bones."

In short, there is continual need, and seldom more than in this present time, that there should be a solid moral impact in all Christian preaching and in the thinking of Christians as they go out of church. There is no use in expounding the gospel of salvation unless people are helped to see the actual sins from which they need to be saved. In an age whose mood is easygoing and sometimes cheap and compromising, "puritanical" is a distasteful word; but the ultimate soundness of any people depends upon the magnificent moral integrity which—in spite of some failings and unpleasantnesses—the Puritans did possess: the same integrity of conscience which John the Baptist preached, with its clear conviction as to right and wrong, and as to the difference between them.

JOHN'S EXPECTATION

As the people were in expectation, and all men questioned in their hearts concerning John, whether perhaps he were the Christ, John answered them all, "I baptize you with water; but he who is mightier than I is coming, the thong of whose sandals I am not worthy to untie; he will baptize you with the Holy Spirit and with fire. His winnowing fork is in his hand, to clear his threshing floor, and to gather the wheat into his granary, but the chaff he will burn with unquenchable fire." (Luke 3:15-17.)

John the Baptist had no megalomania about himself. He repudiated the excited rumor which was stirring in the crowd that he, John, might be the Messiah. But apparently he did have the intense and passionate hope that the Messiah was about to come and that when the Messiah appeared he would bring a deliverance for Israel which would be dramatic and complete. His baptism would be with fire. He would gather up the wheat and throw the chaff into the furnace of his wrath.

At the period of John's ministry and in the decades before and after it there circulated among the Jewish people apocalyptic writings, blazing poetry in which the desire and hope of people long oppressed broke through into fierce expression. In one of these books, The Psalms of Solomon, it was written:

> Behold, O Lord, and raise up unto them their king, the son of David,
>> At the time in which thou seest, O God, that he may rule over Israel Thy servant.
> And gird him with strength, that he may shatter unrighteous rulers,
>> And that he may purge Jerusalem from nations that trample (her) down to destruction.
> Wisely, righteously he shall thrust out sinners from (the) inheritance,
>> He shall destroy the pride of the sinner as a potter's vessel.
> With a rod of iron he shall break in pieces all their substance.
> He shall destroy the godless nations with word of his mouth.
>
> (17:23-25.)

It may have been in such form that John envisioned the Messiah; if so, then the contrast between what he had imagined and what he was to see in Jesus could have been the reason why later he sent messengers to Jesus to ask the wistful question: "Are you he who is to come, or shall we look for another?"

WHEN DISAPPOINTMENT IS NOT DEFEAT

So, with many other exhortations, he preached good news to the people. But Herod the tetrarch, who had been reproved by him for Herodias, his brother's wife, and for all the evil things that Herod had done, added this to them all, that he shut up John in prison. (Luke 3:18-20.)

Luke inserts abruptly into his narrative here a reference that belongs in another time sequence. It was not at this moment, between the first preaching of John and the baptism of Jesus, that John was arrested. That arrest came later. But the shadow of it here accentuates the significance of John's ministry. It brings the sudden realization that greatness in spiritual service is not lessened even when particular expectations have not been fulfilled.

Great crowds had flocked to the Jordan River when John first began to preach. "The kingdom of heaven is at hand!" he had declared, and men listened to the tremendous proclamation at first with breathless awe. "What shall we do, then?" they asked; and John answered with his relentless demand for repentance and his uncompromising word to every kind of person as to what repentance must directly mean for him. It seemed as though the depths in a nation's soul were being stirred, and out of those depths the river of a new life might flow.

Yet that was not to be. John's preaching was brought to an end by one of the evil forces he had denounced. The day came when he was in Herod's prison, and the listening crowds were gone. Where was the kingdom now, and what difference had his preaching made?

That is the sort of seeming defeat which is not unfamiliar in the experience of those who try to be servants of God. A man stands up in his place and time as the spokesman of a new righteousness, denouncing wrongs which have become accepted, in political affairs, in business, or in the church itself. For a time it seems that the power of his own moral indignation may come to the public conscience like a storm that sweeps things clean. Yet that does not happen, and he may feel at last that all he has striven and suffered for has been in vain.

But it is not in vain, as John's ministry was not in vain. He himself might seem to have made no progress, but he had built a road along which someone mightier than himself would come. He had made men conscious of their need—their need for redemption of life. If by himself he could not accomplish that redemption, he had waked the expectation that it could be accomplished, and he had opened the way for the Redeemer. He had brought men to attention in the fear of the Lord. Now he could stand aside for the coming to them of the love of God in Christ.

THE BAPTISM OF JESUS

> Now when all the people were baptized, and when Jesus also had been baptized and was praying, the heaven was opened, and the Holy Spirit descended upon him in bodily form, as a dove, and a voice came from heaven, "Thou art my beloved Son; with thee I am well pleased."
> (Luke 3:21-22.)

This account of the baptism of Jesus reflects one of Luke's particular characteristics. To him the heavenly world was a close encircling reality from which the influences of God were continually coming down with an immediacy not to be expressed in any abstract word. He thought of God as surrounded by his angelic messengers, and so the Gospel narrative is full of angel forms. The angel Gabriel appears to Mary at the annunciation. An angel comes to Zechariah in the Temple with the promise of the birth of John the Baptist. The glory of the heavenly host fills the sky above the plains of Bethlehem. An angel will stand before Jesus in the Garden of Gethsemane. Two men in shining garments will speak to the women at

Jesus' tomb on Easter morning, and the women will tell the disciples that they had seen a vision of angels. With dramatic vividness Luke thus describes the spiritual facts. Here in the account of the baptism, therefore, he is not content to say only what was the experience of Jesus himself. He pictures the event as with supernatural signs manifest to all the throng by the Jordan River. "The heaven was opened, and the Holy Spirit descended in bodily form, as a dove."

But of course the supreme matter is not the form of the description but the substance of the event, and it is evident from all the Gospels that the baptism was a crucial moment in the life of Jesus. Yet at first thought that is surprising. Why should Jesus be baptized by John, when John's preaching had to do directly with people's sins and his baptism was a baptism of repentance? Did Jesus come as a sinner also?

The whole testimony of the Gospels contradicts this. Every reference they contain points to the completeness of Jesus' consecration and to the white purity of all that he thought and did. Why, then, did he come to be baptized?

The answer may be a double one.

In the first place, there is the fact that no life stands in isolation, and for Jesus above all it was impossible that he should have been concerned about himself alone. Born a child of Israel, he belonged to a people in whom a corporate consciousness gave a larger relationship to each single life. From the time of the patriarchs and the prophets there had been the mighty hope that the nation should be saved, and this hope was the passion of Jesus' soul. His whole ministry was to be vicarious: a taking upon his conscience the fact of all human sin, his bearing the burden of it, his full involvement in the consequences of it with a self-forgetful love that could be redeeming. So by coming to John's baptism he made himself at one with the people's needs. Here in his immeasurably greater way and with a spiritual meaning deeper than we can ever fathom, Jesus was expressing the ultimate devotion which Moses had been reaching toward when he cried to God at Sinai, "Alas, this people have sinned a great sin. But now, if thou wilt forgive their sin—and if not, blot me, I pray thee, out of thy book which thou hast written." Jesus would not hold himself apart from the world in privileged detachment. He had come to seek and save sinners, and this meant that he had to enter fully into the evil world they knew and pay the cost of that collision.

Then, in the second place, the baptism becomes more understandable when one considers what sinlessness in Jesus meant and what it does not imply. In the words of the letter to the Hebrews he was "without sinning," but also he was "in every respect . . . tempted as we are." "He had to be made like his brethren in every respect" in order that he might "make expiation for the sins of the people." For Jesus himself, therefore, even though his spirit was beyond the reach of gross temptations, there was always the possibility of what he himself would have considered to be sin: the sin of the second choice. The crucial decisions of the soul do not generally come between black evil on one side and unmistakable right on the other. They come at those crossroads where only a conscience sensitive and alert can perceive which way leads up and which leads down. It was into this sensitiveness that Jesus came to be baptized. He would walk the road of his Father's purpose, wherever it might lead; and the baptism was the seal of assurance that he would not falter.

THE SAVIOR OF MANKIND

Jesus, when he began his ministry, was about thirty years of age, being the son (as was supposed) of Joseph the son of Heli, the son of Matthat, the son of Levi, the son of Melchi, the son of Jannai, the son of Joseph, the son of Mattathias, the son of Amos, the son of Nahum, the son of Esli, the son of Naggai, the son of Maath, the son of Mattathias, the son of Semein, the son of Josech, the son of Joda, the son of Joanan, the son of Rhesa, the son of Zerubbabel, the son of Shealtiel, the son of Neri, the son of Melchi, the son of Addi, the son of Cosam, the son of Elmadam, the son of Er, the son of Jesus, the son of Eliezer, the son of Jorim, the son of Matthat, the son of Levi, the son of Symeon, the son of Judas, the son of Joseph, the son of Jonam, the son of Eliakim, the son of Melea, the son of Menna, the son of Mattatha, the son of Nathan, the son of David, the son of Jesse, the son of Obed, the son of Boaz, the son of Sala, the son of Nahshon, the son of Amminadab, the son of Admin, the son of Arni, the son of Hezron, the son of Perez, the son of Judah, the son of Jacob, the son of Isaac, the son of Abraham, the son of Terah, the son of Nahor, the son of Serug, the son of Reu, the son of Peleg, the son of Eber, the son of Shelah, the son of Cainan, the son of Arphaxad, the son of Shem, the son of Noah, the son of Lamech, the son of Methuselah, the son of Enoch, the son of Jared, the son of Mahalaleel, the son of Cainan, the son of Enos, the son of Seth, the son of Adam, the son of God.   (Luke 3:23-38.)

This long genealogy is to be compared with the parallel one in the first chapter of the Gospel of Matthew, and curious facts then become evident. Many of the names are the same, but many are different. Obviously, therefore, neither one can possess any final authority. Moreover, neither one seems to be an intimate and necessary part of the Gospel in which it is included. The real story in the Gospel of Matthew begins with vs. 18, and the genealogy is like a label pasted in front of it. In Luke the genealogy is an interruption between the account of Jesus' baptism in 3:22 and the account of the temptation with which the fourth chapter opens. Both genealogies apparently had been worked out somewhere in the Christian community, and they had come separately to the two Evangelists. Each included the one that had come down to him because it was part of the tradition which demanded to be preserved. Here in Luke, as more conspicuously in the Old Testament books, there is evident the strong inclination which all the biblical writers had: namely, to put in whatever material had any significance in itself, even if it was not plainly consistent with the rest of the writings. Luke has already put into his Gospel the lovely picture which an adoring wonder had portrayed: Mary, the angel Gabriel, Bethlehem, and the virgin birth. In the divineness of Jesus as thus expressed, Joseph played no essential part. But in order that Jesus should be seen as the promised Messiah, it was important that he should be recognized as the heir to David's line; and so Luke included the genealogy of Joseph, Mary's husband, by which the lineage of Jesus was led back to the great king who was accounted "a man after God's own heart"; and back of David, all the way to Abraham.

The effect of the genealogy then, in the first place, was to identify Jesus with the age-long hopes of Israel. He did belong to Israel. He came not to destroy but to fulfil the law and the prophets. He knew—and all who as Christians call themselves by his name must know—that there can be no complete redemption until the law and the prophets are fulfilled. For the law at its highest meant obedience to the holy will of God; and the message of the prophets was that real religion is not ritual but righteousness, the righteousness of a moral standard made controlling in the everyday actualities of personal and social life. That great legacy of Judaism must be an everlasting part of the Christian gospel. The gospel goes beyond the Old Testament in its proclamation of the Savior; but it must never lose the magnificent Old Testament conception of a covenant with God, nor the intensity of its conviction that morality is one of the marks of being saved.

So Luke would make it clear that in Jesus is the climax of all that began with Abraham. But that is not all. If Jesus is the fulfillment of the mighty hopes of the special people of Israel, he nevertheless does not belong to one people alone. Therefore in his Gospel Luke breaks beyond the particularism of early Jewish thinking, out to new horizons in which the salvation of the Gentiles is included. Jesus is linked with the destiny of the whole human race. He is not only one of the children of Israel. He transcends all distinctions and differences, and his significance goes back beyond all time. He was more than a descendant of Abraham and a son of the covenant. His genealogy should be reckoned in relation to Adam, "the son of God."

chapter 4

JESUS FACES HIS LIFE'S ALTERNATIVES

And Jesus, full of the Holy Spirit, returned from the Jordan, and was led by the Spirit for forty days in the wilderness, tempted by the devil. And he ate nothing in those days; and when they were ended, he was hungry. (Luke 4:1-2.)

The temptation of Jesus in the wilderness is recorded in all the first three Gospels, and its long impact on Christian thinking appears in Hebrews, where it is written of Jesus that he was "one who in every respect has been tempted as we are, yet without sinning." It may be that some day, in one of those periods when Jesus was alone with his disciples, he told them of that crisis for his spirit and of what it meant in his commitment to his Father's will. Certainly if the disciples knew of it, it was only from Jesus that they could have known.

As told in the Gospels, the account of the temptation is cast into dramatic form. It is as though, into the presence of Jesus in the wilderness, there came the sinister figure of the Tempter, an immediate and visible antagonist. That is the picture which in its concrete vividness conveys the deep reality of the inner conflict, the battleground for which was Jesus' thought and will. In the thrilling consciousness of his mission which had illumined him at his baptism, his spirit had been exalted; but always after exaltation there come the crowding questions as to where the road runs next. Can actual life continue on the level of the heavenly vision, or must it come down into the valley of compromising choices if it is to find the realistic way ahead? At the baptism the voice of God had spoken. Out in the bleak solitude the voice of this world's plausibilities was saying, "Listen instead to me."

"NOT BY BREAD ALONE"

The devil said to him, "If you are the Son of God, command this stone to become bread." And Jesus answered him, "It is written, 'Man shall not live by bread alone.' " (Luke 4:3-4.)

"Command this stone to become bread." Such were the words that expressed the first temptation; and for the full meaning of it one must remember that the thought of Jesus always went beyond his personal concerns. He had been fasting, and he was hungry; but the temptation was not to perform some convenient miracle which might turn those stones that lay about him into food for him. It was with issues far greater than this that the real temptation had to do: the temptation to see his ministry first in material terms. He had grown up among the poor. He knew how many there were who—if their world stayed as it was—might continually be hungry. What they wanted was a leader who would change the conditions of their lives: take some of their immediate burdens off, get them more to live on, hand out loaves and fishes. Devote yourself to that, the tempting voice suggested. Serve the obvious desires of the disadvantaged people—this will give you popularity. And when you are popular, they may listen to you when you talk to them of God.

The subtlety of the temptation was in its partial truth. Jesus' great compassion did go out to the poor, and he understood their physical needs. But he could not let men's interest and ambition stop with these. He had to wake, and then feed, a deeper hunger, to show men a purpose for their living which could not be satisfied by bread alone.

"Tempted as we are," says Hebrews. The issues of our little lives cannot be compared with the infinite issues in the life of Jesus; but the same plausibilities that spoke to him speak to us on our lesser level. A man, for example, goes into public life, with a Christian's desire to be in some fine sense a servant of the people. He knows that his finest achievement would be to help create in a community or in the nation a responsiveness to great ideals: moral cleanness, equal justice, defense of the exploited, a citizenship that reaches out beyond mean provincialism to recognize its responsibility for the well-being of all God's children everywhere. But other forces will assail him and demand his subservience: little groups that want some selfish gain, old vested interests, loud demands for the "practical" programs which will answer the question, "What is there in this for me?" The man of Christian conscience knows which way he ought to face. The voice within which tells him that man does not live by bread alone bids him take the high road, but whispered calculations of his immediate advantage may bid him take the low one.

THE KINGDOMS OF THIS WORLD

And the devil took him up, and showed him all the kingdoms of the world in a moment of time, and said to him, "To you I will give all this

authority and their glory; for it has been delivered to me, and I give it
to whom I will. If you, then, will worship me, it shall all be yours." And
Jesus answered him, "It is written,
'You shall worship the Lord your God,
and him only shall you serve.'" (Luke 4:5-8.)

In the account of the second temptation, as in the account of the first, the
profound spiritual fact must be seen beneath the figurative language. The
devil took him up into a high mountain, and showed him all the kingdoms
of the world. That does not mean, of course, that a satanic figure escorted
Jesus to some mountaintop in the Tekoan wilderness and unfolded there
a miraculous panorama of the circle of the earth. What Jesus saw was the
projection of great imaginations which had been in his mind already. From
the hills of Nazareth he had looked out on a landscape which revealed
what the world had become. Once all the country he saw had belonged to
the kingdom of David. Now the shadow of Rome was on it. Cities which
represented Roman ways of life fringed the Lake of Galilee; on the roads
the sunlight glinted on the eagles of some marching Roman legion; on the
distant Mediterranean were the Roman triremes that commanded the sea.
Israel, his people, the people of the covenant whose history went back to
Abraham, was subject now to this Roman rule. Every now and then the
national pride and smothered patriotism burst out in desperate rebellion.
When Jesus was growing up in Nazareth, Judas of Galilee had led the revolt which centered in the nearby city of Sepphoris. The secret fellowship
of those who were called the Zealots continually looked forward to a war of
liberation. The kind of Messiah they wanted was one who could make
himself a conqueror. In *The Man Born to Be King* the penetrating understanding of Dorothy Sayers has dramatized that fierce desire in the figure of
Baruch, captain of a group of spearmen whom he had gathered already in
the Judaean hills. "To every man opportunity comes once and not again"
was the message he and other Zealots would send to Jesus. "The people
are on your side, and I have men and arms. Now is the moment to strike
and seize your kingdom." [1]

"Why should not Messiah be this kind of conqueror the people want?"
said the tempting voice, the voice of the prince of this world and of its
seeming practicalities. Rome has ruled too long. It is time that there should
be another sort of rule and another kingdom. That could be accomplished.
If all the outraged people could be roused, the fury of their rising might
break the yoke of Rome.

[1] Dorothy L. Sayers, *The Man Born to Be King* (New York: Harper & Row, 1949), p. 203.
Copyright 1943, Dorothy L. Sayers.

Was that fantastic, too fantastic to have entered the thoughts of Jesus and to have constituted a temptation? Fantastic to think that he himself might set in motion forces that could change the actual framework of the world? If it should be deemed fantastic, let two facts of history be brought to mind. The first is the fact of what did begin to happen in the first century. Already in the apparent stability of Roman rule there were seeds of disintegration. From the death of Tiberius in A.D. 37 to A.D. 69, the imperial authority was violently disrupted seven times. There were nine different emperors, three of whom were assassinated, and one of whom committed suicide; and three times revolt by some of the legions removed one emperor and set up another. And if it be said that all this has nothing to do with a possible temptation to Jesus because in human terms he had nothing to start from and therefore could not have conceived of winning dominance in this actual world's affair, then there emerges a second fact of history. In this twentieth century one nation in Europe, defeated and occupied, seemed no more formidable than Israel seemed in comparison with Rome. In that nation was one man, who in a material sense appeared to be possessed of nothing. He had no army, no store of weapons, no wealth, no consequential friends. Yet that man, by the terrible power of a burning purpose, very nearly became the master of the world. His name was Adolf Hitler. To link his name with that of Jesus is to be putting darkness next to light, a slough of evil against a mountain rising to the sky. But the reality which nevertheless emerges from his dark history is the incredible power of a single personality when his mind and purpose are on fire. How much more immense could have been the power of Jesus if he had chosen to listen to the cry of the Zealots for a leader, had fanned the smoldering passions of Israel and of other conquered provinces into flame, and had set out to win dominion by the sword.

That was the meaning of the second temptation. It was the allurement which spoke to Jesus' loyalty to his own people and sought to make that loyalty synonymous with his dedication to the kingdom of God. "Advance the fortunes of this nation first, even if it has to be by way of violence. Follow the realistic methods toward achievement. Then from the vantage point of authority and glory, great purposes of human betterment can be carried out." So spoke—and so may speak in every time—the tempting voice which seems to express the wisdom of the world.

But Jesus had a different answer. "It is written, you shall worship the Lord your God, and him only shall you serve." There was a time when the crowds, swept by the vast enthusiasm which the very look of him created, surged round him and would have made him a king. He might have had a kingdom if he had compromised enough; gained what would have seemed

73

great ends if he had been satisfied with doubtful means. But Jesus knew that what the common thought declares to be only sensible may actually be satanic, and to God alone must obedience be given.

THE UNCONDITIONAL COMMITMENT

And he took him to Jerusalem, and set him on the pinnacle of the temple, and said to him, "If you are the Son of God, throw yourself down from here; for it is written,

'He will give his angels charge of you, to guard you,

and On their hands they will bear you up,

lest you strike your foot against a stone.' "

And Jesus answered him, "It is said, 'You shall not tempt the Lord your God.' " (Luke 4:9-12.)

In the Gospels of Matthew and Luke the order of the temptations is recorded differently. In Matthew the climactic temptation is the one symbolized by the vision of the kingdoms of the earth; but here in Luke the climax comes in the suggestion which above all others could be the most beguiling. What that suggestion was may not instantly appear. The description in the Gospel, if read with a bald literalism, might seem to take the whole event outside the field of any recognizable reality. Jesus transported to Jerusalem, put upon a pinnacle of the Temple, urged to leap off and then be saved by a miracle in midair, while all the crowd looked on in stunned astonishment—that is a picture of exhibitionism impossible actually to associate with Jesus. Here, as in the other temptations, one must look for the far-reaching meaning within the pictured symbol. It is as though the tempter said this: "If you are the Son of God, then you have a claim on God. Whatever happens, you should be saved from harm. It is beyond all rationality that you, the Son of God, should suffer. No matter what peril you may have to cope with, even if it should be as deadly as falling from the temple parapets, you will be shielded from disaster."

Read thus, does not the reality of the temptation strike deep into our own recognition? How instinctive it is to assume that goodness must have its obvious reward! Why should not the righteous have a right to think that God will give them guardian angels: against sickness, bereavement, mistreatment, ill chance of any kind? If that is not true, then where is the faithfulness of God?

These were the questions that Jesus met and answered—for himself and for all who would learn from him. In the previous temptations he had committed himself completely to his Father's will. Supremely then it could have seemed that God would make the road smooth before him. Why should he not expect that, and let his own continuing faith be conditional upon what happened? So the tempting voice suggested, and only Jesus could have seen the truth beyond the twisted subtlety. "It is said, 'You shall not tempt the Lord your God,' " he said, which means that God is not to be put on trial. There in the wilderness Jesus had put himself into his Father's hands, without conditions. The great thing was to choose the heroic road, not to ask that the road be kept from being hard. Looking forward to what his ministry would encounter, Jesus knew that faithfulness might have to pay a heavy cost. But, through light or dark, he would trust the love of God for his life's fulfillment, even if at the end of it there might be a cross.

THE RECURRING BATTLE

> And when the devil had ended every temptation, he departed from him until an opportune time. And Jesus returned in the power of the Spirit into Galilee, and a report concerning him went out through all the sur-rounding country. (Luke 4:13-14.)

When the devil had ended every temptation, he departed from him until an opportune time. Thus the description of Jesus' spiritual struggle con-cludes. Here was an end which yet was not an end. The compromising choices which had been brought to Jesus' mind had been rejected, and the Tempter put to silence. In that sense something had indeed been finished and achieved. Jesus' great decisions had been made. But after the decisions had been registered, what then? Was it certain now that no temptation would come again, because the devil "had departed"? A dangerous assump-tion! The devil had departed, yes; but only "for a season," as the King James translation has it; or, in the words of the Revised Standard Version, "until an opportune time." The days would come when the old solicitations of the Tempter would return to Jesus with sudden new persuasion. Those decisions made in the wilderness—would they work? It is all very well to have chosen great ideals, but suppose the hard facts of the world made them seem impossible? Modified choices might after all be necessary: more accommodation to the poor little instincts of the crowd that was interested first in the loaves and fishes, alliance with the fierce nationalism of the Zealots that might put power at his side, cautious adjustments that would keep him safe. Questions like those must have insinuated themselves again and again to Jesus' consciousness. The Tempter who had chosen to make it seem that he was departing was back again whenever the time was oppor-tune; and so not once, but many times, Jesus had to repeat his spiritual vic-tory.

Always there is a double fact about temptation. If at first it is faced and grappled with, then there is growth in inward power. As Robert Browning wrote in *The Ring and the Book,*

> Why comes temptation but for man to meet
> And master, and make crouch beneath his feet?

For that kind of encounter with temptation a man may well thank God, because of what it can develop in his soul. If there were no such encounter, it could only mean that he had never entered the arena where the moral victories of life are won. But when any particular victory has been achieved, then comes the other side of fact: the need for undiminished vigilance. The temptation which had seemed to have been conquered and to have departed may have withdrawn only "for a season," and it will watch for the unguarded moment to return. Many a man who has thought that he had finished with some besetting sin or armored himself against old weakness has found himself surprised and shaken because he had assumed too quickly that he was secure. Moral hardihood is a long-term matter, and for that long term "needs provision be for keeping the soul's prowess possible."

THE DIVINE IN THE ORDINARY PLACE

And he taught in their synagogues, being glorified by all. And he came to Nazareth, where he had been brought up; and he went to the synagogue, as his custom was, on the sabbath day. And he stood up to read.

(Luke 4:15-16.)

Nazareth, where he had been brought up. That brief reference, which the casual reader might pass over, can bring instead a sudden and almost startling realization. Jesus has become for us so transcendently the Lord and Savior that we might be led to suppose that people in Galilee must have looked upon him as a divine figure walking in their midst and that all his appearance seemed supernatural. But the fact was completely different. Nazareth where he was brought up—note the simple and ordinary words —was not disposed to see in him anything astonishing. He grew from a little child into a boy, and then into a man, within the small town and the small town's life. In his spirit there was the very reality of God—in his purity, his joyous goodness, his sympathy, and his self-giving. But it never occurred to most people in Nazareth that these were signs of the divine. Nothing that seemed miraculous had happened. When he came back, they did not think that he was anybody to whom they ought to listen. Who was he, after all, more than merely "Joseph's son"?

It is always possible for our dullness and stupidity not to recognize the presence of God. So many of us assume that the only way in which God would speak to us is in something astonishing. He may be speaking to us all the time, and we do not hear. The spirit of Christ may be reflected in some lovely soul in our town, our family, our house; in the person who wears no outward halo, but who in everyday living and in the familiar place represents what is redeeming.

The same first sentence of the account in Luke reveals another fact concerning Jesus. He went to the synagogue, as his custom was, on the sabbath day. "As his custom was," he went to church—that is to say, not now and then, not on condescending occasions, but habitually. He deliberately associated himself with what was best in the life of the community. The synagogue service there in Nazareth may have been led by men who made it far from inspiring, and in the congregation were certainly very ordinary people. But Jesus went, nevertheless, because in the synagogue the immemorial spiritual heritage of all the centuries was handed down, because even through imperfect human lips the living and present word of God was spoken, and because in being there the people of the town were lifted up together into a common loyalty to what was larger than their little selves.

JESUS IN THE SYNAGOGUE AT NAZARETH

And there was given to him the book of the prophet Isaiah. He opened the book, and found the place where is was written,
"The Spirit of the Lord is upon me,
because he has anointed me to preach good news to the poor.
He has sent me to proclaim release to the captives
and recovering of sight to the blind,
to set at liberty those who are oppressed,
to proclaim the acceptable year of the Lord."
And he closed the book, and gave it back to the attendant, and sat down; and the eyes of all in the synagogue were fixed on him. And he began to say to them, "Today this scripture has been fulfilled in your hearing." And all spoke well of him, and wondered at the gracious words which proceeded out of his mouth; and they said, "Is not this Joseph's son?" And he said to them, "Doubtless you will quote to me this proverb, 'Physician, heal yourself; what we have heard you did at Capernaum, do here also in your own country.' " And he said, "Truly, I say to you, no prophet is acceptable in his own country. But in truth, I tell you, there were many widows in Israel in the days of Elijah, when the heaven was shut up three years and six months, when there came a great famine over all the land; and Elijah was sent to none of them but only to Zarephath, in the land of Sidon, to a woman who was a widow. And there were many lepers in Israel in the time of the prophet Elisha; and none of them was cleansed, but only Naaman the Syrian." When they heard this, all in the synagogue were filled with wrath. And they rose up and put him out of the city, and led him to the brow of the hill on which their city was built, that they might throw him down headlong. But passing through the midst of them he went away. (Luke 4:17-30.)

77

On this particular sabbath Jesus was asked by the leader of the synagogue to speak. He read from the prophecy of Isaiah concerning what one possessed by the spirit of God would proclaim—God's mercy and redemption for all needy souls who turn to him, good news for the poor and the forgotten, release for those in bondage to misery and sin, new sight for those who had been blind, liberty and larger life for all who had been oppressed. He brought his message home to the people there before him by illustrations which they could not fail to understand. They could be in danger of the narrow-mindedness which conventional religion is so apt to fall into: the narrow-mindedness which makes men and women want to hold on to their own special privilege and care nothing for those outside their supposed superior group. But the love of God as the prophets knew it went out, he said, to those outside the covenant: to the widow in Sidon, to Naaman who came from hated Syria. They also were dear to God, and the good news of God's redeeming purpose belonged equally to them.

The congregation in Nazareth did not like that kind of preaching. They resented the suggestion that other people might rate as high in God's sight as they did. So they were filled with wrath—as some modern congregations are when a preacher champions the unprivileged or defends the rights of Negroes in a segregated town. They tried to get rid of Jesus, as some churches get rid of ministers who preach what he preached that day. They led him to the brow of the hill on which their city was built, that they might throw him down. But the power of his spirit is forever stronger than those who would destroy it. Passing through them, he goes his way.

A DAY IN CAPERNAUM

And he went down to Capernaum, a city of Galilee. And he was teaching them on the sabbath; and they were astonished at his teaching, for his word was with authority. And in the synagogue there was a man who had the spirit of an unclean demon; and he cried out with a loud voice, "Ah! What have you to do with us, Jesus of Nazareth? Have you come to destroy us? I know who you are, the Holy One of God." But Jesus rebuked him, saying, "Be silent, and come out of him!" And when the demon had thrown him down in the midst, he came out of him, having done him no harm. And they were all amazed and said to one another, "What is this word? For with authority and power he commands the unclean spirits, and they come out." And reports of him went out into every place in the surrounding region. And he arose and left the synagogue, and entered Simon's house. Now Simon's mother-in-law was ill with a high fever, and they besought him for her. And he stood over her and rebuked the fever, and it left her; and immediately she rose and served them. Now when the sun was setting, all those who had any that were sick with various diseases brought them to him; and he laid his hands on every one of them and healed them. And demons also came out of many, crying, "You are the Son of God!" But he rebuked them, and would not allow them to speak, because they knew that he was the Christ. (Luke 4:31-41.)

Capernaum, as a town where people lived, has vanished. Archaeologists, who have excavated ancient foundations on the shore of the Lake of Galilee, can only guess where it may have been. All its fabric, like that of far greater cities of the Roman Empire and its provinces, has gone down into dust. Nevertheless, the name of Capernaum is immortal, for it was there that much of the ministry of Jesus centered. The spiritual history of mankind would be impoverished if it should lose remembrance of what happened in that little town.

It is the nearly unanimous belief of New Testament scholars that the earliest written Gospel was the Gospel of Mark and that both Matthew and Luke possessed and used it. Here at the beginning of this fourth chapter Luke incorporates almost verbatim three vivid incidents which had been described by Mark, and their significance is heightened by the fact that Mark may have been told about them by the one who would have remembered them most surely. The strong tradition in the early church, as recorded by Papias, a bishop of the first quarter of the second century, was that "Mark, having become the interpreter of Peter, wrote down accurately everything that he remembered"—wrote it down sometime after the middle of the first century when he met Peter and was with him, perhaps in Rome. One of the incidents, as we shall see, is recounted as having happened in Peter's own house.

In Capernaum, as in Nazareth, when the sabbath came, Jesus was in the synagogue. There is no account this time of what he said, but there is a clear echo of the impression he made. "They were astonished at his teaching, for his word was with authority." There is an authority which can belong to any superlative human personality, and the people could have recognized that in Jesus, even if they had been conscious of nothing more. Here was one who could speak to a group of hardy fishermen and by the sheer fascination of his presence make them ready to leave everything they had and follow him. Here was strength that did not flinch before any danger and under the shield of which all the troubled or the timid could feel secure. When his eyes looked into their eyes, people felt that somehow he was seeing everything that was in their minds and hearts: every wrong thing which they suddenly were ashamed of, and also every longing after goodness that his trust woke to life. "No man ever spoke like this man," they might have said—as, according to the Gospel of John, another group would say at a later time. He did not have to claim authority of rank or title, as the priests and rabbis did. He had authority because of what he was himself.

Yet the fact was more than that. As Jesus stood there before them, men knew that he was not thinking of himself. There was a vaster dimension in what spoke through him. Those who listened, hushed and awed, would not have had any sure words to express what they were feeling. If anyone had asked them whether they believed in the divinity of Jesus, they would not have known what the question meant. But in the emotions which he woke in them, another world was breaking through. While they were near him they knew that their souls were coming near to God.

How do we discover the reality in the church's great affirmations concerning Christ: God of God, Light of Light, Very God of very God? Not by reciting phrases. Not by any arguments. Not by any outward signs. No, but by what happens within.

> Thou shalt know Him when He comes
> Not by any din of drums.
> Nor the vantage of His airs
> Neither by His crown, nor His gown.
> Nor by anything He wears.
> He shall only well known be
> By the holy harmony
> That His coming makes in Thee.

In the synagogue there was a man who had the spirit of an unclean demon. This is the first reference in the Gospel of Luke to the affliction that will become familiar in the whole narrative of this Gospel, and in that of the others. Great numbers of people in Palestine were haunted by the fearsome belief that evil spirits existed, hiding in desert places or in ravines, or in graveyards, and coming out invisibly but in horrid fact to invade human beings. Once that belief became established, it could spread in hysterical contagion—as belief in witches was to spread in Salem in a century long afterwards. Some person otherwise normal but torn by suppressed anxiety and remorse for some hidden guilt could be seized by physical spasms and by wild vagaries of mind. The person thus afflicted might so identify himself with the demon who he thought possessed him that he stood in terror of being changed, lest the demon in a last wild struggle might kill him. So the man in the synagogue cried out to Jesus, "Have you come to destroy us?" But there was a power in Jesus, a power of strength and calm, that hushed the possessed man's cry. He did not brush aside the man's agony as though it were nothing but imagination. He treated it as if it were the demonic reality which the man felt it to be. Therefore he spoke as though to that. "Come out of him," he said. Before the gaze of Jesus the burden of the man's distress was lifted, and into his tormented spirit came the assurance of a mercy that set him free.

It was not only in conspicuous places that the compassion of Jesus was unfailingly expressed. From the synagogue he went to Simon Peter's house. Someone told him that Peter's mother-in-law was sick. Jesus went in and stood beside her; when she heard his voice, her fever left her, and she rose up and went about her work. There was nothing exciting about that, and the people in Capernaum might have forgot it after a time. But not Peter. He would remember; and that perhaps is how the story of it got into Mark's Gospel and then into Luke's.

Since this was the sabbath, the rigid Jewish law prohibited anything that looked like labor. Therefore sick and infirm people could not be picked up by their friends and brought to Jesus. But in the Jewish reckoning the day ended with the sunset; and when the sun was going down, they came. Henry Twells, in his hymn of a hundred years ago, has expressed what that scene was like; and he has made it a symbol of a reality which can continually be true.

> Once more 'tis eventide, and we
> Oppressed with various ills draw near.
> What if thy form we cannot see?
> We know and feel that thou art here.

THE WIDER MINISTRY

And when it was day he departed and went into a lonely place. And the people sought him and came to him, and would have kept him from leaving them; but he said to them, "I must preach the good news of the kingdom of God to the other cities also; for I was sent for this purpose." And he was preaching in the synagogues of Judea. (Luke 4:42-44.)

It had been a long day, and for any ordinary strength an exhausting one. The people of Capernaum wanted to keep Jesus in their midst. The next morning when he had gone to a quiet place to pray, they followed him; and when they found that he was going on to other towns, they tried to persuade him not to go. An unending number all down the years has argued in the same fashion: "Why let benefits get away? Why missions, when there is so much that needs to be done right here at home? Let Christianity finish saving us. Those people off yonder somewhere do not matter."

But the voice of Christ will say again that the message of the kingdom of God must be as wide as the field of human need.

chapter 5

THE WINSOMENESS,
AND YET THE AWESOMENESS, OF JESUS

While the people pressed upon him to hear the word of God, he was standing by the lake of Gennesaret. And he saw two boats by the lake; but the fishermen had gone out of them and were washing their nets. Getting into one of the boats, which was Simon's, he asked him to put out a little from the land. And he sat down and taught the people from the boat. And when he had ceased speaking, he said to Simon, "Put out into the deep and let down your nets for a catch." And Simon answered, "Master, we toiled all night and took nothing! But at your word I will let down the nets." And when they had done this, they enclosed a great shoal of fish; and as their nets were breaking, they beckoned to their partners in the other boat to come and help them. And they came and filled both the boats, so that they began to sink. But when Simon Peter saw it, he fell down at Jesus' knees, saying, "Depart from me, for I am a sinful man, O Lord." For he was astonished, and all that were with him, at the catch of fish which they had taken; and so also were James and John, sons of Zebedee, who were partners with Simon. And Jesus said to Simon, "Do not be afraid; henceforth you will be catching men." And when they had brought their boats to land, they left everything and followed him.   (Luke 5:1-11.)

In the passage with which this chapter of the Gospel opens, the Evangelist has combined two matters: one is the tradition which had come to him of an astonishing miracle, and the other is a description of the call of the first disciples. The resulting impression is that it was the miracle which made the disciples follow Jesus.

But in this connection it is helpful to remember that there was a Gospel which was written earlier than the Gospel of Luke and which possesses at some points a special authority. This first Gospel was the Gospel of Mark; and a strong tradition which has come down from the early church is that Mark had "become the interpreter of Peter" (as Papias of Hierapolis reported in the second century), and that therefore in some of Mark's descriptions the remembrance of Peter is shining through. Certainly there would have been nothing that Peter would remember more particularly than the day and the scene when Jesus called him to be a disciple, and nothing that he might have been more likely to describe to Mark. When we turn to the opening chapter of Mark's Gospel, there the description is: so simple, so straightforward, so free from elaboration and yet so graphic, that it seems to bear the marks of an eyewitness. Four fishermen are near the shore of the Lake of Galilee; and the picture of what happened is etched with a convincing sharpness of particular facts—facts which in themselves were insignificant, but would have been unforgettable to Simon Peter. The four men are in two groups: Simon and Andrew, his brother, casting what—in the Greek word—was a scoop net and therefore walking in the shallow water; James and John in their boat mending the larger seine. Jesus speaks to the men by the shore; he calls to the men in the boat. Then there is the incidental reference at the end of Mark's description to Zebedee and the hired servants—a reference which just because it has no importance whatever conveys more strikingly the impression that Peter was describing the scene that way for the simple reason that that is the way the whole scene was.

There was no miraculous shoal of fishes, and there was no need of one. The power of Jesus over the men who were to follow him did not depend on miracles. It had to do instead with the immense attractiveness of his spirit. His passion for the kingdom of God, his courage, his strength, and his winsomeness gave to his manhood a magnetism which these virile fishermen could not resist. They had no definitions yet in which to tell what he meant to them. They only knew what they felt. Not in extraordinary things he might do, but in what he was as he stood there calling them to his companionship, they felt themselves gripped by the immediate reality of God.

This will always be true. The same Jesus who became the Christ for the disciples becomes the Christ again, and he becomes such most surely when men realize that his divinity is expressed through his complete humanity. Ernest Gordon, now Dean of the Chapel at Princeton University, an officer in the Argyll Highlanders of the British Army in the Second World War and captured by the Japanese at Singapore, was one of the prisoners forced to build "the Railroad of Death" which he has described in *Through the Valley of the Kwai*. In the horrors of that prison camp men had to find something better than an abstract Christianity whose "doctrines and practices seemed irrelevant." Said Ernest Gordon,

Through our readings and our discussions we came to know Jesus. He was one of us. He would understand our problems because they were the sort of problems he had faced himself. . . .

He, too, had known bone-weariness from too much toil, the suffering, rejection and disappointments that are part of the fabric of life. . . . The friends he had were like our own and like us.

As we read and talked, he became flesh and blood. We saw him in the full dignity of manhood. He was a man we could understand and admire; the kind of friend we would like to have guarding our left flank; a leader we could follow.[1]

But what about the picture of Jesus which appears in this chapter of Luke? That is part of the reality also—though it may be that Luke has combined here two elements which do not belong together. In the Gospel of John there is an account of a miraculous draught of fishes which occurred in Galilee after the resurrection, when the disciples were in the presence of the risen Christ; and New Testament scholars have surmised that the call to launch out into the deep for the great catch that could be gathered represented not any words of Jesus at the actual Lake of Galilee but what the early church took to be the message of the risen Lord concerning the missionary adventures it must undertake. Luke may be reflecting that Johannine story here as a framework for his portrayal of the shattering emotion which sometimes could overwhelm a man like Simon Peter as he stood in the presence of Jesus. This is the message of spiritual importance which comes to us from Luke. Whatever may have happened about the fish, it is certain that there were occasions when the greatness of Jesus filled the disciples with such awe that they could only stammer out words as humbled and abased as those which Luke here puts upon the lips of Simon Peter: "Depart from me, for I am a sinful man, O Lord."

WHEN A LEPER WAS CURED

> While he was in one of the cities, there came a man full of leprosy; and when he saw Jesus, he fell on his face and besought him, "Lord, if you will, you can make me clean." And he stretched out his hand, and touched him, saying, "I will; be clean." And immediately the leprosy left him. And he charged him to tell no one; but "go and show yourself to the priest, and make an offering for your cleansing, as Moses commanded, for a proof to the people." (Luke 5:12-14.)

The discoveries in modern medicine have made leprosy no longer the hopeless horror it used to be. Many lepers are cured, and those who still have the disease can be in colonies where their treatment is carried on under conditions of kindness and encouragement. But in earlier times leprosy meant not only physical disintegration; it meant also such an exclusion from all decent human contacts that it must have seemed to the leper that

[1] Ernest Gordon, *Through the Valley of the Kwai* (New York: Harper & Row, 1962), pp. 118, 137.

to the world and its regard he was no more than a dead soul. He was not allowed to come where people were. If anyone approached him, he must give his warning cry, "Unclean!"

In the narrative here, Luke is reflecting both Jesus' power of healing and his unfailing compassion for any human being who came to him in need. The story of the leper illuminates these facts first. But there is a sidelight also, which had to do with Jesus' relationship to established customs. He told the leper to go and show himself to the priest and make the offering which was required of anyone who believed he had been cleansed and wanted that cleansing certified. The fact that Jesus directed the leper thus makes plain that he did not ignore the value of sensible regulations which the Jewish community had set up. He never hesitated to break through old codes and customs when these had become cramping to life. But there ought to be respect—and impatient reformers in any century should remember that—for the orderly processes and methods which long social experience may have evolved.

BODY AND SOUL

> But so much the more the report went abroad concerning him; and great multitudes gathered to hear and to be healed of their infirmities. But he withdrew to the wilderness and prayed. (Luke 5:15-16.)

It is easy to understand that multitudes gathered to hear and to be healed of their infirmities—more eager, no doubt, to be healed than to hear. We poor human creatures live in mortal bodies, and the primal instincts have to do with what these bodies feel. "Touch his bone and his flesh," said Satan in the book of Job, and it will be seen what a man is most concerned with. Respectable numbers of people go on Sundays to church to listen to the Word that is spoken to their spirits, but a great many more will go that same week to doctors' offices. And when some exponent of a self-appointed healing ministry comes to town, crowds will flock to have him lay his hands upon them—as also the crowds of wistful sufferers flock to Lourdes in France. The nature we have been born with has its double aspect: the eyes of the spirit look upward to the sky, but the feet walk the dusty earth.

Jesus was always sensitive to these plain realities. His heart went out to all the pathetic people who were sick or crippled. But there was danger that the physical needs might be so clamorous as to eclipse all other values and that there might grow up a crowd hysteria which could be satisfied only by sensational miraculous signs. He must keep his own spirit tuned to the heavenly purpose for the wholeness of men's life. Therefore he went away alone to pray.

THE POWER OF THE SON OF MAN

On one of those days, as he was teaching, there were Pharisees and teachers of the law sitting by, who had come from every village of Galilee and Judea and from Jerusalem; and the power of the Lord was with him to heal. And behold, men were bringing on a bed a man who was paralyzed, and they sought to bring him in and lay him before Jesus; but finding no way to bring him in, because of the crowd, they went up on the roof and let him down with his bed through the tiles into the midst before Jesus. And when he saw their faith he said, "Man, your sins are forgiven you." And the scribes and the Pharisees began to question, saying, "Who is this that speaks blasphemies? Who can forgive sins but God only?" When Jesus perceived their questionings, he answered them, "Why do you question in your hearts? Which is easier, to say, 'Your sins are forgiven you,' or to say, 'Rise and walk'? But that you may know that the Son of man has authority on earth to forgive sins"—he said to the man who was paralyzed—"I say to you, rise, take up your bed and go home." And immediately he rose before them, and took up that on which he lay, and went home, glorifying God. And amazement seized them all, and they glorified God and were filled with awe, saying, "We have seen strange things today." (Luke 5:17-26.)

This passage, like the preceding one, is the description of a healing, but it is full of rich suggestions that go beyond the principal fact.

To begin with, there were the friends who brought the sick man into Jesus' presence. We are not told whether the bringing of him was at his entreaty, or whether it was their own idea. However that may be, they had a warmth of interest and a determination which would not be turned aside by any difficulty. More ordinary persons might have started out well enough on what they thought was a proper duty and then given up when the effort looked unreasonable.

"Sorry, we wanted to get you there"—they could have had excuse to say —"but you can see for yourself how it is. The street is jammed with people. Jesus is inside that house: and there's no way of getting you on this pallet through the crowd even as far as the door. Nothing left but to turn round and take you home."

But that was what they emphatically did not say. They went up by the outside stairs that led to the flat roof of the Palestinian house, they made an opening in the roof, and they let their friend down directly into the presence of Jesus. This was friendship that really amounted to something. And out of it comes a contemporary question. How many of us have the spiritual devotion that will go the whole never-to-be-discouraged way to bring some man closer to the living Christ?

The second arresting fact in the story has to do with Jesus himself. The scene, which was first described in the Gospel of Mark and is reflected— but with not quite the same vividness—in this passage of Luke, is lighted by Jesus' quick compassion. According to Mark his words had a special tenderness. Looking at the man lying there on his pallet, paralyzed, he said to him: "My son"—as though he spoke the comforting pity that one might bring to a hurt child.

Then he said what might not have been expected first. It was the man's body that everyone was looking at, but Jesus said, "Your sins are forgiven you."

It is not to be inferred from this that all bodily illness is the result and sign of sin—so much suffering weighed out as the equivalent of so much sin. That is the hard idea which Job's counselors insisted upon and which Job so desperately denied. But it is true that the body does reflect the mind and spirit, and that underneath the physical symptoms may be the smothered anxiety and remorse which come from sickness of the soul. Looking at the man before him, the deep-seeing eyes of Jesus recognized his hidden need. Therefore he brought him first the overwhelming message of God's forgiving mercy. Once he was grasped by that, hope and courage would break through the paralysis that bound him.

Some of the Pharisees who stood near muttered indignantly. Who was this that blasphemously presumed to declare a man's sins forgiven? And where was any sign that his sins *were* forgiven? Easy words to say—and also empty.

Then Jesus answered. They wanted to know whether he had the authority to forgive sins? He said to the man who was paralyzed, "I say to you, rise, take up your bed and go home." And immediately he rose before them, and took up that on which he lay, and went home, glorifying God.

For the first time in the narrative of Luke, Jesus speaks of himself as the Son of man. Exactly what those words meant to him no one can presume to know. The most thoughtful and reverent pondering of New Testament scholars can only piece together the inferences that come from the Gospels and their background. Son of man in Aramaic might mean only man; but certainly Jesus was not saying here that man, *any* man, can speak with the authority of God. In the book of Ezekiel Son of man is the prophet standing in his imperfect humanness before the glory of the divine. In the book of Daniel it was written: "I saw in the night visions, and behold, with the clouds of heaven there came one like a son of man, and he came to the Ancient of Days and was presented before him. And to him was given dominion and glory and kingdom, . . . an everlasting dominion which shall not pass away." All the partial realities which those words reflect may have been woven together in the consciousness of Jesus: the fullness of his humanity and at the same time the completeness of his consecration as the Father's instrument which made the power of God operative in him beyond all ordinary human limitations. Such certainly was the Son of man whom the Gospels picture: Jesus whose presence in any circle of men and women and in every scene seemed invested with a dominion and a glory. It was no wonder then that Luke's account of the healing of him who was paralyzed comes to this climax: Amazement seized them all, and they glorified God and were filled with awe, saying, "We have seen strange things today."

THE CALL OF MATTHEW

> After this he went out, and saw a tax collector, named Levi, sitting at the tax office; and he said to him, "Follow me." And he left everything; and rose and followed him.
>
> And Levi made him a great feast in his house; and there was a large company of tax collectors and others sitting at table with them. And the Pharisees and their scribes murmured against his disciples, saying, "Why do you eat and drink with tax collectors and sinners?" And Jesus answered them, "Those who are well have no need of a physician, but those who are sick; I have not come to call the righteous, but sinners to repentance."
> (Luke 5:27-32.)

In the Gospels of Mark and of Matthew there are accounts almost identical with this of the call by Jesus of a particular man to be one of his disciples. Here and in Mark his name is Levi. In the First Gospel he is Matthew. How the difference in names arose, and which is right, remains uncertain—and also unimportant. The significant matter is that Jesus called a man out of a class whom the people in general looked upon with hatred and contempt.

In the King James translation these men were called publicans. What that meant becomes more specific in the plain word of the Revised Standard Version—tax-collectors. The Roman authorities, or perhaps Herod Antipas to whom they had given the local privilege, farmed out the right of collecting taxes to the most acceptable bidder. Then the man who had the contract paid to the authorities the sum they set, and kept for himself what he could collect in addition. For two reasons therefore tax-gatherers were despised: they served the alien rulers whom everybody who called himself a patriot was supposed to hate, and their business seemed to the people who were gouged in the tax-collecting to be so much a thing of greed and graft that no decent person would be in it. Yet it was one of these men whom Jesus takes into the circle of his disciples.

But the thing that seemed most incredible to stereotyped opinion was exactly what was characteristic of Jesus. He did not look at men according to their labels. His understanding eyes could see what the individual person really was, in his true self: the hidden man of desires and possibilities that did not show in the surface facts by which the crowd judged. And what he saw in this tax-collector was what Dorothy Sayers, with her flashing insight, has imagined as Matthew's description of his own response.

I shan't forget my first sight of him neither. You don't know me, mister—well, I'll tell you, I was a tax-gatherer. You know what to think about that: I can see it in your face. One of the dirty dogs that works for the government and makes his profit out of selling his countrymen. That's so, and you're dead right. . . . Well, see here. When he came down our street the other day, I don't mind telling you I'd had a pretty good morning. . . . And I looked up—and there he was. "Hullo!" I thought, "here's the Prophet. I suppose he'll start calling me names like the rest of 'em. Let him. Hard words break no bones." So I stared at him, and he stared at me—seemed as though his eyes were going straight through me and through me ledgers, and reading all the bits as wasn't for publication. And somehow or other he made me feel dirty. That's all. Just dirty. I started shuffling my feet. And he smiled—you know the way he smiles sometimes all of a sudden—and he says, "Follow me." I couldn't believe my ears. I tumbled out of my desk, and away he went up the street, and I went after him. I could hear people laughing—and somebody spat at me—but I didn't seem to care. . . .
I said to him, "Master, I'm coming with you." And he said, "Come along." [2]

To call the man seemed to proper people bad enough. To sit down in his house with a lot of his questionable intimates seemed worse. No wonder the Pharisees and scribes were shocked. They did not come directly up to Jesus with their challenge, but they relayed their sense of outrage through the disciples: "Why do you eat and drink with tax-collectors and sinners?"

Jesus' answer has come down as one of the supreme expressions of the meaning of his life and ministry: "Those who are well have no need of a physician, but those who are sick; I have not come to call the righteous, but sinners to repentance." How undeniable and final his illustration was, and yet how easy it is to forget what ought to follow from it. Of course a doctor does not sit around discussing pleasantries with people who are well; he must be listening to the distressed and is on his rounds among them. But what of priests and pastors who are supposed to be physicians of the soul, and what of the Christian church in general? Always there is the subtle temptation to act as though the righteous—not to say the self-righteous—were the ones that matter, and to make the church a satisfied conventicle of the pious, with no passion of evangelism for the human crowd that would be dear to the heart of Christ.

[2] *The Man Born to Be King,* pp. 109-10.

THE GOSPEL OF JOY

> And they said to him, "The disciples of John fast often and offer prayers, and so do the disciples of the Pharisees, but yours eat and drink." And Jesus said to them, "Can you make wedding guests fast while the bridegroom is with them? The days will come, when the bridegroom is taken away from them, and then they will fast in those days." He told them a parable also: "No one tears a piece from a new garment and puts it upon an old garment; if he does, he will tear the new, and the piece from the new will not match the old. And no one puts new wine into old wineskins; if he does, the new wine will burst the skins and it will be spilled, and the skins will be destroyed. But new wine must be put into fresh wineskins. And no one after drinking old wine desires new; for he says, 'The old is good.' "   (Luke 5:33-39.)

The resistance to Jesus' spirit which was voiced in connection with the tax-collector found another ground for complaint. Jesus could have no excuse for ignorance as to the standards that were supposed to mark religious people. The requirements of Judaism called for fasting on specified days. John the Baptist knew that, and his disciples fasted. Why didn't Jesus' disciples have any regard for that?

If the sentences which Luke records as Jesus' answer are to convey their specific meaning, one must recognize who it was that each sentence refers to—Jesus' own disciples, or John's?

In vs. 34 Jesus is obviously speaking of his own. As they gathered round him and listened to his message of the kingdom of God, such a mood as that of fasting would be as unthinkable as it would be for friends of the bridegroom on a wedding day. Verse 35, on the other hand, may express Jesus' understanding sympathy with John the Baptist's disciples and their inevitable sadness if his ministry had been brought to its end. And vs. 39 also may refer to them. They had drunk the old wine and were accustomed to it. It could not be expected of them quickly to like the new.

But vss. 36 and 37, like vs. 33, have to do with those who had been caught up into Jesus' purpose that "my joy may be in you, and that your joy may be full." For them all life was new, and there could be no sense in going back to the moods that were old and gray: no sense in tearing up the wedding garment of fellowship in the kingdom to make patchwork with yesterday's forms; no sense in thinking that old wineskins could hold the exultant ferment of the new spiritual wine. Whenever the church forgets that and tries to contain the Gospel within the dry traditions which have no flexibility, its living power is lost. The message of Jesus is forever one of good news; his only authentic witnesses are those whose faces show it.

chapter 6

LIFE MORE IMPORTANT THAN LAW

On a sabbath, while he was going through the grainfields, his disciples
plucked and ate some ears of grain, rubbing them in their hands. But some
of the Pharisees said, "Why are you doing what is not lawful to do on the
sabbath?" And Jesus answered, "Have you not read what David did when
he was hungry, he and those who were with him: how he entered the
house of God, and took and ate the bread of the Presence, which it is not
lawful for any but the priests to eat, and also gave it to those with him?"
And he said to them, "The Son of man is lord of the sabbath."

(Luke 6:1-5.)

As the disciples went through a grain field on a sabbath day, they broke
off some of the heads of ripening wheat, rubbed the kernels between their
hands, and ate them. They were breaking the law, said some of the Pharisees who saw them. As one reads the account, the first supposition might
be that what the Pharisees objected to was the disciples' helping themselves
to somebody else's grain. But as a matter of fact, it was not this that they
complained of, for they knew that in the book of Deuteronomy it was
written, "When you go into your neighbor's standing grain, you may pluck
the ears with your hand"—a commonsense flexibility of the law which
meant that anything as trivial as the picking up of a few grains of a neighbor's wheat should not be treated as invasion of his property.

What was wrong, then, in what the disciples did? Nothing, the ordinary
man might have said; but not so the Pharisees. "This is the sabbath day,"
they would have argued. "The law says that no work shall be done on the
sabbath day, and the learned rabbis have specified what that word *work*
includes. It includes reaping, threshing, winnowing, and preparing food.
These disciples of Jesus have violated every one of those prohibitions: reaping when they took the grains of wheat, threshing when they rubbed the
kernels out, winnowing when they threw the husks away, and getting a meal
ready by the whole of what they did."

How would Jesus dispose of a fantastic legalism such as that? He did it
by a double answer. As lawyers, the Pharisees based everything on prece-

dent. Well, he would give them a precedent which they could not belittle: the precedent of David seeming to violate the sanctity of the tabernacle by taking the holy bread which only the priests were supposed to touch. No liberty the disciples took could be as conspicuous as that.

And why had David dared to do what he had done? Because of the urgency of actual need. This, said Jesus, means more than frozen forms of law. The Son of man can be lord of the sabbath, which is to say that the living instinct of the spirit is a more sensitive guide to what God would sanction than any inflexible code can be.

To the rigid literalist that seemed then—and always seems—to be a dangerous and subversive doctrine. How can there be any proper religious conduct unless lines are drawn hard and fast? To make new interpretations is to upset everything. But opposed to this timid narrowness, Jesus saw the more inclusive truth. He reverenced every commandment and custom which embodied the best that was already believed. He reverenced—for particular example—the real holiness of the sabbath day. But he saw that the only interpretation of a law which is true to the will of God is that which ensures that within it the life of the spirit will not shrink but expand.

WHEN THE SPRINGS IN THE HEART GROW BITTER

> On another sabbath, when he entered the synagogue and taught, a man was there whose right hand was withered. And the scribes and the Pharisees watched him, to see whether he would heal on the sabbath, so that they might find an accusation against him. But he knew their thoughts, and he said to the man who had the withered hand, "Come and stand here." And he rose and stood there. And Jesus said to them, "I ask you, is it lawful on the sabbath to do good or to do harm, to save life or to destroy it?" And he looked around on them all, and said to him, "Stretch out your hand." And he did so, and his hand was restored. But they were filled with fury and discussed with one another what they might do to Jesus. (Luke 6:6-11.)

The scene which Luke describes here is an example even more conspicuous than the one preceding it of how that which was supposed to be religious loyalty can turn sour. The scribes and Pharisees ought to have been the best men in the community. They thought they were, and the people in general were inclined to the same idea about them. They were the inheritors of a long tradition of devotion to the church establishment, and they made it their business to represent everything that was ecclesiastically correct. They believed that they knew the patterns which God meant all the people to conform to, and as far as lay within their power they meant to see to it that everybody did conform. What could be more desirable than that, and what could be better for religion than for the scribes and Pharisees to have their way? So it seemed; but the fact was lamentably different.

The trouble was that their convictions had become cantankerous. They were so sure they knew what was good that it never occurred to them that they might learn better. Nothing could be good if it cut across their previous judgments. So when they came into contact with Jesus, they were not going to believe that any new light might come through him. He was different, and that was enough to show that he must be wrong.

That had been their attitude in the matter of the disciples eating the grain on the sabbath day. Now they were to express themselves again. Once more it was a sabbath, and this time Jesus was in the synagogue. Also in the synagogue was a man with a paralyzed hand. If their hearts had been compassionate, the first thing they might have thought about was this man's affliction, and the first wish they might have had was that somehow he could be healed. They did notice the man's affliction, but not with any resultant concern for the man himself. A healing on the sabbath would be unlawful; that was the one grim idea they held to. Then, knowing that Jesus was reputed to have healing power, they watched to see what he would do—a baleful watching that had no love in it but only an obsession for the abstract law. When Jesus told the man to come forward and stretch out his hand, and then when he asked the penetrating question, "Is it lawful on the sabbath to do good or to do harm, to save life or to destroy it" the scribes and Pharisees still refused to listen. The man could stay crippled for all they cared, and they would rather he did stay crippled than that they should admit that their harsh idea about the law was wrong.

When the divine mercy in the touch of Jesus did heal the man, did this produce any response in them? Yes, it did; but in a reverse direction which showed to what tragic degree prejudice and belligerent pride can poison the spirit of men who are supposed to be good. The piety which might have been in them a well of living water had become a bitter pool. So the account in the Gospel comes to its shadowed climax. "They were filled with fury and discussed with one another what they might do to Jesus."

And the troubled question rises: Are there still those who, because their churchmanship outweighs their Christianity, have made themselves antagonists to the outgoing grace of Jesus?

THE MEN WHOM JESUS CHOSE

In these days he went out into the hills to pray; and all night he continued in prayer to God. And when it was day, he called his disciples,

> and chose from them twelve, whom he named apostles; Simon, whom he named Peter, and Andrew his brother, and James and John, and Philip, and Bartholomew, and Matthew, and Thomas, and James the son of Alphaeus, and Simon who was called the Zealot, and Judas the son of James, and Judas Iscariot, who became a traitor.   (Luke 6:12-16.)

Imagination lingers upon the picture which appears as one reads the first sentence of this passage from the Gospel. Jesus goes up into the hills to pray: up to the heights where the tumult of the day and the confusion of the world's voices were left below, up where the great perspectives widened and he could be alone with God. When we think of prayer, we often instinctively think of it as saying something; and we wonder what Jesus could have been saying and what words he used when—as the Gospel tells —he continued all night in prayer. But the heart of prayer is listening; and what Jesus must have done that night was to lift up his mind and heart for the light and strength that come when the soul is hushed before the infinite.

There was a particular reason for his praying. He was about to choose twelve men to be nearest him and to carry on his ministry for the kingdom of God. The next day he chose them, and the list which the Gospel records stands as the answer to his prayer. To the ordinary estimate it might not have seemed a conspicuous answer. What he sought when he was praying was that there might be men fit for the great purposes of God and that those he was about to name as his disciples would prove to be such men. Then comes the list of those whom he selected, and on the surface it certainly did not look promising. A few obscure fishermen from Galilee, a tax-collector, and some others who seemed equally unimportant; what divine achievement could come through a group as commonplace as that? According to human probability, nothing. But the very fact of these men's seeming insignificance was to make room for the limitless power of the grace of God. Before long what the world held to be incredible would happen. These men, in themselves of such small capabilities, became the instruments of a spirit so transforming that their impact has been upon history ever since.

Consider who they were as individuals, these twelve whom Jesus chose.

The first in the list is Simon Peter, whom Luke has already named in chapter 5. His subsequent record, as the Gospels will describe it, was made up of lights and shadows—with the shadows sometimes more obvious. One day on the Lake of Galilee he would plunge out of a boat to go to Jesus and then grow panic-stricken and begin to sink. The last night of Jesus' life he would vehemently declare that nothing could make him fail his Master, but in the courtyard of Caiaphas he would deny that he ever knew him. A poor sort of person, it would have seemed, to be made into the chief apostle. But that was what he became; and the reason was twofold.

In the first place, Peter had qualities in his nature that were better than the moments of his failure showed. He was inconstant in behavior, but not in the deep desire underneath. He was capable of a devotion that wanted to be faithful and was overcome with shame when he was not. His vehemence, which could be his weakness, was also his potential strength. There was nothing tepid in him, nothing calculating and halfway. Fires were always burning in him, if only they could be kept at steady flame.

That was one side of the double fact which made it possible for Peter to become a bigger man. The other was more important. By himself he would never have been transformed. But the power of Jesus' spirit laid hold upon him. At first it made him shrink, as in the encounter described in the preceding chapter when he cried out, "Depart from me, for I am a sinful man, O Lord." That is the way supreme and shining goodness is bound to affect the man who knows his lack of goodness but has at least a hunger for it, which makes him feel the awful contrast between what he might be and what he is. For Peter, as for every man, there was the impulse to get away—or to have the divine challenge go away. Yet the real Peter, the Peter that he had not yet fully known to be himself, wanted exactly the opposite of that. He wanted to stay where Jesus was. So he would learn and exemplify in his life at last what is the heart of the whole Gospel: that it is not what we are at the beginning and not what anyone by himself can resolve and do; but it is the love of God which will not let us go, that at last can redeem us and make us new.

The next two in the list of the disciples (except for Andrew, who will be remembered presently) were James and John. They were brothers and at the beginning apparently much alike. But one of them would become an example of how a man's spirit can be transformed. According to the almost unanimous belief of New Testament scholars, John is the one not named but meant when the Fourth Gospel speaks of "the disciple whom Jesus loved." Something in his spirit made a relationship between him and his Master that had a quality all its own. And what that quality was shines also in the First Letter of John, where it is written, "Love is of God, and he who loves is born of God and knows God. . . . Beloved, if God so loved us, we also ought to love one another."

Yet the curious fact is that in the early part of the Gospel narrative John does not appear as an exemplar of love or of any kind of tenderness. He and his brother James were both called "sons of thunder." Presently he would be among the disciples as they came seeking shelter for the night in a Samaritan village, only to be rebuffed and turned away. And what did John do then? He flared with anger, as did James. He wanted to curse the churlish villagers and to call down God's lightning to blast their whole town.

So it is plain that John was no lukewarm man, incapable of fierce reactions. On the contrary, there was plenty of fire in him, but fire that could be destructive unless he learned a new self-discipline. "You do not know what manner of spirit you are of," said Jesus to him and James that day in Samaria. If he was ever to become the apostle of love, he would have to learn the hard way.

But it is this sort of man, and not the soft man, who is capable at last of the sort of love that will reflect the love of God. In the latter part of the nineteenth and the beginning of the twentieth century there was a great headmaster of a school, whom some men still living knew and never can forget. He had a blazing temper which could terrify. He had a holy wrath against anything that was mean or false or lazy. Sometimes his judgments were impetuous, and he could launch his hot rebuke without sufficient cause. But if he saw that he was wrong, he would turn to the one he had hurt with a great flood of remorseful eagerness to make amends. And so when all was said and done, the boys and men he dealt with knew that in him there was a concern for their full selves, which made a bond that no mere affability could ever have created.

Perhaps it was this sort of love that John learned from Jesus: a love that would never compromise with truth, but grew continually more understanding, patient, and compassionate; not warmhearted only, but deephearted. And perhaps it was because John had begun thus to sense, at least a little, the depth of the divine love that he could be closest to his Lord.

Peter and James and John: these were the three men who would be often and intimately with Jesus. It would seem that there might have been another also. The account in Mark's Gospel of the calling of the first disciples includes a fourth: Andrew, Simon Peter's brother. But in Mark's Gospel and in the Gospels of Matthew and Luke, Andrew reappears almost not at all. Yet he lingered in the memory of the early church; and in the Gospel of John, written probably at or about the end of the first century, he appears in very winsome aspects.

According to this evangelist some of the men who were afterwards to be called to be Jesus' disciples were in the Jordan valley where John the Baptist was preaching and baptizing; and there Andrew, having seen Jesus, went and told his brother Simon and first brought him to Jesus' notice. Later, in

Galilee, when Jesus was surrounded by a hungry multitude, it was Andrew who observed that there was a lad there who had five barley loaves and two fish. His practical mind went on to say, "What are they among so many?" but all the same he told his Master what there was to begin with, as though in the hands of Jesus the impossibly little might somehow be enough. Still later, according to this Gospel of John, some Greeks in Jerusalem wanted to see Jesus. They came to one of the disciples, Philip, with their request; and Philip went and told Andrew (as though Andrew could carry their appeal better than he), and Andrew went with Philip to tell Jesus.

Such, then, was the tradition as it developed and was handed down. Yet the fact remains that in the earlier, Synoptic narratives Andrew has no conspicuous place. Why that was we cannot know, and there is an element of human pathos in the lack of public record of this one among the two sets of brothers who followed Jesus first. But then one remembers that in the final accounting of human lives it is not only those in the foreground who have been significant. Thought goes back to the beautiful Old Testament story of David and Jonathan. It was David who would play the great role in history, but it was the self-forgetting love of Jonathan that made it possible for him to play any role at all. So also it may have been that back of what some of the other disciples and especially his brother Simon Peter did, there was the warmth of Andrew's faithful spirit. Certainly that is often true in any group of human souls. From the one in the background may come much of the strength and encouragement which has fortified those who stand in front.

In the rest of the list of the disciples two names that stand out are those of Matthew and Thomas. Both men are good to remember; for if Matthew was the tax-gatherer who is also called Levi, then he showed how the fascination of Jesus could have a stronger pull than all the money and possessions a man might have wanted to hold to; and Thomas was the disciple who had his doubts, and yet—to the everlasting encouragement of all honest questioners—kept being loyal to the best he knew, and at the end found the doubts disappear in a blaze of living faith.

James the son of Alphaeus, Simon the Zealot, Judas the son of James— of them we know next to nothing. So far as the record goes, they seem to have had no conspicuous abilities—which is likely to be true always of most of those who try to be disciples of Jesus. But there are men whose value is not in anything dramatic that they will ever do, but in the mere fact that they are just plain good. There is in them a transparency of spirit which lets a sense of God's reality come through. When we talk with them, we feel the better for it. A kind of brightness shines on everyday life from them like the brightness of spring as it falls upon the ground. Perhaps some of these men whom Jesus chose were men like that, and that was why he chose them.

At the end of the list comes "Judas Iscariot, who became a traitor." One reads those words and remembers the awful fatefulness that is wrapped up in the freedom of the will. No human individual is constrained to goodness. God sets before each man the motivation to the highest; but if he chooses, he can turn his back upon it and walk the other way into the dark.

THE EVERLASTING NEED FOR CHRIST

> And he came down with them and stood on a level place, with a great crowd of his disciples and a great multitude of people from all Judea and Jerusalem and the seacoast of Tyre and Sidon, who came to hear him and to be healed of their diseases; and those who were troubled with unclean spirits were cured. And all the crowd sought to touch him, for power came forth from him and healed them all.   (Luke 6:17-19.)

The multitudes came to hear him and to be healed of their diseases. For both reasons people still turn toward Christ. Although the bodily presence of Jesus is not in the world today to lay his visible hands upon the sick, his life-giving touch continues. It is mediated through doctors, nurses, and hospitals which are the instruments of the compassion that glowed in him and by which the best in the Christian world has been inspired; and the thought of him has given to innumerable sufferers the quietness and trust which have helped them to get well. In that deep sense the reality expressed in the words of Whittier's hymn, "We May Not Climb the Heavenly Steeps," is again experienced: "The healing of his seamless dress is by our beds of pain."

But that is not all. As Whittier went on to say, "We touch him in life's throng and press, and we are whole again." If men need Christ for their infirmities, so they need him even more to inspire and direct their strength. In the hurry and confusion of life, his voice can teach what we have to know if the things we do are to have any worthwhile meaning in the light of the kingdom of God.

THE DIVINE
CONCERN FOR THE TROUBLED

> And he lifted up his eyes on his disciples, and said:
> "Blessed are you poor, for yours is the kingdom of God. Blessed are you that hunger now, for you shall be satisfied. Blessed are you that weep now, for you shall laugh.

"Blessed are you when men hate you, and when they exclude you and revile you, and cast out your name as evil, on account of the Son of man! Rejoice in that day, and leap for joy, for behold, your reward is great in heaven; for so their fathers did to the prophets. But woe to you that are rich, for you have received your consolation.

"Woe to you that are full now, for you shall hunger. Woe to you that laugh now, for you shall mourn and weep.

"Woe to you, when all men speak well of you, for so their fathers did to the false prophets."

(Luke 6:20-26.)

Here Jesus is speaking not to the crowd in general but directly to his disciples. There must have been times when they needed his encouragement, and this may have been one of those times. Did they get homesick now and then for the Lake of Galilee and for the familiar and friendly little towns where their lives had centered? What had happened to their fishing boats, their houses, and other possessions they had left behind? It was wonderful to be with Jesus, but sometimes they must have been anxious. None of them—unless it was Matthew—had ever reached even the fringes of being rich, but now they were getting poorer. They could not always know one day where they would find something to eat the next. And being with Jesus meant accumulating plenty of enemies. These sullen Pharisees and scribes, with the high priests and the suspicious Herod in the background, made the future look ominous. So, perhaps it happened that one day they looked depressed and that Jesus saw it.

If so, it is good to imagine what followed: good to imagine how Jesus' quick compassion reached out to rally them. It is as though he said: "I know all about it. You are bothered about what you left behind and what you do not have. You get so discouraged you could almost cry. Sometimes you are afraid. A little more and you might pity yourselves. But do you know what the truth is? You are the ones on whom the blessing rests. You are the ones who can be glad. Look up, and look ahead. Yours will be part of the victory of the kingdom of God; and having been poor and hungry and sometimes scared will seem to have been nothing in comparison with the joy of that!"

And what Jesus said to them had also a wider reference. Though he spoke primarily to the disciples, his message was for all those who could be called poor. In that Oriental world of the first century to be poor meant not only to have no money; it meant to have no justice either. The rich and powerful could exploit the little people as they pleased, and the poor were synonymous with the afflicted. So one of the psalms pleads with God that he "defend the cause of the poor of the people, give deliverance to the needy and crush the oppressor." Jesus had grown up among the poor, and he knew

99

what was often the bitterness of their lot. He understood what it could be like for some helpless individual to stand—as one of his parables pictured —before an unjust judge. He saw the quality of soul that could sometimes develop in these little people: their patience, their courage, their reaching up toward God. In his sermon in the synagogue at Nazareth he preached good news to them. And those who presume to preach in his name today had better be concerned for the poor and the afflicted, concerned for social righteousness, and possessed by Jesus' indignation against all callousness and cruelty of the strong against the weak, if they themselves are not to stand rejected by their Lord.

After the promise to the poor there follows in vss. 24-26 a contrasting indictment of the rich. The spirit of it will be better understood when it is read not as a blanket condemnation of all who have wealth—for Jesus did not condemn Zacchaeus—but as a condemnation of those for whom their wealth destroyed any longing for the kingdom of God. Such was the sort of man whom Jesus would picture in one of his parables, concerned with nothing except to store up more wealth in bigger barns, to eat, drink, and be merry—and forgetting that before the day ended his soul would be required. Such was Dives, indifferent to the hunger of Lazarus at his gate. The deadlines in wealth can be that they destroy the upreach of the soul. The rich man has so much to satisfy his earthly appetite that he may have no higher aspiration. What else should he hunger for when he is already full? And when all men speak well of him and fawn upon him for his favors, why should he disturb his complacency and consider some sort of inconvenient commitment to the kingdom of God?

Well then, where does the woe come in? Nowhere, in the rich man's immediate perception. And that is his peril, and in the end his perdition. For he does not see that as he builds the glittering shell of things around him he himself is shrinking. And when the shell is broken, where large thoughts and generous purposes might have been, there is only emptiness; and the man himself has no more substance than the handful of his dust.

THE COMMAND THAT SEEMED IMPOSSIBLE

"But I say to you that hear, Love your enemies, do good to those who hate you, bless those who curse you, pray for those who abuse you. To him who strikes you on the cheek, offer the other also; and from him who takes away your cloak do not withhold your coat as well. Give to every one who begs from you; and of him who takes away your goods, do not ask them again. And as you wish that men would do to you, do so to them. If you love those who love you, what credit is that to you? For even sinners love those who love them. And if you do good to those who do good to you, what credit is that to you? For even sinners do the same. And if you lend to those from whom you hope to receive, what credit is that to you? Even sinners lend to sinners, to receive as much again. But love your enemies, and do good, and lend, expecting nothing in return; and your reward will be great, and you will be sons of the Most High; for he is kind to the ungrateful and the selfish. Be merciful, even as your Father is merciful."

(Luke 6:27-36.)

In the words which begin this passage, we are confronted by the same breathtaking ideal which the Gospel of Matthew has included as part of Jesus' Sermon on the Mount: "Love your enemies, do good to those who hate you." That charge of Jesus must have staggered the imagination of the men in Israel who first heard it. "Love these Romans who have conquered us; love these tax-collectors who have sold themselves to be the agents of the Romans and of Herod, that pawn of Rome; love these teachers of the law who bind burdens on us which they do not assume themselves—how can we be expected to do that?" The whole idea seemed incredible to those who listened to Jesus nineteen hundred years ago. It seems incredible to the average person now. But all the same we have not been able to get rid of Jesus' words. They keep sounding like the summons of some great bell to which we can never be quite deaf. Yet how can we ever answer what he seems to be requiring?

Our first approach may be by trying to understand specifically the meaning of the word in the Gospel which, translated into English, stands as *love*. Our trouble is that we have in English only one word immediately available; whereas the Greek vocabulary which the Evangelist could employ had three. One word meant romantic love. A second meant the kind of devoted loyalty which is instinctive toward those who are most near and dear. But the third word did not carry that strong emotional content. Instead it had to do with the direction in which thought and will are deliberately turned. It meant the active purpose of a helpfulness which may not begin with an emotion, but goes ahead to positive expression. It is the sort of love which a person may be said to have for himself. He does not sit down and reflect upon how likeable—or unlikeable—he may be. But what he does do is to value himself enough to be always seeking for himself the best that his world can offer. And this sort of love a man can rise to in his relationship to someone else, even to the someone who but for the will to have it otherwise he might have regarded only as his enemy.

Yet the general principle is not the whole of what the Gospel presents. There are specific injunctions of Jesus which make new difficulties for the conscience that wants to be obedient: Turn the other cheek; give your coat also to the man who snatches your cloak; if you are robbed of something, do not try to get it back. If we acted like that, it seems to us that society would only disintegrate into an evil chaos; and since human naure is as far off as it now is from the kingdom of God, perhaps it would.

What shall we say then, and within our poor human limits what shall we do? This at least: we must want to come as close to Jesus' commandment as we can. It is possible for imagination to kindle more and more concerning what love, as unwearying good will, can actually achieve. One looks at Francis of Assisi, gaining a whole new world of wonder and joy because he was ready first to give everything away. One remembers the bishop, in Victor Hugo's *Les Miserables,* melting the heart of the convict Jean Valjean and turning him into a redeemed man when he would not let the police arrest him for what he had stolen. Mixed with the evil that is in men there may always be the little spark of possible goodness which a perceptive trust may kindle into flame. When one is trying thus to love, even though the particular expressions of love which Jesus held up as examples cannot be literally carried out, the would-be Christian may still be living in the spirit of his Lord. It is what a man purposes in his heart that counts for most. It was never the way of Jesus to lay down rigid laws or to cramp the wings of the ideal in a cage of literalism. If a man is really trying to be caught up into the purpose of Jesus, then the love he is beginning to learn can find its ways of being made effective through such faithful choices as may be the best that his imperfect world presents. Meanwhile, because love is absorbed in helpfulness, it has no time for the harshness of attempted judgment; and because it gives out with unstinted measure, life and love come back to it in great return.

WHEN THE IMPULSES OF THE HEART EXPAND

Judge not, and you will not be judged; condemn not, and you will not be condemned; forgive, and you will be forgiven; give, and it will be given to you; good measure, pressed down, shaken together, running over, will be put into your lap. For the measure you give will be the measure you get back.
(Luke 6:37-38.)

Conventional ideas often estimate the goodness or badness of human beings in terms of the flesh, but Jesus looked at the inward disposition. In his eyes, freedom from gross sins did not of itself make a man's life what it ought to be. A man might be respectable and correct, and yet be only an irritant to other people; and that is what he will be if he is absorbed in his own self-righteousness. When he assumes that he is better than others, and is entitled in his superiority to pass judgment on others, he embodies hostility and invites it in return. His life will be walled off from the general life in a kind of sour isolation.

Equally it is a mistake to suppose that a man gets enrichment from what he clutches to himself. It is in giving that we gain. The life which pours itself out in generous service will win at last what no money can buy: its own expansion, and the inestimable reward which comes from the gratitude and love it has awakened. At the end of any life it can be a true self-judgment that says, "What I spent, I had; what I kept, I lost; what I gave, I have."

THE BLIND WHO THINK THEY SEE

He also told them a parable: "Can a blind man lead a blind man? Will they not both fall into a pit? A disciple is not above his teacher, but every one when he is fully taught will be like his teacher. Why do you see the speck that is in your brother's eye, but do not notice the log that is in your own eye? Or how can you say to your brother, 'Brother, let me take out the speck that is in your eye,' when you yourself do not see the log that is in your own eye? You hypocrite, first take the log out of your own eye, and then you will see clearly to take out the speck that is in your brother's eye.

"For no good tree bears bad fruit, nor again does a bad tree bear good fruit; for each tree is known by its own fruit. For figs are not gathered from thorns, nor are grapes picked from a bramble bush. The good man out of the good treasure of his heart produces good, and the evil man out of his evil treasure produces evil; for out of the abundance of the heart his mouth speaks." (Luke 6:39-45.)

The sayings of Jesus which follow one another in this paragraph are like sudden illuminations from a moving searchlight, bringing into sharp visibility facets of human life which once seen are unforgettable.

The first shaft of swift disclosure falls upon the fatuousness of pretended knowledge. Jesus was continually encountering pompous authorities who claimed to be able to tell people the roads of thought and behavior on which they ought to walk. Such were some of the scribes. They had learned the law by rote and memorized all the directions. But when they got out into the actual world, their astigmatic eyes could not recognize what they were looking at. For all practical purposes they were no better than blind men assuming to lead those who were also blind. In this respect, the past can be repeated in the present. Professional churchmen may have their rigid traditions as to what everybody has been supposed to believe and do, and at the same time lack any prophetic vision of what life requires now. And the trouble grows worse when everyone who is fully taught becomes like his teacher. Some great man—a Martin Luther, a John Calvin, a Karl Barth—appears as the witness-bearer for some immense conviction; but the little man who tries to echo him shouts the great man's slogans and goes bumbling along with no perception of the exaggerations into which he strays as inevitably as the blind man strays into the ditch.

Then Jesus lets the light fall on another picture of how pretentious a man can be. Here is a person who says to someone else, "Did you know you have a speck of something in your eye? Just let me get at it, so that you can see." All the while he does not realize that his own eye has no more sight in it than if he were looking through a plank. This is the man who is always ready with advice and correction for the other man, but is quite oblivious to what needs to be done to himself.

What needs to be done is to feel the truth. Presumptions are of no use: it is no use to say you will guide other people when you are blind yourself, no use to see what is wrong in someone else when you cannot see what is wrong in you. The question is what is happening in the heart. Unless a man's heart is humble and his purpose clean, nothing that is of genuine worth can happen. You don't pick grapes from a bramble bush. There must be goodness in a man's essential self if there is to be any goodness in the fruit his life produces.

WHEN THERE ARE NO FOUNDATIONS

"Why do you call me 'Lord, Lord,' and not do what I tell you? Every one who comes to me and hears my words and does them, I will show you what he is like: he is like a man building a house, who dug deep, and laid the foundation upon rock; and when a flood arose, the stream broke against that house, and could not shake it, because it had been well built. But he who hears and does not do them is like a man who built a house on the ground without a foundation; against which the stream broke, and immediately it fell, and the ruin of that house was great."

(Luke 6:46-49.)

No house is stronger than its foundations. Everybody knows that theoretically, but it is possible to be stupid enough or casual enough to ignore the fact. When the skies are clear, sand appears to be enough for a house to stand on. But what happens when torrential rain pours its flood down that which had seemed to be the safe valley, or the hurricane beats in from the sea? Then there will be very little left of any house not built on rock.

That is the way it is with life, said Jesus; and always it is possible to see examples of what his parable expressed. A man may think that a superficial decency is foundation enough for character and conduct to be built on. If he has behaved himself respectably heretofore, he assumes that he will continue to behave that way. He has not dug down to anything deep in thought or purpose, for why take extra trouble when everything seems secure? But then the weather changes. The jerry-built structure of the character he thought he had is assailed by forces he had not reckoned on. The muddy waters of some unexpected moral temptation swirl about him. The strong wind of some public opinion which he knows is false beats upon him. If he had any profound convictions they would hold him; but actually he has none, and down he goes in ignominious disintegration, like a house ripped to pieces in a storm.

Jesus came to make men trust in something more profound than their shallow self-assurance. Their lives could be grounded in the purposes of God, built on loyalties that would be like rock foundations. And to make sure of those foundations must be no matter of easy assumption, but of continual faithfulness to see to it that the foundations are still there. Early in this century the ancient cathedral at Winchester in England was found to be in danger of collapse because the hidden piles on which its walls had rested had mouldered away. So it was necessary to go beneath the walls and towers to make sure that they were anchored now in foundations that would not fail; and this fact concerning the cathedral can be a modern parable for the need in each man's soul.

chapter 7

FACING A PROBLEM

This seventh chapter of the Gospel begins with the account of two
miracles before which contemporary minds will stand perplexed.
In one instance Jesus heals the slave of a Roman centurion without even
going where the sick man was; according to the second and still more
astonishing story he brings back to life a young man who had died and
whose body was already being carried out for burial.

As the Christian reads this narrative, his thought will be like the disturbed
waters of a river at the point where two strong opposing currents meet.
There is his instinctive reverence for the Gospel record and for whatever
it may tell of Jesus; but there is also his consciousness that events such as are
here described simply do not happen anywhere in the world he knows.
So an inescapable question rises: Is Luke's narrative to be read as actual
fact?

"What! Will you hesitate to accept the plain words of Holy Scripture?"
the literalist may ask. The necessary answer is that to find God's truth
the Christian must first of all be truthful. He will not cover up uncertainties
with insincere assertions. He will be humble to admit what he is not sure
of, and patient to find the honest way for mind and heart which leads from
the half light he knows to the full light that may be ahead.

Some facts bearing upon the story of the healings we do know surely.
Who is there who has not experienced the life-giving power of some strong
personality? You are sick and miserable. Then the doctor whose knowledge
and tenderness you know and trust comes and stands by your bed and
looks at you with his reassuring eyes. Or the great surgeon lays his exploring hand upon you, and at the touch of his fingers the fear you had is gone.
From that moment you were on the way to being made well. And if that
can be true in our contacts now, how much more vastly was it true when
the surcharged personality of Jesus touched the sick and the despairing?
Only a brash conceit of skepticism would set fixed limits to what he may
have done or to the factuality of what the Gospels say he did. It was not
anyone with a Christian prepossession but the eminent Jewish scholar,

Joseph Klausner, who has written in his *Jesus of Nazareth*, of "this force which Jesus had," comprising "some secret, some mystical element, still not properly studied by the ordinary psychologists and physicians and scientists, who are conversant only with the laws of nature so far determined by science." [1]

But that is not all that needs to be considered. Before Luke's Gospel was written there had been a long growth of tradition. Rumor and report enlarged the outlines of the record. What men had seen in Jesus towered up so mightily above the common level that their imaginations gathered round their recollection of him as mists gather round some stupendous mountain and are themselves the evidence of how near the mountain reaches to the sky. If special wonders had been told concerning great figures in the earlier history of Israel, such as healing at a distance or raising the dead, the impulse was to assume that in the life of Jesus these must have been equalled or surpassed.

Luke himself, so far as we know, was not there when the healings happened. He tells what had been told to him, which may mean that he is reproducing a picture which included the mists as well as the central mountain. If we could get back to the objective facts, the record might be simpler and physically less miraculous. The description as we have it would need to be "demythologized." But what Luke is expressing transcends any modification of details. He is reflecting the conviction which had come to him from men who had known Jesus, that no report of what Jesus might have done could be too great a representation of what he had done. He did work extraordinary bodily healings; and whether or not the son of the widow from Nain was actually dead, there were others with worse than physical death who could say: "We can tell you what happened to us. He cured the sickness in our souls and made what was dead in our spirits rise to life."

THE WIDENESS OF THE GOSPEL

After he had ended all his sayings in the hearing of the people he entered Capernaum. Now a centurion had a slave who was dear to him, who was sick and at the point of death. When he heard of Jesus, he sent to him elders of the Jews, asking him to come and heal his slave. And when they came to Jesus, they besought him earnestly, saying, "He is worthy to have you do this for him, for he loves our nation, and he built us our synagogue." And Jesus went with them. When he was not far from the house, the centurion sent friends to him, saying to him, "Lord, do not trouble yourself, for I am not worthy to have you come under my roof; therefore I

[1] Joseph Klausner, *Jesus of Nazareth*, translated by H. Danby (New York: The Macmillan Company, 1925), p. 270.

did not presume to come to you. But say the word, and let my servant be healed. For I am a man set under authority, with soldiers under me: and I say to one, 'Go,' and he goes; and to another, 'Come,' and he comes; and to my slave, 'Do this,' and he does it." When Jesus heard this he marveled at him, and turned and said to the multitude that followed him, "I tell you, not even in Israel have I found such faith." And when those who had been sent returned to the house, they found the slave well.

(Luke 7:1-10.)

The account of the healing of the centurion's servant reflects a special interest which marks this third Gospel—an interest that had two aspects, one defensive and the other more positive and outgoing.

First, defensive. Rome had been notably tolerant of the religious convictions of the people in the empire, including the Jews. At first the Christians had been regarded as merely another Jewish sect, the existence of which was a matter of indifference. But by the time Luke wrote his Gospel, something else had happened. Christians had refused to burn incense before the symbol of the emperor in the Roman temples and thus began to be looked upon as subversive. The emperor Nero, unprincipled and vicious, searching for a scapegoat for the great fire which destroyed much of the city of Rome in A.D. 64, had accused the Christians of setting it. In recording this incident of Jesus' response to a Roman centurion, Luke was illustrating the falsity of the idea that the spirit of Jesus was a threat to what was best in Rome.

But his purpose was more than a defense against hostility. It was the positive evangel of making every man, including every Roman, know that there was a life-giving power in Christ that was reaching out to him. Luke was reflecting here what he had learned from the great apostle Paul, that in Christ Jesus there was neither Greek nor Jew, circumcision nor uncircumcision, Barbarian, Scythian, bond nor free" (Col. 3:11 KJV). Wherever there was a human heart ready to receive it, there the redemption of Christ could enter.

UNDERSTANDING THE HUMAN HEART

Soon afterward he went to a city called Nain, and his disciples and a great crowd went with him. As he drew near to the gate of the city, behold, a man who had died was being carried out, the only son of his mother, and she was a widow; and a large crowd from the city was with her. And when the Lord saw her, he had compassion on her and said to her, "Do not weep." And he came and touched the bier, and the bearers stood still. And he said, "Young man, I say to you, arise." And the dead man sat up, and began to speak. And he gave him to his mother. Fear seized them all; and they glorified God, saying, "A great prophet has arisen among us!" and "God has visited his people!" And this report concerning him spread through the whole of Judea and all the surrounding country.   (Luke 7:11-17.)

In this passage another characteristic of this Gospel comes into view. It is sensitive to all the facts of human life, including its pathos and pain. It is concerned with people not because of their supposed importance, but because they are human souls. Most history, especially pre-Christian history, has had to do with men. Women were subordinate. Although they might have their usefulness, they were not treated as being of consequence in themselves. But the Gospel of Luke has often been called "the Gospel of the women," because the eyes of this Evangelist were open always to the loveliness that women bring to life.

Here in the account of the miracle at Nain it is "the young man" who is the center of the story, but here also we catch Luke's instinctive recognition of what may be happening in a woman's heart. The lad who had died was "the only son of his mother, and she was a widow." No more than that in the way of words, and no more is needed; for in that one poignant sentence is revealed Luke's awareness of the anguish of motherhood and the pathos of the woman left alone. The beauty of this Gospel is not only in what is written; it is in the reflection given of the man who wrote it: a man whose emotions had become conformed to Christ's compassion.

THE PURSUIT OF HOPE

The disciples of John told him of all these things. And John, calling to him two of his disciples, sent them to the Lord, saying, "Are you he who is to come, or shall we look for another?" And when the men had come to him, they said, "John the Baptist has sent us to you, saying, 'Are you he who is to come, or shall we look for another?' "   (Luke 7:18-20.)

The question which John the Baptist was moved to ask will have a different tone according to how one thinks of it in terms of two opinions which New Testament scholars hold. It is an unquestioned fact that John had made a powerful impact upon the people and that a generation later there were still those whose religious loyalties were centered in him. Acts 19 is evidence of this. Some scholars believe that the express proclamation by John at the Jordan River of Jesus as the Messiah, which has found its way from popular report into the early chapters of the Gospels, could not have been the fact, and that John did not foresee that Jesus would play a mightier role than he himself had filled. In any case, his work had been brought to a cruel end. He was shut up in Herod Antipas' grim prison of

Machaerus. Then the news of Jesus' ministry comes to him like a light shining in the darkness, and the question he asked would represent what Sherman Johnson in the Interpreter's Bible has called "the faint dawn of a new faith."

But if John actually had believed that Jesus would be the Messiah and had proclaimed that with exultant certainty, then his question would represent an aching disappointment. Although his own ministry had been frustrated, he could endure that and look beyond it if what he had preached was about to be fulfilled. The kingdom of God is at hand, and all flesh shall see the salvation of God! That is what he had declared. The tyranny of the world's wickedness would be broken, and God's mighty redemption for the righteous enter in. If this should be brought to pass by Jesus, then the passionate hope that John had held would not have been in vain.

But where were any sure signs that the Kingdom was coming? Where were any mighty shakings of the earth? Herod still held his evil power. An arrogant Roman procurator ruled Jerusalem. The people of the covenant still waited for the deliverer whom the prophets had said would surely come. Jesus would be the deliverer, excited crowds were saying. John's heart cried out to believe it. But there ought to be some adequate indication. Was there any? Or was the expectation only an illusion—Jesus not the deliverer and the future only a long waiting for one who had not come?

"Shall we look for another?" That is what men may ask again. Some call our age "a post-Christian era." They mean that the influence of Christianity, which once seemed a decisive power in universal history, is fading now into a beautiful but dim tradition. The forces that shape our destiny now are no longer Christian, except in name. How shall we continue, then, to hold Jesus as the center of our hope? Is there some different and more modern voice that must be heard instead?

John the Baptist did not know the answer to that question. Contemporary uncertainty, sometimes wistful, sometimes cynical, does not know it either. But the important fact about John the Baptist was that his uncertainty did not drive him into hopelessness. If he was uncertain, he would still reach out to where there might be assurance. He would try to find out if the facts about Jesus might be greater than in his discouraged moments he could see. So he sent messengers to observe and listen, and to bring him word of what they found.

THE LONG ANSWER

In that hour he cured many of diseases and plagues and evil spirits, and on many that were blind he bestowed sight. And he answered them, "Go and tell John what you have seen and heard: the blind receive their sight, the lame walk, lepers are cleansed, and the deaf hear, the dead are raised up, the poor have good news preached to them." (Luke 7:21-22.)

On the surface of things it might have seemed that John's messengers had little to report that would dispel his doubt. What could they tell him? Only that there were great crowds listening to Jesus and that there were healings of the sick. Nothing dramatic or tremendous. No instant signs of a conquering Messiah, no reversing of the world's hard realities, nor in place of old evils any new heaven or earth. The messengers might have said what those who talk of "a post-Christian era" may repeat now: "Where is the promise of his coming? For ever since the fathers fell asleep, all things have continued as they were from the beginning of creation."

But have they continued so? Only to those who would recognize nothing unless it should be cataclysmic change, who cannot see the working of leaven and the silent growth of seed. The Jesus about whom John made his troubled inquiry would die upon a Roman cross; but in a few centuries his disciples would carry their faith in him through all the Roman empire. Christianity in the monasteries would keep the lights burning for human life through what otherwise would have been only the Dark Ages. Patrick, Columba, Boniface, Benedict would bring the spirit of Jesus as a gradual transformation to the pagan peoples beyond the old frontiers. Great souls in many centuries would be witnesses to the resurgent power of Christ: Francis of Assisi, Martin Luther, John Wesley, Wilfred Grenfell, Albert Schweitzer. That same power of Christ has dimensions in our present time which the uninformed may not see and the fainthearted may forget. And if it be asked why, after all is said, it still seems that redemption comes so slowly and that the spirit of Jesus is as a light lifted only here and there, the first element in the answer is that "with the Lord one day is as a thousand years, and a thousand years as one day." The eternal purposes transcend our hurry and our fret.

Listen to what Jesus said: "The blind receive their sight, the lame walk, lepers are cleansed, and the deaf hear, the dead are raised up, the poor have good news preached to them." Jesus spoke always in relation not to one world only, but to two. He was intensely alive to all immediate realities: to human life in every aspect—its day-by-day relationships, its needs and hopes. He knew how hard the people in little towns like Nazareth had to work, and his quick compassion went out to those who carried heavy loads. When he launched his blazing indictment against some of the Pharisees who "devour widows' houses," his indignation was on behalf of all the little people to whom justice and mercy were denied.

Wherever his spirit was or is, it means good news for the poor: the good news of a social gospel which is directly concerned with changing the conditions under which any people have been exploited and abused. In that sense the gospel is in and of this world. But there is also its mightier dimension. The kingdom of God is not made up of material things. More food, larger houses, more conveniences do not of themselves make greater souls. It was for souls that Jesus supremely cared. That is what his gospel meant that day when the messengers from John the Baptist heard him, and it is what it always means. Because of him men who have been deaf to anything except the clamor of this world have heard the heavenly voices; those who have stumbled have stood erect and walked on the roads of lofty purpose; those who have had some leprosy of sin have been made clean; and the divinely given spark within them which might have seemed dead has been quickened to immortal life.

WHY WAS THERE ENMITY TOWARD JESUS?

"And blessed is he who takes no offense at me."   (Luke 7:23.)

But as a matter of fact they did take offense. Hostility sprang up against Jesus from the first. In the midst of the excitement and wonder which many felt, there was increasing disaffection. It was of a double kind. On the one hand there were those who took offense because Jesus and his ministry seemed to them of no consequence. Sermons preached to the crowds, some healings here and there—these were all very well, but what did they amount to after all? What most people wanted was something more dramatic. Everybody knew and could complain about the conditions of the time: the Roman rule, the petty tyranny of Herod, the humiliation of old pride of blood and nation. Where was the deliverer who would come and set their world straight and get them the satisfaction they were not finding for themselves? When John the Baptist had prophesied that one mightier than himself would presently appear, whose fork was in his hand, who would gather up the wheat but burn the chaff with fire unquenchable, their hopes leaped up in expectation. If Jesus should be like that, all would be well. But he was not.

It was not only in the first century that there was the desire for Christ to be like that. It would be so convenient now to have everything made different without the trouble of having to be made different ourselves. So it happens that men may take offense, if not with Christ then with Christianity, that the world does not suddenly become better. Why does not some divine stroke put an end to war, confusion, and evil generally? When this end does not come about, shallow thought becomes impatient. It is not impressed by the quiet truth expressed in such words as those of Jesus: "Go and tell John what you have seen and heard."

But it had better be impressed. Individuals who genuinely listen to Jesus are made over, healed of their inward sickness, renewed in mind and soul. Thus, and thus only, can the kingdom of redemption come. There was a time in the history of this planet when the glaciers covered much of the surface of the earth. A change of climate melted the ice sheet so that most of it disappeared; but it is estimated that an average temperature drop of ten degrees would begin to bring the ice sheet back. The mortal ice sheet of suspicion, hatred, and disaster could come in that same way. Only a better warmth in human souls can prevent it. Because that warmth of the spirit of Christ is a silent thing, it may be regarded as of no consequence. But destiny depends upon it.

On the other hand, there were those who took offense at Jesus for exactly the opposite reason: not because they thought he was of no consequence but because they knew the consequence of recognizing him would be very formidable. They were a long way from the pallid idea of Jesus which our tame and easygoing notions sometimes hold: a long way from the picture of him which had been produced in the mind of a certain small boy who had been to Sunday school and looked at the chromos of a soft figure with long silken hair, dressed in pink and white and baby blue. One day the Sunday school teacher asked his little sister why her brother had stopped coming, and the answer was: "To tell the truth, he says he can't stand Jesus!" He could not stand the Jesus he imagined: somebody so meek and mild as to be capable of nothing except to be pushed around. But no one who actually encountered Jesus thought of him that way—certainly not the officers of the church one sabbath in the synagogue who resented his authority and on whom he "looked . . . with anger, grieved at their hardness of heart." They could not stand Jesus either, but for a very different reason. Men of that sort did not want to face the tremendous challenge of his spirit—and do not want to now. To pride, cruelty, and stubborn vested selfishness he always gives offense. When anyone faces the reality of Jesus, he faces a decision which will be of drastic consequence. If he deliberately resists the power of that demanding but redeeming love, then the judgment of Jesus may fall upon the hollow shell of what he is, like a rock that will grind it to powder. But that same rock may be the foundation stone on which his life may be built into a temple of the Lord.

NOT CLOTHES, BUT CHARACTER

When the messengers of John had gone, he began to speak to the crowds concerning John: "What did you go out into the wilderness to behold?

A reed shaken by the wind? What then did you go out to see? A man clothed in soft raiment? Behold, those who are gorgeously apparelled and live in luxury are in kings' courts. What then did you go out to see? A prophet? Yes, I tell you, and more than a prophet. This is he of whom it is written,
'Behold, I send my messenger before thy face,
who shall prepare thy way before thee.' " (Luke 7:24-27.)

It was rightly written of Jesus that "he knew what was in man," and here in his words to the people after he had talked with the messengers from John he expressed one obvious fact about human nature. There is something in every man that would like to have things easy: to be clothed in soft raiment, to be gorgeously apparelled, and live in luxury in king's courts. The general instinct is to think that the man who is born into such conditions, or who has managed to attain them, is the man to be envied—and admired too. The crowd will flock around the figure who wears the trappings of what seems to be importance.

But that is no right estimate of greatness, Jesus is saying. The stature of a man is made up not of what he wears but by what he is. John did not need to be dressed up in order to have authority. On the other hand, there is no use being outwardly impressive if a man is hollow inside. A touch of scorn is in Jesus' question to the people as to whether what they were looking for was somebody like a reed shaken by the wind. John the Baptist did not have to live in luxury in kings' courts in order to be great. His royalty was in himself. And the words of Jesus about kings' courts wake a sudden recollection of another figure who was a supreme exemplar of the values that really matter in the final meaning of a life: Moses. Moses did live in a king's court, and he could have stayed there; but he chose instead to be, as John would be, a messenger of the Most High. He confronted Pharaoh, as John would confront King Herod. He gave up what John would not have, luxury and soft raiment, for a hard life that would gain no personal reward. But there is no doubt what Jesus thought of him, and no doubt as to how Jesus would rate the man in any time who lays aside his own advantage in order to serve the purposes of God.

WHAT JOHN THE BAPTIST HERALDED

"I tell you, among those born of women none is greater than John; yet he who is least in the kingdom of God is greater than he." (Luke 7:28.)

"Yet he who is least in the kingdom of God is greater than he." Those words of Jesus might seem to disparage the greatness of John; but it is not so.

F. W. H. Myers, in two verses of his "Saint Paul," has put into one superb simile the truth about John the Baptist—and about men like him—whose own ministry may have seemed fruitless but who nevertheless have turned the world's eyes to something mightier that would come:

> John, than which man a sadder or a greater
> Not till this day has been of woman born.
> John, like some lofty peak by the Creator
> Fired by the red glow of the rushing morn.
>
> This, when the sun shall rise and overcome it
> Stands in his shining desolate and bare,
> Yet not the less the inexorable summit
> Flamed him his signal to the happier air.

John did stand a lonely figure. Viewed by itself, it might have seemed at the end that his ministry was desolate and bare. But his glory was that he had seen long before others that "the sun of righteousness shall rise with healing in his wings." He had made men hope and believe in a new day dawning for their souls.

His limitation—and that of some of the earlier prophets—was that he did not fully grasp what the light of that new day should be. It must come, he thought, with the rising of the sun of righteousness. God's rebuke to wickedness should be a blazing fire. Therefore the warning he would bring must be inexorable. Men must repent, or they would surely perish. But in his magnificent moral sternness he had not yet perceived the wonder of the gospel: that there can be a righteousness which no man in his own strength and self-sufficiency can win and only the undeserved grace of God can give. It was this that the least in the kingdom of God would know. The white light of God's goodness, which might be terrible, yet comes with healing in its wings. The everlasting mercy reaches out to the undeserving in the love of Jesus, who came not to call those who thought that they were righteous, but to be the friend of sinners and to save them.

WHEN PRIDE RESISTS THE TRUTH

> When they heard this all the people and the tax collectors justified God, having been baptized with the baptism of John; but the Pharisees and the lawyers rejected the purpose of God for themselves, not having been baptized by him. (Luke 7:29-30.)

If he who is least in the kingdom of God is greater than John, then to have received John's baptism was obviously not the end of spiritual experience, but it did represent what was a necessary beginning. The people who had been moved by John could understand Jesus when he spoke of the purpose of God, and those who had been contemptuous of John could not. John's preaching had called men to repentance, and repentance meant that men had first to be conscious of the sins for which they needed to repent—conscious not only in cool and abstract recognition, but conscious enough to be concerned. Many were concerned. They had the honesty to look at their real selves and the moral decency to be ashamed of what they saw. But there were others, as there always are, for whom that sort of honesty would be too uncomfortable—not because their sins were more gross than those of the crowd, but because they lived within the shell of their superior pretense, and they could not bear to have that shell broken and the hollowness inside exposed. In the general opinion, they were men of eminence, the super-respectable pillars of society. That was how they preferred to think of themselves, and so they shut their ears to what John had to say. It would cost too much to their pride to come down, as they thought, to the level of common people, to admit their own discreetly hidden sins, to admit their own need of inner cleansing. Thus they rejected the purpose of God for themselves, because they would not bow their stiff necks enough to go through the strait gate of repentance and confession, even for the great chance for expansion of their souls that waited on the other side.

THE PEOPLE WHOM NOTHING SUITS

"To what then shall I compare the men of this generation, and what are they like? They are like children sitting in the market place and calling to one another,

'We piped to you, and you did not dance;
we wailed, and you did not weep.'

For John the Baptist has come eating no bread and drinking no wine; and you say, 'He has a demon.' The Son of man has come eating and drinking; and you say, 'Behold, a glutton and a drunkard, a friend of tax collectors and sinners!' Yet wisdom is justified by all her children."
(Luke 7:31-35.)

Sometimes when we think of Jesus, a tame would-be piety makes our conception of him only a ghostly semblance of what must have been his full reality. We are rightly anxious to be reverent; but what we mean as reverence can produce a gray stereotype from which the glow and color of his spirit have been lost. In our solemn purpose we make him solemn and are almost afraid to imagine that he ever smiled. But here in the moment which Luke describes Jesus looks with a sort of amused pity upon what can be the foolishness of people who think that they are grown. John the

Baptist had come with his formidable message, calling the nation to put on mourning for its sins. Jesus himself had brought his message of the forgiving love of God, which could fill men's hearts with joy. But most of the people had not responded to either one. John was too gloomy, they said, and demanded too much; Jesus was not solemn enough and did not confine his interest to those who were respectable. So they had their pompous reasons why they did not have to listen to the call of God—just as people of the twentieth century may have their so-called reasons for avoiding commitment to the Christian church. But for Jesus all this lofty talk was and is deflated. The substance of what he said is this: that religious unresponsiveness which tries to sound mature may be nothing better than the mood of grumpy children, who will not play funeral or wedding either. No matter what the invitation might be, they will sit in their corner and sulk.

THE GRATITUDE OF THE FORGIVEN

One of the Pharisees asked him to eat with him, and he went into the Pharisee's house, and sat at table. And behold, a woman of the city, who was a sinner, when she learned that he was sitting at table in the Pharisee's house, brought an alabaster flask of ointment, and standing behind him at his feet, weeping, she began to wet his feet with her tears, and wiped them with the hair of her head, and kissed his feet, and anointed them with the ointment. Now when the Pharisee who had invited him saw it, he said to himself, "If this man were a prophet, he would have known who and what sort of woman this is who is touching him, for she is a sinner." And Jesus answering said to him, "Simon, I have something to say to you." And he answered, "What is it, Teacher?" "A certain creditor had two debtors; one owed five hundred denarii, and the other fifty. When they could not pay, he forgave them both. Now which of them will love him more?" Simon answered, "The one, I suppose, to whom he forgave more." And he said to him, "You have judged rightly." Then turning toward the woman he said to Simon, "Do you see this woman? I entered your house, you gave me no water for my feet, but she has wet my feet with her tears and wiped them with her hair. You gave me no kiss, but from the time I came in she has not ceased to kiss my feet. You did not anoint my head with oil, but she has anointed my feet with ointment. Therefore I tell you, her sins, which are many, are forgiven, for she loved much; but he who is forgiven little, loves little." And he said to her, "Your sins are forgiven." Then those who were at table with him began to say among themselves, "Who is this, who even forgives sins?" And he said to the woman, "Your faith has saved you; go in peace."

(Luke 7:36-50.)

So the truthfulness of Jesus could be very devastating. But this chapter of the Gospel comes to its climax on another note: not of rebuke, but of redemption.

Jesus is invited to the house of a Pharisee, and he accepts the invitation. It is well to remember that, as a corrective to the idea that all Pharisees had made themselves his enemies. This Pharisee, Simon by name, was capable of an interest which was at least polite, even if perhaps a little patronizing. It was not Simon, however, but someone else, who would learn the infinite gift that could come from Jesus.

While Jesus was at Simon's table, there slipped into the room a woman from the streets. Before any of the astonished company could stop her, she had come to Jesus' feet; and with tears flooding from her eyes, she anointed his feet from an alabaster box of ointment which she had brought. Simon was shocked. Did Jesus know what sort of woman this was; and if he did know, why did he let her touch him?

What was the woman's name? The Gospel does not give it, and we do not know. Some have surmised that she was Mary Magdalene, from whom —as is said in the next chapter—"seven demons had gone out." Also one commentator has suggested that it may have been the woman—also un-named—told of in chapter 8 of the Gospel of John: the woman taken in adultery whom Jesus saved from her grim judges and told to go and sin no more. Whoever the woman was, she had evidently come into contact with Jesus before and had found in him a great compassion and a divine forgiveness which filled her heart with adoration. Because she had been for-given much, she could love much. And this—notwithstanding some phrases in the Gospel narrative which are puzzling—is the central message which Jesus brought home to Simon the Pharisee. In Simon's treatment of Jesus there was no emotion. He received Jesus with casual hospitality, and that was all. He did not think that he had any particular need of him. But this woman had been down in the depths, and Jesus had lifted her out of them. She had known sin and darkness and desperation, and the mercy of Jesus had redeemed her. Therefore, her soul had a passion of emotion which the cool Pharisee could not know. It is not intended that a child of God should sin; but to have felt sin as an agony when one has fallen into it, and then to have been found by the undeserved love of God which the heart responds to with a flood of gratitude, is better than a shallow and com-placent goodness which has never experienced the awful depths and heights which make up the reality of life. That is perhaps one answer to the poignant question of a contemporary novelist: "Why is it that virtue goes always with a sour sound in the mind and it is the wayward and lost who make the lovely music we want to listen to once again before the lights go out"? [2]

---

[2] Elick Moll, *Memoir of Spring* (New York: G. P. Putnam's, 1961), p. 56.

chapter 8

SOME WHO FOLLOWED JESUS

Soon afterward he went on through cities and villages, preaching and bringing the good news of the kingdom of God. And the twelve were with him, and also some women who had been healed of evil spirits and infirmities: Mary, called Magdalene, from whom seven demons had gone out, and Joanna, the wife of Chuza, Herod's steward, and Susanna, and many others, who provided for them out of their means. (Luke 8:1-3.)

Jesus had preached in the synagogue at Nazareth, but the congregation there had been so offended at his preaching which cut across their prejudices that they drove him out. Conceivably there were other synagogues which did not welcome him, as he went on through cities and villages. Not only synagogues but Christian churches may find his words disturbing. That was what happened to one of his great disciples, John Wesley, who sought, as Jesus himself had done in Nazareth, to preach good news to the poor. When he went back to his father's old parish in Epworth, he was forbidden to come farther than the graveyard; and outside another church he was given a note that read, "Our minister, having been informed that you are beside yourself, does not care you should preach in any of his churches."

It is striking to note who were with Jesus as he went on his way: the twelve, some others who are not named, and three women who are named. One of them was Mary Magdalene. It is because she is spoken of here immediately after the description of what happened in Simon the Pharisee's house that many have assumed that the unnamed woman there who anointed Jesus' feet was Mary. There is no certainty of this; but Mary Magdalene, from whom seven demons had gone out, may well have been the one who loved much because her many sins had been forgiven. Now she was in the company of those who followed Jesus with closest faithfulness, and in company with a woman of high rank, the wife of Herod's steward. The spirit of their Master could weld into one group individuals who before might have been separated from one another by a great gulf.

THE SEED, THE FIELD, AND THE SOWER

And when a great crowd came together and people from town after town came to him, he said in a parable: "A sower went out to sow his seed; and as he sowed, some fell along the path, and was trodden under foot, and the birds of the air devoured it. And some fell on the rock; and as it grew up, it withered away, because it had no moisture. And some fell among thorns; and the thorns grew with it and choked it. And some fell into good soil and grew, and yielded a hundredfold." As he said this, he called out, "He who has ears to hear, let him hear."

And when his disciples asked him what this parable meant, he said, "To you it has been given to know the secrets of the kingdom of God; but for others they are in parables, so that seeing they may not see, and hearing they may not understand. Now the parable is this: The seed is the word of God. The ones along the path are those who have heard; then the devil comes and takes away the word from their hearts, that they may not believe and be saved. And the ones on the rock are those who, when they hear the word, receive it with joy; but these have no root, they believe for a while and in time of temptation fall away. And as for what fell among the thorns, they are those who hear, but as they go on their way they are choked by the cares and riches and pleasures of life, and their fruit does not mature. And as for that in the good soil, they are those who, hearing the word, hold it fast in an honest and good heart, and bring forth fruit with patience."   (Luke 8:4-15.)

This parable is usually called the parable of the sower. It might equally well be called the parable of the seed, or the parable of the soil; for all three factors are essential to the total picture.

Jesus was speaking both to his disciples and to the people at large who crowded round him. The parable would carry a particular meaning for each of these two groups. For the crowd the thrust of it would come through the description of the seed and the soil.

The seed, said Jesus, can represent the word of God, and the soil the human heart. The first thing one should do is to realize the marvel that is wrapped up in what might seem insignificant. One who has no knowledge might look at a seed and throw it away as of no consequence. What value can there be in this tiny thing, so fragile and so colorless? But out of a grain of wheat can unfold the life that will be the beginning of an endless harvest; and out of a word from God can come the power that will turn the barren ground of a man's existence into fruitfulness. A single thought which the mind has caught and the heart has cherished, a single perception of the beauty and wonder of the spiritual world, one new resolve, one new response to a heavenly purpose, carries the promise of a result that can be limitless.

120

Provided that the seed falls where it has a chance to grow. So there comes the part of the parable which describes the different kinds of ground.

To begin with, there is the field which is crisscrossed by paths, so that sections of it are flattened and compacted by the coming and going of many feet. Whatever falls on those paths has little chance to grow. Similarly for the human being the ground of his awareness may have been trampled upon by alien influences, by the rude invasion of other people's ideas, and the continual pressure of the crowd opinion; and when some seeds of the thoughts that come from God fall there, they cannot germinate. They lie on the hard surface unable to take root, until doubt, uncertainty, and discouragement come like a flock of marauding birds to carry the seed away.

Or the field may be underlain by a stratum of rock. Above the rock the soil looks promising enough, and the seed falling there takes root. The grain begins to grow. But when the hot suns come and the roots cannot go deep, the grain begins to shrivel. So it is with the spiritual grain. A man's reception of the word of God may be only a shallow curiosity, as it was with some of the crowd who came to listen to Jesus, and as it is with the casual and the careless in every time. Then whatever the first seeming may be, at the end there will be only barren ground.

Furthermore, as Jesus pointed out, there may be yet a third kind of failure. The life of the spirit may seem genuine. Good impulses are really growing. But they are choked by the cares, riches, and pleasures of life, and their fruit does not mature.

The lesson of it all for those who choose to hear is plain enough. The field must be made ready by the kind of cultivation that gets down beneath the superficial thought to the deep levels of conviction. Then the honest and good heart will bring forth fruit with patience.

Such, then, was the message which the crowd had need to hear. In their kinship with all other human beings the disciples needed it too. But there was another aspect of the parable which Jesus meant especially for them, an aspect not of exhortation only but of encouragement. As he sent them out to spread the message of the Gospel, they would be in the position of the sower. They would see that much of what they tried to do would appear to have no result. Why keep on when so large a part of the seed they sowed was wasted? But Jesus had them know that as servants of God's lavish love they must carry on with trustfulness. Somewhere the seed would fall into hearts where it would bring forth harvests a hundredfold.

In the midst of the parable, however, there is one baffling sentence. How could Jesus ever have said (as in vs. 10) that the parables were told in order that people might *not* see and might *not* understand? Teaching by parables was his characteristic way of making truth so clear and vivid by illustration that it could be grasped by everybody. Certainly this parable of the sower was no riddle or enigma, nor ever meant to be such.

What, then, shall we think concerning vs. 10? This: that here we have not a direct report of what Jesus said, but an interpretation of what happened as Luke reflected upon it a generation later and as he repeated what Mark had already written in his Gospel. All the Evangelists were writing from the perspective of a time when it was clear that Jesus had not been listened to. They knew that the people of Israel had rejected the Lord of Life and had crucified him; but they saw also that because of that rejection and through the crucifixion there had come the ultimate sacrifice of Christ which alone could bring about the world's redemption. So it seemed to them that the whole drama must have been foreordained, that it was the purpose of God that the people should not have been enlightened enough beforehand to have prevented the crucifixion. Jesus therefore spoke to them in terms which would leave them unenlightened.

TRUTH WILL PREVAIL

"No one after lighting a lamp covers it with a vessel, or puts it under a bed, but puts it on a stand, that those who enter may see the light. For nothing is hid that shall not be made manifest, nor anything secret that shall not be known and come to light. Take heed then how you hear; for to him who has will more be given, and from him who has not, even what he thinks that he has will be taken away." (Luke 8:16-18.)

Whatever conception the Gospel writers had as to the inevitability of the history they were recounting, it is as certain as anything can be that Jesus spoke to men of God's kingdom not to mystify them but to make God's invitation clear. Every ordinary person could understand the parable of the seed and the field and the sower—even though the tragic stubbornness which is in human nature made many fail to apply it to themselves. What he meant and what he wanted stands unmistakable in his words reported by Luke in vss. 16-18, which follow immediately after the parable. Concerning these John Knox has written luminously in *The Interpreter's Bible* that all his teaching was intended

to be not a vessel or other object for hiding the light, but a stand to enable the light to shine more clearly and widely. . . . Even if the truth is for a time hidden from our sight (this is true to some degree for all, and for some altogether), it will ultimately be made manifest . . . in the actual stuff of our experience. Truth *will* prevail. . . . [We] shall not be able to escape the final judgment by saying simply, "I did not know," if we shall have slighted our opportunities for learning. . . . Take heed then how you hear.[1]

[1] Exposition of Luke, VIII, 151-52.

FAILURE TO UNDERSTAND

Then his mother and his brothers came to him, but they could not reach him for the crowd. And he was told, "Your mother and your brothers are standing outside, desiring to see you." But he said to them, "My mother and my brothers are those who hear the word of God and do it."

(Luke 8:19-21.)

The reply which Jesus made when it was told him that his mother and brothers were there on the edge of the crowd, desiring to speak to him, gave new and vivid emphasis to the parable he had just spoken. He had been seeking to bring home to the understanding of the people the rich promise that would belong to those who listened to the word of God and planted it in their hearts. Now he would have them know how strong the bond could be for all who sought God's kingdom, with himself and with one another. There was a divine relationship which could go deeper than the relationship of birth and brotherhood.

But in Jesus' words there may have been the reflection of another fact which had its undertones of sadness. In the Gospel of Mark, just before the parallel record of this effort of his mother and his brothers to see him, it is written that "his friends . . . went out to seize him, for they said, 'He is beside himself.' " There is no indication that this was the specific purpose of his mother and brothers when they came, but neither is there any sign that in the time before the crucifixion any of Jesus' brothers followed him. It would seem that on this particular day when they wanted to talk with him and had brought his mother with them, they were moved by the desire—not "to seize" him, as the so-called friends were ready to do—but at least to persuade him to come home. In all likelihood, his brothers were not convinced that he had a divine mission, and they were disturbed at the notoriety he was acquiring. They recognized the hostility which was rising against him in influential quarters. Things might get worse, and they did not want to be involved in the risks that he was running; this may have been what they wanted him to know that day when they stood on the fringes of the crowd. If so, there was added poignancy in what Jesus said in the synagogue at Nazareth: "No prophet is acceptable in his own country"; and in that darker saying in Matthew, "A man's foes will be those of his own household."

THE STORM ON THE LAKE

One day he got into a boat with his disciples, and he said to them, "Let us go across to the other side of the lake." So they set out, and as they sailed he fell asleep. And a storm of wind came down on the lake, and they were filling with water, and were in danger. And they went and woke him, saying, "Master, Master, we are perishing!" And he awoke and rebuked the wind and the raging waves; and they ceased, and there was a calm. He said to them," Where is your faith?" And they were afraid, and they marveled, saying to one another, "Who then is this, that he commands even wind and water, and they obey him?" (Luke 8:22-25.)

In this account of what the Evangelist regarded as miraculous, the stilling of a storm at sea, there are two elements. There is first the scene itself; second, there is the interpretation of it.

On that inland water which was sometimes called the Sea of Galilee, there could be sudden and dangerous storms. Winds, sweeping without warning through the gaps in the surrounding hills, could churn the waters with a violence which put small boats into instant peril. Such a storm broke while Jesus and the disciples were on their way across the lake. The disciples were terrified. They called to Jesus, "Master, Master, we are perishing!" But they did not perish. The wind blew past as suddenly as it had come, the waves went down, and the boat got through to the shore for which they were headed.

That was the bare framework of the event. But when the story of it reached the Evangelist, it was invested with a wondering awe. Men said that the storm had ceased because Jesus had stood up and commanded it. They told one another that even winds and waves obeyed him.

But it is to be remembered that in Palestine of that first century men had no notion of natural cause and effect such as a later "scientific" age would have as the framework of its thinking. They assumed that every amazing event for which they were thankful was a miraculous act of God. So Jesus must have stilled the storm. That was the way their instinctive imagination had to see it. It was not dramatic enough to see the whole picture in terms of where the quiet power really was: the power of Jesus to so transmit his sure faith and courage to the disciples that the tumult of their fears subsided. They handled the boat as it needed to be handled and presently it was as though there had been no storm at all.

Whatever the full fact was, the picture in this Gospel makes one thing break through like a blazing light—the feeling which the disciples had that nothing was impossible for Jesus and that when he was with them, no danger could prevail.

THE MAN WHO HAD BEEN POSSESSED

Then they arrived at the country of the Gerasenes, which is opposite Galilee. And as he stepped out on land, there met him a man from the city who had demons; for a long time he had worn no clothes, and he lived not in a house but among the tombs. When he saw Jesus, he cried out and fell down before him, and said with a loud voice, "What have you to do with me, Jesus, Son of the Most High God? I beseech you, do not torment me." For he had commanded the unclean spirit to come out of the man. (For many a time it had seized him; he was kept under guard, and bound with chains and fetters, but he broke the bonds and was driven by the demon into the desert.) Jesus then asked him, "What is your name?" And he said, "Legion"; for many demons had entered him. And they begged him not to command them to depart into the abyss. Now a large herd of swine was feeding there on the hillside; and they begged him to let them enter these. So he gave them leave. Then the demons came out of the man and entered the swine, and the herd rushed down the steep bank into the lake and were drowned.

When the herdsmen saw what had happened, they fled, and told it in the city and in the country. Then people went out to see what had happened, and they came to Jesus, and found the man from whom the demons had gone, sitting at the feet of Jesus, clothed and in his right mind; and they were afraid. And those who had seen it told them how he who had been possessed with demons was healed. Then all the people of the surrounding country of the Gerasenes asked him to depart from them; for they were seized with great fear; so he got into the boat and returned. The man from whom the demons had gone begged that he might be with him; but he sent him away, saying, "Return to your home, and declare how much God has done for you."　　　　　(Luke 8:26-39.)

To read this account in the terms which the Gospel uses might seem at first as though we were listening to something quite outside the reality of the world we think we know. A man "who had demons"; we do not talk like that, and the phrase may sound to us like ancient superstition. We are abundantly familiar with mental disorders, but we use learned names such as "psychosis," "schizophrenia," "paranoia"—*not* possession by "unclean spirits." Nevertheless, the description in the Gospels, if clinically less sophisticated, may come closer to the felt reality. To the distraught person it may seem that he actually is possessed by an alien influence other than himself, an influence the horror of which can be described only as demonic.

In *Jesus and His Ministry*, by W. E. and M. B. Rollins, there is a perceptive comment:

To feel in the grip of demons was a very real experience for many whom Jesus' ministry touched. The tensions of the political and economic situation produced such insecurity and fear and hatred and fanaticism that countless minds were unbalanced to some degree. The ancient world had no institutions for the care of the mentally ill, and if they had no home they were left to roam about and keep alive as best they could. The violently insane, like the Gerasene among the tombs . . . were driven out of the settled communities into deserted places. He and the "man with an unclean spirit" in the Capernaum synagogue (Luke 4:31-32) had both so lost the sense of their own individuality as to feel that the demons were speaking through them.[2]

Such a person was this poor madman whom Jesus encountered in the country of the Gerasenes. He was a victim not only of his own illness but also of the ignorant human cruelty with which all insanity then was treated. People of the neighborhood had put chains on him to keep him from getting loose. Now in front of him stands the figure of Jesus, with his calmness, his strength, his great compassion, and his mighty trust in the transforming grace of God. The power of that new authority reached through to the distraught consciousness of the demoniac. He heard the voice of Jesus speaking straight to the center of his own obsession, to the demon he believed was there; and suddenly the grip of the hideous old fear was broken, and he was free. And presently he was sitting at the feet of Jesus, like a rescued child.

The astonished bystanders interpreted the whole event in ways which reflected their general thinking. The cries and clamor of the madman, when he first saw Jesus, had frightened a herd of pigs, so that they stampeded and fell into the lake and were drowned. The demons had gone out of the man, but demons would not vanish into thin air. Driven from one refuge, they would find another. Cast out of the man, they had entered into the pigs; and Jesus must have told them that they could.

That particular supposition did not matter too much, but there was a resultant thought which the people had that reflected a pitiable twist in all human nature. There had been too much excitement, and the people asked Jesus to depart. It was all very well that the madman should be healed, but look what it had cost! *He* might be healed, but their pigs were dead. It was not the last time that men would conclude that they did not want the unpredictable influence of Jesus to linger in their community. Benefits to men's souls are desirable, of course; but what about the material price that may have to be paid in the process of saving a human being?

THE RAISING OF JAIRUS' DAUGHTER

Now when Jesus returned, the crowd welcomed him, for they were all waiting for him. And there came a man named Jairus, who was a ruler of the synagogue; and falling at Jesus' feet he besought him to come to his house, for he had an only daughter, about twelve years of age, and she was dying.

As he went, the people pressed round him. . . .

While he was still speaking, a man from the ruler's house came and

[2] (New York: The Seabury Press, 1954), pp. 134-35.

said, "Your daughter is dead; do not trouble the Teacher any more." But Jesus on hearing this answered him, "Do not fear; only believe, and she shall be well." And when he came to the house, he permitted no one to enter with him, except Peter and John and James, and the father and mother of the child. And all were weeping and bewailing her; but he said "Do not weep; for she is not dead but sleeping." And they laughed at him, knowing that she was dead. But taking her by the hand he called, saying, "Child, arise." And her spirit returned, and she got up at once; and he directed that something should be given her to eat. And her parents were amazed; but he charged them to tell no one what had happened.

(Luke 8:40-42, 49-56.)

In this account of the bringing back of the little girl whom all those around her thought to be dead there is a double beauty.

In the first place, there is the fact that Jesus was answering an appeal from a ruler of a synagogue. It is sad to read so often in the Gospels of ecclesiastical leaders who chose to feel toward Jesus only hostility and aversion. They felt their self-importance and prestige threatened, and they wanted no contact with him. But here was one instance in which a man's human affections were strong enough to overcome his prejudices. Jairus' daughter was in danger, and because of that he came with his appeal to Jesus.

And then of course there is the main fact described at the chapter's end. Down the road from Jairus' house there came a messenger with the bleak tidings that there was no use for Jesus to come; the child was already dead. But Jesus said to Jairus, "Do not fear; only believe, and she shall be well." When Jesus and Jairus arrived at the house and found the mourners weeping and lamenting, Jesus said, "Do not weep; for she is not dead but sleeping." Then in spite of their bitter disbelief he went in and took the little girl by the hand and said to her, "Child, arise"; and then, in the words of the Gospel, "Her spirit returned, and she got up at once, and he directed that something should be given her to eat."

Here we stand at the edge of mystery. How far the child had slipped over the borderline between physical life and death we cannot know. Suffice it to believe that in Jesus there was a power beyond our definition. In more ways than one he is the resurrection and the life.

THE POWER OF A GREAT DESIRE

And a woman who had had a flow of blood for twelve years and could not be healed by any one, came up behind him, and touched the fringe of his garment; and immediately her flow of blood ceased. And Jesus said, "Who was it that touched me?" When all denied it, Peter said, "Master, the multitudes surround you and press upon you!" But Jesus said, "Some one touched me; for I perceive that power has gone forth from me." And when the woman saw that she was not hidden, she came trembling, and falling down before him declared in the presence of all the people why she had touched him, and how she had been immediately healed. And he said to her, "Daughter, your faith has made you well; go in peace."   (Luke 8:43-48.)

This description—thrust by the Evangelist into the midst of the story of Jairus' daughter—is one of the many accounts of how the power in Jesus and his great compassion reached out to heal someone who was sick; but through this particular description there comes—like a sudden flash of light—an indication of what is needed if his healing is to be conveyed.

A great crowd of people were pressing round Jesus. As in any miscellaneous throng, individuals in it must have come from many different motives. Some may have been drawn merely by curiosity to see this man of Nazareth who had stirred up so much excitement. Some may have wanted as a matter of general interest to compare his teaching with what the rabbis taught. Others may have had a vague idea that somehow they might benefit in being where he was. At any rate, there they were—looking over one another's shoulders, shoving forward, crowding in closer to Jesus in their midst. No wonder that the disciples were astonished when Jesus asked, "Who was it that touched me?" Wasn't that what the whole multitude was trying to do? How could anybody specify *who* touched him?

But Jesus knew something different. There had been a touch so yearning that the sensitiveness in him had responded to it instantly. And a woman, trembling, knelt at his feet and confessed that she had touched him, and that an illness from which she had suffered for twelve years was healed.

Physical healing by direct spiritual power lies in a realm which is beyond our full knowledge. To this particular sufferer Jesus said, "Daughter, your faith has made you well." In a number of Christian churches there are special services to which men and women come to pray that the living Christ will do for them what Jesus did for the sick and sad in Galilee. We dare not say to any one of them, "If you believe it positively enough, then your bodily infirmity assuredly will be healed." It may be that the greater purpose which the love of God holds for some human life is to enable it to become radiant through accepted suffering. But this is certain: there is a grace for body and soul which will be found by those—and by those only—who reach out for it with the most intense desire. In this scene from Luke the crowd whose interest in Jesus was no more than curious and casual never made contact with his reality. But the woman did, because her soul was hungry for what only God could give; and that sort of hunger the divine compassion will recognize and answer, as Jesus responded to the woman's touch with his outgoing power and bade her, "Go in peace."

chapter 9

APOSTOLIC RESPONSIBILITY

And he called the twelve together and gave them power and authority over all demons and to cure diseases, and he sent them out to preach the kingdom of God and to heal. And he said to them, "Take nothing for your journey, no staff, nor bag, nor bread, nor money; and do not have two tunics. And whatever house you enter, stay there, and from there depart. And wherever they do not receive you, when you leave that town shake off the dust from your feet as a testimony against them." And they departed and went through the villages, preaching the gospel and healing everywhere. (Luke 9:1-6.)

When Jesus sent the twelve out, they entered upon a new chapter of experience. Hitherto they had been disciples, which primarily meant learners. Now they were to be apostles, made responsible to carry to others the power of the gospel which they had begun to know.

There are parts of Christendom which lay large emphasis on the apostolic succession—the authority in the ministry which has come down in a straight line of ordination since the apostles' times. A more important matter is to make sure that all those who are ordained in the name of Christ stand in the line of succession of doing what he had told the apostles to do. No men and no churches are real representatives of Jesus if they sit still and nurse their own spiritual privilege and have no missionary eagerness. "The church is not a club or an association of like-minded and congenial people," the worldwide representatives of one Christian communion have acknowledged, at the Anglican Congress of 1963. "The church exists," the Congress continued, "to witness, to obey, and to serve." And John A. T. Robinson, in *Honest to God* has put in one sentence what all would-be Christians should know about the church, that "its charter is to be the servant of the world." [1]

The gallant slogan of the Student Volunteer Movement at the beginning of the twentieth century was *The Evangelization of the World in This Generation*. That great ideal was not achieved, but it should stand as a

[1] (Philadelphia: The Westminster Press, 1963) , p. 134.

continuing challenge. It breathes the urgency which belongs to each critical time. Certainly as these words are written, the time is critical and is likely to continue so through the years immediately to come. A world with a multitude of new nations in Africa and the Orient struggling toward identity, a world shadowed by the atomic peril and yet possessed at the same time by possibilities unprecedented for the enlargement of human life: *this* is the world whose needs cry out for a gospel that can preach hope and faith and courage, cast out the evil spirits of hate and bitterness, and bring the healing touch of Jesus to the sickness of our human race.

THE HOSTILITY OF HEROD

Now Herod the tetrarch heard of all that was done, and he was perplexed, because it was said by some that John had been raised from the dead, by some that Elijah had appeared, and by others that one of the old prophets had risen. Herod said, "John I beheaded; but who is this about whom I hear such things?" And he sought to see him.

On their return the apostles told him what they had done. And he took them and withdrew apart to a city called Bethsaida. When the crowds learned it, they followed him; and he welcomed them and spoke to them of the kingdom of God, and cured those who had need of healing.

(Luke 9:7-11.)

This Herod—Herod Antipas—was the individual in the whole Herodian family who could fairly be regarded as the one least deserving of respect. His father was Herod the Great, a man of violent and cruel passions, but of unquestioned ability and personal power, who won the favor of Rome and kept it. When he died, his will divided the sphere of his authority into three parts, assigning one of these to each of three sons; and Antipas was given rulership over the province of Galilee. He was the one, therefore, with whom Jesus had to reckon: a cheap worldling, who had divorced his first wife and married the wife of one of his brothers, and had caused John the Baptist to be executed—according to the Gospel of Mark, because John had denounced his adultery. Now he hears of Jesus; and in his mind there was a mixture of curiosity and superstitious unease. He had the worldling's cynical contempt for matters of the spirit, which made him think of the reported activity of this prophet from Nazareth as something he might be amused by; but at the same time there rose out of the dark recesses of his consciousness that which was not amusing. Even he could have some troubling sense of guilt that gave him a momentary shudder when he heard the popular rumor that this might be John the Baptist risen from the dead. If Jesus of Nazareth was indeed to be like John the Baptist, then Herod could have bad dreams. And the cure for that? Perhaps to get rid of Jesus as he had got rid of John.

It is that apparent threat from Herod which has made thoughtful students of the Gospel attach a special importance to the reference in vs. 10. Jesus and the disciples with him are reported to have withdrawn to a city called Bethsaida. There was a little hamlet named Bethsaida on the western shore of the Lake of Galilee in Herod Antipas' jurisdiction; but it is now known that a more important Bethsaida had been built by Herod Philip, Antipas' brother, to the north of the lake. Going there, Jesus would be beyond Herod Antipas' reach; and, according to the Gospel of Mark, Jesus and the disciples "went away in the boat by themselves."

THE FEEDING OF THE MULTITUDE

Now the day began to wear away; and the twelve came and said to him, "Send the crowd away, to go into the villages and country round about, to lodge and get provisions; for we are here in a lonely place." But he said to them, "You give them something to eat." They said, "We have no more than five loaves and two fish—unless we are to go and buy food for all these people." For there were about five thousand men. And he said to his disciples, "Make them sit down in companies, about fifty each." And they did so, and made them all sit down. And taking the five loaves and the two fish he looked up to heaven, and blessed and broke them, and gave them to the disciples to set before the crowd. And all ate and were satisfied. And they took up what was left over, twelve baskets of broken pieces.   (Luke 9:12-17.)

Then follows the account of the feeding of five thousand people by Jesus. It is the one miracle story which appears in all four Gospels, and it reflects therefore the deep conviction of the early church that something of immense importance had happened. Yet across the gap of nineteen centuries it is impossible to know, or to try to say categorically, what it was.

The first possible answer is that here was a physical miracle which could have been brought about only by supernatural power. Jesus is seen as taking in his hands the little store of bread and smoked fish which the disciples brought him, and by his touch making this food multiply until it became enough to feed a multitude. Yet it is a striking fact that no one of the four Gospels states in explicit words that Jesus multiplied the food; here in Luke this comes simply as an inference from the conclusion that "all ate and were satisfied." Few would be so lacking in reverent humility as to assert brashly that a kind of miracle beyond our understanding could not have happened. But it is true that Jesus more than once disparaged supernatural signs. And it is to be remembered that in the wilderness the first temptation which Jesus resisted was the suggestion that he turn the stones into bread. It was the soul and not the body that he had come supremely to feed.

A second interpretation of the narrative is that Jesus saw that here and there in the crowd food had been brought which would be enough to meet everybody's immediate need if it was shared; and so with quiet trust he told the disciples to have the people sit down and then to begin by distributing what they themselves had, after they had brought it to him to be blessed. This possibility has been expressed by a contemporary writer in an imagined dialogue between a minister and a young theological student, anxious and bewildered, who had come to pour out his spiritual distress.

"It's the miracle of the feeding the five thousand. . . . I found I couldn't believe that. . . . I prayed night and day, but it didn't help. I still can't believe it!"

Then the minister described the scene as it seemed to him that it might have been, and he concluded:

"I am only telling you how I have always liked to interpret this story. I think that Jesus' sublime faith in them touched the selfish hearts of the crowd so that suddenly all those who had brought food turned it over to the disciples, and when it was divided and distributed it proved to be enough for all."

The young man stared in amazement, but he did not speak.

"Which interpretation of the incident seems to you to have the deepest meaning for us, the greatest motivating power? The belief that Jesus by pressing some sort of supernatural button increased three loaves to the amount needed to feed a multitude, or that by his teaching and the inspiration of his personality he caused several thousand people to win a victory over selfishness and share their food with those who had none? Which?"

The young man moistened his dry lips, "The latter," he answered.

"It seems so to me," Hilary said quietly. Then he added. "I'll tell you the verse that has helped me in this connection. It's this one: 'The letter killeth but the spirit giveth life.' When you try to believe the Bible according to the *letter*, you will find you have killed much of its truth. If you read it only in search of the spiritual, you will find life on every page." [2]

The third approach to the story of the feeding is through remembering the account in the sixth chapter of the Gospel of John of how Jesus said to the multitude, "I am the bread of life; he who comes to me shall not hunger, and he who believes in me shall never thirst." So it may be that

---

[2] Agnes Sligh Turnbull, *The Bishop's Mantle* (New York: The Macmillan Company, 1947), pp. 192-93. Used by permission of the publishers.

what he did that day near Bethsaida was to anticipate the Holy Communion and to use the loaves and fishes as the sacramental symbols of his continuing fellowship in the spirit with these people of Galilee whom he was leaving now. Later the tradition in the Christian church may have surrounded the event with a miraculous framework; but certainly the enduring miracle of Christ comes not through the temporary satisfaction of nourishment of the flesh but through the invisible bread by which souls are fed.

WHO DO YOU SAY THAT I AM?

Now it happened that as he was praying alone the disciples were with him; and he asked them, "Who do the people say that I am?" And they answered, "John the Baptist; but others say, Elijah, and others, that one of the old prophets has risen." And he said to them, "But who do you say that I am?" And Peter answered, "The Christ of God." But he charged and commanded them to tell this to no one, saying, "The Son of man must suffer many things, and be rejected by the elders and chief priests and scribes, and be killed, and on the third day be raised." And he said to all, "If any man would come after me, let him deny himself and take up his cross daily and follow me. For whoever would save his life will lose it; and whoever loses his life for my sake, he will save it. For what does it profit a man if he gains the whole world and loses or forfeits himself? For whoever is ashamed of me and of my words, of him will the Son of man be ashamed when he comes in his glory and the glory of the Father and of the holy angels. But I tell you truly, there are some standing here who will not taste of death before they see the kingdom of God." (Luke 9:18-27.)

If the feeding of the five thousand did represent a sacramental parting of Jesus from those who had followed him in Galilee and the end of his ministry there, then the scene which follows in the Gospel record brings to climactic expression what that ministry, and all of Jesus' ministry, was and is. When he asked the disciples how the people in general thought of him, they told him the groping answers the people gave: another John the Baptist, Elijah come back to earth, or some other one of the old prophets. Then when he asked, "Who do *you* say that I am?" Peter burst out with his impulsive answer: "The Christ of God!" All he knew was that Jesus seemed more wonderful than any comparisons men had used could ever suggest.

Almost certainly he thought that Jesus as the Christ would bring some sort of splendid deliverance. But there came to him the shocking words of Jesus that the Christ must be a suffering Christ and that those who followed him must suffer also.

A strange way, it seems, for the redemption of God to have to come; but that is the way it is. If men are to be saved—saved not in the matter of passing circumstance but in the response of their own souls—it can only be by the awful sacrifice of a love that comes to them in the midst of their sinfulness and endures all the cost of winning them at last to *want* to be delivered from their sins. The price of complete devotion might have to be a cross. That would be true for Jesus; and he made his disciples know that if they followed him, it would be on a hard way. If they would win their place in the kingdom of God, they must be ready to subordinate everything else to the glory of trying to be like their Lord.

Christian discipleship was never meant to be easy; and if it is genuine, it will not be easy now. For the first disciples it involved physical danger, and martyrdom for some of them. In the dark periods of history all down the years there have been others who have dared to pay that ultimate price. Men like Dietrich Bonhoeffer, executed by the Nazis for his Christian witness, did so in this century. From them has come the sort of message which Pastor Paul Schneider, murdered in the Buchenwald concentration camp in July 1939, had written to his wife: "Those who still want to avoid suffering . . . had better take care lest they be rejected among men and cast off by God."

In times of crisis the great souls—and many who until the test came would never have been imagined to be great—have accepted suffering and have shown that human beings can be heroic. But in ordinary times and in sheltered circumstances it is possible to forget that there is any need of hardship—let alone of heroism. Every now and then there is a so-called "revival of religion." More churches are built; more people go to church; crowds flock out to hear some popular evangelist, to sing hymns, and in response to his exordiums to "confess Christ" as the climax of the "crusade." But what will confessing Christ mean; and what is the crusade for, and what is it against? Is it an enlistment against the deep-rooted evils which most powerfully contradict the kingdom of God: the evils which may be dangerous for a man's popularity, for his business interests, his established reputation, dangerous to criticize and combat? Filthy slums which the people in the pews have never noticed, the cruelties which can go on behind the walls of jails and prisons, perversions of justice, brutal oppression of Negroes, the misery of the poor and the unemployed—will Christian discipleship take up the cross of some costly effort on behalf of these? If not, then a passion for crowds and inflated church membership rolls may represent nothing but escape from the drastic demands of the spirit of Christ. For individuals and for the churches the great words go on sounding: "Whosoever would save his life will lose it, but whosoever loses his life for my sake, he will save it."

Our ordinary instincts flinch, as the first disciples did, from the realization that there is no smooth road to "being saved." It is not a matter of some sort of verbal loyalty that will get us into heaven. It is life that lays the daily foundation of obedience on which God may build the New Jerusalem of a heavenly purpose made manifest on earth. Again the voice of Jesus comes to us as it came long ago to the disciples who also could not understand at first how a crucifixion could be the way to conquest. Albert Schweitzer wrote:

He speaks to us in the same words: "Follow thou Me!" and sets us to the tasks which He has to fulfil for our time. He commands. And to those who obey Him, whether they be wise or simple, He will reveal Himself in the toils, the conflicts, the sufferings which they shall pass through in His fellowship, and, as an ineffable mystery, they shall learn in their own experience who He is.[3]

As to the meaning of vs. 27, we from our distance of time and place cannot speak categorically. The promise as here expressed was that disciples standing there as Jesus spoke would "see the kingdom of God" before they should "taste of death." Would this realization of the kingdom be in the transfiguration of Jesus, which some of the disciples were presently to witness; or in the resurrection; or in the creation of the Christian church? We cannot surely know. But this we do know: that among disciples of Jesus then and now there have been those who have experienced the kingdom of God as having come in their own transformed devotion.

THE TRANSFIGURATION

Now about eight days after these sayings he took with him Peter and John and James, and went up on the mountain to pray. And as he was praying, the appearance of his countenance was altered, and his raiment became dazzling white. And behold, two men talked with him, Moses and Elijah, who appeared in glory and spoke of his departure, which he was to accomplish at Jerusalem. Now Peter and those who were with him were heavy with sleep but kept awake, and they saw his glory and the two men who stood with him. And as the men were parting from him, Peter said to Jesus, "Master, it is well that we are here; let us make three booths, one for you and one for Moses and one for Elijah"—not knowing what he said. As he said this, a cloud came and overshadowed them; and they were afraid as they entered the cloud. And a voice came out of the cloud, saying, "This is my Son, my Chosen; listen to him!" And when the

[3] Albert Schweitzer, *The Quest of the Historical Jesus* (London: A. C. Black, Ltd., 1910), p. 401.

voice had spoken, Jesus was found alone. And they kept silence and told no one in those days anything of what they had seen.   (Luke 9:28-36.)

This description of what happened when Jesus went up on the mountain to pray is linked directly with the new awareness of Jesus as the Christ which had come like a sudden revelation to the mind and heart of Peter. But the real meaning of this revelation he still had to learn. Jesus as the Christ, yes; but a Christ so different from Peter's instinctive expectation that it was hard for him to realize the truth. According to the earlier Gospel of Mark, when Jesus told him and the other disciples that he would be rejected by the authorities of the nation and put to death, Peter was shocked to the point of vehement protest and contradiction. It simply could not be—that the one appointed by God to be the Savior should suffer!

Yet that was to be the fact; and the reality of it came home to Peter, James, and John—the three disciples who were closest to Jesus—when he took them with him as he went apart to pray. They went through an experience then which no flat words could describe, and of which the Gospel narrative can give therefore only an ineffable suggestion, as of the infinite world breaking through into the finite consciousness which for the moment is lifted up above its mortal limitations. They could not forget what Jesus had told them of all that might await him in Jerusalem. They must have been trying to grapple with the awfulness of that ever since he had spoken to them. And now when they saw him pray, they could sense that he must be grappling with it too. He must be facing decisions which would seem to them to be only terrible.

Then as they looked at Jesus, they saw that there was no gloom about him. Instead, the exaltation of his spirit gave a radiance to all his face and form, as the inner light shone through. And then the truth came to them as in a vision: a vision of Moses, through whom had come the law of God, and Elijah, greatest of the prophets of God's living word, on either side of Jesus. They appeared in glory and spoke of his departure, which he was to accomplish at Jerusalem. So this was the glory that should be the fulfillment of all the purposes of God—not the glory of greatness as the world counts greatness, but the glory of their heroic Master who was ready to take upon himself the consequences of the world's sins and through his suffering be the world's Redeemer! They did not understand this yet, but they began at least to know that this was the way it would have to be. If they tried to speak, they could only stammer out incoherent, blundering words like those of Peter. The cloud of mystery that overshadowed them made them afraid. But out of it all there came a voice saying to them what they could never henceforth forget or disobey: "This is my Son,

my Chosen; listen to him!" Jesus who would set his face to go to Jerusalem, Jesus who had said that only he who loses his life shall find it, was
the Lord whom they must follow to the end.

WHERE THE FINAL POWER IS

On the next day, when they had come down from the mountain, a great
crowd met him. And behold, a man from the crowd cried, "Teacher, I
beg you to look upon my son, for he is my only child; and behold, a spirit
seizes him, and he suddenly cries out; it convulses him till he foams, and
shatters him, and will hardly leave him. And I begged your disciples to
cast it out, but they could not." Jesus answered, "O faithless and perverse
generation, how long am I to be with you and bear with you? Bring your
son here." While he was coming, the demon tore him and convulsed him.
But Jesus rebuked the unclean spirit, and healed the boy, and gave him
back to his father. And all were astonished at the majesty of God.

But while they were all marveling at everything he did, he said to his
disciples, "Let these words sink into your ears; for the Son of man is to
be delivered into the hands of men." But they did not understand this
saying, and it was concealed from them, that they should not perceive
it; and they were afraid to ask him about this saying. (Luke 9:37-45.)

While three of the disciples were on the mountain with Jesus, the rest of
the disciples down below were appealed to by a man who had an epileptic
son. That, at least, is the term by which we would describe what seems to
be the malady which the father said was a spirit that convulsed him
till he foamed, shattered him, and would hardly leave him. The father
begged the disciples to heal the boy, and they could not. All the more
desperately, therefore, when he caught sight of Jesus coming, he appealed
to him. The power that was in Jesus did heal the boy; "and all were
astonished at the majesty of God."

The majesty of God *was* there. One stands in awe before the sovereign
strength that was in Jesus whenever the sick in body—as also the sick in
soul—were brought to him. There is a divine healing which goes beyond
what the faithless can believe. But the words which follow the account of
this particular healing are very striking. "While they were all marveling
at everything he did," Jesus said to his disciples, "Let these words sink
into your ears." And the words which he then spoke, the words that
were to be implanted in their heads, had to do with what did not seem to
be majesty. He said he would be delivered into the hands of men. He who
in Galilee had gone about doing good was going up now to Jerusalem to
face crucifixion by men who had forgot God. Against what might be our
shallow supposition stands the fact that the power of God, which can

work its marvels for the eager and receptive, will not break down by force the resistance of evil; for that would leave the spirit of evil still unchanged. It will allow itself to be rejected, until men who see at last the consequences in themselves of that rejection turn in shame and repentant sorrow toward the goodness they had denied. *That* is the majesty of God, the ultimate, strange power which had to be embodied in the cross.

GREATNESS THROUGH SERVICE

And an argument arose among them as to which of them was the greatest. But when Jesus perceived the thought of their hearts, he took a child and put him by his side, and said to them, "Whoever receives this child in my name receives me, and whoever receives me receives him who sent me; for he who is least among you all is the one who is great."

(Luke 9:46-48.)

It ought to have been impossible that this argument among the disciples could follow what Jesus had just said to them. He had told them that his own life was moving toward a climax of suffering and sacrifice. It is recorded (in vs. 45) that they did not understand what he was saying and that they were afraid to ask him. Perhaps the reason why they were afraid to ask was because they were afraid of what they felt they might have to understand, and did not want to. The kind of disaster which Jesus had suggested was too intolerable to believe. So they did what the human mind is prone to do: they suppressed the disturbing idea by talking about something completely different. Instead of suffering, they would think about success. And once they had shifted to that ground, it was easy to begin an argument as to who would deserve to succeed the most. Who would have the highest place in the kingdom which—in spite of every uneasy question—Jesus must surely mean to establish?

Jesus perceived the thoughts of their hearts, and in that perception there had to be again—as there had to be so often—a patient pity for their blundering. He did not rebuke them. He would show them something which might stir their better imagination and help them to understand. So he took a child and put him by his side. A child can give no honors. A child can give no rewards—except the one most precious reward of a love that will answer love. Yet in the heart of every decent man there is the instinct to forget himself and his own advantage when a child needs him; and when he follows that instinct, he knows that he is a better and a bigger man. Think of yourself that way in relation to all human needs is what Jesus in effect was saying. Not in self-assertion but in service you will find that life can be made great.

TRYING TO MONOPOLIZE THE SPIRIT

> John answered, "Master, we saw a man casting out demons in your name, and we forbade him, because he does not follow with us." But Jesus said to him, "Do not forbid him; for he that is not against you is for you."
> (Luke 9:49-50.)

How like all the rest of us those first disciples were! It seemed sometimes that they had caught the spirit of their Master, and then the next day they would have to learn all over again the lesson they were supposed to have learned the day before. A while before they were arguing about their prestige as individuals; now they wanted to assert their prestige as a group. They had seen a man casting out demons in Jesus' name. They might have been glad that demons were cast out, glad that the power of God which Jesus had inspired had spread to others than themselves. But no. What they thought about was that their prerogatives had been invaded. This kind of irregularity must be all wrong. Ministry outside the proper channels ought to be forbidden.

But Jesus did not forbid it. The inclusiveness of his spirit is always wider than that of some of his followers is likely to be. The arrogance of ecclesiastical closed corporations, the rigidity of denominations, the refusal to recognize that the Spirit can really operate outside the boundaries of what may be pronounced to be "the one true church" have plain precedent among those first disciples who were on the way to becoming saints. But when they wanted to forbid the other man who was casting out demons, they were a long way from having arrived at sainthood; and what they needed and what they got was their Master's quick correction.

THE GOAL OF THE GREAT DESIRE

> When the days drew near for him to be received up, he set his face to go to Jerusalem.
> (Luke 9:51a.)

One can see again the picture which those brief words suggest: Jesus with his mind made up to reject all safer choices; setting his face inflexibly now to go up to Jerusalem for the climax of his ministry, even when he knew it meant the risk of almost certain death; moving on ahead of his disciples who, according to Mark's Gospel, followed, but "were afraid."

Concerning such a choice as that of Jesus there is a memorable passage in one of Phillips Brooks's great sermons, "Going up to Jerusalem."

Every true life has its Jerusalem, to which it is always going up. At first far off and dimly seen, laying but light hold upon our purpose and our will, then gradually taking us more and more into its power, compelling our study, directing the current of our thoughts: . . . so every live man's Jerusalem, his sacred city, calls to him from the hill-top on which it stands. . . . The man who is going up to no Jerusalem is but the ghost and relic of a man. . . .

Would it not be a vast thing for us if we could be far more aware than we now are of some such great Christlike sweep of our lives toward a purpose? . . . A friend comes to you and says, "Do this with me!" And you quietly reply to him, "I cannot. . . . I am going up to Jerusalem." There is an end of it. You have not to sit on a stone on the road side, . . . until you have decided just whether the thing is wrong, and just how wrong it is. . . . Simply the thing is not on the way to Jerusalem, and so you press on . . . and leave it far behind.[4]

WHEN THE GATES ARE CLOSED TO CHRIST

And he sent messengers ahead of him, who went and entered a village of the Samaritans, to make ready for him; but the people would not receive him, because his face was set toward Jerusalem. And when his disciples James and John saw it, they said, "Lord, do you want us to bid fire come down from heaven and consume them?" But he turned and rebuked them. And they went on to another village.

(Luke 9:51*b*-56.)

Jesus had made his ultimate decision. He must carry the challenge of his ministry to the center of his people's life, and so he sets his face to go to Jerusalem.

On the way he must pass through Samaria. Between the Samaritans and the Jews there had been a long estrangement, the more bitter because the Samaritans were partly Jewish. In the ninth and eighth centuries B.C., the city of Samaria had been the capital of the northern kingdom of Israel. Then in 722 B.C., the Assyrian armies had captured and sacked the city, ravaged the country round it, and carried off most of the population of the whole north country, "the lost ten tribes," as captives into the East. Among those who were left of the people, and among some of those brought in, there was still a kind of Judaism, based upon the Pentateuch alone; but the fact that the Samaritans had this partial basis of agreement with the Jews made all the more rancorous the points at which they disagreed. To the Samaritans the Temple in Jerusalem and the whole cult that centered there were an idolatrous aftergrowth. They said that Gerizim in their territory was the holy place appointed in the law of Moses. In the words of the woman of Samaria, in the Gospel of John, "Our fathers worshiped on this mountain; and you say that in Jerusalem is the place where

[4] Found in *The Excellence of Our Calling,* an abridgment by T. F. Chilcote of *Lectures on Preaching* by Phillips Brooks (New York: E. P. Dutton & Company, 1954), pp. 177-78, 186.

men ought to worship." In the antagonism which grew from that differ- ence, the Jews and the Samaritans had no dealings with one another.

Now Jesus and the disciples find themselves at evening near a Samaritan village. To him, Samaritans also were children of his Father. He would seek welcome in their town that night. But they gave an answer which has an ironic echo in our contemporary world. The Samaritans would not receive him, because his face was set toward Jerusalem. Similarly today the Arab countries round the present Israel will not admit anyone whose passport shows that he means also to go to Jewish Jerusalem. Religious bitterness is a long and stubborn thing.

Then and now it can impoverish life. If Jesus had entered that Samaritan village, he could have brought to people there what many would have had reason to be grateful for all their days. Sick folk might have been healed, little children taken up into his arms and blessed, men and women given a chance to listen to the message of the love of God which would have made their whole existence different. But the Samaritans were blind to all that. Jesus and his disciples seemed to them only alien and un- welcome strangers. Who were these Galileans that they should bother to take them in?

James and John were indignant. They wanted Jesus to call down fire from heaven and blast these stupid and insulting villagers. They had not learned yet the great compassion of their Master. Some of the ancient manuscripts of the Gospel, as the King James Version accepted and trans- lated them, include these words of his answer: "Ye know not what manner of spirit ye are of. For the Son of Man is not come to destroy men's lives, but to save them." He called down no avenging fire. Simply, they went to another village; and the churlish people of the first village were left in their own refusal.

But in that fact which sounds so inconsequential, there is an eternal parable—a parable of the tragedy that can come unrecognized to human souls. The Samaritan villagers had lost the benediction that would have come to them if they had welcomed Jesus. But they did not know they had lost anything, and they did not care. So it may be again. When the mes- sengers of God are rejected, the result may not show in some sudden and dramatic way. There is no lightning from an angry heaven, and so there may be no awareness that anything disastrous has happened at all. But the lack of that awareness is itself the disaster. A man who is contemptuous of religion may say, "What of it? I have the things I want. I don't need anything more"; and when the spirit of Christ comes knocking at his gates, all he recognizes is that something unfamiliar is there which he need not bother to let in. When it goes to another village, what has he lost? Nothing, he would say. But the truth is that he has lost the fulfillment of his life. He has not been thrust down to hell, but he has condemned himself to the shrinking of his soul which can become the most desperate inner hell. In this hell the bitterest torment is not fire, but the awful finality of failure. The man's spiritual self is left in its mean emptiness, and the blessing that might have been his is gone beyond recall.

THE HIGH DEMANDS FOR DISCIPLESHIP

As they were going along the road, a man said to him, "I will follow you wherever you go." And Jesus said to him, "Foxes have holes, and birds of the air have nests; but the Son of man has nowhere to lay his head." To another he said, "Follow me." But he said, "Lord, let me first go and bury my father." But he said to him, "Leave the dead to bury their own dead; but as for you, go and proclaim the kingdom of God." Another said, "I will follow you, Lord; but let me first say farewell to those at my home." Jesus said to him, "No one who puts his hand to the plow and looks back is fit for the kingdom of God." (Luke 9:57-62.)

This concluding passage is in tune with the deep note of the major chord which has dominated this whole chapter: the inescapable reality of suffering that must be faced by all who would belong to the kingdom of God.

Jesus himself had set his face to go to Jerusalem, where all the influences which threatened him most were centered. He had confronted his disciples with a decisive choice: they could stay in the relative security of Galilee where their whole lives had been, or they could risk everything by going with him all the way. Greatness of living—and perhaps of dying—lay ahead, but every lesser thing to which they had held on might have to be sacrificed if they were to gain what he called them to.

Henceforth, the conditions for any man's discipleship would be drastic; and the abrupt descriptions which the Gospel gives of the three men who fell short show how drastic those conditions could be made.

The first man came to Jesus with large protestation. He would follow Jesus wherever he might go. But he had not reckoned on the fact that this might mean being stripped of every comfort and protection, with not so much refuge into which to escape from danger as the hole that a fox might have. And he flinched at the thought of that.

The second man was met with what seemed an even more stern demand. He said he wanted first to bury his father. "Leave the dead to bury their own dead," said Jesus, by which he meant that those who were the spiritually dead already, the people who had no spark of eagerness for the kingdom which this man seemed to have, could take care of burials. It has been noted that the man's first words may not have meant that his father was dead at that moment, but that the man thought it was proper to make sure that he was around to see that everything was arranged properly and in order beforehand. In any case he was putting his family bond ahead of his immediate commitment.

The third man wanted to go home and tell everybody where he was going—and maybe get their advice on whether he had better go. He did not want to decide until he had thought a little more. Jesus answered him, "No one who puts his hand to the plow and looks back is fit for the kingdom of God."

All three men were rejected. Jesus had made the terms so hard that it might well have been asked, as Peter asked on another occasion, "Who then can be saved?" And the answer perhaps is that none of us can be, except as there comes to us grace from God which lifts our human weakness up above its insufficiency. There can be critical moments in life when a man can choose the kingdom of God only if he has at least the willingness to be taken hold of and made heroic.

chapter 10

UNRESERVED OBEDIENCE

After this the Lord appointed seventy others, and sent them on ahead of him, two by two, into every town and place where he himself was about to come. And he said to them, "The harvest is plentiful, but the laborers are few; pray therefore the Lord of the harvest to send out laborers into his harvest. Go your way; behold, I send you out as lambs in the midst of wolves. Carry no purse, no bag, no sandals; and salute no one on the road. Whatever house you enter, first say, 'Peace be to this house!' And if a son of peace is there, your peace shall rest upon him; but if not, it shall return to you. And remain in the same house, eating and drinking what they provide, for the laborer deserves his wages; do not go from house to house. Whenever you enter a town and they receive you, eat what is set before you; heal the sick in it and say to them, 'The kingdom of God has come near to you.' " (Luke 10:1-9.)

This description of the sending out of seventy others is a close parallel to what is told at the beginning of chapter 9 about the sending out of the twelve. It is possible that Luke had heard or read two reports of a mission which Jesus had appointed, and got the impression that there were two missions; whereas, in fact, both reports were describing the same one. But there is no reason why there may not have been two; and if there were, this second mission, described at greater length and with more detail, had features of significance which were new and special.

To begin with, it gives no names. We know the names of the twelve, but not a single name among the seventy. That might seem at first thought to make the whole event less interesting and important; in a deeper sense it makes it more so. We are sometimes disposed to think that the great service for God has been done—and must be done now—only by the conspicuous people. But the fact is that great service in the sight of God is not measured by our earthly notoriety. There are names not carried down in lasting remembrance which nevertheless are written in heaven: the names of the men and women who in their quiet ways have done their duty, the everyday saints—some of whom we know—who have been obedient, as the seventy were, to the voice of Christ.

The seventy went out two by two. The truth of Christ can best be learned, and work for Christ can best be done, in comradeship. The two great commandments, love to God and love to neighbor, interact. It is not in solitariness that we most surely find God. We find him and he finds us when whatever is in our thought and purpose is enlarged and brightened by what comes to us through the mind and heart of someone else who also is trying to be a Christian.

The seventy traveled light. They were not bogged down by thinking that first they had to make elaborate preparations. They were not encumbered with a lot of baggage. Nothing diverted them from the urgency of what they had to do: no thought about needing money, no hunting about for good accommodations, no fastidious concern about what they had to eat. They might run into situations where it would seem that their mission had no more value than lambs among wolves. Never mind. Go on. There were souls out there who needed them, houses where they could say, "Peace be to this house" and God's peace would be there.

The great advances for the kingdom of God have not been made by those who thought that nothing could be accomplished without the right equipment. They have been accomplished by men who went out possessed of nothing but the fire in their souls. John Wesley carried his redemptive gospel through the length and breadth of England, and all the equipment he had was his saddle and the horse on which he rode a quarter of a million miles. When the pioneers pressed the American frontier farther and farther to the west, the established churches, accustomed to conventional ways and soft surroundings, did not follow them; but the circuit riders did. They made it possible that the frontier, which might have been only lawless, wild, and pagan, should have the leaven of the word of God.

Again and again it has been the call of the difficult service which has enlisted the men who have been the glory of the gospel. Francis of Assisi, wealthy, pleasure-loving, careless, and unconcerned, heard one day in the little church of Santa Maria degli Angeli the priest read as the Gospel for the day the passage from Matthew that parallels this charge to the seventy in Luke: "As ye go, preach, saying, 'The kingdom of heaven is at hand.' Heal the sick, cleanse the lepers, cast out devils: freely ye have received, freely give. Provide neither gold, nor silver, nor brass in your purses, nor scrip . . . , neither two coats, neither shoes, nor yet staves: for the workman is worthy of his meat." (Matt. 10:7-10 KJV.) To Francis, the words came with the blazing authority of heaven. Here was his commission! He would be stripped of every thing which the world reckoned as its resources. Empty-handed, he would go out to preach the gospel of him who said, "He that seeketh his life shall lose it, and he that loseth his life for my sake and the gospel's, shall save it."

In his new life of dedication he went with such a shining joy that other men caught the contagion of his spirit, and there grew up around him the Franciscan Order, or the Brothers Minor, as Francis chose to call them, committed to humility, simplicity, poverty, and prayer, in uncalculating service to the poor. So he made evident that although the world may seem full of men who pass through life with souls asleep, there are always those who are waiting for some tremendous message, at the sound of which their wakened spiritual energies will stand up in thrilling answer.

THE TRAGEDY OF THE LOST CHANCE

"But whenever you enter a town and they do not receive you, go into its streets and say, 'Even the dust of your town that clings to our feet, we wipe off against you; nevertheless know this, that the kingdom of God has come near.' I tell you, it shall be more tolerable on that day for Sodom than for that town.

"Woe to you, Chorazin! woe to you, Bethsaida! for if the mighty works done in you had been done in Tyre and Sidon, they would have repented long ago, sitting in sackcloth and ashes. But it shall be more tolerable in the judgment for Tyre and Sidon than for you. And you, Capernaum, will you be exalted to heaven? You shall be brought down to Hades."

(Luke 10:10-15.)

There is always a dark other side to opportunity, and that darkness may be terrible when the opportunity ignored has had to do directly with men's souls. Cities in Galilee, and all the people in them, had had the chance to learn a new meaning for their life. Possibilities were open to them beyond anything they had known before. "Know this," said Jesus, "that the Kingdom of God has come near." But when men shrug off the heavenly influences as though they did not matter, then they are worse off than if their conscience had not once been stirred. The darkness is deeper because it stands in contrast to what might have been the light.

"Woe to you" was the judgment that Jesus pronounced. There are inexorable consequences which follow upon the choices men make, and the consequences are more dire when the low choice is made by those who have known what the high choice could be. Tyre and Sidon could have the excuse of comparative ignorance. Even Sodom, proverbial in the Old Testament history for its wickedness, could say in its defense that it had never been appealed to by a voice like that of Jesus. But Bethsaida and Capernaum had heard him, and had gone on in their stodgy ways as though nothing he had to say to them need make much difference.

And Chorazin also. What town was Chorazin, and where was it? Nobody surely knows, for except in this passage there is no other mention of it. So Chorazin is an illustration of the fact that the written narrative of Jesus' life is fragmentary, and there may be many places to which he went that are not named. That was true of the world he walked in nineteen centuries ago. There are many more places where his spiritual presence walks today: places which wait for the identifying names that we can give them. Is one of them *your* city; is one of them *your* life? Who will dare wave these questions aside with a brash dismissal? The fact is that what we like to call our Christian civilization stands under more searching judgment because of the privileges we have had. We have known what Paul called the mind of Christ. We have been aware of the beautiful but disturbing challenge of his spirit—for our personal living, for public affairs, for every relationship of men to men: as between the strong and the weak, the favored and the disadvantaged, the white man and the Negro. Public orators are glib enough in declarations that this is "God's country," and therefore entitled to assured supremacy over all "godless" societies and nations. But down the centuries does there not come the continuing echo of the iron bell of judgment which rang in Jesus' words: "You Capernaum, will you be exalted to heaven? You shall be brought down to Hades"—or, as the King James Version puts it in syllables more grim, "You shall be thrust down to hell."

BEYOND THE HUMAN LIMITATIONS

"He who hears you hears me, and he who rejects you rejects me, and he who rejects me rejects him who sent me." (Luke 10:16.)

In the Revised Standard Version this single sentence stands by itself, as though it represented what Jesus would be saying not only to the seventy, but to those who would be his witnesses at any time. When Luke wrote his Gospel, Christians in many places were facing persecution. Even when they were not in danger, they might grow discouraged in face of the indifference of those to whom they tried to preach. What could their small abilities accomplish? But when they were tempted to ask that, they were to remember the great companionship in spirit by which they were undergirded. Jesus, their Master, had been heard by those whose souls were sensitive; and if they were faithful to him, they also would find in every crowd some at least who would respond. But there had been times and places where Jesus himself had been rejected. They need not feel lonely, then, and need not be dismayed when the best they knew how to do fell short. Only let them be sure that in all they did and in all they said they tried to their utmost to express their Master and not themselves: not their anxieties but his assurance, not self-consciousness or any self-assertion, but such a complete devotion as would let their little selves be lifted up to meet the strength of Christ. If they did that, then they could leave the result to God.

THE PERIL OF PRIDE

The seventy returned with joy, saying, "Lord, even the demons are subject to us in your name!" And he said to them, "I saw Satan fall like lightning from heaven. Behold, I have given you authority to tread upon serpents and scorpions, and over all the power of the enemy; and nothing shall hurt you. Nevertheless do not rejoice in this, that the spirits are subject to you; but rejoice that your names are written in heaven."

(Luke 10:17-20.)

The seventy disciples returned from their mission with a glad report. "Even the demons are subject to us in your name," they said to Jesus. The terms they used in their description were not those which might be used today, for "possession by demons" is not a part of customary modern diagnosis (though sometimes it might seem closer to the stark reality than more complacent scientific terms!). Be that as it may, the substance of the disciples' report is clear. Their preaching had been with power. People had listened and had been moved. Their message of the renewing love of God had been able to bring back hope and even sanity to some of the poor demented souls who in the Palestine of that first-century world were all too common.

The joy of his disciples woke a mightier joy in Jesus. What they had done was a sign that his spirit could catch fire in others. Through them the gospel and its redeeming power would be carried far. They symbolized the coming triumph of the purposes of God. He saw it in a flashing vision, a vision of Satan overthrown.

That, then, is the most immediate interpretation of what Jesus was expressing: exaltation of spirit because of what God had wrought, and a great comradeship of gladness with these disciples who thus had experienced what the grace of God could do.

But it may be that there is another meaning in his words. The disciples were full of wonder and excitement. This was natural, and could be beautiful and good. But not if pride crept in. It was possible that they might begin to think of themselves with satisfaction. So they would need to be reminded that even at the moment when one seems very near to God, there may be the self-glorying which alienates one from him. Isaiah the prophet had written, "How art thou fallen from heaven, O Lucifer, son of the morning!" (KJV) He was echoing there the magnificent symbolism in which religious imagination had dramatized the origin of evil. How did the world's rebellion against the goodness of God begin? Not through some influence ugly and malignant. No, but from one who had been "son of the morning." Lucifer, the archangel, had wanted to assume as his own the greatness that belongs only to God. So he had lost his place in heaven, and he who had belonged to the morning went down into the night.

By such a reminder Jesus in his quick solicitude for the men he loved was seeking perhaps to protect them from the peril of thinking so much about themselves that they might break conscious touch with God, through whom alone they could do anything. They had brought back the story of their achievements. "Nevertheless, do not rejoice in this," he said. Let them not be looking about for earthly credit. "But rejoice that your names are written in heaven."

Whatever may have been true of the seventy disciples, certainly there are souls in every generation who need a warning against self-assertion. Once in a lecture which had to do with the perversions which can creep into public affairs, Reinhold Niebuhr began with this sentence: "It is sometimes asked, 'Does the state belong to God or to the devil?' The answer is that the state belongs to God, but it is in danger of becoming the devil by imagining that it is God." So can it be not only with institutions but with individuals, and not least with individuals who are meant to be God's witnesses in the community and in the church. As long as they keep their humility before the Highest, they can be sons of the morning; but when they begin to assume importance as though they were little gods, then they too have become children of the night.

THE DIVINE REALITY

In that same hour he rejoiced in the Holy Spirit and said, "I thank thee, Father, Lord of heaven and earth, that thou hast hidden these things from the wise and understanding and revealed them to babes; yea, Father, for such was thy gracious will. All things have been delivered to me by my Father; and no one knows who the Son is except the Father, or who the Father is except the Son and any one to whom the Son chooses to reveal him."

Then turning to the disciples he said privately, "Blessed are the eyes which see what you see! For I tell you that many prophets and kings desired to see what you see, and did not see it, and to hear what you hear, and did not hear it." (Luke 10:21-24.)

The seventy who had come back to Jesus rejoicing because they had experienced what God could do through them were the unpretentious men. In comparison with the scribes and Pharisees, who had no doubt that they themselves were wise and understanding, these men could seem like babes in spiritual knowledge. They were not versed in books of the law. They would not have got far in a religious argument, for they had no conventional learning: the kind of learning that bred in some of the scribes and Pharisees—and can breed in professional ecclesiastics in any time—a rigid self-assurance. But lacking that, they had something better. They had simplicity. Because they were not cased in by prejudice and presuppositions, they could be sensitive to new truth. Listening to Jesus, they had believed that his trust could make something out of hem. They had gone out, when he told them to, to help people; and in doing that they had found God.

No wonder Jesus rejoiced in the Holy Spirit; and no wonder that he could say to the disciples that they were seeing what kings and prophets had longed to see. They were beholding the power which alone can give meaning and glory to life. "God is love." In that supreme sentence the disciple nearest Jesus' heart was afterward to express what he had learned from his Master. Jesus, who had come not to be ministered unto but to minister and to give his life a ransom for many, was making men understand now who and what the Father is. The world could have its twisted thought of what should be Lord of heaven and earth: pride, power, self-assertion; but Jesus knew and was known by an infinite and more gracious will. "All things have been delivered to me by my Father." That is to say, if human life is to be redeemed, it will be by the measure in which it yields itself to the redeeming love that was and is in Jesus.

GREATNESS FROM THE UNEXPECTED

And behold, a lawyer stood up to put him to the test, saying, "Teacher, what shall I do to inherit eternal life?" He said to him, "What is written in the law? How do you read?" And he answered, "You shall love the Lord your God with all your heart, and with all your soul, and with all your strength, and with all your mind; and your neighbor as yourself." And he said to him, "You have answered right; do this, and you will live."

But he, desiring to justify himself, said to Jesus, "And who is my neighbor?" Jesus replied, "A man was going down from Jerusalem to Jericho, and he fell among robbers, who stripped him and beat him, and departed, leaving him half-dead. Now by chance a priest was going down that road; and when he saw him he passed by on the other side. So likewise a Levite, when he came to the place and saw him, passed by on the other side. But a Samaritan, as he journeyed, came to where he was; and when he saw him, he had compassion, and went to him and bound up his wounds, pouring on oil and wine; then he set him on his own beast and brought him to an inn, and took care of him. And the next day he took out two denarii and gave them to the innkeeper, saying, 'Take care of him; and whatever more you spend, I will repay you when I come back.' Which of these three, do you think, proved neighbor to the man who fell among the robbers?" He said, "The one who showed mercy on him." And Jesus said to him, "Go and do likewise."   (Luke 10:25-37.)

"What shall I do to inherit eternal life?" That certainly was an important question, and it could have been a genuine one. But in this case it seems to have been asked by the sort of man who has his imitators in every age —the man who is not actually seeking truth but is bent upon what he thinks will be a clever argument. He would put Jesus to the test. Did this teacher from Nazareth have anything to say that would stand analysis?

Luke calls the man a lawyer, for that was the word which would have most immediate meaning to Gentiles whom he wanted his Gospel to reach. The more usual word would have been *scribe,* for the scribe was the ecclestical lawyer, interpreting the Jewish law which had come down from Moses and was continually being defined and particularized by rabbis. Lawyers have their necessary place in any ordered society, but they are always subject to a danger. They are dealing constantly with precedents and prescriptions, and their legalism may so fence in their minds that they do not recognize the expanding facts of life. What do you *have* to do in order to be respectable? This may be the question they are most concerned to answer. There must be a code precise enough to include all that conscience needs to be concerned with.

"Very well; you know the law," said Jesus. "What do you read when you turn to it?"

Inadvertently, the lawyer made an answer which was to put his intended argument in trouble. Before he saw the consequences, his mind remembered and repeated the principle which lay back of all right living and which the complicated legalisms he was accustomed to had so often frozen into formalities. He had to admit that the heart of the law was something deep and simple. "You shall love the Lord your God with all your heart, and with all your soul, and with all your strength, and with all your mind; and your neighbor as yourself." This was right, said Jesus. Whoever reflected what those two commandments taught him would indeed have learned the meaning of eternal life.

But now the lawyer thought he saw his chance for argument again. All very well to talk about loving one's neighbor. But it is necessary to be specific. How is anyone to know where his duty begins and where it ends. "Who *is* my neighbor?"

Jesus answered—as was so characteristic of him—not with some abstract statement but with a picture of life so vivid and so inescapable in its meaning that the parable of the Good Samaritan has become immortal. A man on the dangerous road from Jerusalem to Jericho is set upon by robbers, beaten, stripped of his possessions, and left half dead. A priest comes by, looks aghast at the bleeding figure in the road, gives him a wide berth, and goes on. Another supposed representative of religion, a Levite from the Temple, comes next—and scurries past exactly as the priest had done. But then comes a man of whom nothing would have been expected, a Samaritan; and between Samaritans and Jews there was the old, inveterate hatred. He was certainly no neighbor to this poor beaten-up creature on the Judean road. But he acted as though he were. As soon as he saw him, he went straight up to him and dressed his wounds. Not only that; he interrupted his whole journey long enough to take the wounded man to an inn, pay the innkeeper to take care of him, and promised to come back on his return and pay whatever more might be owing then. Now, said Jesus, "Which of these three, do you think, proved neighbor to the man who fell among the robbers?"

That was not the question the lawyer had asked. He had asked, "Who *is* my neighbor?"—which in actual meaning was to say, "Who are the people I am bound to bother with?" But what Jesus made the lawyer look at was the difference between two men who did not want to find themselves in the neighborhood of anybody who needed help, and one other man whose spirit made him choose to be a neighbor. The lawyer had no wish to answer the question which Jesus had reversed, but he had to. When Jesus asked, "Which of these three, do you think, *proved* neighbor?" there was nothing he could do but say, "The one who showed mercy." And he had no more room for argument when Jesus told him, "Go and do likewise."

So the first message of the parable is that neighborliness is not a physical fact or a legal obligation. It is an opportunity. It is not a question of who happens to be next to you, but of who needs you and of where you will go and what you will do in answer to that need.

In the United States not many years ago there died at almost the same time two men, who illustrated in stark contrast the unconcern or the concern which a man may have for his fellow men. One of these two was a person of great wealth and privilege, who wrote in his will: "I earnestly request my wife and children and descendants that they steadfastly decline to sign any bonds or obligations of any kind for any other person; that they refuse to make any loans except on the basis of first-class, well-known securities." The other man was Nicola Sacco, who was executed in Massachusetts in what many believed to have been a gross perversion of justice for an alleged crime he could not have committed, but who belonged to a group among the poor against whom a blind hostility of the well-to-do had been inflamed. Before his death he wrote to his son: "Do not cry. Be strong to comfort your mother. . . . Do not seek happiness for yourself. Step down to help the weak ones who cry for help. Help the persecuted, because they are your better friends."

And the second message which comes from Jesus' parable is the fact that the goodness and gallantry which the world needs most may come not from those from whom it might have been most expected. Who had the role of honor on the Jericho road? Not the priest. Not the Levite. Not one of those who might have boasted that he belonged to the covenant people of God. No, but a Samaritan, an alien, belonging to a people despised. Our contemporary world may present a parallel to that. In the 1960's in the United States it has not always been the churches, not "the best people," not "the superior race," which have shown the most generous courage on behalf of the hurt and disadvantaged. The poor have sometimes fought and suffered for the ideals of the country more stanchly than the prosperous; and Negroes—in spite of their handicaps—have shown a moral strength for sacrifice which may win at last for all men the human rights which the Barnetts and Wallaces and too many other whites in power have denied. Out of our Samarias may come the figures for a modern parable; and the historian of the twentieth century be moved to confirm that "there lived a great people—a black people—who injected new meaning and dignity into the veins of civilization." [1]

THE TWO SIDES OF LIFE

> Now as they went on their way, he entered a village; and a woman named Martha received him into her house. And she had a sister called Mary, who sat at the Lord's feet and listened to his teaching. But Martha was distracted with much serving; and she went to him and said, "Lord, do you not care that my sister has left me to serve alone? Tell her then to help me." But the Lord answered her, "Martha, Martha, you are anxious and troubled about many things; one thing is needful. Mary has chosen the good portion, which shall not be taken away from her."
>
> (Luke 10:38-42.)

Here in Luke's description the bright light of commendation seems to fall on Mary. But what about Martha? Surely a good case could be made for what she did. Granted that she was annoyed; but what made her annoyed?

[1] Martin Luther King, *Stride Toward Freedom* (New York: Harper & Row, 1958), p. 63.

What else except that too much of the load had fallen on her because her sister had left her to serve alone. If there was to be supper that night, if the Lord was to be received with the hospitality that ought to be accorded him, then somebody had to do the work. And Martha did it.

Rudyard Kipling, in *The Sons of Martha,* has expressed what many might consider to be the practical truth. It is the men who embody the spirit of Martha—he would have us acknowledge—who make the world's great achievements possible.

> It is their care in all the ages to take the buffet and cushion the shock.
> It is their care that the gear engages; it is their care that the switches lock.[2]

How would the everyday processes of life go on without the people who are efficiently and steadily on the job? It is all very well for preachers to sit serenely in their studies and for monks and nuns to follow "the contemplative life"; but how would they be sheltered and clothed and fed if the sons of Martha were not always working?

There is reality in that, and people who go to church had better never forget it: never forget that the breakfast they eat, the automobile or bus they ride in, the paved street they travel on were made possible by workers they have never seen but without whom their smooth existence would not be a fact. In our actual society there may be reason for protest akin to that which Martha made. She said she had been left "to serve alone." Men and women who carry the heavy end of the labor that keeps things going will not speak in biblical language, but they can ask plain questions all the same. "How much do the people who talk religion measure up to the tough responsibilities? Can they be relied upon to take the dirty job and see it through? And do they care anything about the lot of the men and women who can and do?"

Certainly Jesus, who grew up in a little town and in a carpenter's shop, had a sure understanding that work could be part of man's service to God. It is a mistake to imagine that he would ever have belittled what Martha did. Neither did he say—as some have thought he said—that Mary had chosen "the better part." He said that Mary had chosen "the good portion"; and so she had.

For when life is complete, it has two aspects. There are things to be done, and there are quiet things to be understood; and sometimes it is the latter which are more imperative. The trouble with Martha was not in what she did, but in what she failed to see. She meant only to be devoted,

[2] Used by permission of The Macmillan Company of Canada, Ltd., Mrs. George Bambridge, and Doubleday & Company, Inc.

but what she had let herself become was just distracted. She forgot that preparations in the kitchen could have their real value only as they contributed to the comradeship of people. She acted as though the best thing she could give to Jesus was something special to eat; but what Jesus wanted most was that the minds and hearts of those he loved should be open to the great realities of God which he was there to share with them. That was what Mary knew, and that is what all men and women need to comprehend. Man doth not live by bread alone. When all is said and done, when all the framework of existence which work can build is finished, the meaning of life is fulfilled only when a soul takes time to come into touch with another soul.

chapter 11

THE LORD'S PRAYER

He was praying in a certain place, and when he ceased, one of his disciples said to him, "Lord, teach us to pray, as John taught his disciples." And he said to them, "When you pray, say:

'Father, hallowed be thy name. Thy kingdom come. Give us each day our daily bread; and forgive us our sins, for we ourselves forgive every one who is indebted to us; and lead us not into temptation.' "

(Luke 11:1-4.)

The reason why the disciples asked Jesus to teach them how to pray was that they saw what prayer meant to him: serenity, poise, and recruited power. They had noted how again and again he separated himself from the confusion of the crowd and went apart to be alone with God. There are many things that men will want to learn, and many of them seem worth desiring; but most of them are secondary. We may say to some person whose abilities we admire, Teach us that trick of skill you have. Teach us to succeed in business. Teach us what you have read in books. Teach us how to get on with people. But when our deepest selves are stirred, what we would say is this—teach us how to come close to God.

Jesus answered the request by giving to his friends that which has come down through all the centuries as the Lord's Prayer. The form of it here in Luke is shorter than that given in the Gospel of Matthew. In Matthew it seems to represent the more liturgical rhythm in which the early church had shaped it, and in which it has been repeated ever since. The stripped phrases of Luke may reflect more closely what Jesus meant to do. He was not concerned to give the disciples finished phrases for them to memorize. He was showing them the essential way of faith, hope, and dedication by which their own praying might reach up to God.

The supreme conviction upon which the whole prayer is built is in the single opening word, *Father*. *Is* there really at the heart of the universe one who is to be more loved and trusted than all that we know in human fatherhood at its best? Sometimes it is hard to believe so. Life may seem so often in the grip of evil, so shadowed by inexplicable sorrow, that would-

156

be faith stumbles toward a desperate questioning. May the dark fact be that there is nothing at last but blind fate, or a God who does not care? Looking at Jesus' life, men might have asked that question; for as the days moved on toward Jerusalem and the cross, it seemed that evil and not good was the ultimate power. But Jesus himself in his own praying rose above that contradiction. His spirit moved into such mighty contact with the Eternal Goodness that he came back from his prayer with the heroic certainty that this Eternal Goodness was invincible. Beyond the clouds, there was the sun. Beyond all uncertainties he had seen what was to him his Father's face.

Look toward that, he was telling his disciples. Trust in that, and live in the light of it. Then you can believe that God's kingdom is coming, and that if you are faithful, you shall have your daily bread.

Then comes the petition, "Forgive us our sins, for we ourselves forgive"; or according to the Gospel of Matthew, "as we have also forgiven." What is the meaning of those last words? Is God's forgiveness something that he deliberately withholds until we have been virtuous first? No, not that. The forgiveness of God, as the whole redeeming love of Jesus expressed it, reaches out to all whose stained lives stand in need of it. But the deep fact is that this forgiveness cannot be felt until a man tries to make himself ready to receive it. If he cherishes hatred and resentment, he cannot really believe in love. Unless God's spirit flows through him toward those whom he might forgive, his heart remains like a dead sea which all the waters of God's grace cannot make less bitter. But when he tries to open up new channels of understanding compassion for the follies and sins of some other human being who has offended him, then cleansing currents pour into his own soul.

In Luke's terse record the Lord's Prayer ends with "lead us not into temptation." Here also there could be misunderstanding. If temptation is thought to mean trial and testing, then certainly Jesus would not have desired that his disciples should be shielded from that. When he led them up to Jerusalem, he was leading them into the most searching sort of testing: into dangers that would try them as in a furnace, by which the slag in them would be burned away, and out of which they might come as men refined by fire. That sort of testing can be God's gift to every soul which reaches on to what is at least a beginning of the heroic. Therefore it was not this that Jesus meant by the temptation from which we need to be delivered. He meant instead the temptation of seductive evil into which a man can blunder when he is off guard. It may be the allurements of the flesh, or it may be the beguiling prizes of self-absorbed ambition.

Well may one pray that the paths of life may be so directed as to keep him from the snares of these. And his hope that this may be true goes back to the first great petition of the prayer. When a man is caught up into the positive desire that his soul may be part of the kingdom of God's increasing purpose, then—and only then—is he on the sure road that will lead away from what is mean and sordid.

Such, then, is the mighty faith which the Lord's Prayer expresses. But what when we pray and nothing significant seems to happen? We may want to be drawing nearer to God, but the fact is that sometimes our praying appears to find not any open thoroughfare, but a forest so thick with uncertainties that we cannot get ahead.

Recognizing this, Luke in his Gospel has followed the Lord's Prayer with a parable of Jesus which stresses persistence. The fainthearted may think that all they face is a dead-end road, but those who are in genuine earnest will keep on until they find a way.

WHAT THE ANSWER TO PRAYER MAY BE

And he said to them, "Which of you who has a friend will go to him at midnight and say to him, 'Friend, lend me three loaves; for a friend of mine has arrived on a journey, and I have nothing to set before him'; and he will answer from within, 'Do not bother me; the door is now shut, and my children are with me in bed; I cannot get up and give you anything'? I tell you, though he will not get up and give him anything because he is his friend, yet because of his importunity he will rise and give him whatever he needs. And I tell you, Ask, and it will be given you; seek, and you will find; knock, and it will be opened to you. For every one who asks receives, and he who seeks finds, and to him who knocks it will be opened. What father among you, if his son asks for a fish, will instead of a fish give him a serpent; or if he asks for an egg, will give him a scorpion? If you then, who are evil, know how to give good gifts to your children, how much more will the heavenly Father give the Holy Spirit to those who ask him?"   (Luke 11:5-13.)

As to this parable, like nearly all the others, it must be remembered that Jesus was lifting one single idea into concentrated emphasis. Details are subordinate and should not become beguilements to lead thought off into irrelevant elaborations. In this parable it is not the person appealed to who has any parallel. Most certainly this man who has shut his door and wants to go to sleep does not represent the nature of God. The whole emphasis is on the one who makes the appeal. The point is that if in an ordinary human situation perseverance can prevail, how much more surely will perseverance prevail when the one approached is not a grudging human being but God who is the Everlasting Mercy.)

Then this message of the goodness of God is brought closer home by the comparison in vss. 11-13. (Look at the human life you know, said Jesus, and see what your intuitions learn from that. What does any father do when his child asks him for food? Does he give him nothing at all? Or worse, does he—in cruel mockery—give him a snake when he had asked for fish; or a scorpion when he had asked for an egg? No, even the ordinary human father, imperfect and in some ways sinful though he be, is better than that. He will give his child the best he has.) How much more, said Jesus then, will your heavenly Father give. And what? "The Holy Spirit to those who ask him."

In the light of those last words must vss. 8 and 9 be read. (He who goes to God in patient trustfulness will be given not less but more than he has asked. In our confused human values and in the blindness of our choice the thing that looks to us so shining and desirable may have a snake or scorpion hidden in it; and God, because he is God, will not give us that. This is the reason for what may be called "unanswered prayer." A thoughtful Christian saw the sign, which some fervent evangelist had painted on a rock by the side of the road, *God answers prayer;* and he said, "I wished that someone with a deeper understanding would paint under it, *and sometimes the answer is NO!*" The certainty is that God will increasingly give his Holy Spirit: to purify our desires, enlighten our prayers, open the door to possibilities for our souls which we had not glimpsed when we began to pray.

Such is the central message which comes from the parable and from the words of Jesus added to it.) But in the living picture which constitutes the parable there is a detail which enlarges its spiritual suggestion, like another stream flowing from a fountain. The man who comes knocking at the door with his appeal for bread is stirred not by his own need but by the need of another. "A friend of mine has arrived on a journey, and I have nothing to set before him." Somebody else is depending on him, and he has no resources of his own. For that somebody else's sake he will turn from his own lack to where that lack may be supplied. Not selfishness but concern for his friend makes him knock at another door. So certainly it is with the deepest and most persevering prayer. It is when some other human soul, weary on the pilgrimage of life, comes to us hungry for the bread of the spirit, and we realize how poor our own resources are, that *then* we turn to God with a plea which nothing can discourage.

WHEN EVIL TWISTS THE TRUTH

Now he was casting out a demon that was dumb; when the demon had gone out, the dumb man spoke, and the people marveled. But some of them said, "He casts out demons by Beelzebul, the prince of demons"; while others, to test him, sought from him a sign from heaven. But he, knowing their thoughts, said to them, "Every kingdom divided against itself is laid waste, and house falls upon house. And if Satan also is divided against himself, how will his kingdom stand? For you say that I cast out demons by Beelzebul. And if I cast out demons by Beelzebul, by whom do your sons cast them out? Therefore they shall be your judges. But if it is by the finger of God that I cast out demons, then the kingdom of God has come upon you. When a strong man, fully armed, guards his own palace, his goods are in peace; but when one stronger than he assails him and overcomes him, he takes away his armor in which he trusted, and divides his spoil. He who is not with me is against me, and he who does not gather with me scatters." (Luke 11:14-23.)

The conversation here recounted tells something about Jesus, but more about the little men who dared to think they could entrap him. He had cast the evil spirit out of a man, and here were some who saw him do it and tried to say that the reason he could do it was that he was in league with Beelzebul, the chief of all the demons. It would have been difficult for anyone to put forth a more preposterous notion: that the devil would go out of his way to work against himself.

But the significant fact was that these men who opposed Jesus were so full of rancor that they did not stop to think how stupid what they said might sound. They had gone past the point of wanting to recognize reality, or to listen with an open mind. They were lying in wait (vs. 54) for Jesus; and if their intended ambush of argument turned out to be a failure, that was not for lack of malevolence on their part. They had ranged themselves against Jesus and his whole ministry, no matter what he said or did. And the worst of it is that men of that spirit have their descendants in every generation: in men, and women too, who are so warped by self-interest and bitter prejudice that they will instinctively resent the coming of any inconvenient new ideal. If some strong figure rises above the average conscience in church and state, or anywhere where men make their money, there will be those who try to bring him down. The purposes he represents may be such as reflect, to some degree at least, the values of the kingdom of God; but if he endangers the idols to which the sleek and contented give their orthodox devotion, then they will believe, and assert with passion, that he is not of God but of the devil.

Others, to try him, sought from him a sign from heaven. They were not necessarily opposed to Jesus, but neither were they sure that they believed in him and in the coming of the kingdom. They wanted some sensational evidence. Evidence was there, but they did not see it. Granted that no conspicuous and final overthrow of evil and triumph of goodness had come. Yet already the reality of God was manifest: in Jesus' acts of mercy, in men and women lifted up to larger life. In the great fresco in the Sistine Chapel Michelangelo has depicted the quickening of Adam by one outreaching touch of the finger of God. It was the finger of God which Jesus saw in the transformations that were beginning; and it is nothing less than the finger of God which is present every time in the little things that are redeeming. Wherever there is loveliness in life—the self-forgetfulness of a mother, a man's great devotion to some great cause, truth, honor, and gallant sacrifice—there is the foregleam of God's kingdom.

THE HOUSE LEFT EMPTY

"When the unclean spirit has gone out of a man, he passes through waterless places seeking rest; and finding none he says, 'I will return to my house from which I came.' And when he comes he finds it swept and put in order. Then he goes and brings seven other spirits more evil than himself, and they enter and dwell there; and the last state of that man becomes worse than the first." (Luke 11:24-26.)

This parable grips attention, as a ghost story does, and holds it with a shuddering fascination: the more so because one recognizes here an authentic picture of what may happen to the inner life. It is not enough to free a house from one demonic spirit; something positive and protective must occupy the empty place, or worse influences will come in.

Jesus could see around him men in whom this ugly reality had happened: men who had got rid of particular faults but now represented others more damaging. Many of the leaders in Israel were persons of conspicuous correctness. They had excluded from their habits and practices whatever the Mosaic law and the teaching of the rabbis forbade, and in their prim daily conduct they had abjured association with the Gentile world. In morality they seemed impeccable. Like the Pharisee in the Temple, to be described later in chapter 18 of the Gospel, the best of them could claim that they were not extortioners, or cheaters, or adulterers. It appeared that their souls were swept and garnished. But they had become possessed by pride and harshness—sins of the mind which Jesus knew could be more destructive than the sins of the flesh. Anybody knocking at their hearts' doors and thinking that he was coming to a house of goodness would find instead that cruelty dwelt there.

161

So it may always be when men imagine that if they get rid of one kind of evil, all will be well. The last state may be worse than the first unless some affirmative purpose comes in to occupy the vacant place. A somber and terrible instance is in what happened to a great nation a generation ago. The soul of the German people suffered from humiliation and despondency after the First World War. "I will deliver you from that haunting ghost," said Adolf Hitler. "I will drive out your evil spirit." And so far as that one spirit was concerned, he did. But he had no noble spirit to summon in its place, no conception of a purpose great enough and high enough to be redeeming, no recognition of the need of God. Into the empty house therefore came the demonic spirits which he chose to summon: hatred, revenge, the megalomania of reasserted power, the idolatry of lies; and what he had thought that he would sweep and garnish was turned into a house of horror.

The tragedy comes when any man or men imagine that they can drive out some specific evil and then be safe through what they themselves have done. But men do not possess this sufficiency. "Except the Lord build the house, they labour in vain that build it. Except the Lord keep the city, the watchman waketh but in vain" (KJV). It is only when a man commits his life to the power greater than himself that the house of his soul can be defended. Only when he surrenders to the heavenly Master can he be free.

THE DEMAND FOR REALITY

As he said this, a woman in the crowd raised her voice and said to him, "Blessed is the womb that bore you, and the breasts that you sucked!" But he said, "Blessed rather are those who hear the word of God and keep it!"

When the crowds were increasing, he began to say, "This generation is an evil generation; it seeks a sign, but no sign shall be given to it except the sign of Jonah. For as Jonah became a sign to the men of Nineveh, so will the Son of man be to this generation. The queen of the South will arise at the judgment with the men of this generation and condemn them; for she came from the ends of the earth to hear the wisdom of Solomon, and behold, something greater than Solomon is here. The men of Nineveh will arise at the judgment with this generation and condemn it; for they repented at the preaching of Jonah, and behold, something greater than Jonah is here." (Luke 11:27-32.)

The woman doubtless meant well, but it could be true that all she was expressing was a shallow sentimentality. She may have been fascinated by Jesus' looks, speech, and manner, and so was moved to pay her gushing tribute, half of admiration and half of envy, to the mother who could bear such a son. One can imagine Jesus turning toward her with gentleness, but with a quick correction. He was not there to stir a soft appreciation. He was there to make men and women face deep choices for their souls, to look through him to the Infinite Reality which made him what he was. Emotional feelings about him and those who belonged to him did not go far enough. What mattered was to hear the word of God, and keep it.

Essentially that same message is in the passage about Jonah, though the occasion and approach were different. The woman, as she first regarded Jesus, was satisfied, but for a wrong reason; the crowd was unsatisfied, but for an opposite wrong reason. For the woman it was sufficient that Jesus was so likeable; for the crowd he would not be sufficient unless he did something sensational. Neither the woman nor the crowd had seen yet the supreme fact about Jesus: namely, that through him the word of God was speaking its moral and spiritual challenge to their inner selves. What was the sign of the prophet Jonah? It was not in what he looked like, not in any miracle he wrought or might have wrought. It was in what happened when the truth of God used him as its instrument for the conversion of a whole city. Now one greater than Jonah and with an understanding more profound than that of Solomon had come, and the signs of his authority could be plain to all who had eyes to see—so plain that, for those who could not or would not see it, the men of Nineveh would arise at the judgment with this generation and condemn it. Because of him people who had stumbled along in ignorance were learning the meaning of life; people who had been sinners were turning from their sins; and people who had been weak and purposeless were being lifted into strength. They would know that "blessed are those who hear the word of God and keep it."

THE MANY ASPECTS OF LIGHT

"No one after lighting a lamp puts it in a cellar or under a bushel, but on a stand, that those who enter may see the light. Your eye is the lamp of your body; when your eye is sound, your whole body is full of light; but when it is not sound, your body is full of darkness. Therefore be careful lest the light in you be darkness. If then your whole body is full of light, having no part dark, it will be wholly bright, as when a lamp with its rays gives you light." (Luke 11:33-36.)

Many a preacher has learned that those who have listened to him may remember his illustrations, and after a while quite forget what they were meant to illustrate. So it could have been—and so, apparently, it often was—even with Jesus. The vividness of some swift picture which he awoke

163

in men's minds lingered and could be passed on when they told later of what he said, but without the context which would have showed specifically what he meant. Here in vss. 33-36 Luke appears to have written down some of these recollections of the words of Jesus which were spoken on different occasions and carry different suggestions, and are put together for the one broad reason that they all have to do with light.

Light most naturally is something outside ourselves from which we get the color and meaning of our world, and our own guidance in it. Light is the sun that rises in the morning, or the lamp that is at hand when the shadows fall. Without the light we grope in darkness, and stumble and go astray.

Yet it is possible to ignore the light. We cannot put out the sun, but we can get away from it. There may be times and moods when men love darkness rather than light because their deeds are evil. When crimes are to be committed, it is not generally the daytime that is chosen; and the phrase "night-life" carries its suggestion of haunts toward which it is not the better conscience that has set up the street signs. Or, to use the figure of speech of the Gospel, it is possible in any house to smother the light that might be there: to hide the lamp in the cellar so that it will not shine on things upstairs not fit to be seen.

"I am the light of the world," said Jesus. Some of those who had made their sullen objections to what he said had the uncomfortable sense that this was so, but they did not want to recognize it. They preferred to argue that some miraculous sign had to be shown before Jesus would have any claim on their allegiance. Let him do something stupendous so that they would *have* to believe. But there in him, in what they saw he was and in what he made them deeply know of what life ought to be, there was the sign. He would be the light by which they could walk surely—if what they really wanted was light on the road that led to God.

Then in the analogies of the Gospel light is seen in another aspect: as having to do with the inner eye according to the condition of which the objective light may or may not be truly seen. Even the divine beauty cannot be evident to a warped vision. The terrible fact is that a man may lose his ability to recognize the lovely things that might redeem him. Self-absorption, engrossment with material gains, irritable insistence on what he thinks are his prerogatives, may make a man angry even with his own little child who breaks in upon his sullen mood, harsh and demanding with his wife, indifferent toward his friends. As an infection in the body clouds the physical eyes, so the infection in his spirit blinds him to the real values in everything he looks at. The light that ought to have been in him has become darkness. But on the other hand, if his emotions are kept sensitive, he will have what George Fox preached and the Society of Friends have witnessed to—the Inner Light. There grows a new perception of Christ and of whatever is Christlike in our everyday world. In that illumination of the spirit we can look on all life with a new reverence and a new response to meanings from God which may be shining there.

THE GOOD AND THE BAD IN PHARISAISM

> While he was speaking, a Pharisee asked him to dine with him; so he went in and sat at table. The Pharisee was astonished to see that he did not first wash before dinner. And the Lord said to him, "Now you Pharisees cleanse the outside of the cup and of the dish, but inside you are full of extortion and wickedness. You fools! Did not he who made the outside make the inside also? But give for alms those things which are within; and behold, everything is clean for you."   (Luke 11:37-41.)

Jesus goes to dine with a Pharisee. That may seem surprising, for nearly always in the Gospel narratives the Pharisees appear as in bitter hostility to Jesus, and the assumption might be that he would be hostile to them. But the real picture was in no such blacks and whites. It is true that most of the Pharisees chose to be his enemies, but not all. And Jesus did not blanket men in classes, or read their real selves according to what were supposed to be their labels. He could find men who would respond to him among the tax-collectors and sinners; and he could find some, as certainly ought to have been the case, among the Pharisees. The pity was that he did not find many more. For the Pharisees had a noble lineage. They were descended from the men who in times of peril and persecution—especially during the Maccabean struggles two centuries before—had been most heroic in defense of the religion of their fathers. They represented magnificent fidelity to what they believed to be the will of God. It would seem therefore that no company could have been more congenial to Jesus than that of a Pharisee, and here perhaps was at least one Pharisee of whom this was true.

The difficulty with the passage from vs. 38 to the end of the chapter is that the reader runs into what appears an impossible contradiction. Here is Jesus accepting the invitation of a man who wanted to welcome him, and then at that man's table launching into a scathing denunciation of him and all his friends. Probably the fact is that Luke has put at this point in his Gospel what the early church knew to have been Jesus' indictment not of some individual Pharisee but of the warped spirit which had infected Pharisaism in general. As S. MacLean Gilmour in *The Interpreter's Bible* has rightly said:

The interpreter should keep the fact in mind that the gospel tradition was given its final form by Christian evangelists, teachers, and apologists during a period of acute conflict with Jewish opponents. It is probable that these sayings tell us more about the attitude of the early church to Judaism than they do about the attitude of the Jesus of history toward his Pharisaic contemporaries.[1]

THE HOLLOW MEN

"But woe to you Pharisees! for you tithe mint and rue and every herb, and neglect justice and the love of God; these you ought to have done, without neglecting the others. Woe to you Pharisees! for you love the best seat in the synagogues and salutations in the market places. Woe to you! for you are like graves which are not seen, and men walk over them without knowing it." (Luke 11:42-44.)

Toward his "Pharisaic contemporaries," as individual men and human souls, Jesus had the same outreach as he did to the publicans and sinners whom the hard and bitter among the Pharisees despised. But the hardness which had come into Pharisaism did deserve and did receive his terrible rebuke. And here, as also in the Gospel of Matthew, is that rebuke as it has to do not only with men of the first century but with men in every time for whom religion becomes a thing of brittle forms.

As the Gospel of Matthew described the Pharisees of Jesus' time, "they make their phylacteries broad and their fringes long." The phylacteries were the little leather cases containing Holy Scripture which were bound upon their foreheads, and the fringes on their robes were another evidence of sanctimoniousness; but what they were thinking of and concerned with might be very different from what were supposed to be their prayers. Fashions change. In modern churches one does not see phylacteries, but one may see faultlessly attired gentlemen who go through all the proper motions, sit and stand and kneel according to the pattern, and look solemn —but are thinking more about the shrewd business deal which is coming up tomorrow than about the service or the sermon. Extortion and wickedness—those are the devastating words which Jesus used. He knew that piety can too often be used as a cover for sharp practice. The man who sits at the head of his pew on Sunday may not be the man who on Monday will have any mercy at the bank. He may "devour widows' houses," and do so none the less for the fact that in church on the day before he has recited the accustomed prayers.

This kind of Pharisaism may go on without recognition by the man himself that anything is wrong. He may actually think that he is religious,

[1] The Exegesis of Luke, VIII, 214.

for religion to him is a matter that has its convenient bounds and definitions. It has to do with what the general customs require of a man in his position so that he may be looked upon as a leading citizen. He will make his proper contribution to the Community Chest, or make sure that he has the respectful notice of the other vestrymen or elders when the amount of his contribution to the church's budget is read out. He will see to it that neither he nor his wife has any outstanding bills. He will observe every particularity of conduct which his business and social set expects, including the mint, anise, and cummin of conventional politeness. But the love of God within? That is a different matter.

They love chief seats in the synagogues and calculations in the market places: this description can apply to people in general, but it can strike home more particularly to clergymen. The man in the clerical vest may have much secret pleasure in the deferential way people speak to him. And who can tell how often the genuineness of worship has been overlaid and in the end almost smothered by ostentation in the chancel, parade of vestments and exaggerated ceremonial, or just the petty mannerisms of a man whose thought is on himself?

All these are the hollow men, or worse than that. They may be no more than graves which have in them only dead men's bones.

WHEN RELIGION TURNS INTO LEGALISM

One of the lawyers answered him, "Teacher, in saying this you reproach us also." And he said, "Woe to you lawyers also! for you load men with burdens hard to bear, and you yourselves do not touch the burdens with one of your fingers. Woe to you! for you build the tombs of the prophets whom your fathers killed. So you are witnesses and consent to the deeds of your fathers; for they killed them, and you build their tombs. Therefore also the Wisdom of God said, 'I will send them prophets and apostles, some of whom they will kill and persecute,' that the blood of all the prophets, shed from the foundation of the world, may be required of this generation, from the blood of Abel to the blood of Zechariah, who perished between the altar and the sanctuary. Yes, I tell you, it shall be required of this generation. Woe to you lawyers! for you have taken away the key of knowledge; you did not enter yourselves, and you hindered those who were entering." (Luke 11:45-52.)

One of the lawyers answered Jesus, "You reproach us also." The lawyers were that special group among the Pharisees, also called the scribes, whose business it was to interpret the law into its minute particulars. The lawyer's mind always runs into danger, the danger of a dry legalism which destroys the sensitive responses of the living spirit. It was that sort of legalism which Jesus was continually encountering: the ironbound definitions, for example, about what must be prohibited on the sabbath which made the scribes consider it an outrage that Jesus healed a man who was sick. In the church that rigidity can crop up again and again, as in the conscientious but constricted obsession of ecclesiastical scribism with rubrics and canons which hold the church back from Christian charity and generous communion. Only the other day in an isolated western countryside there was a little wooden church which had long been disused and was apparently abandoned. People living near it began to repair and paint it and wanted to buy it so that they might hold services there. But the bishop of the church to which the building belonged refused, because he thought it was his obligation to see that no kind of ministry and worship except his kind should be permitted there. So he loaded burdens hard to bear on those who wanted to move toward the kingdom of God; and to such as he might be spoken the formidable words: "You have taken away the key of knowledge; you did not enter yourselves, and you hindered those who were entering."

Loyalty to traditions can be noble, but it can also be perverted: noble if the loyalty is to the real values of the spirit, perverted if that imagined loyalty is only a stupid incantation to a shell in which the spirit has been allowed to die. A contemporary preacher described the D.A.R. as "Daughters of Yesterday's Revolutionists, Sisters of Today's Tories, and Mothers of Tomorrow's Reactionaries." They did not like it. Neither do reactionaries in the church like to be reminded that when they invoke the names of the great pioneers of "the faith once delivered to the saints," they may have lost the flaming faith and kept only the charred wood of the torch with which it was delivered. So they honor the tombs of the prophets, but the living prophets walk in their midst no more.

New Testament scholars of high authority believe that vss. 49-51, with the significant use of the word "apostles," represent not a direct reflection of the words of Jesus but the passionate thought of the Christian community after the destruction of Jerusalem in A.D. 70, when it seemed to them that the whole world's calamities were due to the particular generation which was alive when Jesus came, and that judgment for all the evils of all time should fall on it. That was too narrow an indictment. There is a fateful continuity in human life. Each new generation could deserve the judgment unless it tries to reflect whatever greatness there has been in those who have gone before, and to break the entail of their evil.

chapter 12

HONESTY FIRST

In the meantime, when so many thousands of the multitude had gathered together that they trod upon one another, he began to say to his disciples first, "Beware of the leaven of the Pharisees, which is hypocrisy. Nothing is covered up that will not be revealed, or hidden that will not be known. Whatever you have said in the dark shall be heard in the light, and what you have whispered in private rooms shall be proclaimed upon the house-tops."

(Luke 12:1-3.)

In one of Jesus' most familiar parables he used leaven as a symbol of the spirit which can create the kingdom of God. But for the most part in the Bible, and in the general thinking of the people of Israel, leaven represented not something beneficent but something alien and unwelcome. So the Passover was a feast of unleavened bread, and in the book of Exodus it was enjoined that "on the first day you shall put away leaven out of your houses, for if any one eats what is leavened, . . . that person shall be cut off from Israel." It is against that background of associated meaning that there is warning here against "the leaven of the Pharisees."

It is no wonder that *this* sort of leaven should have been considered evil—the leaven which unhappily the Pharisees, or some of them, had brought into religious life; for this leaven, Jesus said, was hypocrisy. The dictionary definition of that word is "playing a part on a stage, simulation, outward show." To play a part on a stage is what is expected of the actor in a theater, but to turn the whole of life into play acting is to make life into a simulation and an outward show. This perversion of truth was the evil which Jesus would not endure. He could have great patience with many kinds of faults, provided there was honesty. He could be the friend of sinners, when the sinners knew what they were and faced up to the fact. Then there was reality and something could be built on that. But when men pretended to be better than they were, traded on their reputation for sanctity but gave it no substance, there was nothing left except for their emptiness to be exposed.

This could be a dismaying thing. As long as a man hides his crooked

169

thoughts and assumes that the world will rate him by his contrived appearance and not by what he actually is, he can manage to be comfortable. But the whole flimsy shell of his reputation collapses when what goes on inside him is brought out into the light. On the other hand, the full blaze of truth can be a blessing to the man who is honestly committed to all that is of good report. If he has been trying to think and speak as God would have him do, he will be jubilant to have the time come when what he has stood for in his little place shall be shouted from the housetops.

THE DEATH BEYOND DEATH

"I tell you, my friends, do not fear those who kill the body, and after that have no more that they can do. But I will warn you whom to fear: fear him who, after he has killed, has power to cast into hell; yes, I tell you, fear him!" (Luke 12:4-5.)

All human beings do fear the death of the body, and that fear may be sharper when there is apprehension that death may come by violence. This was the possibility for the disciples. They knew that danger was thickening round their Master and themselves. He had already told them that he was going up to Jerusalem, where he would be killed. And so might they.

It would be no wonder if they were dismayed. But Jesus lifted the thought of death up into a mightier perspective. In one way or another, death will come to every mortal man. Whether it should be by violence or by some long illness and slow pain, whether it should come a little sooner or a little later, is not the crucial matter. What matters is that the death of the body should not mean that the man himself has died.

"I will tell you whom to fear," said Jesus. Not your enemies or anything that they can do, not anything that can happen to the flesh, but the reckoning of the ultimate reality with what you are. Fear him who has power to cast into hell.

The picture which those words convey may change, but their awful significance does not change. There was a time when hell was conceived as concretely as this surface of the earth on which the living walk—the subterranean region where the devil stoked his fires for the eternal torment of the damned. Dante's *Inferno* only put into more tremendous language what the world at large already believed. In our own time, which considers itself more sophisticated, hell is not thought of in those literal and spatial terms; and the danger is that in a shallow smartness we may imagine that there is no hell at all. But any man who contemplates his own soul knows better. He can understand what the real hell could be; and in the moments when his conscience is most awake, he can have a foretaste of it.

In T. S. Eliot's *Murder in the Cathedral,* the chorus of the women of Canterbury see the men who bring the threat of human violence; but their mind is not on them, and therefore what they chant is this:

> The agents of hell disappear, the human, they shrink and dissolve
> Into dust on the wind, forgotten, unmemorable; only is here
> The white flat face of Death, God's silent servant,
> And behind the face of Death the Judgment
> And behind the Judgment the Void, more horrid than active shapes of hell;
> Emptiness, absence, separation from God.[1]

That would be the final hell: "emptiness, absence, separation from God." To know that all the great opportunities of life have been wasted, to have only emptiness at the end, to have no response anymore to the voice of God which can wake an eternal meaning in the soul: it is *this* that a man may fear—and had better begin to fear in time.

THE VALUE OF EVERY SOUL

"Are not five sparrows sold for two pennies? And not one of them is forgotten before God. Why, even the hairs of your head are all numbered. Fear not; you are of more value than many sparrows.

"And I tell you, every one who acknowledges me before men, the Son of man also will acknowledge before the angels of God." (Luke 12:6-8.)

In these verses, as in vss. 4-5, there is the mighty message that the death of the body is not the final fact. After death—as before it—comes the question of the soul's relationship to God. In vss. 4-5 the aspect of that relationship is what might be the fearful one of judgment. But here the thought is of God's infinite compassion. Every life he has created has value in his sight. In the markets of Palestine nothing could be cheaper than a sparrow. Five of them, said Jesus, could be bought for two pennies. Yet not one sparrow could fall and God not know and care. And if that were true of a sparrow, how much more of a human soul.

The heart reaches out to that immense promise of Jesus and craves to believe it. But the facts of the world we live in seem so different. The sparrows do fall, and so do precious human beings who are of more value than many sparrows. What shall we say of the faith we want to have in the unfailing providence of God when death is actually so inclusive?

So our troubled mortal instinct asks. Then we turn back to the words of Jesus and see that he did not say that death would be escaped. What he

[1] Used by permission of Harcourt, Brace & World and Faber and Faber Ltd.

did say was that beyond the body's death is God, and that in God we are not forgotten. In the words of Paul Tillich: "Everything real comes from eternity and goes to eternity. . . . We are together with everything real in the divine life. . . . This is what 'last judgment' means—to separate in us, as in everything, what has true and final being from what is merely transitory and empty of true being." [2]

THE SIN AGAINST THE HOLY SPIRIT

"But he who denies me before men will be denied before the angels of God. And everyone who speaks a word against the Son of man will be forgiven; but he who blasphemes against the Holy Spirit will not be forgiven." (Luke 12:9-10.)

Time and eternity meet in these words of Jesus. In what he taught of the kingdom of God and of the love of God which is also judgment, there is the touchstone of final destiny. To accept or reject the message he brought is not a passing matter. It is to register a decision one way or the other concerning the values of life which will be certified in the courts of heaven.

Yet at first reading it appears that vs. 10 runs counter to what has just been expressed; for it says that anything spoken against the Son of man will be forgiven—although any blasphemy against the Holy Spirit cannot be forgiven. What is the meaning of this distinction? Apparently this: that through human ignorance or even through rebelliousness a man might turn away at some particular moment from what Jesus said, but this may not mean that he has made the deep and deliberate choice of evil instead of good which is the final sin. It would be this complete perversion of conscience, this insolent preference for falsehood rather than truth, that would be the sin against the Holy Spirit.

Sometimes this passage in the Gospel is misinterpreted; and some pitiable person, who like every other human being has committed faults but yet has a genuine spiritual concern, imagines that he or she has committed the unpardonable sin. Such persons are most certainly those who have *not* committed it, because the very fact that they are troubled shows that they are sensitive toward God and crave above everything not to be separated from him. Only a very few—may God grant it—will be blasphemers against the Holy Spirit. They are those who have so continually stifled their response to goodness and treated all high ideals with increasing contempt that there is nothing left in them that can desire or register forgiveness. It is against this dread possibility that Jesus' warning stands.

[2] Paul Tillich, *The Eternal Now* (New York: Charles Scribner's Sons, 1963), p. 35.

THE HOLY SPIRIT AS INSPIRER

"And when they bring you before the synagogues and the rulers and the authorities, do not be anxious how or what you are to answer or what you are to say; for the Holy Spirit will teach you in that very hour what you ought to say."

(Luke 12:11-12.)

In the written Gospel, as has been noted before, the Evangelist records every precious recollection of Jesus he could gather, even though originally the recollections may have had no close connection with one another. There are sayings succeeding one another on the printed page which stand quite separate. So it is with vss. 11 and 12. Their only relationship to vs. 10 is that they also speak of the Holy Spirit, but of an aspect of the Spirit which is quite different. In vs. 10 it is the Holy Spirit in the dread fact of judgment; in vss. 11 and 12 it is the Holy Spirit as inspirer.

Here Jesus is speaking directly to his disciples. He is encouraging them to trust that when they may be called upon to confess their faith, something greater than they will speak through them. Again and again in Christian history that promise has come true. Men and women who by themselves might have been afraid and tongue-tied have borne their indomitable witness in the face of threats and danger. Peter and John would stand before the hostile council in Jerusalem as "uneducated, common men" but they would manifest a boldness which would leave the council wondering and astonished.

Martin Niemöller was imprisoned by the Nazis during the Second World War, and kept in isolation so long that he seemed for a while to have lost the power of effective utterance. When he was finally released and tried to speak in assemblies of the church, it seemed to him that he could not mobilize his thoughts beforehand. Then he had to rely on the Holy Spirit, and he said that the Holy Spirit did come and prompt him what to say. Also, when later he visited America and spoke to the students in a theological seminary, he told them that what had been true for him could be true for them in moments of genuine need.

Then, however, he went on to say: "But you must not depend carelessly upon that. You are not meant to shirk what is required of you. Reliance on the Holy Spirit must be linked with faithfulness to one's own full duty and responsibility. Once in a meeting of the Evangelical Synod a young minister testified that he never prepared his sermons but trusted the Holy Spirit to put the words upon his lips. Later an older pastor arose. He said, 'I heard our young brother testify that he never prepared his sermons, but depended upon the Holy Spirit to speak to him. As for me, the Holy

Spirit has never spoken directly to me in the pulpit—yes, he did once. Once in the midst of a lamentable sermon the Holy Spirit spoke. And what he said was, 'Heinrich, you're lazy.' "

THE FULL BARNS AND THE EMPTY SOUL

> One of the multitude said to him, "Teacher, bid my brother divide the inheritance with me." But he said to him, "Man, who made me a judge or divider over you?" And he said to them, "Take heed, and beware of all covetousness; for a man's life does not consist in the abundance of his possessions." And he told them a parable, saying, "The land of a rich man brought forth plentifully; and he thought to himself, 'What shall I do, for I have nowhere to store my crops?' And he said, 'I will do this: I will pull down my barns, and build larger ones; and there I will store all my grain and my goods. And I will say to my soul, Soul, you have ample goods laid up for many years; take your ease, eat, drink, be merry.' But God said to him, 'Fool! This night your soul is required of you; and the things you have prepared, whose will they be?' So is he who lays up treasure for himself, and is not rich toward God." (Luke 12:13-21.)

Truth is most effective when it is related to some concrete occasion. The trouble with a good deal of ordinary preaching is that the preacher may be weaving elaborate answers to questions which nobody is actually asking. But with Jesus there was always a quick recognition of the immediate opportunity. A man comes to him with the kind of request which was often brought to the rabbis, who were expected to be authoritative interpreters of the Jewish law. This man wanted Jesus to straighten out a will and make sure that he get his proper part of the inheritance; but that kind of involvement in the man's jealous little calculations Jesus refused. "Who made me a judge or divider over you?" he said. He dismissed the petty question, but he seized upon the greater one which was what the man essentially was asking. "How can I get what ought to be coming to me? How can I manage things so that I shall be satisfied?"

The answer Jesus gave was to point the man to something bigger than his covetousness. He wanted to shock him out of the circle of his mean values and show him where the immortal values lie. So he told him this parable which Luke records of a rich man and of what happened to his riches.

Note what it was that the rich man "thought to himself." Nothing beyond his greediness. No matter how much his land produced, no matter what surplus he accumulated, all he considered was how he could stack it away. He was not interested in using his goods for anyone else. No. He would pull down his old barns, build new and bigger ones, and fill those up. So maybe he would have enough to satisfy him, and he could relax, eat, drink, and be merry. Then he would say, "My soul, take your ease." His soul! Consider the unfathomable irony in that! He would say to his soul, "Take your ease"—when as a matter of fact, he had not even been mindful that he had a soul.

There of course is the peril that may lurk in riches, or at any rate in obsession with them. A man can grow content with what ministers to his body: food, fine clothes, soft surroundings, control of material things. Meanwhile he grows oblivious to what may be happening to his mind and heart: the contraction of his interests, the withering of sympathy, the deadened imagination to other people's needs. And he is so lapped in the luxurious present that he does not bother about the future and the critical reckoning which it may bring.

Even on the bodily level the insensate drive to get more possessions may provoke its disastrous penalty. One single mordant verse suggests it:

> He used his health
> To store up wealth
> To get, and scrimp and save;
> Then spent his wealth
> To get back health,
> And only got a grave.

But the supreme loss is not in what may happen prematurely to the body. The loss is what happens to the man's whole self. He thinks he has plenty of time to find out who he is and what his life is for. He will stop and give attention to all that after a while. But it is not only in the parable that the unexpected bell may toll. "Fool! This night your soul is required of you; and the things you have prepared, whose will they be?" If a man possesses in himself no generous thoughts, no great devotions, no immortal purposes, then certainly nothing which he *thought* he possessed can go with him to give dimensions to the soul that stands thin and naked before God.

Francis J. McConnell, beloved bishop of The Methodist Church, used to tell of a young Methodist preacher assigned to a country church in one of the Western states. In the congregation was a so-called self-made man, who had managed to acquire a great area of rich farmland. He took the young preacher up on a rise of the ground and pointed across the rolling grain fields to the north. "Everything in that direction, as far as you can see, I own," he said. Then turning east, south and west, he said the same thing and clapped the preacher on the back to show his satisfaction.

The younger man looked at him. "I've heard what you said," he answered. "You've turned me to the four quarters of the compass, and told me that everything in each of those directions is what you own. But one thing you haven't told me." He lifted his hand and pointed upward. "How much do you own in *that* direction?"

So is he who lays up treasure for himself on earth and is not rich in the sight of God.

BEYOND MATERIAL THINGS

And he said to his disciples, "Therefore I tell you, do not be anxious about your life, what you shall eat, nor about your body, what you shall put on. For life is more than food, and the body more than clothing. Consider the ravens: they neither sow nor reap, they have neither storehouse nor barn, and yet God feeds them. Of how much more value are you than the birds! And which of you by being anxious can add a cubit to his span of life? If then you are not able to do as small a thing as that, why are you anxious about the rest? Consider the lilies, how they grow; they neither toil nor spin; yet I tell you, even Solomon in all his glory was not arrayed like one of these. But if God so clothes the grass which is alive in the field today and tomorrow is thrown into the oven, how much more will he clothe you, O men of little faith? And do not seek what you are to eat and what you are to drink, nor be of anxious mind. For all the nations of the world seek these things; and your Father knows that you need them. Instead, seek his kingdom, and these things shall be yours as well." (Luke 12:22-31.)

In his parable of the man who spent his life building bigger barns in which to store up more possessions, Jesus was speaking to the rich—or to those who wanted to be rich. Now he turns to the great majority who not only had no thought of ever being rich, but also never could be quite sure of having enough to live on at all.

The Revised Standard Version has a translation of an important word which is more accurate and true than the old translation in the King James Version. The passage used to read, "Take no thought for your life, what ye shall eat; neither for the body, what ye shall put on." But the right translation is not, "Take no thought"; but, "Do not be anxious." Jesus knew life realistically enough to know that men had to take thought: the shepherd for his sheep, the farmer for his grain field, the builder for the foundations of his house. The work of the world could not go if men were unintelligent and shiftless. Everybody must be faithful to what he has to do. But in what spirit? Not with anxiety and tension, said Jesus. No, but with a happy trust in the goodness of God that would not fail.

Look at the living things in the world around you and learn from them, he said. Those ravens coming across the sky yonder, do they spend their time worrying because they have no stored-up food? They do not need to, for in God's abundant universe they will find what they need to eat. And those lilies that make the fields beautiful, do they have to agonize about clothes to wear? No, they do not need to, for God has arrayed them in a glory surpassing the glory of Solomon. They are so perishable that tomorrow they will be feeding a hearth-fire somewhere, but the lavishness of God has been poured out upon them. "How much more will he clothe you, O men of little faith?"

Believe then, said Jesus, that all you need will come to you out of the Father's hand. Keep a quiet spirit. It is what you are and not what you get that matters. For life is more than food, and the body than clothing.

Let it be humbly said that Jesus goes beyond us here, as he so often did. We cannot pretend that we have his trust. We are not really sure that if we seek God's kingdom—that is to say, if we always put the spiritual values first—the material things we have to have will be provided. Most of us are caught in anxieties which we would be bound to confess, and we wonder whether any other attitude is "practical." Yet now and then some person or event reveals a world of spiritual wonder beyond our common world, and it is as though in them "a trumpet sounds from the hid battlements of Eternity." [3]

We see again the winsome figure of Francis of Assisi, with his incredible joyousness and his freedom of soul when he had stripped himself of concern for things. Or we read of one like George Müller, in Bristol, England, a century and a half ago, who built an orphanage for two thousand children out of nothing and did it by a faith which the man of the world might have considered to be absurd. For he committed himself completely and only to the rightness of what he was trying to do, and to prayer that God would sustain it. He never borrowed, he never asked for money, he forbade his helpers ever to tell outsiders of his needs. Often there were evenings when all the food was gone, but by the next day more had somehow come. He had dared to take seriously the promise of Jesus, "Seek his kingdom, and these things shall be yours as well."

THE HEAVENLY TREASURE

"Fear not, little flock, for it is your Father's good pleasure to give you the kingdom. Sell your possessions, and give alms; provide yourselves with purses that do not grow old, with a treasure in the heavens that does not

[3] Francis Thompson, "The Hound of Heaven."

fail, where no thief approaches and no moth destroys. For where your treasure is, there will your heart be also." (Luke 12:32-34.)

The promise of Jesus to the disciples, which had been expressed in the words which the Evangelist has just recorded, is carried on into a still more intimate and loving assurance. They are the "little flock" for whom the divine shepherding will not fail. It may be that the disciples, on the way to Jerusalem and the uncertain future, were wondering what would happen to whatever possessions they were leaving behind. Compared to what God had in store for them, possessions would not matter. They could sell them and give to the poor—as the early church, to be told of in the book of Acts, would actually do. One thing is certain about the things a man owns: they will not last. A thief may steal some of them; and some which seem most securely stowed away the moths may destroy. But there are heavenly treasures that are beyond the touch of time and change.

A man will not have to wait until after death to find that out. A treasure in the heavens can be won—or lost—here and now: lost if a man's life has been a continual contraction into jealous interests that center in himself, so that as the years go on he is left with the bitter consciousness that he is lonely and unloved because he has never been really loving. But if instead he has been committed to great loyalties and has found his values in a self-giving reflection of the love of God, then he will have a lasting joy. He has gained the sort of treasure in which his whole heart can expand.

THE DIVINE SELF-GIVING

"Let your loins be girded and your lamps burning, and be like men who are waiting for their master to come home from the marriage feast, so that they may open to him at once when he comes and knocks. Blessed are those servants whom the master finds awake when he comes; truly, I say to you, he will gird himself and have them sit at table, and come and serve them. If he comes in the second watch, or in the third, and finds them so, blessed are those servants!" (Luke 12:35-40.)

For those who listen to Jesus, life can never settle down into a dull somnolence. In effect he was always saying to his disciples, and is saying now, "Be vigilant! For God's thrilling visitation may at any moment be knocking at your doors." We cannot tell if as he went up to Jerusalem he expected some sudden end of the present age and the perfected kingdom of the Son of man. But what he surely did proclaim is that life is continually subject to new and wonderful invasions of the transforming grace of God, and of which it has been truly said that they may come "not so quickly as impatience, not yet so late as carelessness, supposes." Our great need is to be ready to welcome these at whatever hour they may appear. The picture in which Jesus dramatizes the spiritual fact is put into colors that go beyond our ordinary likelihood, for that is exactly how he wished the transcendent self-giving of God to appear. We human beings are like servants who know that their Lord may come home. When we open the door for him, we are doing only our duty and have no reason for any special reward. But in Jesus' picture, the incredible happens. The Lord has the servants sit down, and he serves them. Such is the boundlessness of the blessing which may be given to those who have kept the lamps of great desire burning. To be eager that something divine may come to us, and to be ready to receive it whenever it is at the door, is to have God bring himself to us in a completeness which we could not have dared to think.

THE NEED FOR ROUTINE FAITHFULNESS

"But know this, that if the householder had known at what hour the thief was coming, he would have been awake and would not have left his house to be broken into. You also must be ready; for the Son of man is coming at an hour you do not expect." (Luke 12:39-40.)

It may well be thought that it would have been right and helpful if the translators of the Revised Standard Version had separated these verses from vss. 35-38 and put them in a distinct paragraph; for they appear to be the Evangelist's record of a saying of Jesus which was not a part of what immediately precedes it on the Gospel page. The central emphasis in vss. 35-38, with its symbol of the master coming home from the wedding feast, is of the blessedness that may be in welcoming him. But in these vss. 39-40, with its symbol of the thief, the emphasis is upon the suddenness and the shock of the event.

Here—as at other times and in other ways—Jesus was stressing the fatefulness which may be in every moment of time. The Son of man is coming at an hour you do not expect. It is not a matter of waiting for a last judgment so evident that its approach can be foreseen. Every hour of life is a last judgment, in that every hour represents some possible faithfulness which is or is not achieved, some opportunity fulfilled or neglected which will never come again. At every instant eternity is breaking into time.

Full of significance also is the truth which speaks through all of vss. 35-40, and will speak again in vss. 41-48. What is it that the Lord desires to find in his servants when he comes? It is that they shall be carrying on the work which they were supposed to do. As the master of the house was

179

absent in the parable which Jesus used, so in spiritual experience it may often be that the presence of God is not immediately felt. But each man has some awareness of what the duty is which God has given him. And when the divine does draw near in some special way, the benediction it brings may depend not upon a man's being rapt in some mystic contemplation but upon the fact that he is carrying his thought of God into the routine faithfulness of the common day.

THE PERIL OF MISUSED OPPORTUNITY

Peter said, "Lord, are you telling this parable for us or for all?" And the Lord said, "Who then is the faithful and wise steward, whom his master will set over his household, to give them their portion of food at the proper time? Blessed is that servant whom his master when he comes will find so doing. Truly I tell you, he will set him over all his possessions. But if that servant says to himself, 'My master is delayed in coming,' and begins to beat the menservants and the maidservants, and to eat and drink and get drunk, the master of that servant will come on a day when he does not expect him and at an hour he does not know, and will punish him, and put him with the unfaithful. And that servant who knew his master's will, but did not make ready or act according to his will, shall receive a severe beating. But he who did not know, and did what deserved a beating, shall receive a light beating. Every one to whom much is given, of him will much be required; and of him to whom men commit much they will demand the more." (Luke 12:41-48.)

As usual, it was the impulsive Peter who broke out with a question which the other disciples may also have been asking in their own thoughts. Jesus had been speaking of servants whose responsibility was that they should be alert to meet the unexpected. Was he saying this to everybody, or did he have special reference to the twelve?

Jesus answered him not with a direct yes or no. He described a scene that might happen and let Peter draw his own conclusion. This time he spoke not only of servants in general, but also of a steward who had been given special responsibility and trust. If that steward presumed upon his office and abused the confidence his master had put in him, there was bound to be a stern accounting. If the man were well-meaning and in his intention faithful, but had blundered through honest misunderstanding of his master's instructions, the rebuke given him would be compassionate. But if he grew drunk with power and began to indulge himself and to treat the other servants with domineering pride and harshness, then his punishment would be severe. Did Peter remember how a little while before he had been one of those who were disputing who should be the greatest? Let him ponder that; and let him remember also that to whom much is given, of him much will be required.

THE BAPTISM OF FIRE

"I came to cast fire upon the earth; and would that it were already kindled! I have a baptism to be baptized with; and how I am constrained until it is accomplished! Do you think that I have come to give peace on earth? No, I tell you, but rather division; for henceforth in one house there will be five divided, three against two and two against three; they will be divided, father against son and son against father, mother against daughter and daughter against her mother, mother-in-law against her daughter-in-law and daughter-in-law against her mother-in-law."

(Luke 12:49-53.)

One cannot read these words of Jesus without awe. It is as though one were permitted for a moment to look into the infinite arena where Jesus wrestled with the terrible issues which his soul confronted. "I have a baptism to be baptized with." Not a baptism now of water, but of blood. He was going up to Jerusalem to face hostility and fury, to precipitate a conflict that would cast fire on the earth. That fire would be the devastating challenge of God's spirit to the pride and sin of men, and he who carried that fire would have to be baptized in a devotion unto death.

Jesus knew now what he had to face, and he was constrained until it was accomplished. Who can estimate the cost he had to pay for that accomplishment? All that was human in him must have recoiled from the dreadful possibility of crucifixion; for life was beautiful to him in the world of sun and sky and Galilean hills, and in the love he had for men whom he had drawn into his comradeship, and in that wider love that he had for all of Israel, his own people—whether they loved him or not. Yet what he must do now was to become not a focus of unity but a sword of division. He had come to bring peace, but Israel would not accept the only peace which can belong to human souls: reconciliation with the redeeming will of God. Now he must be ready to suffer and to die, that the full awfulness of men's rejection of the love of God might be manifest, but also that through the power of his sacrifice might come salvation.

READING THE SIGNS OF DESTINY

He also said to the multitudes, "When you see a cloud rising in the west, you say at once, 'A shower is coming'; and so it happens. And when you see the south wind blowing, you say, 'There will be scorching heat'; and

181

it happens. You hypocrites! You know how to interpret the appearance
of earth and sky; but why do you not know how to interpret the present
time?" (Luke 12:54-56.)

"Why do you not know how to interpret the present time?" The tragic
fact is that men so seldom do. When Jesus came to Jerusalem, the people
in general had no conception of the infinite issues that were at stake. They
did not know that they were at the crossroads of time and that in the man
of Nazareth God was seeking to reconcile the world unto himself. They
did not see that in rejecting him they rejected the reason for their existence, and that within a generation Jerusalem and the nation of Israel
would be destroyed.

And today? How well do we of this later century read the signs that
appear in the winds and clouds of destiny? Some things we can read well
enough: advertisements of bargain sales, quotations on the stock market, the
rise or fall of our investments, the next chance for easy profit. But the
ominous forces which may be gathering in a world that seems so bright and
prosperous—the hot desire to make money which can have its poisonous
growth in economic cruelty and political corruption, the sensuality and
sexual license which can disintegrate the moral fiber of a people, racial
bitterness that perverts justice, nationalistic pride which is blind to the
selfishness that ignores the awful oneness of human destiny—how many
read *these* signs and interpret their fateful meaning?

BEFORE THE TIME RUNS OUT

"And why do you not judge for yourselves what is right? As you go with
your accuser before the magistrate, make an effort to settle with him on
the way, lest he drag you to the judge, and the judge hand you over to
the officer, and the officer put you in prison. I tell you, you will never
get out till you have paid the very last copper." (Luke 12:57-59.)

The stern climax of this chapter needs no elaboration. There is a moment
when recognition of reality and clear decision in the light of it is still in
time, and there is another moment when it will be too late. There may be
wrongs in a man's life which he should rectify, obligations he owes which
he can discharge now before the crisis of final reckoning comes. Otherwise,
there may be a judgment from which there is no more appeal.

chapter 13

THE RIDDLE OF SUFFERING

There were some present at that very time who told him of the Galileans whose blood Pilate had mingled with their sacrifices. And he answered them, "Do you think that these Galileans were worse sinners than all the other Galileans, because they suffered thus? I tell you, No; but unless you repent you will all likewise perish. Or those eighteen upon whom the tower in Siloam fell and killed them, do you think that they were worse offenders than all the others who dwelt in Jerusalem? I tell you, No; but unless you repent you will all likewise perish." (Luke 13:1-5.)

The references here to actual events which had just occurred were familiar, of course, to those who listened to Jesus, and therefore needed no elaboration so far as they were concerned. From our distance of time we cannot know exactly what happened, or why; but we do know of acts of Pilate which were like this one in ugly cruelty. Flavius Josephus, Jewish historian of the first century, wrote in his *Antiquities of the Jews* that on one occasion Pilate undertook to bring water to Jerusalem; and in order to do it he appropriated revenues of the Temple. "And many thousands of the people got together, and made a clamor against him, and insisted that he should leave off that design." Foreseeing trouble, Pilate not only ordered out his legionaries, but he had each man wear a dagger concealed under his cloak. When the Jews defied his command to disperse, he gave a signal; and the legionaries closed in upon the protesting crowd. "They equally punished those who were tumultuous and those who were not, nor did they spare them in the least; and since the people were unarmed, and were caught by men prepared for what they were about, a great number of them were slain." [1]

This act of Pilate in Jerusalem may or may not have been the killing of Galileans to which vs. 1 specifically refers; but in any case there had been a brutal killing, and the people wanted to know what Jesus had to say about it. It may be that some of his enemies were trying—as they tried later—to provoke him into some indignant denunciation of the

[1] Book 18, chapter 3.

183

Roman power which would bring swift Roman punishment. It may be instead that some who hated Rome were hoping that he might encourage actual revolt in Galilee. But aside from any other motive, there was the general impulse which always stirs in people to understand the reason for conspicuous tragedy. Why did these particular Galileans and these particular workers on the tower of Siloam have to die?

One answer might have been that these men were flagrant sinners whom God singled out for the visitation of his wrath. This was the sort of answer which Job's counselors would have given. If calamity came, it was because there had been wickedness; and the calamity must be in proportion to what that wickedness deserved.

But Jesus rejected that explanation. Life is not as simple as that. There are purposes of God which cannot be measured by our glib arithmetic, and mysteries which as yet we cannot fathom. The danger is that men may so involve themselves in perplexities about life in general that they ignore what is imperative for themselves. Their bodily existence, and the length of it, must be left in the hands of God. The crucial matter is that the soul should be ready to meet whatever comes. "Unless you repent, you will all likewise perish."

THE JUDGMENT ON THE NATION

And he told this parable: "A man had a fig tree planted in his vineyard; and he came seeking fruit on it and found none. And he said to the vine-dresser, 'Lo, these three years I have come seeking fruit on this fig tree, and I find none. Cut it down; why should it use up the ground?' And he answered him, 'Let it alone, sir, this year also, till I dig about it and put on manure. And if it bears fruit next year, well and good; but if not, you can cut it down.' " (Luke 13:6-9.)

The stringent message of vss. 1-5 is carried forward into its meaning not only for individuals but for the nation as a whole. Israel had had its long history of relationship to God. It was the people of the covenant. In its spiritual privilege it was like a fig tree planted in a vineyard, its branches lifted to the sunlight of its heavenly opportunity. But the years had gone, and there was no adequate fruit. Now the day of accounting must come.

There is the necessity of judgment, but those who warn of it will not be welcomed. Six centuries earlier, the prophet Jeremiah had seen the moral disintegration of the kingdom of Judah and had predicted its fall. He had been met by hatred and malignant punishment. Anyone who runs counter to a nation's pride and self-assurance in any century is likely to meet that same fate. Let such a man as Dietrich Bonhoeffer in our own time stand as witness to that truth.

Jesus' parable had to do with judgment, but also with mercy. God has infinite patience, or else what nation could endure? These United States of America have had a spiritual opportunity in the new world such as Israel had in the old. But the time could come when the voice of God might say, "Lo, these . . . years I come seeking fruit on this tree, and I find none." Or else the voice might say what would be an equal condemnation: that among the fruit which God does find is the blighted and bitter fruit of material engrossment, moral laxity, racial hatreds and perversion of justice, political slander, and violence bred by lies. It may be that the time is short in which a better purpose can rid the ground of the poisonous growths which have infected the roots of the tree, before there come the words of final judgment: "If it bears fruit . . . , well and good; but if not, you can cut it down."

STRAIGHTENING THE BENT BACKS

Now he was teaching in one of the synagogues on the sabbath. And there was a woman who had had a spirit of infirmity for eighteen years; she was bent over and could not fully straighten herself. And when Jesus saw her, he called her and said to her, "Woman, you are freed from your infirmity." And he laid his hands upon her, and immediately she was made straight, and she praised God. But the ruler of the synagogue, indignant because Jesus had healed on the sabbath, said to the people, "There are six days on which work ought to be done; come on those days and be healed, and not on the sabbath day." Then the Lord answered him, "You hypocrites! Does not each of you on the sabbath untie his ox or his ass from the manger, and lead it away to water it? And ought not this woman, a daughter of Abraham whom Satan bound for eighteen years, be loosed from this bond on the sabbath day?" As he said this, all his adversaries were put to shame; and all the people rejoiced at all the glorious things that were done by him.   (Luke 13:10-17.)

Jesus was in one of the synagogues on the sabbath, and the curious thing is that everytime he was teaching there, some kind of angry consequence happened. When he preached in the synagogue in his own town of Nazareth, as told of in chapter 4, the congregation was so offended by what he said that they "put him out of the city" and actually tried to push him over the cliff at the top of the hill. On another sabbath in another synagogue people were "filled with fury," and began to plot what they could do to get rid of him. And now again in this chapter 13 we come upon another outraged group, with the ruler of the synagogue voicing their general indignation.

Obviously this is very much out of line with what some present-day church members like to assume. Surely the Christian gospel must be quiet and comforting, they think. The last thing that ought to be expected is anything controversial in the pulpit. Why should any Christian preaching ever stir up trouble? But the fact is that Jesus stirred up trouble nearly every time he spoke. And the reason was that he brought the word of God with its shock of awakening life to people who had wrapped themselves in their own ideas and gone to sleep.

Moreover, many of those who resented him most were men who were supposed to be good, and *were* good according to their notion of what proper religion required. Look at the scene which the Gospel is describing. Jesus has healed a crippled woman on the sabbath day. That ought to have seemed to everybody what the love of God would always do. But the traditionalists said that it was not according to the law. Anyone claiming to perform a ministry for God must carry it out their way and according to their accepted rules of time and manner, or it was wrong.

The trouble with men like the ruler of the synagogue was that they thought their ideas were unquestionable. Whenever that is true, there can develop a fanaticism which is cruel—in religion, in social relationships of every kind. The immediate opportunity to express the will of God in a new and living way is rejected because it does not fit into patterns to which hard intolerance holds.

That was the shadowed side of this incident in the synagogue, but the beauty in it came from the fact that Jesus could not be deterred. His spirit broke through then—and always will break through—the barriers of a frozen orthodoxy. He would set God's mercy free to act, even when men who thought they were being pious insisted that it should operate only in their own way.

There is a brightness in every passage of the Gospel which tells of Jesus' healings. We do not see in our world a healing power which we could dare to say is the same as his. Through him something beyond our measurements flowed in from the world that is above our world. But the good thing to remember is that there is a continuing power which is the direct fruit of his compassion. Where the influence of his spirit has touched any land or people, there has been pity for all the sick and suffering, and the kind of concern which could turn that pity into effective deed. Consider the contrast between the countries which in part at least are Christian and the non-Christian countries where human misery may go unnoticed. Hospitals, doctors, surgeons, nurses—who will say that their ministry of mercy would ever have arisen if it had not been for the gospel of the compassionate Christ?

This particular account of the healing of the woman who "was bent over" has a lovely echo in a modern act of service. It is described in *The Ugly American,* a book which in the midst of other and less pleasant revelations showed what some individuals in the foreign service personnel have done to bring a blessing to poor and ignorant people in the little countries of Asia.

Emma Atkins was a simple and straight-forward person. She was not a busybody; but she had learned that when she wanted to know something the best way to find out was to ask a direct question. . . .
"Why is it that all the old people of Chang 'Dong are bent over?" Emma asked. "Every older person I have seen is bent over and walks as if his back is hurting." [1]

Presently she found the answer. The old people did all the sweeping. Wood was too scarce for broom handles. Nothing was available except reeds tied together, and the reeds were short. So the people, generation after generation, had to sweep stooped over, and all of them as they grew older had crooked spines.

So what did Emma Atkins do? She got her husband to go with her to hunt in the mountains—until one day they came upon a patch of reeds that grew with a long strong stalk. She transplanted some of them to the yard of her house in the village. She made a tall strong broom and swept where the villagers could see her.

At length they caught the idea. She told them where they could find the tall reeds and make themselves brooms which they could use while they stood up straight.

Four years later, when she was back in Pittsburgh, she had a letter from the headman of the village of Chang 'Dong. It said:

Wife of the engineer:
I am writing to thank you for a thing you did for the old people of Chang 'Dong. For many centuries, longer than any man can remember, we have always had old people with bent backs in this village. And in every village that we know of the old people have always had bent backs. . . .
But, wife of the engineer, you have changed all that. . . . You showed us a new way to sweep. It is a small thing, but it has changed the lives of our old people. . . . You will be happy to know that today there are few bent backs in the village of Chang 'Dong. . . . No longer are their bodies painful during the months of the monsoon.
I know you are not of our religion, wife of the engineer, but perhaps you will be pleased to know that on the outskirts of the village we have constructed a small

[1] William J. Lederer and Eugene Burdick, *The Ugly American* (New York: W. W. Norton & Company, 1958), pp. 232-33. Copyright © 1958 by William J. Lederer and Eugene Burdick.

shrine in your memory. It is a simple affair; at the foot of the altar are these words: "In memory of the woman who unbent the backs of our people." [2]

THE PARABLE OF THE MUSTARD SEED

He said therefore, "What is the kingdom of God like? And to what shall I compare it? It is like a grain of mustard seed which a man took and sowed in his garden; and it grew and became a tree, and the birds of the air made nests in its branches." (Luke 13:18-19.)

One of the briefest of the parables, yet in its few words a width of spiritual suggestion. If the kingdom of God is like a seed, then it is lifted up above the level of any human contrivance. No man ever made a seed. In the hidden miracle of its potency for growth and fruitfulness, it comes out of the abundant mystery of the universe upon which all human life must be dependent. So the spirit which can create the kingdom comes from God alone. It can only be a gift; and our part is to reach out for it with desire and to accept it whenever and wherever it is given.

It may come in small beginnings. In the Gospel of Mark there is a phrase which is not in Luke: a grain of mustard seed which is "the smallest of all the seeds on earth." That may not be exactly the fact, but the mustard seed is small enough. Beside some great object like a rock or a log of wood it seems insignificant. So may seem the little things in which the kingdom of God can come. Often it would appear that the dead weight of the world's grossness and actual evil is overwhelming. Where are the signs of God in the reports which make the headlines in the morning papers?—war or threats of wars, violence, murder, dishonesty, infidelity, divorce? Yet all the while in ways that are not sensational the spirit of the kingdom is planted here and there: in the steadfastness of ordinary men who go about their duty, in the daily devotion of women in their homes, in those who carry on the agencies of mercy in great cities, in the young people who volunteer for the Peace Corps in the difficult places.

"The birds of the air made nests in its branches," said the parable. The fellowship which gathered round Jesus at first was only as the seed. But the worldwide Christian church which was grown from this fellowship does draw to itself the hope and faith of people out of every land.

THE PARABLE OF THE LEAVEN

And again he said, "To what shall I compare the kingdom of God? It is like leaven which a woman took and hid in three measures of meal, till it was all leavened." (Luke 13:20-21.)

[2] *Ibid.,* pp. 237-38.

As a symbol of the spirit from God which can create his kingdom, the leaven is like the seed in that at first its power is not apparent. No one looking at a seed would know the possibilities of growth wrapped up in its littleness, and no one looking at leaven can see beforehand what can happen when it begins to work.

In order for leaven to be of use it must be kneaded into the dough. Without that kneading, the leaven would produce only a little corner of sourness, and the bulk of the dough would remain untouched. It is the permeation of the leaven that makes the dough ready to be baked into bread. So it is the permeation of the heavenly purpose which can turn what would be our common life into the substance of the kingdom of God. The so-called religious and secular must not be kept apart. When they *are* kept apart, then the possibilities everywhere are frustrated. That is what happens when men imagine that their relationship to God is a matter of conventional churchgoing on Sunday in a particular building which has been "consecrated," while their everyday activities are of different material. The Sunday leaven is of little use unless it is kneaded into the whole week. It is not chiefly in church that men show whether or not they are Christians. It is in the spirit they carry into the farm, the factory, the schoolroom, the lawyer's office, and the doctor's office that the evidence is given. Then when thought and action are thus all leavened, the kingdom of God begins to be made real.

THE NARROW DOOR

> He went on his way through towns and villages, teaching, and journeying toward Jerusalem. And some one said to him, "Lord, will those who are saved be few?" And he said to them, "Strive to enter by the narrow door; for many, I tell you, will seek to enter and will not be able."
>
> (Luke 13:22-24.)

Jesus was not inclined to answer superficial questions. "Lord, will those who are saved be few?" This could have been only a dabbling in generalities, the kind of question people ask who like to talk about the great issues of life but are not concerned to meet them. It is as though the Lord replied: "The crucial matter is not about numbers, many or few—the crucial matter is what about you?"

The door to the kingdom is narrow. A man cannot get through it if he tries to carry with him all his encumbrances. He cannot get through it if he has let himself grow fat and soft. There must be some measure of self-discipline and hardihood if a man is to go through that door. And that stern truth is underlined by what Jesus himself was doing as he spoke to the man who questioned him. He was "journeying toward Jerusalem." He himself faced decisions so demanding, and with dangers which crowded so close, that only the resolute could follow on his way.

THE HOLLOW CLAIM

"When once the householder has risen up and shut the door, you will begin to stand outside and to knock at the door, saying, 'Lord, open to us.' He will answer you, 'I do not know where you come from.' Then you will begin to say, 'We ate and drank in your presence, and you taught in our streets.' But he will say, 'I tell you, I do not know where you come from; depart from me, all you workers of iniquity!'" (Luke 13:25-27.)

It is an ominous note that sounds in vs. 27, the same note that sounded in Matthew's Gospel in the parable of the careless bridesmaids who let their lamps go out and came too late to the wedding feast. The shutting of a door may be a devastating thing to hear. There is a harsh finality in the sound of it; and there is a deeper shock when it becomes the symbol for an increasing reality in the whole realm of the spirit's life. As the years go on, there may be many doors which we know we shall not go through again: the doors to opportunities which are now forever lost.

Here the picture of the man knocking for admission is a parable of the soul knocking at the door of the house of God. As with all the parables it must be read for its broad suggestion, not pressed at every aspect as though the parable must be complete. Obviously no human "householder" can exemplify the fullness of the meaning of God. But the man who comes knocking at the door of an earthly house can exemplify that same man as he might knock at last at the final haven for his soul. The point of the parable is that the man's plea for admittance is hollow and pretentious. He claims friendship because of some casual contact which meant nothing to him at the time. Many who had heard Jesus now and then were of that sort. In the final judgment they might try to pretend association with the kingdom of God because Jesus had preached about it in their town and they had watched with curiosity when he went down their street. But what had they done about it? Nothing. Their lives had been no different. Whatever glib words of acquaintance they might try to utter concerning the kingdom of the spirit, they still belonged outside it among the workers of iniquity.

REVERSALS IN DESTINY

"There you will weep and gnash your teeth, when you see Abraham and Isaac and Jacob and all the prophets in the kingdom of God and you yourselves thrust out. And men will come from east and west, and from north and south, and sit at table in the kingdom of God. And behold, some are last who will be first, and some are first who will be last."

(Luke 13:28-30.)

The preceding parable is given here an application which has in it an echo of the preaching of John the Baptist. John arraigned those who thought that their status was guaranteed because of their religious ancestry and their excellent associations. All their family traditions were impeccable. Who could doubt that they belonged to the elect?

But John had said, "Do not begin to say to yourselves, 'We have Abraham as our father'; for I tell you, God is able from these stones to raise up children to Abraham." Now Jesus is reminding some of these same people that they might fail to hold their places in the covenant which God had promised to Israel. Abraham, Isaac, and Jacob would be in the kingdom, and also the prophets, though the prophets, with their living and disturbing truth, had been rejected and despised by some of the forerunners of the particular men to whom he was speaking now. All sorts of unexpected people would find their way into the kingdom: Samaritans, Mary Magdalenes, publicans and sinners. They would come from strange places and conditions, north, east, south, and west; some who had heard of it last would enter, and some of those who had known all about it would be left outside. The self-satisfied and assured would stand and see these strangers go by them, and ask one another in outrage how this riffraff could get into the kingdom which they had supposed was meant to belong to *them*.

FREEDOM THAT
CAN FRUSTRATE THE DIVINE

At that very hour some Pharisees came, and said to him, "Get away from here, for Herod wants to kill you." And he said to them, "Go and tell that fox, 'Behold, I cast out demons and perform cures today and tomorrow, and the third day I finish my course. Nevertheless I must go on my way today and tomorrow and the day following; for it cannot be that a prophet should perish away from Jerusalem.' O Jerusalem, Jerusalem, killing the prophets and stoning those who are sent to you! How often would I have gathered your children together as a hen gathers her brood under her wings, and you would not! Behold, your house is forsaken. And I tell you, you will not see me until you say, 'Blessed be he who comes in the name of the Lord!'" (Luke 13:31-35.)

Jesus was not concerned with Herod now. Herod could not prevent him from going to Jerusalem, and to Jerusalem he would go. But Jerusalem did concern him. It was the Holy City. It was the central shrine of his own people and of all their mighty history. For it to be involved in rejection of God's message again, to meet with hatred and violence the gospel he would bring, perhaps to crucify him as it had stoned and killed the prophets in other generations—this would be the ultimate spiritual tragedy. He had been speaking a moment before of judgment, but it was not judgment that he desired. The sin of Jerusalem and of the people who represented it weighed heavily upon him. His great compassion reached out to save, if it were possible, even the most obdurate from the consequences of their stubbornness and stupid pride. On one side was the outreaching love of God; on the other side, the fatefulness of the human will that would not listen. "How often would I have gathered your children together as a hen gathers her brood under her wings, and you would not!" The dread fact was that Jerusalem could determine its own destiny. Because God had given to men the awful dignity of human freedom, even the Christ could not bring salvation to a city that did not want to have him come.

chapter 14

WHEN RELIGIOUS REALITIES ARE TWISTED

One sabbath when he went to dine at the house of a ruler who belonged to the Pharisees, they were watching him. And behold, there was a man before him who had dropsy. And Jesus spoke to the lawyers and Pharisees, saying, "Is it lawful to heal on the sabbath, or not?" But they were silent. Then he took him and healed him, and let him go. And he said to them, "Which of you, having an ass or an ox that has fallen into a well, will not immediately pull him out on a sabbath day?" And they could not reply to this.
(Luke 14:1-6.)

It is a sorry fact that nearly every time the sabbath day is mentioned in the Gospel it had to be in connection with some scene in which men who ought to have known better were trying to take the beautiful meaning out of it. Keeping the sabbath holy was part of the noble inheritance of Israel. It was written among the Ten Commandments, and in the book of Genesis woven into the creation story. There should be a day in every week which men should keep free in order that they might remember again and again the greatness and goodness of God; and very early in the history of Israel it was provided that concern for people must go hand in hand with worship offered to God. So it should be a day of rest for all servants, a day for the lifting off of burdens generally.

But little by little rules and definitions had smothered the living purpose. Pious literalists became so engrossed with their particularities as to *how* the sabbath should be observed that they lost any sensitive perception of *why*. The result was that what was meant to be a blessing had become a bondage. Rules had to be observed as to what should *not* be done, even if that meant not doing an act of mercy. So the objectors watched Jesus, not in desire to see God's goodness manifested in some new and happy way, but with crabbed determination that he must stay within their regulations. They could not answer when Jesus asked them whether or not they would not actually rescue something that belonged to them if it needed rescue on the sabbath. That was another matter, they considered. Anyhow, they were going to lay down the law for him—an impulse which has found frequent imitators among the hidebound in every age.

THE RIGHT WAY TO HONOR

Now he told a parable to those who were invited, when he marked how they chose the places of honor, saying to them, "When you are invited by any one to a marriage feast, do not sit down in a place of honor, lest a more eminent man than you be invited by him; and he who invited you both will come and say to you, 'Give place to this man,' and then you will begin with shame to take the lowest place. But when you are invited, go and sit in the lowest place, so that when your host comes he may say to you, 'Friend, go up higher'; then you will be honored in the presence of all who sit at table with you. For every one who exalts himself will be humbled, and he who humbles himself will be exalted."

(Luke 14:7-11.)

The vanity of protocol is both ancient and modern. Men who want to be important, especially if they are not sure that everybody thinks they are, will be looking jealously for all the deference they have demanded as their due. But this self-assertion may overreach itself. The man who has marched up to the high seat may have the humiliation of being asked to take a low one.

Whether or not that happens, there is no dignity in trying to reach out for the place of honor; and great dignity in not being concerned about it. What this means was embodied in an incident which is stamped unforgettably upon the memory of a man who saw it. In the 1940's, when Harry Emerson Fosdick was preaching in the Riverside Church, New York, great throngs poured in on every Sunday. One Sunday morning when the church was already nearly full, an usher came up the center aisle with a gentleman and a lady. Pausing opposite a pew, the usher said: "I am sorry, but there are no two vacant seats together. If you will go in here, I will take her to a seat farther forward." The husband smiled assent and entered the pew, while his wife went on alone. When the man already in the pew looked up, he saw to his surprise that the one who had now sat down beside him was John D. Rockefeller, Jr. It was Mr. Rockefeller who first envisioned the possibility of this great church, and it was his unbounded generosity which turned the vision into fact. The whole building would not have existed except for him. If any man deserved the right to preferential treatment, it was he; and a lesser man might have demanded it. But he was too big for that. With complete simplicity he took the seat he happened to be given. For him there was no priority in the house of God.

BANQUETING THE POOR

> He said also to the man who had invited him, "When you give a dinner or a banquet, do not invite your friends or your brothers or your kinsmen or rich neighbors, lest they also invite you in return, and you be repaid. But when you give a feast, invite the poor, the maimed, the lame, the blind, and you will be blessed, because they cannot repay you. You will be repaid at the resurrection of the just." (Luke 14:12-14.)

The meaning and message of these words of Jesus are plain enough. They were his vivid way of reminding people not to be thinking all the time of their own pleasures and of what might benefit them among their prosperous friends; but, instead, of what they might do for the poor, the lonely, and the friendless.

Peter Marshall, who in his brief and brilliant ministry at the New York Avenue Presbyterian Church in Washington, D.C., touched the minds and hearts of multitudes, preached a sermon one Sunday entitled, "By Invitation of Jesus." [1] It told of a wealthy man who sat before the blazing log fire in his handsome house on a wintry night and happened to read this very passage from the Gospel. He began to think about the dinner which Jesus described, and then he thought about the dinners and parties in his own home and the sort of people he invited.

Most of them were listed in "Who's Who in Washington"; and there were those whose names were household words in business, finance, clubs, and in government circles. . . .

> But *they* were not poor
> or maimed
> or lame
> or blind.

What, then, if he should try to carry out something like what Jesus pictured? He determined that he would. So what he did was to have cards engraved, which began this way:

> JESUS OF NAZARETH
> *Requests the honor of your presence*
> *at a banquet honoring*
> *The Sons of Want.*

[1] *Mr. Jones, Meet the Master* (New York: Fleming H. Revell Co., 1949), pp. 117-28. Used by permission.

Under that was the date for the dinner and the place where the guests were to meet.

A few days later as he went downtown with the invitations in his hands, he gave them to the sort of people he was inviting this time to his dinner: to an old man trying to sell pencils, to the blind man at the corner newsstand, to any forlorn person he met on the winter street. They looked at the cards with puzzlement, and some with disbelief. But if you are hungry and cold, you don't pass up a possible chance to be fed. So when evening came a line of men were waiting at the Central Union Mission as was printed on the card. What they found there, though, were cars to take them to the home of the man who had issued the invitation—to be received by him and to sit down with him to the sort of dinner he would have given to his most honored friends. And when all the shyness and strangeness had melted away, he read them the words of Jesus and said to them:

"If I have given you one evening of happiness, I shall be forever glad to remember it, and you are under no obligation to me.

"This is not my party. It is His!

"I have merely lent Him this house.

"He was your *Host*. He is your *Friend*.

"And He has given me the honor of speaking for Him."

Said Peter Marshall, as his sermon moved toward its end, "Of course, that never happened. It is only a piece of imagination." Imagined, yes, according to the particular picture which Peter Marshall drew. But not imagination only. The words of Jesus have waked their echo in many real people. There is hardly a community in America, especially at Christmastime, where one cannot read in the newspapers the account of some party to which the sick or the crippled or the forlorn, and those only, were invited.

Nor is that the only way or indeed the greatest way in which the spirit that came from Christ has led men to give the best they had—not to those to whom they had some obligation, but to the poor and needy of the earth. It may be a rich gift when a man shares his material possessions; it can be a richer one when he shares the very substance of himself. That is what some of those who have been inspired by Christ have done. They have fed people with more than food; they have fed them with a devotion of the whole of life. Wilfred Grenfell, when he had seen the poverty and the bitter hardships of the fisherfolk on the bleak coasts of Labrador, wrote home: "How could any human being with a heart of flesh, after seeing such sights, enjoy a Christmas dinner in old England . . . with minds haunted by these hungry pale faces of people of our own race and blood?" [2] And so he came back to Labrador to give it his magnificent ministry in medicine, and to change the meaning of existence for the people of a whole land. Dr. Tom Dooley, moved by the pitiableness of the refugees in Southeast Asia at the end of the Second World War, established his mission hospital in Laos; and when one of his naval corpsmen, who had responded for service in that hard place, was asked why he did it, he answered, "We just want to do what we can for people who ain't got it so good." [3] And Dr. Gordon S. Seagrave, "the Burma Surgeon," who made the hospital he built from nothing at Namkham a beacon of hope for a whole nation, said on his sixty-fifth birthday, "I will keep on working as long as I can help sick people get well, assist doctors to learn surgery, or teach nurses to care for the sick." [4]

Such men do "give a feast." They have made the gospel live, and they have found the fulfillment of the promise of Jesus, as James Russell Lowell expressed it in *The Vision of Sir Launfal:*

> Who gives himself with his alms feeds three,
> Himself, his hungering neighbor, and me.

THE NEGLECTED INVITATIONS

When one of those who sat at table with him heard this, he said to him, "Blessed is he who shall eat bread in the kingdom of God!" But he said to him, "A man once gave a great banquet, and invited many; and at the time for the banquet he sent his servant to say to those who had been invited, 'Come; for all is now ready.' But they all alike began to make excuses. The first said to him, 'I have bought a field, and I must go out and see it; I pray you, have me excused.' And another said, 'I have bought five yoke of oxen, and I go to examine them; I pray you, have me excused.' And another said, 'I have married a wife, and therefore I cannot come.' So the servant came and reported this to his master. Then the householder in anger said to his servant, 'Go out quickly to the streets and lanes of the city, and bring in the poor and maimed and blind and lame.' And the servant said, 'Sir, what you commanded has been done, and still there is room.' And the master said to the servant, 'Go out to the highways and hedges, and compel people to come in, that my house may be filled. For I tell you, none of those men who were invited shall taste my banquet.'" (Luke 14:15-24.)

[2] J. Lennox Kerr, *Wilfred Grenfell, His Life and Work* (New York: Dodd, Mead & Co., 1959) , p. 70.
[3] *Doctor Tom Dooley, My Story* (New York: Farrar, Straus & Co., 1960) , p. 63.
[4] From a leaflet sent by the American Medical Mission to Burma.

Twice Jesus had used a feast as the central illustration of circumstances which would show the sort of person a man might actually be. The first time he was making plain that the vanity of claiming the seat of honor could result in losing the very dignity the man wants to assert. The second time he had pictured the kind of feast which a warmhearted man might choose to give: not to friends and kinsmen and rich neighbors, but to the poor, the maimed, the lame, the blind.

Now one of those who heard him broke in with the sort of remark which some parrotlike person in any group is likely to make in order to get into the conversation. Feasts, ah yes—but how wonderful to think of feasting in the kingdom of God! It was a current belief that when the new age came all the redeemed would sit down together at the Messiah's banquet. The man who spoke up was no doubt thinking of that, and perhaps at the same time, by his pious exclamation, conveying the assumption that a person like himself would naturally be one of those who would belong to the Messiah's kingdom.

Jesus took instant occasion to hold this assumption up to scrutiny. He would make this man, and all other men, understand that the hope of being admitted to the heavenly feast was not something to be dealt with by glib phrases. The list of those who expected to be invited might be very different from the list of those who would ultimately get in. So he drew his picture of a host whose great banquet had been made ready—and of what happened then.

His servant went out to carry a reminder of the dinner hour to those who had been invited. All of them were supposed to be ready to respond. But as a matter of fact, they were not. They all alike began to make excuses —excuses which in cold type look so inexcusable, but which sounded so plausible and sufficient to the men who made them.

That was not the way they sounded to the host. All the impediments that the invited guests alleged could have been foreseen and adjusted to the acceptance they had already given. But they treated their promise to be there as a trivial matter, to be moved aside if something else seemed more important. So the host was finished with them. Others to whom his banquet might be a thrilling opportunity should take their places. "Go out quickly to the streets and lanes of the city," he said to his servant, "and bring in the poor and maimed and blind and lame"; and when even these did not fill the banquet hall, the invitation was to be carried into the highways and the hedges.

The parable was addressed to men in Judaism who thought that they had an assured relationship to God. These were the religious upper classes, educated in all proper ecclesiastical conventions, who looked down on the common people, "this people that does not know the law," with aloof superiority. This common crowd—in the words of the parable—would be the lame and blind. But beyond them were those outside of Israel altogether and outside the line of religious respectability, the Samaritans and the Gentiles, who belonged in the highways and the hedges. Whoever would say that *they* had any chance of being invited into the kingdom of God? And yet that is exactly what Jesus was saying.

So it was in ancient Israel, and so it may be wherever the old inclinations are repeated. Men may lose their place in the kingdom of God, lose the supreme relationship which has been offered to their souls, simply by letting lesser things get in the way.

There are two words continually heard on radio and television which unintentionally express a fact that may be devastating. Those words are: "But first—." No matter what the news to be announced may be, no matter how crucial some impending world decision, something else must interrupt. "But first"—cigarettes; but first, beer; but first, lipstick; but first, "what doctors recommend."

From the irritation of this particular "but first" on the radio, one can try to turn away. But the obsession which it symbolizes besets us everywhere. To what do we really give priority? Is it to try to hear through the general clamor the summons of the Highest, and to answer it? Or is it to have so many things we are obsessively pursuing that we make excuses from the purposes of God? If so, it may be the unexpected and the seemingly unlikely who will find places in the kingdom of God. And many who in social and religious privilege have had every chance to be fed at the table of a heavenly inspiration may hear the voice that says, "I tell you, none of those men who were invited shall taste of my banquet."

THE CROSS OF SEPARATION

> Now great multitudes accompanied him; and he turned and said to them, "If any one comes to me and does not hate his own father and mother and wife and children and brothers and sisters, yes, and even his own life, he cannot be my disciple. Whoever does not bear his own cross and come after me, cannot be my disciple." (Luke 14:25-27.)

This chapter moves on to an increasing climax. In the story of the banquet invitations that were neglected, Jesus had made clear that a casual response to the kingdom of God is no response at all. Now his emphasis becomes more drastic. If one is to be a committed disciple, it will have to be by way of decisions that cut deep.

When Jesus spoke, he used words which compelled attention. When he said that a man might have to "hate" members of his own family, he did not mean angry repudiation. What he did mean was that a moment might come when a man would have to stand as squarely opposite to what they were standing for as he would stand against his enemies. That kind of collision might already have been experienced by some of his disciples. It certainly has occurred again and again in Christian history, when some soul drawn by the love of Christ has had to face the bitter protest and even persecution of his non-Christian family or community which was determined not to let him go. Nor is it only from avowedly pagan influences that the would-be disciple may have to separate himself. Families which by convention at least would call themselves Christian may be outraged and indignant if a boy or girl decides upon some career of sacrificial service in the name of Christ, which seems to them not in keeping with the family interest and prestige; and in that case the would-be disciple may have to suffer a cleavage which could seem as deep as hate. The stubborn selfishness and blindness of the uninspired must not block the path for one who is trying to follow the light. Such a one must go ahead even at the cost of separation, and with the sadness of knowing that there will always be those who, like friends of Albert Schweitzer who tried to keep him back from Africa, are "so far from perceiving that the . . . love preached by Jesus may sweep a man into a new course of life." [5]

So the words of vs. 27 follow understandably. A breach with those whom he has loved but who will not recognize the new ideal he is constrained to follow may be the hardest cross the Christian has to carry.

COUNTING THE COST OF FAITHFULNESS

"For which of you, desiring to build a tower, does not first sit down and count the cost, whether he has enough to complete it? Otherwise, when he has laid a foundation, and is not able to finish, all who see it begin to mock him, saying, 'This man began to build, and was not able to finish.' Or what king, going to encounter another king in war, will not sit down first and take counsel whether he is able with ten thousand to meet him who comes against him with twenty thousand? And if not, while the other is yet a great way off, he sends an embassy and asks terms of peace. So therefore, whoever of you does not renounce all that he has cannot be my disciple.

Salt is good; but if salt has lost its taste, how shall its saltness be restored? It is fit neither for the land nor for the dunghill; men throw it away. He who has ears to hear, let him hear." (Luke 14:28-35.)

[5] Albert Schweitzer, *Out of My Life and Thought* (New York: Henry Holt & Co., 1933) , p. 108.

Again the unflinching message which Jesus has been expressing is driven home. For a man to be a disciple, it is not enough to have an emotional glow and an unspecified enthusiasm. Let him consider what the adventure will actually mean to him, and whether he is prepared to pay the cost. It may seem all very well to dream of some noble structure and to be so excited about it as to gather a few building stones and to manage one hasty level of its walls; but this sort of procedure may end in nothing but frustration and the fragment of an unfinished tower. Let a man reckon what will be required not only today, but tomorrow; not only a fleeting impulsiveness, but long patience, resources of energy and devotion that will not fail.

And let him take account not only of what he wants to do and what he might do if unhindered, but also of the opposition he will meet. To wage spiritual war on behalf of the kingdom of God will not be a smooth maneuver in an open field. It will be the shock of real encounter with forces of evil that may seem to outnumber a man's good purposes and that are already entrenched. Seeing this, a man may conclude that there is no sense launching a one-sided battle; it is better to make a truce, compromise with evil; and as to an all-out struggle for the best he has believed in—call it quits.

But on the other hand, that man may be the kingly warrior who sees that he has an army of only ten thousand as against an enemy of twenty thousand, but nevertheless is not dismayed. Not dismayed because he knows there is an ultimate power in righteousness which no adversaries can finally resist. So every soul that fights under the banner of God may be able to say what Judas Maccabeus said: "The victory of battle standeth not in the multitude of an host; but strength cometh from heaven."

That can be possible if the salt has not lost its saltness. The issues of life do not depend on quantitative measurements, or on the powers of this earth. They depend upon whether or not there is in the men of God a quality of divinely given strength which nothing can destroy.

chapter 15

THE BOUNDLESS LOVE OF GOD

> Now the tax collectors and sinners were all drawing near to hear him. And the Pharisees and the scribes murmured, saying, "This man receives sinners and eats with them." (Luke 15:1-2.)

If the Gospel of Luke comprised only this one chapter, it would still be precious beyond all estimate; for here, to a degree hardly equalled in any other passage, one feels close to the divine compassion made known through Christ.

Note first the introduction. "Now the tax collectors and sinners were all drawing near to hear him." Thus Jesus attracted to himself the sort of people who are not usually supposed to be most interested in hearing about God. The tax collectors were despised because they had become part of the machine of the hated Roman government: men who had sold out what ought to have been their natural loyalties for the sake of graft from the system in power. If they had been described in modern language, they would have been called "those dirty politicians." The "sinners" were the general run of people: not notorious evildoers, but the careless and unconcerned about religious proprieties, whom the sanctimonious looked down upon as an uncovenanted lower class. But these were the men to whom Jesus had an appeal which they had not encountered before. They sensed that he was concerned with realities, not with false fronts; with human beings as they were, not as they might think they had to pretend to be. If they had ever pretended, they had long since stopped; for they knew it was no use. They knew, and everybody knew, that they were not as good as they ought to be. But in all honesty they knew something else, too. There was something in them that wanted to be better. The spark of a right conscience still glowed under the dust of old neglect, and what they saw in Jesus made it come alive. Some wistful instinct made them dare believe that this poor little spark in them belonged to the flame that was in Jesus.

But the Pharisees and scribes resented the very thing for which the tax gatherers and sinners all were grateful. Did Jesus have no sense of right distinctions—no knowledge of what among proper people simply was not done? It was bad enough that he preached in a fashion that seemed to make the riffraff want to listen. He actually went to their houses, sat down at the same table with them. If he had ever expected to have any standing among the upper classes—they murmured among themselves—he had certainly lost the chance for it by all this contact with the disreputable.

The sad fact is that there are always Pharisees who murmur in that same way—Pharisees in church and state. In church they are the men and women in the fashionable congregation who are uncomfortable if the poorly dressed stranger gets into their pew, and worse than uncomfortable if they think their minister is reaching out to welcome families who live off the avenue on the other side of the tracks. In the community they are those whose angry racial pride would keep the Negro "in his place." In their bitter obsession with their own privilege it is true of them as the prophet Amos said of people like them in ancient Israel, "they are not grieved for the affliction of Joseph" (KJV). The deprivations, the injustices, the denials of opportunity under which the disadvantaged suffer do not concern them. The one thing that matters is that they maintain their own position.

No doubt the Pharisees soon stopped listening and turned disgustedly away. This was no message that they chose to hear.

But the rest of Jesus' audience did choose to hear. The three parables which Jesus told are keyed to one haunting word, *Lost!* Among "the sinners" a quick emotion must have been waked at the sound of that one syllable: a sense of emptiness, of something gone, and the blank frustration of not knowing where to look for it. That was the wistful minor chord which reflected what for them was part of the whole reality of life. But there was also the major chord of a great assurance: the assurance of a love which reaches out to the lost, that it may be found again.

What is it like—this being lost, and being sought for, and ultimately found?

As always, Jesus made the divine facts plain not in any abstract terms, but through pictures and parables which every human being could recognize and understand. And his first parable was a simple story of a lost sheep.

THE LOST SHEEP

So he told them this parable: "What man of you, having a hundred sheep, if he has lost one of them, does not leave the ninety-nine in the wilderness, and go after the one which is lost, until he finds it? And when he has found it, he lays it on his shoulders, rejoicing. And when he comes home, he calls together his friends and his neighbors, saying to them, 'Rejoice with me, for I have found my sheep which was lost.' Even so, I tell you, there will be more joy in heaven over one sinner who repents than over ninety-nine righteous persons who need no re-pentance." (Luke 15:3-7.)

In the Galilean country there was no one to whom sheep and shepherds were not familiar. They knew how frequently, and as it seemed how stupidly, a sheep could get lost—as human beings also can. George A. Buttrick, in *The Interpreter's Bible,* has a paragraph so vivid that once read it cannot be forgotten.

The farmer came down the lane. "Got a stray," he said. "How do they get lost?" asked the city man. "They just nibble themselves lost," said the farmer; "they keep their heads down, wander from one green tuft to another, come to a hole in the fence—and never can find the hole by which to get back again." The city man answered, "Like people, like every generation of foolish men." [1]

So men do get lost: their heads down, their thoughts only on the next little satisfaction, dumbly unaware of where their impulses are leading them, and at the end of the day caught out alone in the dark.

But the major emphasis in the parable is not on the sheep but on the shepherd. Arithmetically, one lost sheep might not seem to amount to much. If that one goes, there are still ninety-nine left. But the shepherd of course does not think that way. The one sheep has value, not only as a hundredth part of the whole flock, but because that one particular sheep has an individuality of its own. In the words of Jesus, as the Gospel of John presents them, the shepherd "calls his own sheep by name and leads them out, . . . for they know his voice," and he knows them. So the love of God embodied in Christ knows human souls one by one and cannot rest when any single one has gone astray.

In the baptismal service in *The Book of Common Prayer* the first sentence before the actual baptism is, "Name this child." Thus is symbolized the fact that the child to be baptized has the dignity of his own selfhood in the eyes of God. Wherever the spirit of Christ prevails, this divine worth of every single person becomes a fact demanding all men's recognition. No one can read the Gospels thoughtfully without being struck by the way in which Jesus never treated people miscellaneously, but always with a quick and sensitive regard for the needs and hidden possibilities of every individual soul, whether it was one of the disciples with their various

[1] Exposition of Luke, VIII, 265.

temperaments, Peter, John, Matthew, Thomas; or the woman of Samaria; or the blind man by the Pool of Siloam; or Mary Magdalene in Simon the Pharisee's house. One cardinal difference between any society which means to be Christian and a society which repudiates the Christian ideals is that in the former the single human being is respected, whereas in totalitarianism that has gone pagan, whether it be Nazi or Communist, the individual is reduced to a gray nonentity. Freedom of thought, freedom of speech, freedom of a man to be himself are cut down to the drab stereotype of mass conformity. The state is everything, the person comparatively nothing. Any system of government which recognizes no higher authority than the manipulation of power for its own fanatical ends will inevitably degrade the human person. It is only when a society holds itself accountable to the Divine Shepherd that each single soul, like the single sheep, is prized.

THE LOST COIN

"Or what woman, having ten silver coins, if she loses one coin, does not light a lamp and sweep the house and seek diligently until she finds it? And when she has found it, she calls together her friends and neighbors, saying, 'Rejoice with me, for I have found the coin which I had lost.' Even so, I tell you, there is joy before the angels of God over one sinner who repents."

(Luke 15:8-10.)

The second of the three parables is based upon a comparison even more familiar than the first. Not everyone has ever lost a sheep, but there is no person anywhere who has not lost some particular thing that just had to be found again. What woman having ten silver coins, if she loses one coin, does not light a lamp and sweep the house and seek diligently until she finds it? A house turned upside down for one coin. A trivial reason for so much search?

Yes, a trivial reason, it might seem. But the very point of the parable is in what seems the triviality—and yet was not. To the Galilean hearers of Jesus' words, one silver coin represented far greater value than it suggests to modern reckoning. It was half the annual sum that had to be paid as tax to the Temple treasury by every head of a Jewish household. For a woman it would represent a great part of any savings she might have managed to put aside. To the poor, therefore, the loss of one coin could be a major calamity, and Jesus knew the lot of the poor. He had grown up among them. It may be that he was remembering his own mother in the little house in Nazareth, with a family of children to provide for and next to no money to do it with, when he spoke one day of a woman mending clothes and of how sometimes "the patch tears away from the garment, and a worse tear is made." That was what did happen sometimes: children's clothes cost so much to make or buy that they had to be worn and patched until the patches no longer held together. A household where this was true knew well enough the value of one silver coin, and how a woman who had lost it would light a lamp and sweep into every corner until she found it.

When she did find what she was searching for, she would call together her friends and neighbors, and say, "Rejoice with me, for I have found the coin which I had lost." Jesus said, "Even so, I tell you there is joy before the angels of God over one sinner who repents."

Before the angels of God. And what about before the church? That is a question which needs to be asked. L. P. Jacks, a former editor of the *Hibbert Journal,* once wrote a little book called *The Lost Radiance of the Christian Religion.* If that radiance at any time is lost, it may be because the church becomes complacent with what it has, wrapped up in its comparative well-being and indifferent to what has drifted away. Radiance comes to any Christian fellowship only when it has a great concern for souls, and therefore can know the heavenly rejoicing that wakes when the lost is found.

THE HEADSTRONG YOUNGER SON

And he said, "There was a man who had two sons; and the younger of them said to his father, 'Father, give me the share of property that falls to me.' And he divided his living between them. Not many days later, the younger son gathered all he had and took his journey into a far country, and there he squandered his property in loose living. And when he had spent everything, a great famine arose in that country, and he began to be in want. So he went and joined himself to one of the citizens of that country, who sent him into his fields to feed swine. And he would gladly have fed on the pods that the swine ate; and no one gave him anything. But when he came to himself he said, 'How many of my father's hired servants have bread enough and to spare, but I perish here with hunger! I will arise and go to my father, and I will say to him, "Father, I have sinned against heaven and before you; I am no longer worthy to be called your son; treat me as one of your hired servants." ' And he arose and came to his father. But while he was yet at a distance, his father saw him and had compassion, and ran and embraced him and kissed him. And the son said to him, 'Father, I have sinned against heaven and before you; I am no longer worthy to be called your son.' But the father said to his servants, 'Bring quickly the best robe, and put it on him; and put a ring on his hand, and shoes on his feet; and bring the fatted calf and kill it, and let us eat and make merry; for this my son was dead, and is alive again; he was lost, and is found.' And they began to make merry."   (Luke 15:11-24.)

The third parable is of course the one in which the double theme of human lostness and the love of God becomes most near and poignant. Here is not only an illustration applicable to human life. Here is life itself in its unmistakable reality.

Sermons beyond count have been preached on the parable of the prodigal son, and it is true that this title is printed at the top of the page in the King James Version of the Bible. But the curious fact is that the word "prodigal" does not occur in the parable as Luke has recounted it; moreover, one may search the Bible from end to end, and still that much-echoed word is not there. In its literal meaning the word is an accurate description of the boy who is the central figure in the parable story, for the dictionary definition is "addicted to wasteful and extravagant expenditure." This younger son did have his wild period when he was wasteful and extravagant. But "prodigal," as it has been elaborated in the fervent exordiums and warnings of ten thousand pulpits, has come to mean something more than this. The word has been surrounded by a cloud of suggestion which is sinister. "The prodigal son" is made to sound like someone who by his very nature was dissolute, if not debauched.

The result is that often the parable—or the preaching of it—has lost its sure and inescapable thrust. Those who most need its message can ward it off. Decent young people may listen to it unconcerned because they think its label does not belong on them. "I don't claim to be as good as I know I ought to be," one of them may say, "but I am not a 'prodigal.' A prodigal must mean some sort of a rotter, and I don't intend to be that. This sermon may be pious and good, but I do not have to suppose it applies to me."

But the real parable does apply to him: to the boy who means to be decent, but has in him impulses the perilous drift of which he does not know. What he is at the moment seems blameless enough. The disaster that may happen to him is still in "the far country." Not denunciation but illumination is what he needs first. Not wickedness but wrongheadedness is his immediate danger. What must be brought home to him is not a "parable of the prodigal son," but the actual parable of the *foolish* son and the unfailing father.

For in the parable as it has come to us from Jesus there is no adjective whatever that is derogatory of the younger son at the beginning of the story. The seeds of trouble were in him, but there was no gross fruitage of them yet. He had the possibilities both for good and for evil that belong in the exuberance of youth. He had the instinct to find himself and to be himself, and that could be good. It could be indeed the necessary gateway to maturity. But his trouble was that he thought he knew it all. He must "see life," and see it on his own terms without any interfering advice. He wanted to be on his own, no matter if he did not stop to think where his own came from or what it really meant. "Just let me go!"

So he brashly asked his father to give him right there and then the part of the inheritance which he assumed that someday he would properly have, and the father gave it to him. Then off he went in his satisfied irresponsibility to what he thought would be his brave new world.

He did not feel that he was doing anything evil. But it is not only flagrant and conscious evil that can make havoc of a life. As Edward Rowland Sill wrote in "The Fool's Prayer":

> 'Tis not by guilt the onward sweep
> Of truth and right, O Lord, we stay;
> 'Tis by our follies that so long
> We hold the earth from heaven away.

Yet it is true also that there is no such separation between folly and guilt as Sill's lines imply. Even though the younger son did not at first feel guilty, there was evil in what he had done. "Original sin" is no abstract idea of theologians; it is the dark current of a tendency that runs through all human life. It is the self-will and rebellion against the Highest which has been dramatized forever in the story of Adam and Eve in the garden. There are everlasting laws of accountability which cannot be broken without dire results. Sooner or later those who think there can be nothing wrong in having their own way will find this out.

And they will find it out no less inevitably, although the discovery may be not immediate. When the younger son first left home, there seemed to be no cloud in the auspicious skies. The lad had plenty of money, and because of it he had plenty of companionship. To eat, drink, and be merry: that was what suited him, and it more than suited the crowd who flocked around him—as long as the money lasted. But the time came when it was all used up. Then the supposed friends vanished; and so far as the lad who had feasted them was concerned, he could shift for himself. He could find something to live on, or starve to death for all they cared. He had thought he was on top of the world, and now he had struck bottom. Where he found himself was out in the field of a man who hired him to feed his hogs.

Then in the Gospel story there comes that unforgettable and searching phrase, "When he came to himself." He had thought he was being himself before. That was the whole restless idea in demanding what he supposed to be his freedom, so that he could go it alone. Let everybody take their hands off him, and he would show them who he was.

Now for the first time he began to know who he really was. He was his father's son. It was in forgetting this that he had played the fool. By his stupid self-assertion he had betrayed his deepest self. Perhaps he could never claim it again. But he could get back to the fringes of it. His father was still the person he had always been, who treated even his servants well.

He would go home now and be a servant, if he was not fit to be a son. Hard facts had stripped him of his vanity. He knew that he was not the smart and self-sufficient somebody he had so jauntily taken himself to be. His supposed independence had led him only into the wasteland, where he had fed on husks that the hogs had finished with. He had got beyond the point of telling himself, "What I did was only natural"; beyond the point of saying only, "I did not mean any harm." Looking at himself in honesty at last, he could acknowledge, "I have sinned." *admits error*

So he starts back from the far country. And now the spotlight of the story shifts to the father.

All the while the son had been lost, but it was the father rather than the son who had felt more the suffering involved in lostness. For much of the time the son did not even recognize that he was lost, but for the father the wistfulness of the real fact never ceased. Love cannot forget. In Dickens' *David Copperfield,* when "little Emily" had been led astray by the seducer Steerforth, Mr. Peggotty who loved her more than his own life, went out to seek for her. And as he left, he said, "Every night, as reg'lar as the night comes, the candle must be stood in its old pane of glass, that if ever she should see it, it may seem to say, 'Come back, my child, come back!'"

Likewise, with the father in the parable the candle was always burning—burning not in a window, but in his heart. When at last the day should come when the son turned home again, the unfailing love would be there to welcome him. So when the son did turn his steps that way, the watching father saw and recognized him far down the road, and had compassion, and ran and embraced and kissed him. And presently he called to the servants, "Bring quickly the best robe, and put it on him; and put a ring on his hand and shoes on his feet; and bring the fatted calf and kill it, and let us eat and make merry, for this my son was dead, and is alive again; he was lost, and is found!"

"What, no punishment?"—some have objected. "Was this the way to reward recklessness, recklessness that had led through evil associations to humiliation and disgrace? Was there to be no suffering as the consequence of sin?"

Ah, but there had been suffering, and punishment too, and something else of far deeper consequence. The punishment was in what the son had experienced and in the scars that he would always wear. But what was crucial was the fact that already there had happened the one supreme thing which punishment is meant to bring about. The boy who had been guilty was chastened now. Something real had happened in his soul. The words of the parable quoted above do not follow in that unbroken order. Before the father's command to bring the best robe, there had been the cry of the boy, "Father I have sinned against heaven and before you; I am no longer worthy to be called your son!" Now at last he knew the goodness he had offended. At last his pride and willfulness were gone. When he had left his father's house, he had done so with confident demands. He came back only with confession.

Here, then, the great major chord of the three parables reaches its climax. Over against all human lostness there is the untiring love of God. That is the eternal wonder of the Christian gospel. The saving compassion comes not because we deserve it, but when we know we need it, because all our life is emptiness without it.

This is what Mary Magdalene knew, and what Paul had learned when he wrote: "Wretched man that I am! Who will deliver me from the body of this death? Thanks be to God through Jesus Christ our Lord!" And it is what Martin Luther had discovered when he cried: "Lo to me, an unworthy, condemned, and contemptible creature, altogether without merit, my God of His pure and free mercy has given in Christ all the riches of righteousness and salvation, so that I am no longer in want of anything except faith to believe this is so." [2]

THE PRIM ELDER BROTHER

"Now his elder son was in the field; and as he came and drew near to the house, he heard music and dancing. And he called one of the servants and asked what this meant. And he said to him, 'Your brother has come, and your father has killed the fatted calf, because he has received him safe and sound.' But he was angry and refused to go in. His father came out and entreated him, but he answered his father, 'Lo, these many years I have served you, and I never disobeyed your command; yet you never gave me a kid, that I might make merry with my friends. But when this son of yours came, who has devoured your living with harlots, you killed for him the fatted calf!' And he said to him, 'Son, you are always with me, and all that is mine is yours. It was fitting to make merry and be glad, for this your brother was dead, and is alive; he was lost, and is found.' " (Luke 15:25-32.)

[2] A. C. McGiffert, *Martin Luther, the Man and His Work* (New York: The Century Co., 1911), p. 175.

The parable might have ended with the joyful return of the younger son; but, to our enrichment, it does not. It has described a human love which can represent the love of God in that it welcomes the wanderer home. But what about the kind of person who does not care whether the wanderer comes home or not, and indeed prefers that he stay where he is and take the consequences of his rebellion? Why should we be concerned with anyone who has made himself disreputable? That, in effect, was what the Pharisees had been saying when they "murmured" against Jesus because he received sinners and ate with them. Now he brings the parable to a climax in a portrayal that was meant to come home to them.

Besides the son who had gone astray, there was another one, the elder brother. He was in the field when the prodigal returned; and as he drew near the house, he saw that something important had happened, but he did not know what. He called one of the servants and inquired, and was outraged at what he heard. The boy who had disgraced the family had come back, and a great commotion of welcome had been set on foot. He was so angry that he would not go into the house; and when his father came out to entreat him, he answered with an indignation that grates through every word he spoke. "These many years I have served you," he exclaimed. "I have never disobeyed your command." And then his resentment poured out in words the bitterness of which can be realized only when the contrasts among them are underlined. "You never gave *me* a *kid,* that I might make merry with *my* friends. But when *this* son of yours came, you killed for *him* the *fatted calf!*"

He thought his anger was completely justified. What justice was there in treating the bad man more generously than the good man? *He* was the good man. And what special favor had been shown to him? If anybody wanted to welcome this wastrel, *he* would have no part in it. "This son of yours, this precious son of yours, is no brother of mine anymore!"

How truly representative that elder son is of many persons in every time —the good and proper people. They have never done anything conspicuously wrong. They never went off on wild adventures. They have never been mixed up with an unsavory crowd. As members of the church or the community they have kept the commandments and the conventions. They ought to be recognized for their moral excellence; and they ought to be able to expect that they will not be asked to establish or reestablish relationships with those who have not behaved themselves.

So the modern elder brothers might repeat, on the basis of what appeared to be the legitimate protest of the elder brother in the parable. But, when looked at again, that protest begins to fall apart. That tale of having wanted to "make merry" with his friends! When would that grudging nature of his have wanted to make merry, and what is the likelihood that he had any friends? And the imputation that his father never gave anything to him: the truth was that everything his father had was at his disposal. The tragedy lay in this: that he never really wanted the best that his father could have given him. He wanted to hold on to the material inheritance, but he had no warm desire to inherit his father's spirit. If the analogy were taken up into the Christian churches, the parable would apply to those men and women who want the church to be a nice ecclesiastical club, with no responsibility to bring in the souls that stay outside.

Thus in the parable Jesus portrayed the Pharisaic spirit as it was and is. But there was no harshness in what he said; instead, there was a gentle understanding that might melt an icy self-esteem. In the Greek text the word the father uses is more tender than the usual word for son. It is as though he said, "My child"—his child who had not grown up to his full self—"My child, I love you for your rectitude and your faithfulness to what you have felt to be your duty. All that I seek is to save you from self-righteousness, and to have your goodness be the kind of goodness that will help others to be good."

One further thought arises out of the parable, certainly not written into it, yet blossoming from it. It is the thought of what the elder brother might have been. Suppose that instead of wrapping himself in his own contentment, he had sought the one who had gone away: sought him, found him, and brought him home. That was what the divine Elder Brother did, in Galilee, in Jerusalem, in Gethsemane, on Calvary.

Out of the First World War there came a recollection of two brothers. They were in the foremost trenches at the worst point of the Flanders battlefront. The younger brother ventured out at dusk into no-man's-land, was caught in a burst of enemy machine-gun fire, and collapsed into a shell-hole, helpless. His older brother, seeing what had happened, determined to go and help him. His comrades in the trench tried to hold him back. He would only be shot himself, and do no good. But he did go out; and though he was wounded, he did get to his brother's side. When darkness came, they were both brought in, the older brother with wounds deeper than the younger. And what the younger brother had said to him was this: "I knew that you would come!"

So the human heart expresses its instinct when it thinks of Jesus. "I knew that you would come." That is the way it must be with the love of God. Through all risks and sacrifices, it will be coming to seek and to save the lost.

chapter 16

THE MATERIAL IN THE GOSPEL

In this chapter Luke gathers together two parables and some other
sayings of Jesus which had come to him from the recollections of
the Christian community. Luke had not been among the "eyewitnesses" to
whom he refers in the prologue of his Gospel, nor among those who
might be called the "earwitnesses," either. He had not himself listened to
Jesus. He had to depend upon men and women who could tell him, "This
is what I heard Jesus say"; or perhaps sometimes on those who could say
only, "This is what a friend of mine told me that he heard him say." Consequently, it must be recognized that some of what Luke wrote down had
come to him in broken bits; and when these bits were put together, they
did not always make a consistent whole. Words of Jesus spoken at different
times and in different connections may have been reported in ways that
overlap, and in our reading of them they have to be unraveled if the meaning is to grow clear. That leaves us with uncertainties of interpretation
which we should prefer not to have to admit, but the road to truth always begins with honest facing of the facts. One cardinal fact is that
the mind of Jesus outranged the minds of the average people who listened
to him, and so it is inevitable that we do not get a full, certain reflection
of what he said.

All the more impressive, therefore, is the realization that even through
the fragmentary reports which Luke and the other Evangelists collated,
there comes an impression of Jesus which is self-authenticating. "Never
man spoke like this man"; and no other could. His sayings which have
been handed down—or, rather, the imperfect memories of those sayings—
are like the broken colors that come through prisms; but, all the same,
they reflect the sovereign light. No matter what difficulties may be here and
there, the reports of his teaching make clear the surpassing uniqueness of
Jesus in the width, depth, and height of what he said and what he was:
his keenness of perception, his understanding of human nature, his blazing
moral authority and yet his infinite compassion, his greatness that was
most manifest in that he stooped to serve.

THE MAN WHO
WAS UNPRINCIPLED BUT CLEVER

He also said to the disciples, "There was a rich man who had a steward, and charges were brought to him that this man was wasting his goods. And he called him and said to him, 'What is this that I hear about you? Turn in the account of your stewardship, for you can no longer be steward.' And the steward said to himself, 'What shall I do, since my master is taking the stewardship away from me? I am not strong enough to dig, and I am ashamed to beg. I have decided what to do, so that people may receive me into their houses when I am put out of the stewardship.' So, summoning his master's debtors one by one, he said to the first, 'How much do you owe my master?' He said, 'A hundred measures of oil.' And he said to him, 'Take your bill, and sit down quickly and write fifty.' Then he said to another, 'And how much do you owe?' He said, 'A hundred measures of wheat.' He said to him, 'Take your bill, and write eighty.' The master commended the dishonest steward for his prudence; for the sons of this world are wiser in their own generation than the sons of light." (Luke 16:1-8.)

The first parable in this chapter is a special example of some of the ambiguities we have noticed. At first reading it can sound incredible. Did Jesus really say what it seems he is made to say?

For here is the story of a rascal who appears to have been commended for his rascality. He was the executive manager of a rich man's property. He had begun to think that everything was easy and safe for him, and had handled affairs with careless extravagance. Suddenly his employer discovers this, and confronts the agent with his record. "What is this that I hear about you?" he demands; and without waiting for any elaborate answer, he tells this man, who up until then had held his position of trust, to hand in his accounts and get out.

So the former manager has lost his job; and, in light of the facts, he knows well enough that no one is likely to give him another one. Where, then, shall he turn next? His pride will not let him be a beggar; and he has been in his soft berth too long to think that he can work with his hands. He must frame up some special answer for his emergency, and do it quick.

What he does is to call together some of those who are in debt to his employer. "How much do you owe on that account of yours?" he says to one man; the man answers that he owes for a hundred measures of oil. "We'll fix that bill," says the agent, "to show that you owe for only fifty."

Then to the next man: "What do you owe?"

"A hundred measures of wheat."

"Sit down there and change it to eighty," says the agent.

It can be assumed that the debtors did not take it upon themselves to ask any questions. This was a lucky break, and doubtless they went away delighted. That was exactly what the ex-manager was counting on. He had lost his job, but he figured that he was establishing credit in a new bank. He had done favors to some people, and put them under a lasting obligation. When he needed help, they would have to help him. He had met an emergency which might have been a total loss, and he had used it in such a way as to give good hope for future dividends.

So the employer, when he heard about it, commended the dishonest steward. Commended him for what? For his dishonesty? No: but for the fact that if he was dishonest, he was also smart. Instead of falling into a panic, he was cool enough to make a plan. He could look ahead and use the present moment to serve the future.

If, nevertheless, the question remains why, and under what circumstances, Jesus chose to tell this particular parable, we can give no dogmatic answer. But we can make a guess—and a guess based upon the fact that Jesus, with his sure perceptiveness into all the complex reality of human life, saw the ironic humor in its contradictions. Here was a crook who had one great asset: his quick wit. And the good people? "The sons of this world are wiser in their own generation than the sons of light." In other words, the rascals are sometimes more intelligent than the would-be righteous. There is no reason why this should be. And so perhaps what he meant was to remind his often blundering disciples that in addition to good hearts it was important that they also use their brains. What would *they* do in a crisis? How far could *they* look ahead and find new possibilities when what they had depended upon before was swept away?

THE EVERLASTING VALUES

"And I tell you, make friends for yourselves by means of unrighteous mammon, so that when it fails they may receive you into the eternal habitations."
(Luke 16:9.)

Verse 9 may or may not have been an original part of the parable. It sounds as though it might have been one of the fragmentary echoes of the words of Jesus which came to the Evangelist from an unspecified connection, but which he added here to the parable because the idea of making friends suggested a relationship to what the unrighteous steward had done. In any case, the verse as a whole strikes a wider note than that of praise for worldly cleverness, which was the central emphasis of the parable. In these words of Jesus there is an eschatological dimension. He is thinking of what may happen to men not only at some passing crisis of their earthly fortunes, but at the end of life itself, when its ultimate accounts are balanced. The man in the parable might hope to find a temporary welcome in the houses of those with whom he had established a specious friendship; but how will a man find welcome in "the eternal habitations"? By having created friendships—but friendships built not on sordid schemes but on the outreach and upreach of his soul. Let him use his money and his possessions with responsibility for others, with compassion for the poor, with a love for God and man that might make him at length fit for the communion of the saints. Then their fellowship might be his welcome in God's house.

Here, as again and again in the Gospels, there come into sudden view the vistas which are infinite. It is easy for our thoughts to become earth-bound, easy to settle down into an unthinking existence which ignores the great beyond. But outside our curtained windows lies the untraveled road that we must walk when Death, the awesome messenger from God, has opened the door; and the great truthfulness of Jesus must make men conscious of that road and of the certainty that they will go out upon it. At the end of the road will they find "the eternal habitations," a fulfillment of life where all that is beautiful and best will be secure and strong? It will depend upon the values they have been seeking here. Life on the other side is not an unrelated gift; it is the goodness and greatness of soul which men have longed for—*if* they have longed for it—made real at last in the presence of God. In the Greek text of the Gospel, there is a striking conjunction of unexpected words which kindle a wondering imagination. What both the King James Version and the Revised Standard Version translate as "habitations" is actually the Greek *skenai,* or "tents." But how can a tent be an eternal habitation? A tent is by nature a transient thing, a shelter for one stage of a journey that is still continuing. Perhaps it is in exactly this seeming contradiction that the meaning of eternal life is found—the eternal life which souls may already anticipate if their desires and devotion turn increasingly toward the things of God. It is as the lines of the old hymn by James Montgomery put it:

> Yet nightly pitch my moving tent
> A day's march nearer home.

If mind and heart are making such daily journeys as they can in God's direction, then the angel that summons us for the final pilgrimage will seem benignant, and the end of the road the arrival home.

FAITHFULNESS

"He who is faithful in a very little is faithful also in much; and he who is dishonest in a very little is dishonest also in much. If then you have not been faithful in the unrighteous mammon, who will entrust to you the true riches? And if you have not been faithful in that which is another's, who will give you that which is your own? No servant can serve two masters; for either he will hate the one and love the other, or he will be devoted to the one and despise the other. You cannot serve God and mammon."

(Luke 16:10-13.)

Verses 10-13 seem at first to make an abrupt transition from the parable and the particular picture of human character which it so vividly presents. Standing by itself, the parable might seem just an intriguing bit of realism, the main effect of which is to win wry admiration for a rascal's cleverness. But the Evangelist is concerned that the parable shall not be left with this effect. It would of course be a perversion of Jesus' total interpretation of the values of human life if anyone were left with the impression that crooked dealing might be glorified. So the Evangelist incorporates here what Jesus had said once about the kind of faithfulness in material matters which the steward had conspicuously lacked. That man had been irresponsible in regard to what another man had entrusted to him; he would be equally irresponsible with the whole of what God had entrusted to him— namely, his entire life and his soul. A man's character comes out in the decisions of every day. If he is dishonest in the little things, he will be dishonest all along the line.

Particularly, Luke is emphasizing here the corrupting power which obsession with money may always have. All through his Gospel Luke reflects his sense of the peril which riches—or the desire to get rich and to stay rich—may present. And who will say that he is not right? It is possible for a man to be rich and to use his riches with humility and magnificent devotion; but what is *not* possible is for the man to retain his real manhood when his wealth becomes his ruling passion as the symbol of his self-importance. Little by little he is engrossed in what he has and unaware of what he is: self-absorbed, satisfied, and hollow. He has an idol now, and under the influence of that idol his generous imagination withers. He may think that the idol is not his master and that all the while he has a more proper loyalty. Does he not sit in his pew on Sundays, send his children to Sunday school, say his memorized grace at dinner? He likes to consider himself a Christian—if it does not cost too much. But in the decisive matters, he cannot serve God and mammon; and gradually God fades out.

MAN'S JUDGMENT, AND GOD'S

The Pharisees, who were lovers of money, heard all this, and they scoffed at him. But he said to them, "You are those who justify your-

217

selves before men, but God knows your hearts; for what is exalted among men is an abomination in the sight of God." (Luke 16:14-15.)

It would perhaps have been more precise if Luke had said *some* Pharisees instead of *the* Pharisees. The origin of Pharisaism had been noble, and in many of the Pharisees there was an unselfish devotion to what they believed to be the covenant which God had made with Israel, and the meticulous law for life and worship which they were bound to obey. The love of money was not a fault more characteristic of them than of other groups. But the fact that it could be attributed to them reveals what sometimes can be true: that the pious may fall into the subtle falsehood that their piety entitles them to prosper. If they serve God—or seem to— why should they not be visibly rewarded? And if they do prosper, then it is an easy and pleasant assumption that their prosperity is a sign that God has taken note of how deserving they must be. So more and more their outward seeming may hide their essential hollowness. With their religious orthodoxy they have justified themselves, and the supposition they have created in their community that such pious men must naturally be good has exalted them further in their self-esteem. "But God knows your hearts; for what is exalted among men is an abomination in the sight of God."

THE OLD AND THE NEW

"The law and the prophets were until John; since then the good news of the kingdom of God is preached, and every one enters it violently. But it is easier for heaven and earth to pass away, than for one dot of the law to become void.

"Every one who divorces his wife and marries another commits adultery, and he who marries a woman divorced from her husband commits adultery." (Luke 16:16-18.)

Once again Luke has remembered sayings of Jesus which had come to him from somewhere and which he incorporates here to expand the message which had been expressed in the preceding words. At first sight it is difficult to perceive what connection there is between vss. 14-15 and the seemingly quite disconnected sayings of Jesus in 16-18 which Luke adds so abruptly. The particular association in the Evangelist's thought, and the exact meaning of vs. 16, can only be a matter of conjecture; for the words of Jesus which he quotes were spoken on some special occasion which he perhaps knew but we cannot know, and which stand now in the written Gospel abbreviated and without the framework of time and circumstance which would have made their immediate relevance clearer to us.

But there is suggestion in the fact that Luke has just been recounting what Jesus had said to some Pharisees. As was evident so often, they were men who plumed themselves for their religious standing. In their own regard they were justified. But there may be a vast and tragic difference between what a man likes to believe about himself and what God sees him actually to be.

Then come the words of vs. 16: "The law and the prophets were until John; since then the good news of the kingdom of God is preached, and every one enters it violently." What does *that* mean? one asks in a moment of bewilderment. Certainly the beginning of the meaning is in the fact that with the ministry of John the Baptist, the forerunner of Jesus, there came a crucial turning point in history. Before John, the best that men had known was the message of the Old Testament, "the law and the prophets." It was of this that the Pharisees made themselves the proud exponents—and especially of the law. But in the proclamation of John, and in the ministry of Jesus, there was a new message: the message of the love of God which reaches out to those who could never in themselves attain the righteousness—or the supposed righteousness—of the men who thought they kept the law. To the Pharisees, what Jesus said and what he did seemed nothing short of outrageous. He went out among the sinners. He appeared to be opening the doors of the kingdom of God to people who had no proper standing according to the codes which the rabbis and scribes interpreted as the divine commandments. What would happen to respectable religion if this sort of violence went on? What except the destruction of all the distinctiveness which had been the pride and glory of Israel?

Well, there were some things that had to be destroyed: self-righteousness, the idea of exclusive privilege, and the hard conviction that living within the fixed prescriptions of the law was the same thing as being good. The truth was that the law might freeze those intuitions of the heart in which the living word of God is speaking. Where there is no love, law can be manipulated until it becomes an instrument of cruelty. That is what Jesus was recognizing when he said that everyone who divorces his wife and marries another commits adultery, and he who marries a woman divorced from her husband commits adultery. In the Old Testament book of Deuteronomy it had been written that a man might divorce his wife "because he hath found some uncleanness in her"; and Hillel, one of the great rabbis and teachers of the law, in interpreting that scripture had said that a man could divorce his wife for spoiling the dinner. Against that coldhearted legalism Jesus lifted up the standard of the heavenly spirit by which alone human relationships can be made secure. In this one

219

sentence about divorce—which Luke has interjected so suddenly and without interpretation into his narrative—Jesus was not pronouncing some inflexible dictum for twentieth-century churchmen to enact into canon law. He was exalting the ideal by which marriage can be delivered altogether from any wretched question of divorce: the ideal of a faithful love which can be possible for those who have entered into the kingdom of the love of God.

Thus in discounting the law of the scribes and rabbis where it had become mean and pettifogging, Jesus did not separate himself from the conviction which was at the heart of the Jewish law: namely, that there is a sovereign will of God to which all life is meant to be obedient; and for him "all life" encompassed not only the outward act, but the inner motive. Not by compulsion, but by the spontaneous answer of the heart, men should choose for their allegiance those standards of living which would not fall short of, but rather go beyond, the highest which the law had bid men serve.

"It is easier for heaven and earth to pass away, than for one dot of the law to become void," said Jesus. Thus, as he often did, Jesus set forth a truth with broad emphatic strokes and by magnified illustration, in order that there might be no doubt as to the positiveness of what he said. A *dot*—or a *title* as the King James Version has it—was "one of the little horns or minute projections which distinguish Hebrew letters—one from another." The rabbis believed that it was a sacrilege to change one of these minutiae of the sacred text; and the different and greater thing which Jesus is saying in his figure of speech is that the real law, the essential moral message of life to be lived in the light of God which the Old Testament represented, is eternal. The ethical imperatives do not change, and men's everyday behavior must be built upon the proved rock foundations: honesty, faithfulness, self-discipline, purity of body and of mind.

There is need today that this should be remembered. Theological fashions of speech may throw truth out of balance. In some circles one may hear the term "moralism" bandied about as by a circle of parrots which have glibly got hold of a disparaging word. The original meaning of "moralism" for those who used it thoughtfully had to do with something that was real. It was a word of rebuke for the kind of stuffed-shirt respectability which can make a man imagine that he is religious because he has been conventionally decent. His self-righteous soul may desperately need to be humbled and to be made new by the grace of God. But he does not think so. He supposes that he is good enough already. This kind of "moralism" does deserve to be condemned. But back of the chattering use of the word there may grow up a dangerous falsehood. Because men must be "saved by grace" and not through their own deserving, it may be assumed that they have no personal responsibility. What they do or do not do will not matter much. Therefore, why be too strict with one's self? A little dissipation, a little illicit dabbling in sex—God will forgive that. Maybe morals are only "moralism" anyhow. So the easygoing may try to tell themselves, but the end of that sort of slipperiness can be damnation.

DIVES AND LAZARUS

"There was a rich man, who was clothed in purple and fine linen and who feasted sumptuously every day. And at his gate lay a poor man named Lazarus, full of sores, who desired to be fed with what fell from the rich man's table; moreover the dogs came and licked his sores. The poor man died and was carried by the angels to Abraham's bosom. The rich man also died and was buried; and in Hades, being in torment, he lifted up his eyes, and saw Abraham far off and Lazarus in his bosom. And he called out, 'Father Abraham, have mercy upon me, and send Lazarus to dip the end of his finger in water and cool my tongue; for I am in anguish in this flame.' But Abraham said, 'Son, remember that you in your lifetime received your good things, and Lazarus in like manner evil things; but now he is comforted here, and you are in anguish. And besides all this, between us and you a great chasm has been fixed, in order that those who would pass from here to you may not be able, and none may cross from there to us.' And he said, 'Then I beg you, father, to send him to my father's house, for I have five brothers, so that he may warn them, lest they also come into this place of torment.' But Abraham said, 'They have Moses and the prophets; let them hear them.' And he said, 'No, father Abraham; but if some one goes to them from the dead, they will repent.' He said to him, 'If they do not hear Moses and the prophets, neither will they be convinced if some one should rise from the dead.' "

(Luke 16:19-31.)

As this chapter began with a parable, so it ends with another one, the parable of a rich man and a beggar. In the Greek text of the Gospel, the first man is not named; but when Jerome in the fourth century translated the New Testament into his Vulgate version, the Latin word he used for rich was *dives;* and from that adjective has come the traditional name.

The parable is in two scenes, and both of them are vivid. The first scene is on this earth; the second is in that world beyond our seeing to which the dead go when the business of this earth is finished.

In the first scene there is a contrast which every line of the description accentuates. Dives lives in his palatial house. His clothes are elegant; his food is sumptuous—not only occasionally, but every day. Outside the gates of his house and grounds lies a beggar, half-naked, sick and miserable,

221

so weak that he cannot drive off the scavenger dogs that come smelling at his sores. There is no evidence that Dives was conspicuously cruel. He did not send out orders to get rid of the beggar. He was willing that his servants should throw out the scraps of food from his table when he had finished. But beyond that he did not disturb himself. Lazarus meant nothing to him. If he went out through the gate where Lazarus was, he could look the other way.

Thus Dives was a type of those who exist in every age—the padded rich. He did not want to come into contact with what would disturb his sensibilities. Not infrequently rich people may be charitable in a distant and perfunctory way: sit at a directors' meeting of some welfare organization, tell a secretary to send a check to the "100 Neediest Fund" at Christmas. But close contact with the actual poor would be too uncomfortable. Let Lazarus stay outside the gates.

One thing that was forever true of Jesus was his instant compassion for the poor and forlorn. The common people heard him gladly, because his heart was tuned to the common lot. And Luke reflects all through his Gospel this spirit of his Master. So in his telling of the parable, as elsewhere, Luke is the champion of the poor: not that he supposed that being poor made a man good and being rich made a man wicked, but because he knew that out of poverty may actually come humility and patience; and the poor, having no surfeit of material things, may be more sensitive to the value of the things that are unseen. Moreover, in the portrayal of Lazarus and Dives, Luke is reflecting the passionate conviction that sometime, and in God's greater world, the bitter inequities of this world will be set right. So the parable moves on to the second scene in which Lazarus is comforted and Dives, who before had wrapped himself in his self-indulgence, is in anguish.

As one considers this second scene, it is important not to be led into unwarranted assumptions. In what Jesus said, we do not have a sort of roadmap to that which lies on the other side of death. According to the Jewish thinking of the time, Hades, or Sheol, was the place where all souls must wait for the final judgment, with Gehenna and its fires on one side, and Paradise with its fountains on the other. And between the two a great chasm had been fixed. That was the background Jesus used for the eternal drama of the parable, but he was not giving a categorical description of the future life. Some of the facts he suggested in symbols, but the ultimate realities are veiled in mystery still. As it is recorded by Mark that he said of the coming of the end, "No one knows, not even the angels in heaven, nor the Son, but only the Father."

Through the second part of this parable great solemn warnings glow,

222

like signals in the night. The first of these is the certainty of judgment and the dreadful finality of what may be its verdict. In this life Dives had everything; when the material satisfactions in which he had wrapped himself were stripped away by death, he had nothing—and was nothing. "Son, remember," said the voice of Abraham to him. To remember—what awful inner torment may be in that! To remember what one *might* have done and *might* have been, the opportunities forever lost, the human relationships neglected, the stirrings of conscience that used to come but then were smothered until they came no more! When it is too late we may wish that all were different, wish that the light of the Spirit had been kept burning in our souls. But the stark reality may be as in the parable of the wedding feast in Matthew's Gospel. When those whose lamps had flickered out bestirred themselves and came hurrying toward the house of light and life, the final word for them was written in grim monosyllables: *the door was shut.*

So it might have seemed to be for Dives, but at the climax of the parable Dives begs that it may not be so for his brothers who are still on earth. In the fact that at least he was concerned now for somebody besides himself, is there the glimmer of a new spirit by which Dives might begin to be redeemed? Or is his idea that Lazarus might be summoned out of Paradise to go and be a messenger to his brothers only another evidence of Dives' instinctive old assumption that what belonged to him was entitled to special treatment? We cannot tell; but the answer to his request has clear and grave significance. "If they do not hear Moses and the prophets, neither will they be convinced if someone should rise from the dead." It is easy to imagine that if we had some startling revelation, it would save us; and easy also to think that until some such revelation comes along, there is nothing immediate for us to do. Thus the woman of Samaria said to Jesus: "I know that the Messiah is coming; when he comes, he will show us all things." But until that happened, she could shrug off the word of life which even at that moment was speaking to her ears. Men are not saved by waiting superstitiously for signs; and the living signs of God's nearness will be lost upon them if they grow inattentive to the elemental ways in which they learn the truth. John R. H. Moorman, the Bishop of Ripon, has written:

Many people try to by-pass the fundamentals of the spiritual life. . . . They ask themselves . . . "Why does God seem so remote to me? Why are my prayers so dry and formal? Why does my Communion mean so little to me and apparently so much to other people?" And the answer is: Because you have not set yourself to the discipline of beginning where you ought to begin, with the Scriptures, the revelation of the nature and will of God in "the Law and the Prophets," and in the Gospel of Christ.[1]

What then is the final message of the parable? Does it close all doors of redemption and hope for Dives and his brothers—and for those of us who may be their spiritual kinsmen? The soul cries out in longing that it may not be so! God who is the Everlasting Mercy may hold his undefeated purpose that all his children, including the most unfaithful, shall finally be brought home. But even so, it would have to be at cost of heavy anguish, if the turn in the road is ignored too long.

[1] John R. H. Moorman, *The Path to Glory: Studies in the Gospel According to Saint Luke* (London: S.P.C.K., 1960), pp. 198-99.

chapter 17

INCREASE OUR FAITH

And he said to his disciples, "Temptations to sin are sure to come; but woe to him by whom they come! It would be better for him if a millstone were hung round his neck and he were cast into the sea, than that he should cause one of these little ones to sin. Take heed to yourselves; if your brother sins, rebuke him, and if he repents, forgive him; and if he sins against you seven times in the day, and turns to you seven times, and says, 'I repent,' you must forgive him."

The apostles said to the Lord, "Increase our faith!" And the Lord said, "If you had faith as a grain of mustard seed, you could say to this sycamine tree, 'Be rooted up, and be planted in the sea,' and it would obey you."

(Luke 17:1-6.)

Often as we read the words of Jesus which the Evangelist has gathered from the report of others and written down, we wish that we knew more of the circumstances in which they were spoken: who was there, what moved Jesus at the moment, what immediate purpose glowed in his words. Sometimes there is a suggestion, even when there is not a specific account. Here Jesus is speaking to his disciples; and from what has been indicated earlier in the Gospel narrative, it is during the journey that began when Jesus set his face to go to Jerusalem. According to the Gospel of Mark, when the disciples first knew where Jesus meant to lead them, they were amazed, and some of them were afraid. So it may be that they continued to be tense and troubled, apprehensive as to what lay ahead and therefore sometimes on edge with one another.

Trials would have to come, Jesus told them. The days ahead would have their pitfalls: temptations, perhaps, to be discouraged and doubtful. There was no blame in the fact that such temptations might assail them. The crucial matter was in what they did with these temptations—or what the temptations did to them. Let each man be sure that he met his inner test as best he could, that he fought in his private self against his fears and the fractiousness that they might lead to, so that no failure on his part would be reason for a worse failure on the part of those weaker than himself. For a man in his own person to offend against truth and right was bad enough. Yet he might deal subsequently with the consequences of his sin, by repentance and by deliberate change. But if he made another to offend, he has caused something which he cannot correct and given a hurt which he cannot heal. The knowledge of that and the responsibility for it would be like a millstone round his neck.

But what if the facts are the other way—the offense not one that a man has committed, but one committed against him? In the first place the reality has to be faced. There is no use in letting it fester under the surface, keeping silent as though nothing has happened, while secretly brooding over it. The friend who has done a wrong must be helped to know it. The integrity of friendship requires nothing less than that. But then if the one who has done the wrong is sorry, there must be unlimited for-giveness: forgiveness flowing from such depths of understanding and com-passion that like a fountain of clean water it can wash away whatever stain the relationship has had. A hard requirement, that? Yes, but not unthink-able for men who had been in the company of Jesus. Regarding one another as he would regard them, they might attain a sympathy with the wrongdoer which could be the one thing needful to take a millstone from around *his* neck—and help them believe, in their own extremity, that the mercy of God might take away the millstone which they themselves had deserved to wear.

Yet, how could these things be? the disciples wondered. Their Master's expectation seemed so far above their reach. "Increase our faith," they begged him. As they went up toward Jerusalem, they needed mightily to believe in the possibility of what they knew they did not have: steadiness to keep from offending one another, humility and gentleness if they were themselves offended, courage to go on bravely through the dangers they would have to face together. For all that, they needed faith in something bigger than themselves. How could that faith come? *Feeding of 5000 take what have*

The eminent New Testament scholar, C. H. Dodd, of Cambridge, has written a memorable definition: Faith "is an act which is the negation of all activity, a moment of passivity out of which the strength for action comes, because in it God acts." [1] It is an act in that it is the deliberate purpose of the self to be ready for God, but it is a negation of all activity in that it is an end to tension, inward clamor, and futile self-assertion. In quietness, the soul lays itself open to what may come to it from a world beyond its own. Then into its emptiness the power of God can flow, as the

---

[1] C. H. Dodd, *The Epistle of Paul to the Romans* ("The Moffatt New Testament Com-mentary" [New York: Harper and Brothers, 1932]), VI, 16.

tide comes in from the unseen ocean to the shallow, sequestered bay, to lift the stranded ships and set them free.

For that sort of faith there can be no limits. Jesus pictured it, as he so often drew his pictures of spiritual reality, in great sweeping strokes, to express the possible which to tame spirits would seem beyond all possibility. "You could say to this sycamine tree, 'Be rooted up, and be planted in the sea,' and it would obey you." Men might gasp at such a hyperbole as that. Could any faith *they* could obtain ever have results so great as to seem miraculous? "Try, and see," was what Jesus, in effect, was saying. Take what little reliance in God you already have and plant it in the ground of today's direct obedience. Make the next venture in courage that your duty calls for. Out of that seed can come a harvest beyond all your present measurement.

THE UNRELENTING OBLIGATION

"Will any one of you, who has a servant plowing or keeping sheep, say to him when he has come in from the field, 'Come at once and sit down at table'? Will he not rather say to him, 'Prepare supper for me, and gird yourself and serve me, till I eat and drink; and afterward you shall eat and drink'? Does he thank the servant because he did what was commanded? So you also, when you have done all that is commanded you, say, 'We are unworthy servants; we have only done what was our duty.' "

(Luke 17:7-10.)

After what Jesus had said about offenses, forgiveness, and faith, comes this parable. In reading it one needs to remember again the fact that the Gospel is not a continuous journal of what Jesus said and did, but sometimes broken bits of remembrance and report—like pieces out of a mosaic which have their real meaning only when we can relate them to other pieces and to see the whole pattern emerge. This particular parable set forth in vivid color is one, and only one, aspect of the relationship between a human soul and God.

In that relationship there must be no arrant self-assertion. Jesus put his illustration in extreme terms, though in terms which were entirely familiar to his hearers. There was no doubt in that first-century world about the position of a servant. He might be a slave. He belonged completely to his master. So the servant did not have any light and casual idea about what he was bound to do. He might have worked in the fields all day; and when he came out of them at sundown, dog-tired, he would have liked to sit down and eat and rest. But that was not his privilege. Instead, he washed his hands, changed his clothes, and went to get his master's supper. And did he expect any effusive tribute for that? He did not. He knew that his obligation was to give unlimited service, and the last thing he had better do would be to mope about it and to condole himself.

So, said Jesus—with the note of sternness which sometimes he used to stab the easy-going and self-indulgent wide awake—there can be no limits to the devotion which a man owes to God. Who has a right to say, "Thus far and no farther," in his spiritual commitment, and to begin to whimper when life is hard? Yet there are many who are tempted to do just that. "Why do other people, the church, the community, my own inconvenient conscience—God, in short—demand so much of me? I've done my share. Let somebody else take hold." All this can sound reasonable, but it can be perilous. Self-pity can infect the moral nature and sap its strength; complete devotion can release in a man an energy he did not know he had. The great servants of God are those who do not watch the clock or count the cost.

Such, then, may be the message and purpose of the parable. But honesty will not let us pretend to be too sure. The fact is that we do not know exactly under what circumstances and to whom the parable was spoken. If Jesus was speaking primarily to the disciples, what he may have been doing was keeping them from spiritual flabbiness and making them remember that there could be stern requirements for service in God's kingdom. But on the other hand, he may have been speaking to quite another group: men who represented the rigid literalism of Jewish law. In this case he may have meant this parable to describe not what *is* the most real relationship between God and man, but a distorted *idea* of it which is forever insufficient. The religion of some of the men who may have been listening to Jesus was actually a thing which did not rise much above a forced obedience. They had let the law which the rabbis had elaborated become slavery, a bondage of obligations which had no end; and the more they tried to keep the law, the more they discovered new requirements which they had not kept. So in their ecclesiastical loyalty there could be no spontaneous gladness. The burden of commandments which they had to carry got heavier all the time, and God seemed to be only an exacting taskmaster who never could be satisfied.

If we were only slaves in the sight of God, then it would be true that nothing we could ever do would be any more than the drab routine of unwilling duty. There is the great fact of duty, but that is only half the truth; and the meaning of duty is understood only when it is seen in its supreme relationship. What the eagerness of Jesus continually sought to make men understand was that they are not slaves but sons, children of the heavenly Father who would have them enter into the fullness of their sonship. Then all life can become not a dull obedience to law, but the joyous response of love toward him who first loved us.

THE ONE OUT OF TEN

> On the way to Jerusalem he was passing along between Samaria and Galilee. And as he entered a village, he was met by ten lepers, who stood at a distance and lifted up their voices and said, "Jesus, Master, have mercy on us." When he saw them he said to them, "Go and show yourselves to the priests." And as they went they were cleansed. Then one of them, when he saw that he was healed, turned back, praising God with a loud voice; and he fell on his face at Jesus' feet, giving him thanks. Now he was a Samaritan. Then said Jesus, "Were not ten cleansed? Where are the nine? Was no one found to return and give praise to God except this foreigner?" And he said to him, "Rise and go your way; your faith has made you well." (Luke 17:11-19.)

This story of the lepers will have an element of difficulty for readers who bring to it the instinctive analytical questioning of a scientific age. Was this the literal fact—Jesus healing ten men at once, and doing it by words spoken to them while they stood at a distance, as lepers with their warning cry of "unclean" were compelled to do? In the first-century world there was less concern than there would be now for meticulous scrutiny. When men believed in marvels anyway, they did not have prosaic measurement for details. Therefore if some astonishing event happened, the proportions of it might grow as the report of it was passed from one group to another. So the story may have come to Luke magnified in its repeated telling. At the core of it lies the essential fact, reflected throughout the Gospels, that Jesus did have an astonishing power of healing which individuals had experienced and of which the crowd had heard. What mattered most was not the details of the happening, but the light which it threw upon the figure of Jesus who was at its center.

The first impression of him which the Evangelist reflects is his compassion. Lepers in Palestine had become a familiar sight. Their disease was so dreaded that the sight of a leper was likely to produce not pity but revulsion. Lepers were driven apart to exist in their wretched hideouts as best they could. But these lepers recognized in Jesus a different spirit. Here was one who would treat them not as outcasts. "Jesus, Master, have mercy on us!" they cried.

Then, in relation to the compassion of Jesus, the thought of Luke turns to the unhappy fact—which may be all too common—of the human failure to acknowledge it. Whether there were ten healed or not, it had been remembered that among those who *were* healed only one had come back to

Jesus to pour out his gratitude. It was this one alone who received the final blessing. Whether or not the King James translation at this point is as precise a rendering of the Greek text as the Revised Standard Version, there is sudden suggestion in what it says: "Arise, go thy way: thy faith hath made thee whole." Physical leprosy might have been healed for other men, but they might go away as no bigger persons than they were before. To this one man there had come something greater. Because he opened out his heart in gratitude, the realized love of God could come into it to make him feel that his life had been caught up into the unbounded life. Kneeling there at Jesus' feet, he could feel himself the child of God that he was meant to be. For that moment of realization at least, he was made whole.

The truth embodied here is as long as time. No matter what the century may be, it is only when men take the trouble to be grateful that they can be made whole.

"Take the trouble to be grateful"; this may sound mechanical and unreal, but it is not. The emotions of the heart may depend upon the direction in which we deliberately turn our thoughts. Let anyone begin the day by thinking only of what he wants and does not have, or saying prayers which are all asking for more of this and that, and he is likely to go through the day with his spirit tense and arid. Let him stop and think first of what his blessings are—really *think* of them so that they cease to be the taken-for-granted things which have lost their freshness because they have been covered by the dust of his indifference. In the Family Prayer section of *The Book of Common Prayer,* those giving thanks are helped to remember, and so to be grateful for, "our health, friends, food, and raiment, and all the other comforts and conveniences of life"; and above all for the meaning of life which God has brought to us in Jesus. Love is that ultimate meaning; and the one thing that will most surely expand the spirit and fill it with a living joy is to give conscious thanks in the morning, and all day long, for those most near and dear to us whose love, so often undeserved, can help us know and trust the love of God.

Another point which seems to have had especial significance for Luke in the healing of the lepers was the fact that the one man who came back to express his gratitude was a Samaritan. Thus it was the outsider who was most sensitive, and not those who—if, as presumably, they were Jews—had been brought up in more orthodox religious circles. The Gospel had reflected this already in the parable of the man robbed and left wounded on the Jericho road, whom the priest and Levite passed by, and who got no help until a Samaritan came. Here the Evangelist was expressing the new realization which Jesus had brought home to all who heard him, including some who did not want to hear: that goodness may be found not among those where it would be traditionally expected, but among those upon whom the privileged looked down.

THE KINGDOM WITHIN

> Being asked by the Pharisees when the kingdom of God was coming, he answered them, "The kingdom of God is not coming with signs to be observed; nor will they say, 'Lo, here it is!' or 'There!' for behold, the kingdom of God is in the midst of you."   (Luke 17:20-21.)

The question asked of Jesus was an inevitable one. In many times and in many moods men ask it. When shall the world be changed and the sovereignty of God's spirit over it be really seen? It may be an earnest and a wistful question. But in this instance a group of Pharisees apparently asked it as a hostile challenge. Jesus had been preaching and teaching about this kingdom; but what right did he have to be a spokesman for it, and what did he actually know? If he had any actual knowledge, then let him be specific. *When* would the kingdom come, and what would be the signs preceding it?

The answer of Jesus expressed an eternal spiritual fact. The kingdom of God is not some violent change in the framework of things that can be dated as one might date an earthquake. It cannot be seen at first with the outward eye. Two translations have been given to the Greek words of Jesus' reply in the Gospel: "The kingdom of God is within you"; and "the kingdom of God is in the midst of you." The meanings of the two are not identical, but they shade one into the other. The kingdom of God "within you" suggests the Spirit already moving redeemingly in men's responsive souls. The kingdom of God "in the midst of you" suggests that its power is in the world as an influence which some will recognize but many will deny.

It was the latter which seems the more likely answer to the Pharisaic questioners. The kingdom of God "within you," the kingdom of God as the genuine passion in these men's lives, certainly did not appear. Yet nevertheless the kingdom was "in the midst" of them. Jesus himself was the expression of it and the embodiment of its meaning. He represented the love of God which reached out to Samaritans and outcasts, a love which went beyond the jealous particularities of privilege and status which some of the Pharisees clung to, a love which could be manifested in all those who are responsive. In that sense the kingdom in the midst can always become the kingdom within.

Our need is to perceive that fact. Ever since he first came, Jesus has been part of the reality that men must deal with. His spirit confronts our thinking and our choice; and the everlasting question is, How and when and where does his kingdom come? That question may be only a speculation, or it may be an experience; and that experience may be most real to those who are not the ones to whom it might have been supposed to be. Sometimes, for instance, the students in a theological seminary or the ordained minister in his study may be asking themselves about the kingdom, reading books about it, wrestling with all sorts of critical uncertainties as to what passages in the Gospels mean. But all the while the wife at home who does not know so many books may have grasped the inner secret of what the kingdom is. Going on her way among what seem the common things, keeping a house, pouring out her love to little children, making her home a haven of blessing and a peace, she may have found the kingdom as a present possession singing in her heart.

WHEN THE CRISIS COMES

And he said to the disciples, "The days are coming when you will desire to see one of the days of the Son of man, and you will not see it. And they will say to you, 'Lo, there!' or 'Lo, here!' Do not go, do not follow them. For as the lightning flashes and lights up the sky from one side to the other, so will the Son of man be in his day. But first he must suffer many things and be rejected by this generation. As it was in the days of Noah, so will it be in the days of the Son of man. They ate, they drank, they married, they were given in marriage, until the day when Noah entered the ark, and the flood came and destroyed them all. Likewise as it was in the days of Lot—they ate, they drank, they bought, they sold, they planted, they built, but on the day when Lot went out from Sodom fire and brimstone rained from heaven and destroyed them all—so will it be on the day when the Son of man is revealed. On that day, let him who is on the housetop, with his goods in the house, not come down to take them away; and likewise let him who is in the field not turn back. Remember Lot's wife. Whoever seeks to gain his life will lose it, but whoever loses his life will preserve it. I tell you, in that night there will be two men in one bed; one will be taken and the other left. There will be two women grinding together; one will be taken and the other left." And they said to him, "Where, Lord?" He said to them, "Where the body is, there the eagles will be gathered together."

(Luke 17:22-37.)

But the chapter in the Gospel does not end with what we have just considered, and in its concluding part there are admitted problems. Jesus is speaking now of those critical moments when the judgments of God may break upon the world in some tremendous cataclysm. New Testament scholars differ on what Jesus may have thought and said on all earthly history coming to its end. Some believe that in the so-called eschatological sayings the Gospels have incorporated words from Jewish apocalyptic writings which reflected and enlarged the dread picture in the book of Daniel of the Son of man coming in the clouds of heaven. However that may be, the central purpose of Jesus as reflected in this chapter of Luke is unmistakable. What Jesus did not do was to give any countenance to those pathetic folk who now and then, all down the centuries, believe that they have figured out the day and hour of the end, and have staked their faith on their perfervid calculations. What he did instead was to sound the note of the awesome responsibility of all men to be ready when the unpredictable might come. In the Scriptures which he bade them now remember were the warnings they were to take to heart: the careless crowd caught by the flood in the days of Noah, the people of Sodom who drank, bought, sold, planted, and built, and imagined that all their little affairs would go on forever—when destruction was about to fall. Let no one forget the drastic and terrible particularity of what must happen when the days of reckoning begin. No man can be saved by his neighbor then. One will be taken and the other left. With God are the issues of life and judgment. Two people working side by side may seem alike and marked for the same destiny, but it is not so. In a crisis of history, with its dreadful winnowing of human souls, one man will come through and the other fall.

Where will this be? the disciples asked; and Jesus answered with a proverb: "Where the body is, there the eagles will be gathered together." This is to say that wherever there is in human souls the slow disintegration that leads to moral and spiritual death, the dark wings of judgment will be hovering in the sky.

chapter 18

PRAYER THAT CANNOT BE DISCOURAGED

And he told them a parable, to the effect that they ought always to pray and not lose heart. He said, "In a certain city there was a judge who neither feared God nor regarded man; and there was a widow in that city who kept coming to him and saying, 'Vindicate me against my adversary.' For a while he refused; but afterward he said to himself, 'Though I neither fear God nor regard man, yet because this widow bothers me, I will vindicate her, or she will wear me out by her continual coming.'" And the Lord said, "Hear what the unrighteous judge says. And will not God vindicate his elect, who cry to him day and night? Will he delay long over them? I tell you, he will vindicate them speedily." (Luke 18:1-8a.)

The parable with which this chapter begins must be read in the light of what is true with the parables of Jesus almost always. They are like pictures painted in broad colors, setting forth with a few swift strokes some vivid central meaning; and to dwell on every detail as though it had some necessary value is to lose the significance of the whole. The point of this parable is perseverance, and what it can accomplish. To bring the point home, Jesus takes an illustration so extreme that no one could fail to be arrested by it. In the world which his hearers knew only too well, justice was the last thing people could be sure of. The rich and privileged could get verdicts in their favor by favoritism or a bribe; the poor and humble would get nothing. But there was a way, said Jesus, in which the picture could be changed. A poor widow came before a judge who neither feared God nor regarded man. He brushed her aside and paid no attention to her plea for help against someone who had wronged her. That might have been the end, but she did not let it be the end. Day after day she kept coming back. Though he had not listened yesterday, she would try to make him listen today—and tomorrow, and as many tomorrows as might be necessary after that. Her persistence wore him out. Not from any virtuous purpose but just from annoyed impatience to be rid of her, he grants her suit. Her determination has won, in spite of all the odds.

"And will not God vindicate his elect who cry to him day and night?"

234

said Jesus. Does this mean that Jesus is implying that God is *like* the unjust judge? Most certainly not. It is the *unlikeness* that emphasizes the meaning of the parable. It is as though Jesus were saying to those who listened to him, "Sometimes you are discouraged because God does not seem to answer your prayer. Then you might think there is no use to keep on praying. But that would be faintheartedness. Show how steadfast you can be. If perseverance can prevail with an indifferent human judge, don't you know that your Father who is more ready to hear will give you your heart's desire?"

Perseverance in prayer—that, then, is what Jesus is urging. But it is true that this still leaves us with a question. *Why* should it be that God seems sometimes so to delay his answer? Why must it be necessary to pray again and again, to go through days of wistful waiting when we are tempted to wonder whether there really is a God who hears and cares?

There is no glib answer to that question. Job wrestled with it: "I cry to thee and thou dost not answer me; I stand, and thou dost not heed me." So did the men who wrote the psalms. "How long, O Lord? Wilt thou forget me for ever? How long wilt thou hide thy face from me?" There are mysteries before which the soul stands hushed and knows that it cannot see all the way. What we must do is to follow such light as we have, and not to be either surprised or discouraged if our little human understanding cannot spell out in advance the infinite purposes which some day we may learn. Glimpses, at least, we do have into what may be the heavenly purpose for us when we have to keep on praying.

To begin with, we may be helped to learn better what we really want to pray for. Every one of us may have learned a little of the meaning of this through our human relationships. A child comes and asks his father or mother for something he thinks his whole happiness depends on: the little child for a toy he craves, the older boy for a rifle or for the automobile he is not grown-up enough to drive. Or he pleads to do only what he feels like doing. Why does he have to go to school today? Why does he have to study the particular subject that seems too hard for him to endure? The father who loves him cannot say yes to what the son is asking for, but nonetheless he wants him to keep on asking—to keep on coming to the love he can trust, until presently he learns that what he really wants is something bigger than what he thought he wanted. He has begun to understand his father and his father's larger purposes for him; and in a way far beyond the dimensions of his first asking, he is satisfied.

So may it be between us and God in what we might imagine to have been our unanswered prayers. The heavenly love would have us keep on coming with our instinctive petitions, but learning meanwhile that the truest prayer is speaking less and listening more. Then in the spiritual adulthood which develops from that persistence we look back and see

> . . . of what toys
> We made our joys,
> How weakly understood
> Thy great commanded good.[1]

And out of our childishness we are lifted to become the Father's grown-up sons.

Yet that is not the whole fact, and therefore not the whole answer to the perplexity we may have in the face of seemingly unanswered prayer. What if the gift we are asking for is not toys? What if it is the satisfaction of desires which are deep and true?

Then it may be that the postponement of the answer is meant to magnify the earnestness of the one who prays. The effect of anything God gives depends not only upon the gift itself, but also upon the spirit of the one to whom it is given. That which has seemed too lightly won may be casually accepted and indifferently used. But that which is struggled for through a great longing will enlist all the energies of the mind and heart. In Paul Gallico's *Coronation,* an eager small boy on a railroad journey finds himself sitting next to an officer of one of the famous regiments of the British army. Shyly he reveals his passionate ambition to grow up to be someday in a regiment like that.

"Then you must never relent," said the gentleman, and then repeated four times solemnly, "never, never, never, never. The wish must always be with you, battering at the gates like an army that doesn't know the meaning of defeat. Against such an attack, every defence must fail. Do you not agree?"
The glory of being talked to like a man! "Yes, sir," said Johnny.[2]

Is there a parallel here to what God searches for in those who come to him—a determination deep enough to justify a greatly given opportunity, and a strength of purpose ready to be "talked to like a man"?

Certainly it is true that the mightiest answers to prayer are linked with the readiness of praying men to open within themselves the channels for those answers; and God may wait for that. Some miracle from heaven might seem the quickest way to bring the victory for goodness which men crave, but the effect of it could be only superficial. Men must be led

[1] Coventry Patmore, "The Toys."
[2] (Garden City: Doubleday & Company, 1962) , p. 115.

through disciplined patience to become God's instruments, if men—and not momentary appearances only—are to be transformed. Laurence C. Jones, who built at Piney Woods in Mississippi a school for boys and girls who would have known nothing but poverty and ignorance except for him, said: "I prayed as if everything depended on God. And I worked as if everything depended on me."

BUT CAN FAITH ENDURE?

"Nevertheless, when the Son of man comes, will he find faith on earth?"
(Luke 18:8*b*.)

Here is the echo of the cry that had begun to go up when the early church faced persecution and was tempted to let its hope for God's deliverance falter. Can faith last until vindication comes?

This is the question which men may have to face in every generation when the right thing they fight for is imperiled, and they wonder if their courage can hold out. But the great spirits are those who make sure that, however long the trial, there shall be faith on earth.

Martin Luther King, threatened in Montgomery, Alabama, for trying to win even the elementary decencies of human treatment for his Negro people,

bowed over the kitchen table and prayed aloud. . . . "I am here taking a stand for what I believe is right. But now I am afraid. . . . I am at the end of my powers. I have nothing left. I've come to the point where I can't face it alone."

At that moment I experienced the presence of the Divine as I had never experienced Him before. It seemed as though I could hear the quiet assurance of an inner voice saying: "Stand up for righteousness, stand up for truth, and God will be at your side forever." Almost at once my fears began to go. My uncertainty disappeared. I was ready to face anything.[3]

That is the sort of prayer and resultant courage which can make sure that when all is said and done, there *shall* be faith on earth.

THE PHARISEE AND THE PUBLICAN

He also told this parable to some who trusted in themselves that they were righteous and despised others: "Two men went up into the temple to pray, one a Pharisee and the other a tax collector. The Pharisee stood and prayed thus with himself, 'God, I thank thee that I am not like other

[3] *Stride Toward Freedom*, pp. 134-35.

men, extortioners, unjust, adulterers, or even like this tax collector. I fast twice a week, I give tithes of all that I get.' But the tax collector, standing far off, would not even lift up his eyes to heaven, but beat his breast, saying, 'God be merciful to me a sinner!' I tell you, this man went down to his house justified rather than the other; for every one who exalts himself will be humbled, but he who humbles himself will be exalted." (Luke 18:9-14.)

There are two ways of teaching. One of these states truth in generalities and abstractions. It weaves its formulas and deduces arguments. Even among the spokesmen for religion there are some who never get beyond that kind of teaching. Their minds are bookish. They deal with propositions rather than with people. But there is another kind of teaching. It sees life and makes life manifest. Such was the way of Jesus. He never began with theories. He turned men's eyes toward facts which conveyed their own immediate suggestions. It was as though he said, "Look here at life and see its meaning." The result is that many of the things he said are as vivid now as though they were being played on a stage before our eyes. He made truth dramatic because he could draw out of the human existence some scene which showed man as he is, not in idea merely, but in action, with those collisions of character through which men are most unmistakably revealed.

Such a scene in the drama of the spirit is revealed in this short, swift story that begins, "Two men went up into the temple to pray."

We see the background of the Temple and the two figures, the Pharisee and the publican—as the King James Version calls him—or the tax collector, as is the explicit meaning of the word. At the beginning we see the two men as they were supposed to be. At the climax we see the two men as they are. The proud man has been abased, and the man who was abased has been exalted. Who are they, then, these two men whom Jesus has made so unforgettable? Let us understand them as clearly as we can, not only as they once lived in Jerusalem, but as they may live in contemporary figures who illustrate their spirit.

First, the Pharisee. It is possible for us not to be fair to the Pharisee. We read the New Testament, and we hear that name spoken again and again in condemnation. We see that in the end the Pharisaic spirit was a failure. We are likely to think of it then as having been undesirable all the time. But such was not the fact. Not only was the Pharisee for the most part an honored man. He was a man who in the light of all the expectations that gathered round him seemed to be one whose honors were deserved.

For the Pharisees—as we have noted in connection with Luke 11:37-41— were linked with one of the noblest periods in the history of Israel. In the second century before Christ, Israel had battled desperately for its independence—its national independence and its spiritual integrity too. The nation had come under the political dominion of the kings of Syria, who were insolent and cruel in their contempt for all that was most precious in the religious heritage of this Jewish people who believed that they had a covenant with God. Under Antiochus Epiphanes, one of these Syrian kings, the Temple was defiled. Every effort was made by threats, and then by violence, to win the people away from the old observances of Israel, to root out the ancient ways of worship, to destroy the ancient faith. Some of the weaker spirits succumbed. Then there arose the party which came to be called the Pharisees. They were the Puritans of that day, with all the inflexible, moral rectitude and costly commitment to an ideal which the Puritan spirit at its highest can represent. They made themselves champions of the law of Israel which they believed to be God's law. They did not flinch from self-discipline and obedience. They would order worship, work, habits, everything, according to what they believed to be God's ordinance for his people.

Therefore, when the Pharisee stood in the Temple and said, "God, I thank thee that I am not like other men," he was not saying what was a cheap boast. There was an element of reverence in what might have seemed to be only arrogance. It was true that he was not like some other men. He belonged to a particular class, and he had back of him a history of fidelity to what was believed the faith committed to his keeping. He was not like other men in his own behavior day by day. He was more strict, more definite in the requirements he laid upon himself. He had guarded himself from gross sins. He had been responsible to what he thought were his religious duties. When the church commanded him to fast, he fasted. When it told him that he ought to give as much as a tenth of all his income, he gave it.

It was no wonder that a man like this was honored in Jerusalem. He seemed to be the sort of citizen by whom the enduring values of the community were guaranteed.

Religion and morality in every time have owed a debt to the Pharisee, and to the man who is like the Pharisee. In this fellowship may belong the respected laymen who are wardens, vestrymen, deacons, and elders in the churches; these men take their religious obligations seriously, keep their lives clean of moral scandal, go to church and give to the church, and in general want to fortify by their influence the best traditions of belief and conduct which have come down to them from their fathers. They may kneel down in their pews and with some degree of honesty thank God that somehow they have been enabled to keep free from some of the sins into which it might have been easy for them to fall, and have been able to carry out duties which they might have neglected if God had not given them a conscience.

✓ Before we condemn the Pharisee or dismiss him, let us be sure that at least we have risen to his level. If he had his grievous limitations, nevertheless he did have solid virtues which not every man attains. He believed in something strongly enough to be true to it with an inconvenient loyalty. ✓ If his soul lacked grace, he must be given credit for the fact that he had moral iron in his blood. There are plenty of flabby persons who call themselves religious but have never reached the level on which the Pharisee was moving. There were qualities in him which might stare us out of countenance.

Yet when all was said and done, the Pharisee was and is a tragic figure, tragic in the contrast between what he was and what he might have been, but which—because of his self-satisfaction—he would never be.

Even God himself could hardly change the Pharisee and lift him up to his full possibilities, for he had no awareness that he needed to be changed. It was this mood which Jesus encountered again and again in the Pharisaic group—and encounters always in those who have grown complacent. The Pharisees could not seriously believe that anyone might consider their view of life defective. Whoever else might be blind, they could not be blind; but Jesus said, "If you were blind, you would have no guilt; but now that you say, 'We see,' your guilt remains." It was their stubborn pride of supposed spiritual achievement which was their ruin. They thought they knew all that needed to be known, and so they would not learn.

In contrast to the Pharisee stood the tax collector. "God be merciful to me, a sinner!" was his cry. He knew well enough that people in general despised him because of the class he belonged to and the sort of person he was supposed to be. Tax collecting under the Roman occupation often meant collusion between corrupt officials, with resultant graft and fraud. The system made every man who belonged to it suspect. No matter how honest the individual might be, he was looked upon as dishonest. No matter how conscientious, he was regarded as a crook.

How, meanwhile, did this particular tax collector in the Temple regard himself? As a sinner? Yes. But as a sinner of a different sort from what the crowd imagined. He was not thinking of the estimate of him which the people had. It may well be that the people's estimates were wrong. Notwithstanding the evil odor of his profession, he may have been as just as any man in Jerusalem. He was not asking pardon of the people. He was making his appeal to God. It was as measured by the glory of God that he saw himself a sinner. Even if he were a man of average virtue, he could not be content with that. This man's soul was sensitive to the highest. Somehow he had caught a glimpse of what life ought to be, and in the light of that he knew the awful distance between what he saw in himself and what he beheld in God.

Here we perceive the difference between the tax collector and the Pharisee. In terms of moral attainment, the Pharisee might seem to have come farther along the road. But at the point he reached he was content to stay. He looked back and congratulated himself—and was sure God must be pleased—at the distance he had traveled. He did not look ahead and let his soul be humbled by the awful heights of possibility which towered still above him. But the tax collector did look forward and look up. He knew how low was the valley in which he lived, but he had seen and desired the sky.

When a man is of this spirit, he can be saved. He may have a long way to go, but God will lead him. If his one impassioned prayer is, "God be merciful to me a sinner!" then he has opened his heart to the heavenly grace that can lift him above his sin. And so the words of Jesus end with their redeeming promise: "I tell you, this man went down to his house justified rather than the other; for every one who exalts himself will be humbled, but he who humbles himself will be exalted."

THE SPIRIT OF THE CHILD

> Now they were bringing even infants to him that he might touch them; and when the disciples saw it, they rebuked them. But Jesus called them to him, saying, "Let the children come to me, and do not hinder them; for to such belongs the kingdom of God. Truly, I say to you, whoever does not receive the kingdom of God like a child shall not enter it."
>
> (Luke 18:15-17.)

As so often in the Gospel narrative, one incident follows another without obvious connection. What has the bringing of children to do with the scene in the Temple? But there is at least the kinship of suggestion which may have led the Evangelist to put them together: namely, that for Jesus importance and unimportance were very different from the world's idea of them. The general crowd supposed the Pharisee to be an eminent person and scorned the tax collector, but Jesus lifted this scorned man into dignity. The disciples thought that children were too insignificant to be bothered with, but Jesus saw them as having the nature which alone can inherit the kingdom of God.

But how could this be? some harassed adult might ask, exhausted from looking after a houseful of noisy children who may have seemed at times more like limbs of Satan than innocents with angel wings. What was there in them that suggested the kingdom of God? Certainly not everything. The old Adam can crop up in children as well as in grown-ups. But the child does have qualities which are beautiful, and it was these—we may believe—which Jesus meant when he said that only with a childlike spirit could anyone enter the kingdom of God.

The child, in the first place, is full of wonder. For him the world has not become humdrum and common, and to his imagination nothing is impossible. He will listen fascinated to every story that has a triumphant ending. That sense of the wonder and wideness that can belong to life must be the continuing possession of all those who in the midst of drabness will see the heavenly meaning breaking through. For them, if they have kept the childlike spirit, "the earth and every common sight" can be "apparelled in celestial light." [4]

Also the child is teachable. His mind is alert with questions. A whole undiscovered universe is round him, and no hard shell of satisfaction with what he might think he knows already exists to shut him in from learning more. Watch the wide eyes of a child as he looks up at his father who is explaining to him something that he wants to know. Here is a picture of what is needed for entrance into the kingdom: openness of mind and heart to receive from God the living truths which the complacent and conceited can never understand.

And the child is sensitive to love. Abstract reasoning may not get far with him, but he responds when he is loved. As he begins to grow up in a family, he learns instinctively to let the love which has been given him flood through to others, and in that mutual loving he finds his life made happy and secure. So it is with God's kingdom, "for love is of God, and he who loves is born of God and knows God."

WHEN COMMITMENT IS NOT COMPLETE

And a ruler asked him, "Good Teacher, what shall I do to inherit eternal life?" And Jesus said to him, "Why do you call me good? No one is good but God alone. You know the commandments: 'Do not commit adultery, Do not kill, Do not steal, Do not bear false witness, Honor your father and mother.'" And he said, "All these I have observed from my youth." And when Jesus heard it, he said to him, "One thing you still lack. Sell all that you have and distribute to the poor, and you will have treasure

[4] William Wordsworth, "Ode on Intimations of Immortality."

in heaven; and come, follow me." But when he heard this he became sad, for he was very rich. Jesus looking at him said, "How hard it is for those who have riches to enter the kingdom of God! For it is easier for a camel to go through the eye of a needle than for a rich man to enter the kingdom of God."

(Luke 18:18-25.)

Few passages in the Gospel equal this as a sudden drama of critical human choice. Here is a man of wealth and rank who has felt the fascination of Jesus. According to Matthew he was young. According to Mark, the earliest Gospel, there was a winsome eagerness about him, for he "ran up and knelt" before Jesus; and when he began to speak, "Jesus looking upon him loved him." He seemed to have everything he needed, but he was sensitive enough to know that there was an emptiness somewhere within. Hearing Jesus—or having at least heard about him—he caught a haunting glimpse of new dimensions of the spirit, and the best in him reached out to find them. "Good Teacher," he pleaded, "what shall I do to inherit eternal life?"

The first reply of Jesus, "Why do you call me good?" seemed astonishing—so much so that Matthew, when he read what Mark had written, thought there must be an error. So he changed the original report as it stood in Mark to "Why do you ask me about what is good?" lest the other words imply that Jesus had *not* been completely good. But what Jesus was doing to the young inquirer was bringing him up short before the reckoning he must make with the Infinite Goodness. In effect he said to him, "It is not enough that you should politely call me 'Good Teacher,' as though you sought some conveniently acceptable advice. Are you ready to listen to what may be the drastic imperatives of God, those imperatives which begin with the plain commandments of the moral law?"

Yes, the young man had tried to observe all those; and the fact that he had done so established him even more in Jesus' regard. If a life was to stand acceptable in God's sight, it had to rest first on the old foundations of integrity. But it must not stop with the foundations. To rise into the sunlight, it must have larger aspirations. So Jesus continued, "What will you build on the basis of your moral blamelessness? Listen to me, and I will show you how your soul can grow. One thing you still lack—one great thrust of devotion that will deliver you from the littleness that you feel now in your life. Sell all that you have and give to the poor. Then you will have treasure in heaven. Come, follow me!"

We read those startling words, and may stumble between two possibilities. One is the thought that Jesus is condemning all possessions. Must every Christian then give away everything he has in order to be a Christian? So it could be concluded if what Jesus said to this rich young ruler be given blanket application. But one remembers that Jesus did not characteristically speak with blanket applications or lay down inflexible abstract laws. He touched the varying facts of life with sensitive discrimination. There is no record that he told James and John to give away the fishing boats which they left with their father Zebedee, or that he told Mary and Martha to sell their house in Bethany. His words therefore to one particular man who stood before him are not a universal principle. They do not give a fixed answer to everybody who asks what to do with what he has. Here, as in many other instances, the words of Jesus are like the flashing beacon of a lighthouse. They are not eyeglasses through which nearsighted lawyers are to scrutinize their charts and law books. They are signals to the mariner at sea.

It is in the light of this latter fact that the story of the young man whom Jesus loved has its poignant meaning. Here was an actual man whom Jesus saw to be in danger. He had gallant possibilities, like a full-rigged ship that might set out on some great voyage. But the ship was too heavily laden to cross the hidden shoals. It would have to put overboard some of the things that cluttered it and weighed it down if it was to get past the shallows to the open sea. And the open sea was what Jesus coveted for this young man who at first had seemed so eager. Jesus was on his way to Jerusalem and to the ultimate hazard of his devotion to the kingdom of God. Those who went with him would have to pay a heavy cost, but the reward for it would be to have part in something supremely glorious. It was to this that Jesus invited him: "Leave the secondary things behind, and come and follow me!"

The young man flinched from that. He could not bring himself to learn what Matthew the tax collector learned—as Dorothy Sayers has imagined what Matthew might have said when he was questioned. Judas asked him what happened to all his belongings.

I never gave 'em a thought. . . . Then my brother hunted me up and asked me what I thought I was doing. "Sell the whole lot up"; I said, "or do what you like. I've done with it." . . . And I'm having a wonderful time.[5]

This other man never reached any such exultant emancipation of his spirit. The ordinary attachments were too strong. He was sad to turn his back on this immense new opportunity; but sad or not, he did it.

The tragedy in riches thus may not be that possessing this or that is wrong. Rather it is the fact that the comfort and complacency which riches

[5] *The Man Born to Be King*, p. 110.

give may make the fibers of the spirit grow so soft that they cannot respond to noble effort. F. W. H. Myers in his "St. Paul" has put this prayer on the great apostle's lips.

> Never at even, pillowed on a pleasure
> Sleep with the wings of aspiration furled.

But it is possible, as with the young ruler, that the wings of great desire may be folded not only at evening but at morning and noontide too.

LIFE FULFILLED

Those who heard it said, "Then who can be saved?" But he said, "What is impossible with men is possible with God." And Peter said, "Lo, we have left our homes and followed you." And he said to them, "Truly, I say to you, there is no man who has left house or wife or brothers or parents or children, for the sake of the kingdom of God, who will not receive manifold more in this time, and in the age to come eternal life."

And taking the twelve, he said to them, "Behold, we are going up to Jerusalem, and everything that is written of the Son of man by the prophets will be accomplished. For he will be delivered to the Gentiles, and will be mocked and shamefully treated and spit upon; they will scourge him and kill him, and on the third day he will rise." But they understood none of these things; this saying was hid from them, and they did not grasp what was said. (Luke 18:26-34.)

"Who then can be saved?" some of the listeners asked; and Jesus lifted the answer up above this one young man's immediate failure. Even what had been asked of him might some day not be impossible for him, or for another like him. God's inspiration might kindle at length the flame of the heroic choice.

The disciples had already made a costly choice. They had left their homes, friends, and substance back in Galilee. But they were moving toward a fullness of life such as they had never known before. In the fellowship of what was to be the Christian church they would find all human relationships and the complete meaning of existence brought to a new dimension.

That new dimension was what Jesus himself would represent. He was going up to Jerusalem to be mocked and scourged and spit upon, to face the entrenched resistance of the world's stubborn sin. Instead of the shallows where most lives like to move, he would sound life to its depths; its depths of evil, and the completeness of devotion by which alone evil could be overcome. He would be crucified. No wonder that at first the disciples could not see in that anything but tragedy and defeat. But he dared to see beyond the cross the power of his deathless life. Out of the tragedy would come the glory. Someday the disciples would understand that glory and share it with their Master.

THE FAR AND THE NEAR

> As he drew near to Jericho, a blind man was sitting by the roadside begging; and hearing a multitude going by, he inquired what this meant. They told him, "Jesus of Nazareth is passing by." And he cried, "Jesus, Son of David, have mercy on me!" And those who were in front rebuked him, telling him to be silent; but he cried out all the more, "Son of David, have mercy on me!" And Jesus stopped, and commanded him to be brought to him; and when he came near, he asked him, "What do you want me to do for you?" He said, "Lord, let me receive my sight." And Jesus said to him, "Receive your sight; your faith has made you well." And immediately he received his sight and followed him, glorifying God; and all the people, when they saw it, gave praise to God.
>
> (Luke 18:35-43.)

It might have been imagined that on his way to Jerusalem Jesus would be so preoccupied with the awful issues waiting there to face him that he could have no time or thought for some poor, insignificant somebody by the way. But the truth proved exactly opposite.

A blind beggar sitting by the roadside heard the commotion of a crowd drawing near. He could not see, but he knew that something exciting must be happening. People round him told him what it was. "Jesus of Nazareth is passing by." Jesus of Nazareth! That name had already come to the blind man's ears: the name of the one who was said to bring healing and whole-ness to those who were in need. Above the noise of the crowd came his cry: "Jesus, Son of David, have mercy on me!" People near him tried to shut him up; but he cried out all the more: "Son of David, have mercy on me!" Jesus stopped. More important than the crowd excitement was this one pitiful appeal. He commanded the blind man to be brought to him, and he asked him what he wanted. "Lord, let me receive my sight," the blind man answered. And Jesus said, "Receive your sight; your faith has made you well."

Does the scene belong only to the long ago? No. In its essential meaning it belongs to every time. Here was a man who knew acutely what he needed, and reached out for it with a desperate eagerness. Jesus of Nazareth was passing by; the one critical moment must be seized before he had gone. "Lord, that I may receive my sight," he pleaded. Are there not always those who need to receive their sight? Along the road of life there are always the blind: if not blind physically then spiritually, blind to all that might be the beauty and meaning of their world. Then at some unexpected moment may come the awareness that there is a light from God in Christ which if they could gain would make their whole world new. Do they want it— do *we* want it—enough to keep pleading for it before the moment of awakened hope and faith has passed by?

So much for the blind man. Consider also what the scene reveals of Jesus. For him two great dimensions of life were always held in balance: the long perspective and the response to what was near. He who had set his face steadfastly to go to Jerusalem followed the road of complete commitment, but on that road he could be sensitive to the immediate human cry. Where our lives fall short may be in either one of these respects. We have no far purpose, and so our days may be made up of nothing but chance distractions; or, on the other hand, we may be so obsessed with what we think are large responsibilities that we have no time for little kindnesses and compassion. But the great life must be made up, as Phillips Brooks made clear in one of his unforgettable sermons, both of visions and tasks. "It is a terrible thing to have no vision"; but also, "It is a terrible thing to have seen the vision, and to be so wrapped up in its contemplation as not to hear the knock of needy hands upon our doors." [6]

[6] Phillips Brooks, "Visions and Tasks," in *Phillips Brooks: Selected Sermons,* edited by William Scarlett (New York: E. P. Dutton & Company, 1949), p. 149.

chapter 19

JESUS GOES TO ZACCHAEUS' HOUSE

He entered Jericho and was passing through. And there was a man named Zacchaeus; he was a chief tax collector, and rich. And he sought to see who Jesus was, but could not, on account of the crowd, because he was small of stature. So he ran on ahead and climbed up into a sycamore tree to see him, for he was to pass that way. And when Jesus came to the place, he looked up and said to him, "Zacchaeus, make haste and come down; for I must stay at your house today." So he made haste and came down, and received him joyfully. And when they saw it they all murmured, "He has gone in to be the guest of a man who is a sinner." And Zacchaeus stood and said to the Lord, "Behold, Lord, the half of my goods I give to the poor; and if I have defrauded any one of anything, I restore it fourfold." And Jesus said to him, "Today salvation has come to this house, since he also is a son of Abraham. For the Son of man came to seek and to save the lost." (Luke 19:1-10.)

Let the scene reappear in our imagination: Jesus passing through Jericho, people pouring out to see him, among them a little man so short of stature that he had no chance to see above the heads of the crowd, and knowing furthermore that anybody he jostled might spit in his face and push him out of the way; so he climbs up into the branches of a tree. Let him scramble up there then and get himself out from among decent people, the crowd would have said; and if he fell out of his tree and broke his neck, so much the better. For the man was a tax collector; and for one born a Jew to be a tax collector, what did it mean except to have sold out his loyalty to Israel and to have become a moneygrabber for the Roman overlords? Who, then, would want to associate with him?

But to the astonishment of all Jericho it was this tax collector, this Zacchaeus, whom Jesus singled out and spoke to. "Zacchaeus, come down, for I must stay at your house today," he said. Not at the house of a rabbi, or a priest, or some other respectable person; no, but at Zacchaeus' house, of all places! To the general public, nothing could have seemed more outlandish than that.

But it was exactly in character for Jesus. He was not swayed by con-

248

not hold grudges

ventional opinion. He could never be carried away by the crowd to lump men into classes and to suppose that in a given class all men were alike. He looked through names and appearance to reality underneath. For him at that particular moment this tax gatherer was more important than anything else in Jericho.

Because in the first place, here was a soul in need. The crowd did not see that, and would not have cared about it if they had seen. But Jesus saw and cared. Something wistful was looking at him out of Zacchaeus' eyes, and from the midst of all the gaping and curious faces Jesus caught that special look. Need always drew him. He stopped by Jacob's well to talk with the woman of Samaria and to pour out for her discredited life some of the richest and most wonderful teaching which the Gospels contain. Mary Magdalene needed him, and in the house of Simon the Pharisee he responded to her pitifulness, notwithstanding the lifted eyebrows of his host. So now he will go to the house of Zacchaeus, no matter who might be shocked.

He sensed that Zacchaeus was longing for something he did not have. He sensed too that in Zacchaeus there were possibilities ready to respond to the quickening touch of the love of God. In certain parts of the country there are persons who go about with what are called divining rods. A hazel twig held in their hands, by some strange influence which no one quite wholly understands, will bend down toward the earth when they walk across ground beneath which there is water. With these divining rods they locate the places where wells may be dug successfully. This is the way it was with Jesus. In his understanding he had a divining rod for what might lie in the depths of a human soul. He could tell when, underneath even an unpromising surface, fountains of spiritual possibilities lay quivering. So he uncovered depths, which most of the people of Jericho had never dreamed of, in the one whom they regarded as only a mean little man deserving to be despised. When Jesus' eyes looked into his, Zacchaeus knew how different he was meant to be. "Behold, Lord, the half of my goods I give to the poor," he said, "and if I have defrauded anyone of anything, I restore it fourfold." According to *The Interpreter's Bible* this is "the present tense used for the future." [1] In other words this is not what Zacchaeus had already been doing, but what he would do, now that the love of God in Jesus had cared enough for him to make him want God's real fulfillment for his life.

Zacchaeus is long since dead and gone. Jericho and all its streets and walls are tumbled into dust. Jesus of Nazareth went on from Jericho

---

[1] Exegesis of Luke, VIII, 325.

to Jerusalem, died on the cross, and was buried in Joseph of Arimathea's tomb. So there is an aspect in which it would seem that the old story is only a fragrance that lingers round a vanished yesterday. But that same love of Jesus, which went into the house of Zacchaeus to seek and to save that which was lost, exists in the spiritual universe today. The undying Lord still comes with his quickening presence to those who will receive him, and still he brings to us his transformation. There is no human soul today that looks in the direction of Jesus with wistful and desirous eyes to whom he will not say, as he said to Zacchaeus, "I will go home with you."

ON BEING CONTENT
WITH PARTIAL UNDERSTANDING

As they heard these things, he proceeded to tell a parable, because he was near to Jerusalem, and because they supposed that the kingdom of God was to appear immediately. He said therefore, "A nobleman went into a far country to receive kingly power and then return. Calling ten of his servants, he gave them ten pounds, and said to them, 'Trade with these till I come.' But his citizens hated him and sent an embassy after him, saying, 'We do not want this man to reign over us.' When he returned, having received the kingly power, he commanded these servants, to whom he had given the money, to be called to him, that he might know what they had gained by trading. The first came before him, saying, 'Lord, your pound has made ten pounds more.' And he said to him, 'Well done, good servant! Because you have been faithful in a very little, you shall have authority over ten cities. And the second came, saying, 'Lord, your pound has made five pounds.' And he said to him, 'And you are to be over five cities.' Then another came, saying, 'Lord, here is your pound, which I kept laid away in a napkin; for I was afraid of you, because you are a severe man; you take up what you did not lay down, and reap what you did not sow.' He said to him, 'I will condemn you out of your own mouth, you wicked servant! You knew that I was a severe man, taking up what I did not lay down and reaping what I did not sow? Why then did you not put my money into the bank, and at my coming I should have collected it with interest?' And he said to those who stood by, 'Take the pound from him, and give it to him who has the ten pounds.' (And they said to him, 'Lord, he has ten pounds!') 'I tell you, that to every one who has will more be given; but from him who has not, even what he has will be taken away. But as for these enemies of mine, who did not want me to reign over them, bring them here and slay them before me.' " (Luke 19:11-27.)

It was characteristic of Jesus that he almost always taught by parables. Truth can be put forth in abstract statements, and it may touch the sur-

250

face of the mind. But it is only when truth is expressed in terms of some familiar fact, and projected thus as in a picture, that it becomes vivid to the inward eye, and the listener says instinctively, "I *see* it now."

All of Jesus' parables, therefore, were related to what his hearers knew or what from their experience they could immediately imagine. Most of them have to do with realities so typical and universal that their essential meaning is as clear in our time as in another: the good Samaritan, the shepherd and the lost sheep, the leaven kneaded into the flour. But some parables were sparked by happenings which the people who listened to Jesus knew about, but about which we can only guess. And this parable of the pounds is one of them.

With simple honesty, then, let it be admitted that we cannot fully understand it. It may be that Luke is combining recollections which had come down to him of what Jesus said on two separate occasions, and that the overlapping has produced some of the references which are puzzling. There is no virtue in laboring too painfully over details which we cannot surely deal with, and worrying so much about these that we lose the nourishment which the central part of the parable contains. A wise old man of God was traveling once on a railroad train and eating his dinner in the dining car. A fellow passenger, ignorant but self-assertive, of the type who likes to be smart by seeming to be superior to the Bible, came over and sat down at the table with the minister, and began to parade his ideas of certain passages which he said he was not going to believe. The older man looked at him unruffled.

"What am I doing?" he asked.

"Why, eating your dinner," the other answered.

"And what am I eating?"

"You are eating fish."

"Yes, and I eat the good nutritious meat, and leave these bones on one side for somebody—if he wants to—to choke himself on."

Look at verses 14 and 27 of this Lukan passage, which in this case might be like the bones. It is hard to figure out why they are there. The best assumption is that they may reflect what Jesus said one day about a special fact, the echo of which got into this parable, while exactly what he said about that fact was something else. "A nobleman went into a far country to receive kingly power. . . . But his citizens hated him and sent an embassy after him." That was what actually happened with regard to Herod Archelaus, whom his father, Herod the Great, named in his will as his successor to the rulership over Judea. Archelaus went to Rome to try to get the emperor to confirm that appointment, but had the mortification of knowing that a deputation of Judeans came to plead with the emperor that he do no such thing. If Jesus was still in or near Jericho, as the beginning of this chapter 19 implies, it was entirely likely that he might have been reminded especially of Herod Archelaus, for in Jericho was the palace and an aqueduct which Archelaus had built. In the eyes of Rome he had made such a failure of his administration that the emperor had stripped him of his rulership, and the palace stood as a sardonic witness to a man who had lost his chance. And if the reference to the nobleman in the parable is in fact to Herod Archelaus, that would explain the final verse about the treatment of enemies, which would have been quite congenial to this Herod and to his father too.

Leaving out, then, these conjectural references to Herod, which Jesus may have developed in some other specific way, there remains the essential message of the parable: that every man has his urgent responsibility which in his own circumstances he must fulfill.

The first man of the three whom Jesus described was the richly endowed. He had a great deal to begin with, and he used it in such a way that his endowment doubled. There may seem nothing surprising about this. The average person, reading this parable, might say, "Of course, if I were in that man's place it would be easy to make a success of life. If I were born with brilliant abilities, I would use them. Anybody would." But the reality is not so simple. The man who seems to have every advantage to start with may sit down with the lazy assurance that there is no need to make any special effort. He may repeat the old Aesop fable of the hare and the tortoise, in which the hare loses the race because he was sure that he could win it anyway, and so why not sleep awhile before he started?

It has often been observed that in a class graduating from college the men who on the basis of their undergraduate showing seem certain to go far may be back among the undistinguished when the reckoning is made ten years thereafter. It had been too easy at first to do well, and so they had no flaming incentive to do better. It has been with them as it was with Andrea del Sarto, called "the faultless painter" because he had every attribute of artistic genius—except the steady will to use them. "I might get up to-morrow to my work": so Robert Browning has him say. But he never fully did; and in that fact he exemplified the temptation which may beset even those who seem most fortified against all possible failure. The achievement of the first man in the parable therefore was not a matter of course. Great opportunity must be matched by greatness of spirit if it is to win any commendation and reward.

But it is the second man in the parable who is perhaps the most immediately recognizable. The majority of us measure in the middle of the scale, not conspicuous in ability, and yet not too deficient either. Then the tendency may be just to plod along respectably; or, worse than that, to look with frustrated envy on the supposedly more fortunate person, and do nothing at all. It is hard to be in second place, to be given—as it seems —only the mediocre opportunity, to have to manage with five pounds when somebody else has ten.

Yet some of the greatest triumphs of the human spirit have come directly from those who, when they might have become cynical because of what they did not have, went on instead to use with magnificent responsibility what they did have. When the battlefield of Gettysburg was dedicated in 1863 as a memorial to the men who had fallen there, the great oration was to be made by Edward Everett, the man whose gift of eloquence was supposed to be supreme. Abraham Lincoln, President of the United States, was invited to make "a few appropriate remarks." An envious man might have resented that subordination, and refused to do what seemed the trivial thing that he was asked to do. But Lincoln came and spoke what was in his heart, and that brief address he made at Gettysburg will live as long as history lasts, while Everett's three-hour oration has long since been forgotten. The fragment of opportunity given to him was made into more than the ten pounds which belonged to Everett.

When Eleanor Roosevelt died in 1962, her life had borne such astonishing fruit of wide-ranging interests and devoted service that she was accounted the most admired woman in the world. It might be supposed that she was born with native gifts so superlative that there could never be any question of her great development. But that was not the fact. As a little girl, she was "the ugly duckling" of her family, shy, awkward, and unhappy. As she grew up, there was still no sign of any ten-pound endowment. But she used to the utmost whatever she had and whatever came to her. After her seventy-fifth birthday she wrote:

I had really only three assets: I was keenly interested, I accepted every challenge and every opportunity to learn more, and I had great energy and self-discipline.[2]

One can, even without any particular gifts, overcome obstacles that seem insurmountable if one is willing to face the fact that they must be overcome; that, in spite of timidity and fear, in spite of a lack of special talents, one can find a way to live widely and fully. . . .

The fatal thing is the rejection. Life was meant to be lived. . . . One must never, for whatever reason, turn his back on life.[3]

[2] *The Autobiography of Eleanor Roosevelt* (New York: Harper & Row, 1961), p. 410.
[3] *Ibid.*, p. 19.

The tragedy of the third man in the parable was that he did "turn his back on life." He thought the little he had was not worth using, and so he would wrap it up and put it away. When he was asked for an accounting, he would say that he knew that any mistake of his would be judged harshly. Therefore, he had taken no risks.

In the Revised Standard Version there is a slight but exceedingly significant difference from the older King James Version. The former makes clear what was not clear before. According to the King James Version the master accepts the picture of himself which the servant has presented. He *is* a hard man, and the servant had better recognize that and take the consequences. But in the Revised Standard Version, vs. 22 ends not with a period but with a question mark. The master is pressing his searching scrutiny on what the servant really thought: "You knew that I am the kind of man who expects what I had no right to expect? You really thought that? Then all the more you should have felt yourself roused to some sort of accountability in action. On the basis of your own thinking, you are the more condemned."

In other words, if a man actually thinks that life is harsh and cruel, in plain common sense he had better be careful not to commit the failure that results in punishment. But the point of the parable is that life is opportunity; and the tragedy is that a man, by his own neglect, may lose what he was meant to have. This sad reality may be seen in instances everywhere. Gifts which are not used, abilities which are not exercised, begin to shrivel and disappear. Knowledge accumulated from books and studies fades out of the mind unless it is made to be an active stimulus toward further knowledge. Generous emotions not turned into action die down like neglected fire, until the heart grows cold. Even in the most precious relationships, loyalty and love can fade into ashes unless they are continually expressed.

Such, then, is the urgent message of the parable. As has been remembered before, it is a characteristic of the parables that each one is like a searchlight concentrated on one aspect of truth. No one of them gives all the answers concerning God and man. This parable still leaves us with what Paul Tillich has called "the riddle of inequality," the question of why it should be that some have ten pounds, some five, and some only one. "Only in the unity of all beings in time and eternity," he writes, "can there be a humanly possible answer" to that riddle. "We participate in each other's having and in each other's not having." [4]

The upshot of the matter is that we must live with "the riddle of in-

---

[4] Paul Tillich, *The Eternal Now,* p. 45.

equality," even while our finite minds cannot understand it. And the way to live with it is to be sure that each one of us in his own place shall live responsibly.

THE ENTRANCE
INTO JERUSALEM ON PALM SUNDAY

And when he had said this, he went on ahead, going up to Jerusalem. When he drew near to Bethphage and Bethany, at the mount that is called Olivet, he sent two of the disciples, saying, "Go into the village opposite, where on entering you will find a colt tied, on which no one has ever yet sat; untie it and bring it here. If any one asks you, 'Why are you untying it?' you shall say this, 'The Lord has need of it.' " So those who were sent went away and found it as he had told them. And as they were untying the colt, its owners said to them, "Why are you untying the colt?" And they said, "The Lord has need of it." And they brought it to Jesus, and throwing their garments on the colt they set Jesus upon it. And as he rode along, they spread their garments on the road. As he was now drawing near, at the descent of the Mount of Olives, the whole multitude of the disciples began to rejoice and praise God with a loud voice for all the mighty works that they had seen, saying, "Blessed be the King who comes in the name of the Lord! Peace in heaven and glory in the highest!" And some of the Pharisees in the multitude said to him, "Teacher, rebuke your disciples." He answered, "I tell you, if these were silent, the very stones would cry out." And when he drew near and saw the city he wept over it, saying, "Would that even today you knew the things that make for peace! But now they are hid from your eyes. For the days shall come upon you, when your enemies will cast up a bank about you and surround you, and hem you in on every side, and dash you to the ground, you and your children within you, and they will not leave one stone upon another in you; because you did not know the time of your visitation."   (Luke 19:28-44.)

As has been true at other points in the Gospel, this passage is like a flash of light which illumines for a moment a single scene, but leaves us wondering about the background which we do not see. It is hardly likely that Jesus told his disciples to go and untie a colt belonging to someone whom neither he nor the disciples knew and who would therefore ask in astonishment why they were walking off with his property. It must have been the fact instead that Jesus had friends in Jerusalem whose names we do not know, and that they had made ready for him what he would want to use that day. In *The Man Born to Be King* there is a dramatic suggestion of a choice imagined to have been presented then to Jesus: Baruch, head of an armed band of Jewish revolutionists, urging him to ride a horse as the sign to which Baruch and his men would instantly rally in challenge to the Roman power. It was on a horse that a conqueror in arms would ride; but it was not this that Jesus chose. His challenge would not be the kind that the violent would prefer. In the hearts of many of the Jewish people there did burn the passionate desire for a deliverer girded with a sword, a Messiah surrounded by the weapons of this world; but Jesus came to represent a different kind of Christhood. The authority which he represented was not less royal but more so than that which any military conqueror could claim; it was the authority of the love of God to enter into and to rule the hearts of men. In the strength of *this* authority he dared now to make his entrance into Jerusalem. He would come with the spiritual salvation expressed by the symbol which Zechariah the prophet had foreseen:

> Rejoice greatly, O daughter of Zion!
> Shout aloud, O daughter of Jerusalem!
> Lo, your king comes to you;
> triumphant and victorious . . . ,
> humble and riding on an ass,
> on a colt the foal of an ass.

The throngs on the road into Jerusalem were caught up into a sense of excitement over something which they felt to be tremendous, though they could not have told why. All they knew was that there was power in Jesus. Anything might happen. Jesus' own disciples could cry, "Blessed be the King who comes in the name of the Lord," but the general crowd would be more likely to shout—as the Gospel of Mark has echoed—"Blessed be the kingdom of our father David that is coming!" So the multitude, with nationalistic fervor, might hail Jesus on this Palm Sunday; and when he seemed to be not what they expected, they would cry, "Crucify him" in Pilate's court five days later.

It must have been in part because he understood how shallow and fickle the moods of the mass of people could be that Jesus wept over Jerusalem. He had come to tell of the things that make for peace, but the crowd's mind would not be likely to listen. Jerusalem, like many another city and nation since that time, did not have discernment enough to know that it stood at the crisis of its destiny. It would continue in the ways of its stupid unconcern, with no purpose to examine its thought and life and set them right before disaster came.

THE CLEANSING OF THE TEMPLE

And he entered the temple and began to drive out those who sold, saying to them, "It is written, 'My house shall be a house of prayer'; but you have made it a den of robbers."

256

And he was teaching daily in the temple. The chief priests and the scribes and the principal men of the people sought to destroy him; but they did not find anything they could do, for all the people hung upon his words. (Luke 19:45-48.)

Here was the act which would bring down upon Jesus the implacable anger of the entrenched interests in Jerusalem. Halford E. Luccock in his pungent way said that "Jesus was not crucified for saying, 'Consider the lilies, how they grow,' but for saying, 'Look at the thieves in the Temple, how they steal.'" For the changing of various kinds of money for the coinage required in the Temple, and the sale of doves and lambs for sacrifice, had become a cover for privileged graft; and the whole noisy huckstering had made a market out of what was meant to be the house of prayer. When Jesus let loose the storm of his indignation, the merchants and the priests shrank away before him; but their wrath was all the hotter because they had been humiliated. They would have acted against Jesus then, but the crowd was still on his side. They would wait until the wind of popular opinion began to blow from a different direction.

chapter 20

THE SADDUCEES ARE PUT TO SILENCE

One day, as he was teaching the people in the temple and preaching the gospel, the chief priests and the scribes with the elders came up and said to him, "Tell us by what authority you do these things, or who it is that gave you this authority." He answered them, "I also will ask you a question; now tell me, Was the baptism of John from heaven or from men?" And they discussed it with one another, saying, "If we say, 'From heaven,' he will say, 'Why did you not believe him?' But if we say, 'From men,' all the people will stone us; for they are convinced that John was a prophet." So they answered that they did not know whence it was. And Jesus said to them, "Neither will I tell you by what authority I do these things." (Luke 20:1-8.)

This twentieth chapter is different from most of the Gospel in a way that the reader must instinctively feel, even if at first he does not stop to specify just what the difference is. Then if his thought turns back to the preceding chapters, he sees where the difference lies. What Luke has been reflecting almost always is the positive message of the kingdom of God and the outreach of Jesus to all those who responded to it—the living and redeeming message which was to proclaim release to the captives and recovering of sight to the blind. The characteristic descriptions of Jesus' contacts with people have been those which showed his instant compassion—with the poor and the sick and the outcasts, with the woman in Simon the Pharisee's house, with blind Bartimaeus, with despised Zacchaeus. It is the heart of Jesus, and the great encouragement of his love, that has been most evident. Now in this chapter it is as though the Evangelist would have all men remember the strength and mastery of Jesus' mind. So he puts together the record of questions which antagonists asked to try to trap him, and the answers of Jesus by which these men were confounded. In Dorothy Sayers' brilliant drama, *The Man Born to Be King,* one of the most fascinating scenes is that in which these malevolent questioners are dealt with. There was no sincerity of interest in them, only the attempted smartness of men who thought they could be clever in debate. So it is "almost as though he enjoyed playing with these clumsy opponents," and "it is exhilarating to watch the baffled hounds at a check." [1]

It should be remembered that the challengers of Jesus in this particular encounter included people of various sorts, but most particularly the Sadducees. In the earlier part of the Gospel narrative the Pharisees are the ones who most often appear. But Jerusalem was the center where the Sadducees were dominant. They would have claimed, as the Pharisees did, to be devoted Jews, but in their case the kind of devotion they had could be a matter more of convention than of conviction. They recognized the authority of what they called the law of Moses, but they ignored the teaching of the Pharisaic scribes which could make the law too strict a regulation of everyday life. In the main, they were men of wealth, and therefore they had much to gain by keeping the social order free from dangerous disturbance. The Romans were in control of Palestine. That was regrettable, of course, and as Jews they disliked it; but as "practical men" they must recognize things as they were and—like the Quislings and the Lavals of Europe in the Second World War—manipulate matters to their own advantage. They flatly disbelieved in a resurrection. This life, with a respectable conformity to the law of Moses, was the sphere in which a man might reap such rewards as were offered both by religion and by worldly wisdom. So they had collaborated with the Roman power; and by the Romans they had been given the chief appointments as priests and beneficiaries of the lucrative revenues that came from the sacrifices and offerings required of all the people at the Temple.

They had been outraged by what Jesus had done when he drove the traders out of the Temple courts. So they challenged his authority. Who had given him any right to interfere with what they chose to license?

Of course, from their point of view, nobody had given him any right. Nobody in the kind of officialdom which they recognized could. On legal grounds they could prove that he had no case whatever.

His authority was the divine indignation against an intolerable abuse which men of conscience ought to have recognized; but the assertion of this kind of authority he knew they would brush aside—unless he confronted them with a counter question which they could not deal with. Therefore he asked them, "Was the baptism of John from heaven or from men?"

Now John had no legal authority, either. No officials had authorized John to do what he had done; but John had preached a kingdom of God that would be as a consuming fire and as an ax laid to the root of the tree of the things that the Sadducees defended. If the Sadducees could have

---

[1] *The Man Born to Be King,* p. 198.

answered as they wanted to answer, they would have said that John was an intolerable fanatic, and so was Jesus. But Jesus knew well that they would not dare say this about John. The people had recognized the moral power in him that had no need of any Sadducean license, and they had an admiration for him that was passionate. So the Sadducees could not say that John had no authority except what he assumed to himself, for they feared the people. But if they said his authority was from God, then Jesus would ask, "Why did you not believe him?"

He had caught them in an impossible dilemma, and they knew it. All that their angry frustration could answer was that they did not know; and all that Jesus needed to say then was that if they knew no more than that about the authority which comes from God, there was no use interpreting to them the authority that was in him.

THE TENANTS OF THE VINEYARD

And he began to tell the people this parable: "A man planted a vineyard, and let it out to tenants, and went into another country for a long while. When the time came, he sent a servant to the tenants, that they should give him some of the fruit of the vineyard; but the tenants beat him, and sent him away empty-handed. And he sent another servant; him also they beat and treated shamefully, and sent him away empty-handed. And he sent yet a third; this one they wounded and cast out. Then the owner of the vineyard said, 'What shall I do? I will send my beloved son; it may be they will respect him.' But when the tenants saw him, they said to themselves, 'This is the heir; let us kill him, that the inheritance may be ours.' And they cast him out of the vineyard and killed him. What then will the owner of the vineyard do to them? He will come and destroy those tenants, and give the vineyard to others." When they heard this, they said, "God forbid!" But he looked at them and said, "What then is this that is written:
'The very stone which the builders rejected
has become the head of the corner'?
Every one who falls on that stone will be broken to pieces; but when it falls on any one it will crush him." (Luke 20:9-18.)

The question as to the authority of John the Baptist and the sullen unwillingness of the Sadducees to answer it highlighted the fact that the Sadducees had rejected John, and that men like the Sadducees had rejected and would reject God's prophets generally. Therefore Jesus turned to all the people who were listening and spoke a parable which was crushing in its judgment of religious officials who had failed in the trust which had been given them by God.

He drew the picture of a vineyard let out to tenants. The men who heard him recognized immediately that symbol of the vineyard. The prophet Isaiah, centuries before, had used it to represent the life of this people who wished to believe that they were the chosen of God. "Now, O inhabitants of Jerusalem and men of Judah," he said—as though the voice of God himself were speaking—"judge, I pray you, between me and my vineyard. . . . When I looked for it to yield grapes, why did it yield wild grapes?"

But the picture as Jesus shaped it is more grim. He shifted the spotlight from the general fact of unfruitful ground to the specific living persons who were responsible for something worse than the ground's unfruitfulness. They had ignored altogether the fact that the vineyard belonged to God. Instead of trying to produce the fruits of righteousness which would have been their offering to him, they had used the vineyard only for their own advantage. And when the messengers had come to remind them of that which they held in trust, they had treated them with contempt and violence. They had rejected the prophets, and now they would reject one who was greater than the prophets. Jesus was bringing to Israel the ultimate summons of God—a summons away from the hard worldliness of Caiaphas and the bitter narrowness of Pharisees and scribes. They could listen now to the one whom their consciences knew to be speaking out of the heart of God; or they could kill what their entrenched rebellion did not choose to hear. The nation stood on the brink of judgment, and the stone of judgment would be crushing when it fell.

It is a smooth and easy matter to read the Bible as a history of ancient times. Priests, Pharisees, people who made the ecclesiastical and political choices in a society long since dead—what do they matter to us? Nothing—or else everything, according to the measure in which we see the eternal truth in the changing scene. Wherever and whenever men forget the sovereignty of God, forget that they are only tenants accountable to him and act instead with self-assertive arrogance, then the day of reckoning draws near.

It was written long ago in the book of Deuteronomy, "Beware, lest you say in your heart, 'My power and the might of my hand have gotten me this wealth.'" Beware of such boasts as Nebuchadnezzar made when he exclaimed, "Is not this great Babylon, which I have built by my mighty power . . . for the glory of my majesty?" Nevertheless, some individual will say, "I am a self-made man." Also a nation may think that it is self-made—and can be self-maintained: by material affluence, by military power. But if a nation loses its sense of lofty purpose, as Israel did, if in racial pride and nationalistic hardness it exploits for itself alone that which it holds in trust for the human family—then the Owner of the vineyard may come to reckon with those who dared to think they owned it. The great words of Kipling's "Recessional" expressed what every nation needs to echo:

> Lord God of Hosts, be with us yet,
> Lest we forget—lest we forget! [2]

TRIBUTE TO CAESAR?

> The scribes and the chief priests tried to lay hands on him at that very hour, but they feared the people; for they perceived that he had told this parable against them. So they watched him, and sent spies, who pretended to be sincere, that they might take hold of what he said, so as to deliver him up to the authority and jurisdiction of the governor. They asked him, "Teacher, we know that you speak and teach rightly, and show no partiality, but truly teach the way of God. Is it lawful for us to give tribute to Caesar, or not?" But he perceived their craftiness, and said to them, "Show me a coin. Whose likeness and inscription has it?" They said, "Caesar's." He said to them, "Then render to Caesar the things that are Caesar's, and to God the things that are God's." And they were not able in the presence of the people to catch him by what he said; but marveling at his answer they were silent.
>
> (Luke 20:19-26.)

Twice the Sadducees had been infuriated: the first time by being caught themselves in the trap they had tried to spring about Jesus' authority, and then by his devastating parable of the vineyard. It was not strange that they wanted to arrest him then and there, but they were still afraid of the temper of the people. They would try again to tempt him to some pronouncement that would be grounds of accusation to the Roman governor.

So they asked him, with sardonic pretense of respect for his heavenly knowledge, whether or not it was right to pay the Roman tribute. It seemed a crafty and effective question. If he said yes, he would outrage all the violent Jewish patriots. If he said no, he would incur the instant punishment of Rome. But once again his mind was quicker and surer than theirs. "Show me a coin," he said, and they gave him a coin with the emperor's likeness on it. Now the issue of coinage was a mark of rulership, and the fact that men had accepted Caesar's coins was a sign that they accepted the framework of law and order which Caesar represented. In material things, therefore, let them adjust themselves to that. But in and above and

[2] Used by permission of The Macmillan Company of Canada, Ltd., Mrs. George Bambridge, and Doubleday & Company, Inc.

through their ordinary transactions, let them ask what tribute in ideal and effort they were offering to the kingdom of God.

So he expressed the double relationship which can never be pinned down into categorical prescriptions, but within which the sensitive conscience must find its right adjustment. On the one hand, there is the framework of existing social order about which the apostle Paul would later write, "Let every person be subject to the governing authorities. . . . For rulers are not a terror to good conduct, but to bad." On the other hand, there is the spiritual imperative which is ultimately sovereign, and which can lead a man or a people to the sort of allegiance which was expressed by Cardinal Mercier of Malines when in the First World War he wrote to the German occupying powers in Belgium, "There is a barrier . . . behind which is intrenched inviolable right. On this side of the barrier, it is we, the representatives of moral authority, who speak as masters. We cannot and will not let the word of God be shackled." [3]

THE MARRIED HERE AND IN THE LIFE TO COME

There came to him some Sadducees, those who say that there is no resurrection, and they asked him a question, saying, "Teacher, Moses wrote for us that if a man's brother dies, having a wife but no children, the man must take the wife and raise up children for his brother. Now there were seven brothers; the first took a wife, and died without children; and the second and the third took her, and likewise all seven left no children and died. Afterward the woman also died. In the resurrection, therefore, whose wife will the woman be? For the seven had her as wife."

And Jesus said to them, "The sons of this age marry and are given in marriage; but those who are accounted worthy to attain to that age and to the resurrection from the dead neither marry nor are given in marriage, for they cannot die any more, because they are equal to angels and are sons of God, being sons of the resurrection. But that the dead are raised, even Moses showed, in the passage about the bush, where he calls the Lord the God of Abraham and the God of Isaac and the God of Jacob. Now he is not God of the dead, but of the living; for all live to him." And some of the scribes answered, "Teacher, you have spoken well." For they no longer dared to ask him any question.

(Luke 20:27-40.)

Those who were questioning Jesus have been denominated as scribes and chief priests. The chief priests were Sadducees, and so the Saducean beliefs or lack of them have already been involved in the discussion. But only the Sadducees are named as the instigators of the next question, for

[3] John A. Gade, *The Life of Cardinal Mercier* (New York: Charles Scribner's Sons, 1935), p. 181.

the question reflected a specific difference between them and most of the Pharisees and scribes, in that the Sadducees dismissed any idea of a resurrection. Knowing that Jesus believed what they rejected, they thought they might discredit him in the hearing of the crowd by making the belief ridiculous.

So they trumped up a story of something which might happen in this life, and which—if there should be a resurrection—would seem to promise a hopeless snarl in any life hereafter. There was an ancient law in Israel based upon the instinctive longing that if a man died, his name at least, and something of his identity, should continue in the world by way of children. So if he had no children, his brother was to marry his widow; and their children would carry on the name. Now, said the Sadducees, suppose a whole succession of brothers married the widow and one by one died while the widow outlived them all, then she died, and the whole lot of them were in heaven together; whose wife would she be?

The way Jesus answered was to lift the spiritual reality up out of the quibbling cheapness in which the Sadducees had tried to confuse it. The practice they had talked about had nothing to do with the actual souls of people. It was simply a device by which a family name should continue to be propagated. Certainly that sort of marriage would have no place in the world to come. But the world to come, like the world that is, belongs to God; and according to the Scriptures which the Sadducees themselves acknowledged, he is not God of the dead but of the living. Therefore all live to him; and it is what has been deepest and most alive in existence here on earth that goes on to its fulfillment in the immortal realm. The trouble with the so-called marriages which the Sadducees recited was that they were only expedients for a framed-up purpose. There had been in those distorted instances no drawing of heart to heart which could give marriage an immortal meaning.

Some of the scribes answered, "Teacher, you have spoken well." They saw that he had cut through the snare which the Sadducees had thought they could set for him. And may it be also that they glimpsed the great assurance which Jesus at this moment did not put into words but which all his spirit expressed: that God is love, and they who love are born of God and know God, and those who in their souls have been truly married here will have their bond of love forever.

THE MEANING OF THE MESSIAH

But he said to them, "How can they say that the Christ is David's son? For David himself says in the Book of Psalms,

'The Lord said to my Lord,
Sit at my right hand,
till I make thy enemies a stool for thy feet.'
David thus calls him Lord; so how is he his son?" (Luke 20:41-44.)

The antagonists of Jesus had had enough. All their questions and would-be challenges had fallen flat. There was nothing more that they quite dared to ask. So he asked them a question, and left them to arrive at what answer they could.

They read the Scriptures according to accepted tradition, and the tradition was that the psalms had been written by David. Psalm 110 was interpreted as meaning that David foresaw the Messiah who would come and be exalted at the right hand of God. But among the Jewish people there had flamed the hope that some actual descendant of David would arise to be the nation's deliverer, to bring back the glory of David's kingdom by the weapons of this earth. But if the Messiah whom David foresaw was to be one of his own descendants, how could David call him "Lord"? It was inconceivable. Therefore to think of the Christ as primarily "the son of David," and to call him by that name, had no warrant in the Scriptures.

This apparently is what Jesus was saying, though it must be admitted that with the lapse of time and with our only partial knowledge we cannot be sure. If it *is* what he was saying, then perhaps his purpose was to check the ferment that might be rising among some of the people that a son of David might come to conquer with a sword. It was necessary that men should know—as Simon Peter had learned at Caesarea Philippi— that the redemption which could come through Christ must involve much deeper changes, not in circumstance but in men's souls.

THE CONDEMNATION OF THE INSINCERE

And in the hearing of all the people he said to his disciples, "Beware of the scribes, who like to go about in long robes, and love salutations in the market places and the best seats in the synagogues and the places of honor at feasts, who devour widows' houses and for a pretense make long prayers. They will receive the greater condemnation." (Luke 20:45-47.)

The warning against the kind of religion represented by the scribes is an abbreviated parallel to the blistering indictment contained in chapter 23 of the Gospel of Matthew. The scribes were the most learned of the Pharisees, experts in all the particularities of religious law. Politically, the Jews were a subject people; but under the shadow of that political humiliation they cherished the conviction of their spiritual superiority as heirs of the covenant with God which was as old as Abraham. The scribes were the ones who understood all about that covenant and the particular customs and the proper worship which the covenant required. So the average man felt himself dependent on the scribes for the regulations that would keep him in good standing as one of the chosen people, and assure him thus of a future salvation which would never belong to the Gentiles who lorded over him now. He took it for granted that the scribes were entitled to special honors. Of course he must bow to them—or in modern terms, take off his hat to them—when he met them in the market or the streets. Of course he must make way for them and show them to the best seats in any assembly. He felt toward them as the simple person in Mexico or Spain or in an Italian village might feel toward the parish priest. Since the priest has the key to heaven, he must be treated with careful deference and even with instinctive awe.

Now it is possible for men to be religious guides and to retain meanwhile a purity of heart that keeps them humble. But it is also possible for them to become possessed by self-importance, so that they expect and demand the honors which the common folk have been taught to give. Thus it had happened with the scribes. They liked to go about in ecclesiastical robes, and they not only got the salutations and the best seats; they loved to get them. Nor was that all. Pride in appearance could bring them to the point where the appearance was made a cover for deeds which belied their supposed religious dedication. They offered long prayers, and that looked like piety; but when they got through praying, they were busy with something very different. They "devour widows' houses," said Jesus. That is to say, they were ecclesiastically eminent and socially disreputable. One of them might have been described in the same ironic phrase with which Edwin O'Connor labeled a church member who bought dilapidated houses and then rented them as tenements at extortionate rates to the poor: "as fine a man as ever robbed the helpless. . . ." [4]

Sometimes the shallow people who want a comfortable message prate about "the simple Gospel." Religion should have to do with the affairs of the soul, they say, and not with ordinary activities; with getting ready for heaven and not with mixing in this world's tangled business. "Social righteousness" is something outside the church's scope. But the judgments of Jesus are different. His devastating truthfulness sees through the pretense of a Sunday piety which has no consequences in the business of the week. As with the scribes in Jerusalem, so with men in every modern city and town who wear the robes of churchmanship but outside the church are rapacious, hard, and merciless—they will receive in the sight of God not less but greater condemnation.

[4] Edwin O'Connor, *The Edge of Sadness* (Boston: Little, Brown & Co., 1961), p. 368.

chapter 21

THE GREATNESS
OF THE SEEMINGLY INSIGNIFICANT

He looked up and saw the rich putting their gifts into the treasury;
and he saw a poor widow put in two copper coins. And he said, "Truly
I tell you, this poor widow has put in more than all of them; for they
all contributed out of their abundance, but she out of her poverty put
in all the living that she had."

(Luke 21:1-4.)

How like Jesus it was that he should have observed this incident and
spoken of it in such a way that the disciples could never forget it. It was
in the last week of his life, when every day was full of destiny. Fateful
issues were pressing in upon him, and it might have seemed that he must
be immersed in these. But here, as always, he could see the spiritual significance in what no one else had stopped to notice. In the Temple as he
passed through, rich men were putting their contributions into the treasury.
Everybody could see them; but the one whom Jesus saw was a woman
coming timidly to cast in her pitifully meager gift. Two copper coins were
all she gave, and some might have looked at such an offering with super-
cilious unconcern. But Jesus said, "This poor widow has put in more than
all of them; for they all contributed from out of their abundance, but she
out of her poverty put in all the living that she had."

The point of Jesus' words is plain. It is not the size of a gift but the
spirit in it which makes it great. The little that the widow gave was more
lavish—and in God's eyes more beautiful—than what the rich men put in.

Yet sometimes our self-interest can twist even the plainest truth to our
advantage—or at least can try to. It can be very convenient to imagine
that not the lavishness but the littleness of the gift can somehow get to be
meritorious. In a certain congregation there was a rich woman who held
on closely to her money. She wrote to her minister, reciting all the expenses
she said she had to meet, but announcing that in spite of those she wanted
to send something for God's work; and so—in the phrase that the King
James Version has made so familiar—she was enclosing "the widow's mite."
Her minister was moved to remind her that even the poor widow in the
Bible had given *two* mites.

So much for our pitiful little human justifications. But over and above our pettiness shines the greatness of devotion which Jesus recognized in the woman who never knew that he had seen her: never knew, because certainly he let no sound of his words reach her to make her self-conscious about the lovely thing she did. Her soul had won its own reward. And as one considers her, one realizes the immortal value of a great loyalty, regardless of all consequences. Devotion poured out in the name of God creates a spiritual enrichment which nothing can destroy. The woman in whom Jesus rejoiced had given the utmost she had to maintain God's sanctuary in Jerusalem. Yet the time came when that Temple and everything that surrounded it would be in ruins. War and pillage knocked at the gates of the city; and all its glory, including the glory of the Temple, was trampled into dust. It might have seemed as though the gift of the widow, and every other gift like hers, had been utterly in vain. But it is not so. The visible Temple in which she made her offering is gone. Nevertheless, the invisible temple of the spirit of God in human life is more beautiful forever for her offering. Still in the midst of human life, the sanctuary of all lovely thoughts and high devotion is builded more securely through the influence of her example. And so it can be in every generation.

So it may be, in more immediate and personal fact, with some one of us. You may be discouraged sometimes at the apparent destruction of the very thing you have tried to help. The cause you have served does not succeed. The personality upon which you have poured out your devotion does not respond. You cannot carry through the help you wanted so utterly to give. Your sacrifice seems to have been in vain. But look further. Look past the things you see into the long perspective which God is seeing. No self-forgetting generous deed is ever wasted. The indestructible reality of it will be part of the shrine of God's presence in humanity long after the immediate world you know has gone down into the abyss of time.

It is significant that this story of the deathless value of what the widow did is followed by Jesus' words concerning the end of an era.

THE DESTRUCTION OF THE TEMPLE

And as some spoke of the temple, how it was adorned with noble stones and offerings, he said, "As for these things which you see, the days will come when there shall not be left here one stone upon another that will not be thrown down." (Luke 21:5-6.)

Hardly anything could have been more shocking to those who heard it than the words of Jesus that the Temple would be destroyed. It had just been rebuilt in unparalleled magnificence by Herod the Great. Of

Idumaean descent, Herod was only half Jew; but as a matter of policy he chose to cultivate the religious pride of the Jewish people. He stood in high favor at Rome with the emperor Augustus, who had appointed him to rule in Palestine; and he had accumulated great wealth, which enabled him to carry out his lavish plans. What he had done in Jerusalem was breathtaking. On colossal stone foundations he had prepared at the crest of the hill of Zion a paved area, roughly rectangular, the longest side of which measured nearly a quarter of a mile. This great space made up the Temple courts, round three sides of which ran a double row of monolithic marble columns; and on the south front the colonnades were four. The first court within the gates was the Court of the Gentiles, into which people in general could come. Beyond was the Temple itself, with the Holy of Holies as its inmost shrine. Not only were all its walls of marble, but the gates were plated with silver and gold, and underneath the cornice was a golden vine, the special gift of Herod. Flavius Josephus, Jewish historian of the first century, wrote that from a distance the Temple was like a snow-covered mountain, and the reflected light from it was dazzling as the "sun's own rays." This was what Herod had built; and to the priests and all the rest of religious officialdom the Temple seemed to be not only the symbol but also the embodiment of Israel's relationship to God. And Herod, meanwhile, was thoroughly pleased with himself for what he had done. Josephus wrote that Herod esteemed this building of the Temple to be "the most glorious of all actions, and that this should be an everlasting memorial of him"; and when Herod put the matter in his own words, he said that he intended "to make a thankful return, after the most pious manner, to God, for what blessings I have received from him by giving me this kingdom." [1]

Yet this Temple would be destroyed, said Jesus; and within a generation his words came true.

It was as though in the judgment of God the pride and ostentation which men called religion had been weighed in the balances and found wanting, and therefore cast down into the dust. Always there is danger that the outward show may become a substitute for the inner spirit. An impetuous young minister insisted one day that every church building should be planned and built to last only thirty years. This would prevent the accumulation of material adornment, the marble and gilt, the stained glass, the jewelled vessels, and all the continuing enrichment by which an ingrown attachment to what men like to call the house of God may make their worship a soft indulgence instead of a response to life.

[1] *Antiquities of the Jews,* Book 15, chapter 11.

There is not much danger that his idea will be taken literally, and there are values which could be lost if it were. Instinctively men feel that all human gifts must somehow be used to the glory of God: architecture and sculpture and music, so that as there is a beauty of holiness, there may be also a holiness in beauty. If a noble church does bring the spirit into awed awareness of the living God, then it serves its purpose. But the condemnation of the Temple in Jerusalem stands as a continual warning. For a congregation to become engrossed in the building of some more magnificent church, and build it partly through the gifts of some half-Christian Herod, may be to forget—while pretending to honor—the costly challenge of the spirit of Christ. In *Honest to God,* the Bishop of Woolwich has truly written, "The test of worship is how far it makes us *more sensitive* to 'the beyond in our midst,' to the Christ in the hungry, the naked, the homeless, and the prisoner. Only if we are *more likely* to recognize him *there* after attending an act of worship is that worship Christian rather than a piece of religiosity in Christian dress." [2]

WHEN THE END COMES

And they asked him, "Teacher, when will this be, and what will be the sign when this is about to take place?" And he said, "Take heed that you are not led astray; for many will come in my name, saying, 'I am he!' and, 'The time is at hand!' Do not go after them. And when you hear of wars and tumults, do not be terrified; for this must first take place, but the end will not be at once."

Then he said to them, "Nation will rise against nation, and kingdom against kingdom; there will be great earthquakes, and in various places famines and pestilences; and there will be terrors and great signs from heaven. But before all this they will lay their hands on you and persecute you, delivering you up to the synagogues and prisons, and you will be brought before kings and governors for my name's sake. This will be a time for you to bear testimony. Settle it therefore in your minds, not to meditate beforehand how to answer; for I will give you a mouth and wisdom, which none of your adversaries will be able to withstand or contradict. You will be delivered up even by parents and brothers and kinsmen and friends, and some of you they will put to death; you will be hated by all for my name's sake. But not a hair of your head will perish. By your endurance you will gain your lives."   (Luke 21:7-19.)

Every reader of the Gospel who comes to this part of chapter 21 beginning with vs. 7 realizes that he is confronted with material difficult to understand, and the plain fact is that no interpreter can be bold enough to claim

[2] p. 90.

that he understands it fully. What does its symbolic language mean? And how can we grasp what it was that Jesus said to his disciples? The best beginning we can make toward an answer is to remember the expectations which were in the minds of men in that first century.

It was a time that was tense with a feeling of crisis. In the second century B.C., there had been a brief period of pride and exaltation for the people of Israel when the Maccabean leaders had waged their heroic wars that won independence for the nation. But the torch which had been lighted then had flickered out. The irresistible power of Rome had advanced into Palestine, and all the region which once had been the kingdom of David was no more than a Roman province. The hope in Israel turned from the earthly to the supernatural realm. Men looked into the future with the desperate desire that by some tremendous intervention God would enter into the troubled course of human history and set its evils right.

The most vivid expression of this hope was in the so-called apocalyptic books, written and widely read in the last two centuries B.C. and the first century after the birth of Christ. The writers of these books believed that the spirit of God had come to them as revelation so that they could foresee the future and declare the changes that were coming on the earth. God's redemption would bring a Golden Age for Israel; but first there would be a period of upheaval and anguish that must precede the coming of the Messiah, and afterwards the Judgment and the end of this world that men know now. Matthew, Mark, and Luke were all three familiar with this apocalyptic literature; and in all three Gospels, after Jesus' predictions of the destruction of the Temple, there follows substantially the same material concerning the woes that were coming on the earth. It seems quite disconnected from the clear words of Jesus about the impending destruction of the Temple, and is no answer to the immediate question which the disciples asked him about the circumstances surrounding it. Therefore there is persuasive likelihood in the judgment expressed by William Manson, professor of New Testament in New College, Edinburgh, that

there is reason to believe that the material here incorporated by the evangelists must have passed through some independent stage of development, and many scholars therefore see in it a Jewish-Christian apocalypse, based partly on words of Jesus and partly on other traditional materials, which was drawn up for the instruction of Christians in days when excited anticipations of the Lord's return were rife, and which took its present form shortly before or simultaneously with the catastrophe of the year 70.[3]

[3] William Manson, *The Gospel of Luke* ("The Moffatt New Testament Commentary" [New York: Harper and Brothers, 1930]), III, 231.

Thus it is uncertain to what extent this passage conveys the actual words of Jesus, or embodies instead part of some current apocalypse by which men's courage might be lifted. In either case, the spirit of Jesus is here. He is warning those who followed him of dangers they must face, and at the same time assuring them of an immortal power by which they will be protected. And he is making them know that their testimony to their Lord will not depend on any nervously considered words. If they are faithful, the Holy Spirit will inspire them to a kind of living witness which no adversaries can withstand or contradict. The truth is mighty and will prevail. In great crises of history, this has been proved true. Martin Luther, brought before the emperor and the great lords of church and state at the Diet of Worms, had no need of elaborate eloquence. "Here I stand; God helping me, I can do no other!" he said as he risked his life for what he dared proclaim to be the saving gospel. Those words, and the conviction back of them, were enough to let loose a new spiritual force upon his world.

THE FALL OF JERUSALEM

"But when you see Jerusalem surrounded by armies, then know that its desolation has come near. Then let those who are in Judea flee to the mountains, and let those who are inside the city depart, and let not those who are out in the country enter it; for these are days of vengeance, to fulfil all that is written. Alas for those who are with child and for those who give suck in those days! For great distress shall be upon the earth and wrath upon this people; they will fall by the edge of the sword, and be led captive among all nations; and Jerusalem will be trodden down by the Gentiles, until the times of the Gentiles are fulfilled."
(Luke 21:20-24.)

T. W. Manson has indicated that this passage in the Gospel "took its present form shortly before or simultaneously with the catastrophe of the year 70." It is clear what catastrophe he meant. It was the fall of Jerusalem, including the destruction of the Temple, which Jesus had already foreseen and predicted. In the Royal Gallery at Edinburgh, there is a painting which foreshadows the coming fact. Seated on the crest of Olivet at the fall of night is the brooding figure of Jesus. His eyes look across the intervening valley to the walls and towers of what men like to call the Holy City; but he knew it to have so lost its living response to the purpose of God that its light had turned to darkness. He saw the inexorable drift of its moral and spiritual failure which was moving toward its doom. And within a generation the doom had come. Roman legions under Titus invested Jerusalem in a frightful siege, during which the defenders, although reduced to starvation, resisted month after month with such stubborn passion that the mood of the besiegers was merciless when the day of their vengeance arrived. When at length the walls were breached, there was massacre in all the streets; and as Flavius Josephus recorded in his *Wars of the Jews,*

As soon as the army had no more people to slay or to plunder, because there remained none to be the objects of their fury, [the order was given] that they should demolish the entire city and temple, except some towers and a portion of the wall in order to denominate to posterity what kind of city it was, and how well fortified which the Roman valour had subdued. But for all the rest of the wall it was so completely levelled with the ground . . . that there was nothing to make those who came hither believe that it had ever been inhabited. This was the end which Jerusalem came to . . . a city otherwise of great magnificence and of mighty fame among all mankind.[4]

Jerusalem had gone the way of Nineveh and Babylon, as another tragic witness that the mills of God grind slowly, but they grind exceeding small.

FAITH THROUGH THE DARKNESS

"And there will be signs in sun and moon and stars, and upon the earth distress of nations in perplexity at the roaring of the sea and the waves, men fainting with fear and with foreboding of what is coming on the world; for the powers of the heavens will be shaken. And then they will see the Son of man coming in a cloud with power and great glory. Now when these things begin to take place, look up and raise your heads, because your redemption is drawing near." (Luke 21:25-28.)

This chapter, as we have seen, is a mosaic in which the Evangelist has put together separate and different materials. The overall pattern is a picture of judgment, wrapped in cloud, fire, and storm; and in its awful symbolism it is not always possible to discern which aspect of the judgment each particular part of the mosaic represents. Clearly vss. 5-6 are a specific prophecy of the destruction of the Temple, and vss. 20-24 a foreshadowing of the ruin of Jerusalem. But the paragraph beginning with vs. 25 has to do with that which cannot be pinned down within the calendar of time. It is like the opening of a door at the point where mortal history will end, and the ultimate reckoning of God begins. We cannot be sure if Luke is transmitting words spoken in this particular form by Jesus to his disciples, or if he is including some apocryphal writing which expressed in its tremendous imagery the mingled dread and hope of the early church. In

[4] Book 7, chapter 1.

either case, its ultimate message is one of faith triumphant. At the crucifixion men's hearts would faint with fear, and the powers both of earth and
heaven seem shaken; but in the risen and living Christ, the Son of man
would be coming in his glory, and through him redemption would be drawing near.

THE CERTAINTY WITHIN THE UNCERTAIN

And he told them a parable: "Look at the fig tree, and all the trees; as
soon as they come out in leaf, you see for yourselves and know that the
summer is already near. So also, when you see these things taking place,
you know that the kingdom of God is near. Truly, I say to you, this
generation will not pass away till all has taken place. Heaven and earth
will pass away, but my words will not pass away." (Luke 21:29-33.)

In the ordinary world of nature, Jesus said, men can see the signs of
changes which are about to come. Let them use this same perceptiveness
in looking for the signs that foretoken the more critical changes in the life
of men. It is well to know when summer or winter may be approaching;
but it is of vaster consequence to know when the kingdom may be drawing
near.

We cannot be certain of the meaning of the words of Jesus which Luke
records in vs. 32. Did he expect that within what was then the immediate
future there would be the cataclysmic act of God which would bring the
world that we have known to an end, and usher in that new existence
which will be on the other side of the Last Judgment? Or did he mean
that the kingdom of God was already appearing in the transforming
spiritual power which had begun to enter into the lives of his disciples
and would bring a new era of redemption to this earth?

If the words, "till all has taken place," in vs. 32 should be considered
as referring to the awful events foreshadowed in vss. 25-28, then it certainly
was not a fact that the generation living when Jesus spoke was to see those
events fulfilled. The earth as men knew it was not disrupted; and in literal
fashion the Son of man did not come "in a cloud with power and great
glory"—not, at least, to those who could see only the things which were
visible to their eyes. But in the deep realities of the spirit, the power and
the glory did come. It came in quietness, with the gradual wonder of un-
folding life. "Heaven and earth will pass away, but my words will not pass
away," said Jesus. Wherever his words had entered into minds and hearts,
there was a new springtime. If the first leafage of the fig tree was a sign
that the earth was on the way from winter into summer, so the little beginnings here and there of the influence of Jesus and the gospel were the

promise that the kingdom of God was dawning on the earth. Our mortal life and all the fashion of it changes. The little voice of men's imagined shrewdness fades into silence, but the words of Jesus outlast all space and time. As long as human existence continues, men will have to reckon with what he taught concerning God and man.

WATCHFULNESS

"But take heed to yourselves lest your hearts be weighed down with dissipation and drunkenness and cares of this life, and that day come upon you suddenly like a snare; for it will come upon all who dwell upon the face of the whole earth. But watch at all times, praying that you may have strength to escape all these things that will take place, and to stand before the Son of man." (Luke 21:34-36.)

There are times when men are beguiled into imagining that human destiny will be like a tranquil river, with no dangerous rapids nor roaring of even distant falls. So it could seem no longer ago than a half century, when to all superficial appearance the nations could look forward in bland assurance to a future of safety and softness, and no one saw on the horizon the dark portent of what was soon to follow. Remembering such a time, one sees again the picture which John Bunyan drew in *The Pilgrim's Progress.* Christian, moved to escape from the city which did not know it was to be the City of Destruction, "saw, a little out of the way, three men fast asleep, with fetters upon their heels. The name of the one was Simple, another Sloth, and the third Presumption." He tried to wake them and call them to come away, for they were lying, he said, above "a gulf that hath no bottom." But "they looked upon him, and began to reply in this sort: Simple said, 'I see no danger.' Sloth said, 'Yet a little more sleep.' And Presumption said, 'Every tub must stand upon its own bottom.' And so they laid down to sleep again, and Christian went on his way."

Through this whole chapter 21 of the Gospel there sounds the deep and solemn note of warning. Under the shallow complacency of human life at any moment may be the "gulf that hath no bottom."

This sense of crisis has come back again to human consciousness in this troubled mid-twentieth century. The shallow confidence which marked the period of fifty years ago, with its belief in smooth and sure progression, has gone down like a stricken ship. On April 10, 1912, the *Titanic,* the largest and most magnificent passenger liner which then had ever been built, proudly proclaimed to be unsinkable, sailed from England on her maiden voyage. Four days later, with her engines driving the great ship ahead at full power, heedless of warnings that there was heavy ice in the north Atlantic, the *Titanic* struck an iceberg that was seen too late, and went down with most of her passengers to her death in the wintry sea. That particular collision, with its stark reminder of dangers in our universe which could be deadly, was followed within two years by the First World War, and then by the Second; and aspects of our human heritage which were supposed to be more indestructible than the *Titanic* were smashed and broken. We may not have been "weighed down by dissipation and drunkenness"; but the general mind—like the unthinking passengers on the *Titanic,* chatting unconcernedly while the great ship was speeding to its doom—has often been so occupied with trivial things that it cannot see appalling facts which are drawing near.

Raymond Robins was the head of the Red Cross mission which carried relief to Russia at the end of the First World War. He has described what happened there that caused the czarist regime to be overthrown. The imperial court and all the nobility which gathered round it were oblivious to the terrible forces rising among the masses of the people whose poverty and wretchedness had been too long ignored. The rich dined in their lighted banquet halls and danced in their levees with silken curtains drawn against the peril gathering in the ominous streets in the dark Russian night. They had—he said in one unforgettable phrase—"the indoor mind." All they knew or cared about was what went on within the circle of their soft advantage, and in the vainly imagined shelter of that they were oblivious of the terror about to strike.

Whenever any individual or society thus loses the consciousness of moral crisis, the day of judgment will indeed come suddenly like a snare.

The climax of this chapter in Luke's Gospel is the summons to be awake. Events, which may bring the judgment of God upon the destinies of men and nations, come in ways and at times which the careless have not foreseen. "Watch at all times, praying that you may have strength." Only so, in personal thinking and in public decision, can any generation meet its crises in such a way as to accept and not reject its chance to be brought nearer to the kingdom of God.

chapter 22

THE BETRAYAL

Now the feast of Unleavened Bread drew near, which is called the Passover. And the chief priests and the scribes were seeking how to put him to death; for they feared the people.

Then Satan entered into Judas called Iscariot, who was of the number of the twelve; he went away and conferred with the chief priests and captains how he might betray him to them. And they were glad, and engaged to give him money. So he agreed, and sought an opportunity to betray him to them in the absence of the multitude. (Luke 22:1-6.)

The Passover was the most sacred festival of the Jewish year. It commemorated the deliverance of Israel from slavery in Egypt, and was a witness to the faith that God can enter with new, redeeming power into history. The priests and Pharisees held to that faith as a matter of inheritance. They demanded that everybody be orthodox in declaring the reality of God's presence—in some past time. But Jesus was making the divine reality a disturbing immediate fact. As Israel had been delivered from physical bondage long ago, so it needed now to be delivered spiritually from the tomb of religious formalism where the old great hopes lay like dead men's bones. The pity was that the priests and Pharisees, like those in all times whose religion becomes professionalized, did not want to be jolted out of their complacency. So they determined to get rid of Jesus. The only question was the way to do it that would stir up the least excitement.

Help came to the enemies of Jesus from an unexpected quarter. Satan entered into Judas, one of the twelve. Judas could tell where Jesus might be found. He could tell other facts about him which the priests might want to know. And he did. He sold his information for money that the high priest gave him. The money may have been the least inducement, for it was a paltry sum. What else, then, moved him to his treachery? Possibly an element of jealousy that he a Judean had seemed to be less prominent than all the Galileans who made up the rest of the twelve. But perhaps most of all he was secretly disillusioned. Jesus had proclaimed that the kingdom of God was at hand. Well, was not Israel the people of God, bound to him by the age-long covenant? Then the kingdom of God ought to mean something tremendous for the Jewish people: their triumph over enemies, the smashing of the tyranny of Rome. If Jesus was to be Messiah, then he would come as conqueror; and there would be honor and greatness for those who were close to him. That perhaps was what Judas had thought. But nothing was working out as might have been expected. Sermons to crowds of ordinary Galileans, healing of sick people here and there, talking about serving others and loving enemies—how would these build any kind of kingdom that had substance in it? What could Jesus *do?* Judas had followed him in the hope that he would shake the earth. But he had not done it, and now it was time to call a halt. Let Jesus prove his power, or admit that he had none. Therefore he would tell the priests where they could find Jesus if they wanted to arrest him. And if Jesus could do nothing but let himself be arrested, why should Judas keep on believing in him?

So Judas argued plausibly to himself, yet actually with twisted thinking that led him to betray the best he knew. Nor does he stand alone.

Alone in the Gospel record, yes; but not alone in human life. For the essential sin of Judas can reappear in any one of us who turns his back on some great loyalty he once believed in, and says he is through with it because idealism is a washout and good intentions do not pay.

THE REAL PRESENCE

Then came the day of Unleavened Bread, on which the passover lamb had to be sacrificed. So Jesus sent Peter and John, saying, "Go and prepare the passover for us, that we may eat it." They said to him, "Where will you have us prepare it?" He said to them, "Behold, when you have entered the city, a man carrying a jar of water will meet you; follow him into the house which he enters, and tell the householder, 'The Teacher says to you, Where is the guest room, where I am to eat the passover with my disciples?' And he will show you a large upper room furnished; there make ready." And they went, and found it as he had told them; and they prepared the passover.

And when the hour came, he sat at table, and the apostles with him. And he said to them, "I have earnestly desired to eat this passover with you before I suffer; for I tell you I shall not eat it until it is fulfilled in the kingdom of God." And he took a cup, and when he had given thanks he said, "Take this, and divide it among yourselves; for I tell you that from now on I shall not drink of the fruit of the vine until the kingdom of God comes." And he took bread, and when he had given thanks he broke it and gave it to them, saying, "This is my body."

(Luke 22:7-19.)

Many ancient authorities add the following after vs. 19: *"which is given for you. Do this in remembrance of me." And likewise the cup after supper, saying, "This cup which is poured out for you is the new covenant in my blood."*

This description of the Last Supper must be approached not only with reverence of spirit but also with the simple honesty of mind which recognizes that there are questions concerning it which we cannot surely answer. All the Gospels make evident that the Supper came at the Passover season; and Luke, Matthew, and Mark indicate that it was the actual Passover feast that Jesus kept with his disciples. But according to the Gospel of John it had to be on the night before the official Passover that Jesus gathered with his disciples in the Upper Room, for the deadly planning of the priests who hated him had moved so fast that before the Passover he would be crucified. So it may not have been the Passover ritual that Jesus celebrated, although it had been his great desire that he should. The Passover, with its immortal story of the deliverance of Israel, would remind the disciples that God's good purposes can be trusted to prevail. Now in this farewell supper he must help them still believe in victory, even though he himself was about to go out to die.

Another uncertainty is as to just what Luke recorded that Jesus said. Among the different manuscripts which have come down to us, there are some which include vss. 19 and 20; and some which do not. Thus the translators have put these not in the accepted text but in the margin of the Revised Standard Version. But these words in almost identical form do appear in the apostle Paul's first letter to the Corinthians, written about A.D. 52; and Paul's description there of the Supper, being thus much closer in time than Luke's, gives strong evidence that Jesus did speak of a new covenant in his blood.

Certainly that was what the early church proclaimed that Jesus had established. Since the time of Abraham, the Jewish people had believed that they had a special place in the purposes of God; but to live up to it was another matter. It was easy to forget, easy to lose the urge to faithfulness. The disciples knew that well enough. By themselves they were always falling short. Then they had come into touch with Jesus, and everything was different. As long as they were close to him, they could try to measure up to what his trust expected. He knew the desolation that would come to them if they should lose him. So he took the bread and wine, the substance of the common meal, and made these into a sacrament. He was about to go to his cross. His body would be broken, and his blood poured out. But the life which he was offering up would still belong to them and feed them, as surely as did the loaf he broke and the wine he gave to them to drink. Here was the covenant of the love that would not let them go.

No words the disciples might have spoken could have expressed at that hour in the Upper Room what the Last Supper meant to them. Nor can all that has been thought and written about it in the Christian centuries sound the depths of its significance. Before the ultimate mysteries of spirit, mortal flesh keeps silence. But beyond all explanations, and certainly beyond all contentious argument, the Real Presence can manifest itself to our poor human souls. To kneel at a Communion service and to remember Jesus—his life of dedication to the redemptive will of God, his strength and yet his gentleness, his willingness to suffer in himself the consequence of all the evil that was like our evil—might seem to be only a matter of our mental recollection of something that happened nineteen hundred years ago. But the truth is mightier than that. What we do can open the way for what God does. Jesus remembered can become the living Christ. Suddenly we may be aware of a reality before which we cry out, "Depart from me, for I am a sinful man, O Lord," and then with deeper yearning cry, "No, do not depart, but save me, Master, from my sins. Show me the glory that can come through suffering, and by thy presence sanctify for me the bread and wine of every common thing in life!"

Not only to our needs as individuals but to all the troubled relationships of society, the spirit of Christ mediated through the Communion may bring the one influence which can be redeeming. In 1963, William Sloane Coffin, Jr., chaplain of Yale University, was in the Fulton County jail in Atlanta, Georgia, with eighty-two Negroes who had been arrested for a civil rights demonstration. They asked that the Lord's Supper should be celebrated for them there; and concerning that experience, this is what Chaplain Coffin wrote:

> In the waiting room outside, the water came from drinking fountains labeled "Colored" and "White," but behind the bars the wine came to all of us from a common cup. The wrongness of the one and the rightness of the other were quite overpowering. "This is my body, broken for you; this is my blood, shed for you." Somehow in that moment in the crowded cell all the sin and suffering of Atlanta, the South, the nation, and even the world seemed reconciled in the sure knowledge of a God who "so loved the world that he gave his only-begotten son that whosoever should believe in him should not perish but have eternal life."
>
> There was a word from the Lord. And the Word was love.[1]

THE WAY TO GREATNESS

"But behold the hand of him who betrays me is with me on the table. For the Son of man goes as it has been determined; but woe to that

---

[1] From "The Word," in *Sermons to Intellectuals*, edited by Franklin H. Littell (New York: The Macmillan Company, 1963), p. 8.

man by whom he is betrayed!" And they began to question one another, which of them it was that would do this.

A dispute also arose among them, which of them was to be regarded as the greatest. And he said to them, "The kings of the Gentiles exercise lordship over them; and those in authority over them are called benefactors. But not so with you; rather let the greatest among you become as the youngest, and the leader as one who serves. For which is the greater, one who sits at table, or one who serves? Is it not the one who sits at table? But I am among you as one who serves.

"You are those who have continued with me in my trials; as my Father appointed a kingdom for me, so do I appoint for you that you may eat and drink at my table in my kingdom, and sit on thrones judging the twelve tribes of Israel." (Luke 22:21-30.)

How deep and tragic was the contrast in that Upper Room: at the center Jesus, and at the same table one who would betray him! The entrenched evils in church and state might in any case have brought Jesus to his crucifixion. The Son of man went as it had been determined. But that did not mitigate the shame of Judas' choice. His will was free, and he had let it be corrupted.

Nor was the knowledge of Judas' desertion the only thing that brought hurt to Jesus. The other disciples would not betray him, but all the same they were about to show him how far short they fell of what he wished that they might be. They began to question one another, which of them it was that should do this. That may mean that each man knew his own weakness, and secretly felt his own conscience stricken with the possibility that he himself might be a traitor. It could also mean that each man was stifling his own uneasiness by trying to point suspicion somewhere else. Nor was that all. As though to magnify their loyalty, they began to dispute their relative importance. "If anything critical is happening, the Master can turn to me. Put me in charge. I know how to use authority."

Against that self-assertion stands the rebuke of Jesus. Had they learned so little from knowing him? Out in the world which had no concern for the kingdom of God, men might look for place and privilege and demand titles of honor. But it could not be so with men who followed him. Only those who found their joy in lowliest service would be great in the eyes of God.

How shall we understand, then, the words in vss. 28-30, which seem so inconsistent with what Jesus had just said? How could he be promising the disciples now that they would sit on thrones? The answer lies perhaps in the fact that in that whole evening of the Last Supper much more must have passed between the disciples and Jesus than the broken record of the Gospel tells. It may be that the twelve had been humbled and shamed by their Master's rebuke. With his disappointed eyes upon them, their self-assertion went down into the dust. In place of pride they began to think that they were of no worth at all. Then he turned to them with the quick encouragement for which his heart was always ready. He knew that they wanted to be faithful. In spite of blunders they had stood by, he told them, when they might have flinched and failed. To that extent, at least, their example should be a sovereign power by which the discipleship of others would be judged.

WHEN LIFE IS CRITICAL

"Simon, Simon, behold, Satan demanded to have you, that he might sift you like wheat, but I have prayed for you that your faith may not fail; and when you have turned again, strengthen your brethren." And he said to him, "Lord, I am ready to go with you to prison and to death." He said, "I tell you, Peter, the cock will not crow this day, until you three times deny that you know me."

And he said to them, "When I sent you out with no purse or bag or sandals, did you lack anything?" They said, "Nothing." He said to them, "But now, let him who has a purse take it, and likewise a bag. And let him who has no sword sell his mantle and buy one. For I tell you that this scripture must be fulfilled in me, 'And he was reckoned with transgressors'; for what is written about me has its fulfilment." And they said, "Look, Lord, here are two swords." And he said to them, "It is enough." (Luke 22:31-38.)

Looking at the men around him there in the Upper Room, Jesus knew that down deep they loved him; but he knew that they had their weaknesses too. Especially he looked at vehement and eager Simon Peter, so impulsive, so full of good intent, so prone to consider himself more dependable than he was. Jesus must warn him, and also the others, that they would be facing trials heavier than any they had known. The time was critical, and men had to gird themselves to meet it. He put the truth in a vivid simile. They would need every resource they possessed. In the days ahead they would be walking on such a road of peril as men would not venture on without a sword.

So he said to them; and then he must have looked at them with half-amused, half-hopeless pity for their literal-mindedness, as they answered, "Look, Lord, here are two swords." All he answered was, "It is enough!"

But to Simon Peter he must make his warning more specific, because he knew how vulnerable that big warmhearted man could be. He foresaw that the Tempter would sift him as one sifts wheat. He wanted Peter to know that he prayed for him; and looking into the future and knowing that Peter might have his moment of dreadful weakness, he would fortify him against despair by turning his failure into strengthening sympathy for others who like him might fail.

IN GETHSEMANE

> And he came out, and went, as was his custom, to the Mount of Olives; and the disciples followed him. And when he came to the place he said to them, "Pray that you may not enter into temptation." And he withdrew from them about a stone's throw, and knelt down and prayed, "Father, if thou art willing, remove this cup from me; nevertheless not my will, but thine, be done." And there appeared to him an angel from heaven, strengthening him. And being in an agony he prayed more earnestly; and his sweat became like great drops of blood falling down upon the ground. And when he rose from prayer, he came to the disciples and found them sleeping for sorrow, and he said to them, "Why do you sleep? Rise and pray that you may not enter into temptation."
>
> (Luke 22:39-46.)

In that first sentence there is echoed the phrase which occurs only one other time in the narrative of the Gospel. One sabbath morning when he returned to Nazareth, Jesus went to the synagogue, "as was his custom." It was habitual with him to join in the community worship which was meant to draw people near to God, even when without him it might have been only a dull routine among ordinary people in the little town. It was equally habitual for him to go apart to pray alone. The Garden of Gethsemane was a quiet spot. He had been there before. Now he comes again to face the deepest crisis of his life.

What he said to his disciples came out of the depths of his own awareness: "Pray that you may not enter into temptation." They would be tested that night. But in a more awful measure so would he. He had known ever since he entered Jerusalem that each day grew dark with peril. Hatreds were encircling him, like wolves gathering at the fall of night. He may not have foreseen exactly what the end would be, and when. But he knew that what he would have to face was dreadful, and that it was drawing near: not physical suffering only, but the agony of the fact that all he had lived for, and now perhaps would die for, might seem to have been in vain. "Father if thou art willing, remove this cup from me!"

That was the beginning of his prayer; and in that instinctive cry he showed his oneness with all humanity as it faces the awful realities of life and death. But his prayer did not stop with its beginning. Past the emptiness of earth, he reached on to the eternal strength. Beyond the pain, beyond the torturing contradictions, beyond what seemed his own frustration, was fulfillment in the unshaken purposes of God. "Nevertheless, not my will, but thine, be done." And then—there appeared to him an angel from heaven strengthening him.

During the First World War, when many countries were scourged by an epidemic of virulent influenza, a splendid boy of seventeen helped carry ill patients to the hospitals. He caught the influenza and died. He was an only son. Not long afterwards his mother went to one of the makers of stained glass windows to confer about a memorial window for the church to which she, her son, and his father all had been devoted; and the minister of that church, who loved them all, was with her. As the artist was talking of possible designs, her emotion broke out in one bitter cry: "Don't put any guardian angel in that window, for there was no guardian angel with him that day!"

Then into the minister's mind there flashed the sudden recollection of the Gospel words: "An angel from heaven *strengthening him.*" That is the way it was with Jesus: an angel not to shield him from what seemed disaster, not to prevent the crucifixion, but to give him power to face it and to go triumphantly to what waited on the other side. So may it have been with the boy who gave his life in service: an invisible angel of the spirit that did not protect him from physical death, but made him the kind of person for whom in the long balances of eternity what he did will be more important than the length of the mortal life he lost.

All human beings at some time or other go through their Gethsemanes: of pain, or broken hopes, or shattering bereavement, and it has been greatly said that there are three ways of meeting the test which then they face.

There is the way of self-pity. "Why did this have to come to *me?* What did I do to deserve it?" So the thought turns inward with continued brooding, and the mind becomes oblivious to the opportunities for brave, active living in which there might be restoration. Grief festers, and the man or woman sinks into a whimpering disintegration.

The second way is the hardened way of bitterness. The one who is bereaved may set his face against the universe which has seemed so cruel. "So this is what reality is! Beauty, goodness, God—all of them are illusions. The only way to be armed against existence is to have done with expectation. I must never let myself be vulnerable again. Smother any new affections. Recognize life to be the cynical farce it is!"

But then there is the third way: making suffering redemptive. That is what Jesus did. The angel that came, not to keep him safe but to strengthen him, could glorify the cross. In ways beyond all measurement, the sufferings on Calvary have been redemptive for all human life. They have not explained tragedy; but they have enabled human souls to know that what we do with tragedy—instead of what tragedy might hopelessly be allowed to do to us—will be the crucial thing. To let suffering teach us the precious values of the heart and make us more tender and compassionate, more loving and more ready to serve, is to grow toward God's purpose for our greater selves; and in the end it will be worth the pain it cost.

THE POWERS OF DARKNESS

While he was still speaking, there came a crowd, and the man called Judas, one of the twelve, was leading them. He drew near to Jesus to kiss him; but Jesus said to him, "Judas, would you betray the Son of man with a kiss?" And when those who were about him saw what would follow, they said, "Lord, shall we strike with the sword?" And one of them struck the slave of the high priest and cut off his right ear. But Jesus said, "No more of this!" And he touched his ear and healed him. Then Jesus said to the chief priests and captains of the temple and elders, who had come out against him, "Have you come out as against a robber, with swords and clubs? When I was with you day after day in the temple, you did not lay hands on me. But this is your hour, and the power of darkness." (Luke 22:47-53.)

Among the scenes in human history none carries a more sinister shadow than this, and the name of Judas has become a byword for betrayal. What he did was made worse by the way he did it. Not only did he identify Jesus for the armed men who had come to seize him, but he made that act more bitter by what seemed a mockery of the relationship he was breaking. "Judas, would you betray the Son of man with a kiss?"

Judas, in the beginning, could not have been an evil man. The fact that Jesus took him into the circle of his closest friends is evidence of that. The tragedy was, and always will be, that no outward cirmumstances by themselves can save a man's soul from disintegration. Judas had the same opportunity as the others of the twelve: the chance every day to see in Jesus what divineness of life could be, and to love it, and to try to follow it. But somewhere out of the mixed elements which make up human nature he let the dark forces emerge: jealousy, twisted ambition, discontent; and little by little these took possession of him and destroyed the man he might have been.

When a man begins to slip secretly down the path of disloyalty to that which he thinks is best, the terrible end may be that he goes blindly to consequences which he has not foreseen. Judas had become impatient with

Jesus. Who could tell whether he was the Messiah or not? If he was, let him prove it. So he, Judas, will force the issue by letting Jesus' enemies get possession of him. Then if Jesus cannot deliver himself, he will be discredited, to be sure. But he can just go back to Galilee again without any great damage having been done; and Judas will thus get free from his disappointing discipleship.

In a great scene of the Passion Play at Oberammergau it is suggested that it was exactly thus that Judas thought. He had supposed that if the priests prevailed when they put Jesus on trial, all they would do would be to denounce him, consider him harmless, and let him go. Judas had never imagined that they would crucify him. It was when he found, to his shocked astonishment, that *this* was what they meant to do, that he came back and flung the blood money of his betrayal at Caiaphas' feet, and went out and hanged himself. The disloyalty he had thought he could manipulate and keep within shrewd limits had got past his control. When a man has not kept close watch upon his heart, he may become what he had never foreseen that he could be—the instrument through whom the powers of darkness can have their victorious hour.

WHEN PETER DENIED HIS MASTER

Then they seized him and led him away, bringing him into the high priest's house. Peter followed at a distance; and when they had kindled a fire in the middle of the courtyard and sat down together, Peter sat among them. Then a maid, seeing him as he sat in the light and gazing at him, said, "This man also was with him." But he denied it, saying, "Woman, I do not know him." And a little later some one else saw him and said, "You also are one of them." But Peter said, "Man, I am not." And after an interval of about an hour still another insisted, saying, "Certainly this man also was with him; for he is a Galilean." But Peter said, "Man, I do not know what you are saying." And immediately, while he was still speaking, the cock crowed. And the Lord turned and looked at Peter. And Peter remembered the word of the Lord, how he had said to him, "Before the cock crows today, you will deny me three times." And he went out and wept bitterly.   (Luke 22:54-62.)

Not only Judas failed his Master. So did Simon Peter. His guilt was not the same as that of Judas, since what he did was not deliberate. Yet it could also seem less excusable, because he had been one of the first to follow Jesus and had been one of the three closest to him all the time.

What happened to Peter? The same thing that can happen to innumerable others—a failure of nerve in the sudden crisis which has not been prepared for. Peter loved his Lord. The last thing he believed he could ever do was to hurt him by defection. After the shock in Gethsemane he had followed to where Jesus would be. That at least he did, although conceivably he might have run away and hidden. He managed to get into the courtyard of Caiaphas, to come as near Jesus as he could. But then one of the servant girls began to scrutinize him. That suspicious gaze made him uneasy; and when in sudden recognition she exclaimed, "This man also was with him," he burst out, "Woman, I do not know him!" His instinct of avoidance had spoken before his conscience could restrain him; and having lied once, he had to brazen his denial through.

The fault went further back. The trouble with Peter was that he had tried to hide a weakness in himself by acting as though it were not there. Notwithstanding Jesus' warning, he had told himself and everybody that he could be depended on, without the forethought and the discipline that could make him be dependable. After his denial he could have said to Jesus, "Lord, you know I did not mean to!" But his condemnation was in his failure to *mean not to,* with a determination clear and strong enough to make the meaning good.

Then the Lord turned and looked at Peter; and when Peter saw the disappointment in those steady eyes, anguish for what he had done swept over him; and he broke into bitter weeping. He might have gone out and hanged himself, as Judas did. And why not? Only because he was still held by something bigger than himself. He had been faithless, but there was a love that would not fail. This Master, whom in one great moment of illumination he had seen to be the Christ, would reach out to him with a compassion that someday would cleanse him of his shame.

THE QUIET MAJESTY OF CHRIST

Now the men who were holding Jesus mocked him and beat him; they also blindfolded him and asked him, "Prophesy! Who is it that struck you?" And they spoke many other words against him, reviling him. When day came, the assembly of the elders of the people gathered together, both chief priests and scribes; and they led him away to their council, and they said, "If you are the Christ, tell us." But he said to them, "If I tell you, you will not believe; and if I ask you, you will not answer. But from now on the Son of man shall be seated at the right hand of the power of God." And they all said, "Are you the Son of God, then?" And he said to them, "You say that I am." And they said, "What further testimony do we need? We have heard it ourselves from his own lips." (Luke 22:63-71.)

In the Garden of Gethsemane the tumult of armed men and the dark face of Judas on his ugly errand; in Caiaphas' courtyard the shrill accusations of the servant girl and the panic-stricken voice of Peter; the vulgar mockery of the men who guarded Jesus and the cold hostility of priests and scribes as they gathered in their council—and in the midst of all of this was the one figure whose greatness rose above them all. Against their human passions, he had the quiet power which came to him from God. He would not argue. The infinite realities do not convey themselves in words to those who do not want to hear. In the midst of the world's contradictions Christ may seem only a captive to old evils against which his spirit cannot prevail. Those who would deny him or forget him may think that they have finished with him if they ask their brash questions and God's silence does not answer. Nevertheless, the one whom the council of priests and scribes presumed to judge, judges them and all mankind. And he can be more than the authority for conscience. He can be the way, the truth and the life. E. Stanley Jones quoted an "earnest Hindu" as saying, "There is no one else who is seriously bidding for the heart of the world." And Stanley Jones added, "Sweep the horizon—is there anyone else?" [2]

---

[2] *The Christ of the Indian Road* (New York: The Abingdon Press, 1925), p. 46.

chapter 23

THE FORCES WHICH
BROUGHT ABOUT THE CRUCIFIXION

Then the whole company of them arose, and brought him before Pilate. And they began to accuse him, saying, "We found this man perverting our nation, and forbidding us to give tribute to Caesar, and saying that he himself is Christ a king." And Pilate asked him, "Are you the King of the Jews?" And he answered him, "You have said so." And Pilate said to the chief priests and the multitudes, "I find no crime in this man." But they were urgent, saying, "He stirs up the people, teaching throughout all Judea, from Galilee even to this place." (Luke 23:1-5.)

The whole company of them arose and brought Jesus before Pilate. In the brevity of Luke's phrase it is not clear who made up this "whole company." Obviously the members of the assembly who had met in the house of the high priest, Caiaphas, were the center of it. But in the Oberammergau Passion Play there is an imagined scene which suggests another group who may have been in that company. Before the arrest of Jesus, it occurs to Caiaphas to make sure that events move smoothly when that arrest has been made. So he goes privately to Pilate, the Roman governor, informs him that a prisoner will be brought before him, and lets Pilate know that he will be expected to judge and condemn this man whom the priests will bring. The Roman treats him at first with cold hostility. Who are these priests that they should presume to think that they can twist his judgments in advance? He will do what he chooses to do when the moment comes.

Then, not in words but in the grim silence of his own determination, Caiaphas in effect answers: "No, you will not do what you choose. You will do what I choose. You will do it because I shall bring upon you a pressure that this pretended integrity of yours will not stand up against."

Then Caiaphas goes out to rally those who he knows will be his allies, especially those who in our modern phrase would be called the business interests of the city. A few days earlier, Jesus had gone into the Temple and driven out the whole entrenched establishment of the merchants and

289

money changers who used the Temple courts for their legalized extortion. The most privileged circles of Jerusalem were rocked with indignation. Who was this interloper out of Nazareth who thought he could upset the accepted order of things? He might have his queer ideas about religion and do no great harm, but let him keep his hands off matters in which their money was involved. If this sort of interference spread, there was no telling what economic disaster it might bring. This was what the Chamber of Commerce—whether or not it went by that particular name—in Jerusalem was saying. This Jesus must be stopped. And what Caiaphas said was, "Exactly. And you must help to stop him." As a result, when the priests brought Jesus before Pilate, they were not alone. An angry crowd of those who were supposed to be the most solid citizens had joined them. Religious obscurantism and material interests frightened for their security joined hands—not for the last time—to resist the disturbance which both felt to threaten them in the spirit of Jesus.

Therefore when Pilate came out upon the balcony of his judgment hall and looked at the throng gathered in his courtyard, he had reason to be concerned. Many New Testament commentators have marked the fact that Luke, all through his Gospel, seeks to minimize the idea that there was any necessary antagonism between the Christian church and the Roman empire, and therefore he depicts Pilate as having had no active ill-will toward Jesus. But even granted a relative decency of motive, Pilate represents the ignoble surrender which a man may make of such conscience as he has, if the risk of doing the right thing grows too frightening.

The priests and their allies brought against Jesus the charge which they knew the Roman would be obliged to consider most disturbing. "We found this man perverting our nation," they said; "he stirs up the people." That much they did hotly believe. They thought that anyone who stirred up too many new thoughts in people might upset their own comfortable conditions, and so represent what they chose to call perversion—or be a "subversive influence," in twentieth-century language. But the more specific charge they brought was a shrewdly calculated falsehood. Jesus had been preaching the kingdom of God; but what they told the Roman governor was that he had said that he himself was Christ, a king; and this meant that he could be a rebel against Caesar. The Gospel of John reports this charge in words more emphatic than the words in Luke; and it is as though one heard again the angry voices of the enemies of Jesus as they pressed their accusation and their calculated threat: "If you release this man you are not Caesar's friend; every one who makes himself a king sets himself against Caesar."

WHEN THE MORAL VALUES OF LIFE HAVE LEAKED AWAY

When Pilate heard this, he asked whether the man was a Galilean. And when he learned that he belonged to Herod's jurisdiction, he sent him over to Herod, who was himself in Jerusalem at that time. When Herod saw Jesus, he was very glad, for he had long desired to see him, because he had heard about him, and he was hoping to see some sign done by him. So he questioned him at some length; but he made no answer. The chief priests and the scribes stood by, vehemently accusing him. And Herod with his soldiers treated him with contempt and mocked him; then, arraying him in gorgeous apparel, he sent him back to Pilate. And Herod and Pilate became friends with each other that very day, for before this they had been at enmity with each other.   (Luke 23:6-12.)

Pilate was no fool. He sensed something malignant in these accusers. He looked at Jesus, and then he looked at those who were shouting their denunciations of him; and he knew that they were lying. "I find no crime in this man," he said. Thus far he was honest. But he was not disposed to try to be a hero. This case, with its suggestion of possible rebellion against Caesar, could be turned into dangerous consequences for him. Better evade any decisive judgment yet.

Why should he have to be entangled in this twisted business anyhow? This man was a Galilean. Hadn't he heard that Herod, tetrarch of Galilee, was in Jerusalem at that moment? Well, let Herod see what he could make of it.

None of the other Gospels mention Herod as being in Jerusalem, and many New Testament scholars question Luke's report. But if Herod was there and if he did see Jesus, his attitude would have been what Luke describes. He was one of the shallow worldlings who look upon religious matters with no more than a patronizing curiosity. All his life he had known wealth and ease, gadded about in Rome, married one woman and then divorced her to marry adulterously his half-brother's wife, caused John the Baptist to be executed because John had denounced his immorality; and then he began to hear of Jesus as another so-called prophet about whom sensational stories were being told. He wanted to see him, not for any reason that would matter to his life, but just to know what he was like. He had heard that the crowds believed that Jesus worked miracles: tricks, no doubt, but it would be amusing if he could make Jesus work one. He had plenty of sardonic questions he would like to ask.

To such a man's approaches, Jesus gave no answer; for in that empty soul there was nothing that could echo truth. So it can be with men in every generation, whose names do not happen to be Herod but whose natures have become like his. When there is moral unconcern which has left nothing but hollowness where conscience should have been, then no amount of pretended interest in Christ or Christianity, no questions and discussions, no glib theories, can end in anything but mocking rejection of the reality of God.

THE TRAGEDY OF IRRESOLUTION

Pilate then called together the chief priests and the rulers and the people, and said to them, "You brought me this man as one who was perverting the people; and after examining him before you, behold, I did not find this man guilty of any of your charges against him; neither did Herod, for he sent him back to us. Behold, nothing deserving death has been done by him; I will therefore chastise him and release him."

But they all cried out together, "Away with this man, and release to us Barabbas"—a man who had been thrown into prison for an insurrection started in the city, and for murder. Pilate addressed them once more, desiring to release Jesus; but they shouted out, "Crucify, crucify him!" A third time he said to them, "Why, what evil has he done? I have found in him no crime deserving death; I will therefore chastise him and release him." But they were urgent, demanding with loud cries that he should be crucified. And their voices prevailed. So Pilate gave sentence that their demand should be granted. He released the man who had been thrown into prison for insurrection and murder, whom they asked for; but Jesus he delivered up to their will.   (Luke 23:13-25.)

Whatever may have happened with Herod, Pilate still had Jesus on his hands. He would try to bargain now. Perhaps he could get rid of these priests by yielding part of what they wanted. As far as he could see, there was no evil in Jesus. But they claimed there was. So he would give a halfway verdict. Jesus would be let go, but first he should be scourged. He was not guilty; but to satisfy their hatred, he should be treated as though he were.

That poor stratagem came to nothing. Caiaphas and the others with him were quick to see that Pilate was moved now by expediency and caution, not by any resolute conviction. He was vulnerable, and they pressed in for the kill. "Away with this man!" they shouted, as they looked at Jesus and at this Roman governor who was not strong enough to shield him. "Give us Barabbas," they demanded. "Set Barabbas free"—Barabbas, who had caught the crowd's fierce admiration as leader of an insurrection against Rome. He was charged with murder, but what of that? Better a man of violence who was for Israel, first, last, and all the time, than this Jesus who seemed to think that people they hated could get into the kingdom of God.

It is Barabbas that the crowd will generally clamor for. In the passion which he arouses, the Redeemer of mankind can be rejected. "Crucify him, crucify him!" they screamed when Pilate asked what should he do with Jesus.

So Pilate surrendered. He delivered Jesus to those who were determined to be rid of him, and let them work their will. The Gospel of John says that he called for a basin of water and washed his hands as a gesture of disgust at the defilement he had been driven to. He did not realize how futile that gesture would be—to cleanse his hands, or to clear his name. Henceforth, his name would be only the dark shadow cast by a greater name; for all down the centuries the creeds that exalt the name of Jesus would carry also the somber memory, "crucified under Pontius Pilate."

THE SEEMING
EVIL THAT IS OPPORTUNITY

And as they led him away, they seized one Simon of Cyrene, who was coming in from the country, and laid on him the cross, to carry it behind Jesus.   (Luke 23:26.)

To those in the crowd who saw it, the thing done to Simon of Cyrene must have seemed an ugly business, and a mean break of luck for this one man Simon. By what appeared to be pure accident, he was at hand when the Romans chose to seize somebody; and they seized him. Who would want to pick up a cross and have to carry it? Simon might well wish that he had never happened to get near Jesus on that road.

So, no doubt, he did wish at that moment when the cross was laid on his back. But afterwards? Afterwards did he look back and see that the hateful burden he was forced to carry had brought him to what he would thank God for forever? He had to go on to Golgotha, where he would be one of the few who were near enough not only to see Jesus but to hear his words from the cross. In the Gospel of Mark it is said that Simon was "the father of Alexander and Rufus"; and in the letter to the Romans, the apostle Paul sent his greetings to "Rufus, eminent in the Lord." Was this Simon's son, and had Simon and all his family been drawn to Christ by what Simon experienced on that day of the crucifixion?

However that may have been, this wider fact is true. Some event which seems inexplicable may force a human soul to take up a cross: a cross of persecution on behalf of some costly loyalty, a cross of some cruel arrest in what we meant to do, or a cross of broken health. Such a cross might provoke only resentment and bitterness of soul. But it may also be the strange yet blessed means of drawing a life closer to the life of him who made his cross a power of redemption. The cross on which Jesus had to suffer was fashioned by the sins of the world, and Simon helped to carry it. Others in modern times may become the bearers of that cross: for example, the dedicated leaders of the Negroes in the South who have put their shoulders under the cruel weight of the injustice by which their people have been oppressed. And sometimes men have become great in spirit because they have accepted what could seem a still more bitter cross: the cross of some great disappointment heroically borne even when it seemed most unintelligible. Alexis Stein, a brilliant young minister in the 1920's, was struck down by illness which ended what might have been a great career of service; but he kept his faith that some high purpose could be fulfilled even in disaster. Before he died, he wrote:

Oh, fellow-bearers of the load we did not choose, the load we fain would have some others carry if we could, remember this . . . someone must carry that great sadness and great pain, must carry it that others should go free, that mankind should go forward and go up.

To such a soul can come the supreme companionship with him who was wounded for our transgressions and bruised for our iniquities, and who upon the cross became the Burden Bearer of the human race.

THE CHEAPNESS OF SHALLOW EMOTION

And there followed him a great multitude of the people, and of women who bewailed and lamented him. But Jesus turning to them said, "Daughters of Jerusalem, do not weep for me, but weep for yourselves and for your children. For behold, the days are coming when they will say, "Blessed are the barren, and the wombs that never bore, and the breasts that never gave suck!' Then they will begin to say to the mountains, 'Fall on us'; and to the hills, 'Cover us.' For if they do this when the wood is green, what will happen when it is dry?"   (Luke 23:27-31.)

A great multitude swarmed along the road as this procession to the cross went by: the kind of crowd that will pour out from every quarter when any sensational happening is afoot, the curious and the casual, people with no deep concern, susceptible to the mob spirit which can quickly make them cruel. Dorothy Sayers, in *The Man Born to Be King*, has dramatized this crowd with a vividness that makes its clamor seem a frightening present fact. But this crowd was not without its element of comparative decency. There were women who lamented as Jesus went by. Women, when their emotions are poisoned, can be more implacable than men—as with Madame DeFarge in Dickens' *Tale of Two Cities;* but for the most part there is in women enough of the instinct of motherhood to make them feel an instant pity at the sight of suffering. Because some of them along the Via Dolorosa that day did have compassion, they kept the human scene from being completely evil.

Yet the sad fact is that pity may be only a shallow thing: a momentary shrinking from what is terrible without any deep effective purpose to prevent it. That was true in Jerusalem, and may be true in every city. There are always right feelings here and there; and if these are positive and determined, they can create a public mind and public will sufficient to prevent such things as crucifixion. The trouble is that often they have no tidal depth, and are only a ripple on the surface of a shallow lake.

Jesus knew the fickleness of the crowd; but the more important fact is that, whatever the crowd may have been, he was not reaching out for pity. "Do not weep for me," he said to the women. For himself, he would walk on his lonely and intrepid way. It is a poor sort of sentimental piety that approaches him as someone to be cried over, which some hymns in church hymnbooks lamentably do:

> O Jesus, thou art pleading
> In accents meek and low
> "I died for you, my children
> And will you treat me so?"

Can anyone imagine the real Jesus, the Jesus who confronted Caiaphas and stood in kingly silence before the Roman Pilate, making that kind of feeble plea for sympathy and soft treatment? His thought was not upon himself. "Weep for yourselves and for your children," he said. The worst tragedy was not in what he faced deliberately. It was in what the unseeing crowd would be forced to face: "If they do these things when the wood is green, what will happen when it is dry?" With that proverb Jesus foreshadowed the day when the blindness and folly of Jerusalem would lead to the disaster that was coming: the terror of the city's fall, not the cutting down of a single tree, but a fire that would consume the whole forest. He would die now on Calvary, but that would not be all. The awful consequence of the sins which were bringing him to his cross would be the doom of the whole community, so blindly unconscious of its sins.

THE INCLUSIVENESS OF CRUCIFIXION

Two others also, who were criminals, were led away to be put to death with him. And when they came to the place which is called The Skull,

> there they crucified him, and the criminals, one on the right and one on the left. (Luke 23:32-33.)

The procession moved on to the place which is called the Skull. There they crucified him. There—but not only there. On more places than the place of the Skull is the cross set up. The influences that would put to death the spirit of God have no limits of locality or time. Wherever prejudice, passion, and cruel self-assertion flourish, there Jesus is crucified afresh. Out of the sufferings of the First World War Studdert-Kennedy was moved to write much that is remembered, but not many lines of his will be remembered more than, "When Jesus Came to Birmingham." For its message is that there is no use in making pious pretended lamentation over what happened in the Judean city nineteen hundred years ago unless our eyes are opened to the fact that the place *we* live in may again be putting Jesus to open shame.

Along with Jesus, two others were crucified. In the King James Version of the Gospels of Matthew and Mark they are listed as two thieves. Here in Luke they are called more generally two criminals. What their particular offense may have been, therefore, we do not know; but in any case they belonged to that class of the violent and dangerous whom the ruling forces in a self-interested society will hunt down and condemn. They endangered the general level of existence which the safe and comfortable chose to maintain. So the two criminals were crucified. But the bitter paradox is in this: Jesus was crucified with them. A society may be as intolerant of that which would lift its standards higher as of that which will drag them down. As men do not want to have their world too much degraded, so equally they may not want to have it too much improved. The challenge of the ultimate goodness can be intolerable.

THE DIVINE COMPASSION

> And Jesus said, "Father, forgive them; for they know not what they do." And they cast lots to divide his garments. (Luke 23:34.)

Jesus recognized the tumultuous emotions surging in the crowd that had come out to Calvary: curiosity, blind excitement, and then the cruelty which can begin with the vindictive few and spread like an ugly fire through a crowd. Here was human nature at its worst, but even so the spirit of Jesus could look upon it with compassion. We cannot know where Luke got his report of the first words spoken from the cross. His Gospel has sometimes been called the Gospel of the women, because he speaks so often of the women who followed Jesus; and perhaps one among them, who had dared to press nearer than any of the disciples, was close enough to see the lips of Jesus and hear his words. Their sensitiveness knew what sort of words he most instinctively would speak: words tuned to what his whole life had been expressing, an infinite compassion. "Father, forgive them, for they know not what they do."

So it was on Calvary. And so it is on those lesser, repeated Calvaries on which love again is crucified: whenever our preoccupation, resentment, hardness, wounds the relationships through which the grace of Christ might come to us.

> Yet each man kills the thing he loves,
> By each let this be heard,
> Some do it with a bitter look,
> Some with a flattering word.[1]

It is for our follies as well as for our conscious sins that we need the infinite forgiveness of God.

— Who were the ones Jesus meant when he prayed for forgiveness for those who did not know what they were doing? Doubtless the Roman soldiers, to begin with. They had no malicious purpose of their own. They were simply part of the military machine which takes orders and asks no questions, instruments of the regimented cruelty for which each particular individual may claim that he is not responsible. And the general crowd from Jerusalem also. They also had nothing directly to do with condemning Jesus. They had no voice in what Caiaphas and the other priests determined. But they could dumbly assume that if the authorities acted, they probably had reason for what they did. There must be something wrong with Jesus; and if he got himself crucified, it was no business of theirs.

Thus the soldiers, and the Jerusalem crowd alike, had not themselves devised what was done to Jesus. It was not deliberate maliciousness for which they needed to be forgiven. But they represented the fact in human life out of which so much of its evil can arise: the dulling of conscience which results when men ignore their own responsibility, and become participants in some moral outrage by trading on their ignorance; and evade any moral judgment by pretending that they do not know what the matter is all about.

Back of those whose sin was that they created no positive opinion which might have prevented the crucifixion, there were also the men whose more conspicuous sin was that they deliberately willed it. How could it be said of them that they did not know what they were doing? On the face of it,

---

[1] Oscar Wilde, *The Ballad of Reading Gaol.*

they certainly did know. They had looked at Jesus and made up their minds that he was a threat to interests which seemed to them paramount, and so they resolved to be rid of him. But in them also was ignorance: the awful ignorance of men in whom pride and self-assertiveness have so corrupted their sense of values that darkness has become their light. The spirit of the kingdom of God, as it brought its confrontation in Jesus, was anathema to Caiaphas—as everything that Christianity represented was anathema in our twentieth century to the frenzied soul of Adolf Hitler.

How can that kind of perversion be forgiven? We ourselves can have no answer to that question. The human soul, with all the factors which make it what it is, has in it a complexity and a hiddenness which no mortal insight can fully fathom. How much of what a man becomes is due to inheritance or to environment, and how much to his own choice? Who can dare to say? There is a degree of evil which would seem to us unpardonable, but our little judgments stand hushed before the words of Jesus on the cross—words which express a divine compassion that is wider and deeper than our thoughts can go.

One thing is certain. Our great desire and prayer should be that Jesus on the cross—with his spirit lifted above all bitterness and hatred, and speaking the divine forgiveness for our tragic world—may create in us a double fact: humility in judgment concerning the sins of others, and a deep awareness of our own sins which need to be forgiven. Within the broken walls of the cathedral in Coventry, which was destroyed by German bombing in the Second World War, there has been set up a cross made of two charred beams which survived the resulting fire. Underneath that cross is an inscription not of three words, but of only two: *not,* "Father, forgive them." but "Father, forgive—." So the sin of all humanity is implicitly confessed, and God's mercy besought for all peoples alike in the name of the one Savior who alone can bring pardon and peace.

THE UNDEFEATED

And the people stood by, watching; but the rulers scoffed at him, saying, "He saved others; let him save himself, if he is the Christ of God, his Chosen One!" The soldiers also mocked him, coming up and offering him vinegar, and saying, "If you are the King of the Jews, save yourself!" There was also an inscription over him, "This is the King of the Jews." (Luke 23:35-38.)

In the taunts of the priests and the soldiers there might have seemed to be the thrust of bitter truth. If Jesus was indeed King of the Jews and God's chosen one, what was he doing hung up there crucified? All that preaching of his that was supposed to have saved others—where was it now? If God was really with him, let him show it by saving himself. "Come down from the cross!"

It may be that for the moment this mockery sank deep into Jesus' soul. Was it then, perhaps, that he uttered the tragic cry which the Gospels of Mark and Matthew both record, "My God, my God, why hast thou forsaken me?" Death was not far off; but more awful than the fact of death was the possibility that his death was also his defeat.

But it was not defeat, and deep within him Jesus knew it. On the cross was the supreme revelation of what he had said to his disciples—he who tries to save his life is the one who loses it, and he who gives his life to God will save it. Our instinctive selfishness finds that hard to believe, but it is the heart of the Christian gospel, and the growing soul begins to understand it. If a man sets out to save others, in his motive he cannot save himself; in his result, he cannot help but save himself. The self that dies is the weak, the unworthy, the ignoble self; the self that is preserved is the true man God meant should be. Indolence, love of applause, freedom from pain, he cannot save; strength, character, and the insight that comes through sympathy, he saves forever. And even if the work that a man seeks to do for others is seemingly frustrated, it is not so. Only the outward aspect may be hidden. No heroic impulse, no great love, is ever wasted. God is concerned not only with the work accomplished, but with the accomplished worker; and the life which could not save itself from weariness, from loneliness, and from sorrow becomes a part of God's ongoing power.

ON THE THREE CROSSES OF CALVARY

> One of the criminals who were hanged railed at him, saying, "Are you not the Christ? Save yourself and us!" But the other rebuked him, saying, "Do you not fear God, since you are under the same sentence of condemnation? And we indeed justly; for we are receiving the due reward of our deeds; but this man has done nothing wrong." And he said, "Jesus, remember me when you come in your kingly power." And he said to him, "Truly, I say to you, today you will be with me in Paradise."
> (Luke 23:39-43.)

Three figures nailed to three indistinguishable crosses on the hilltop: in their outward circumstances the same, but how different in their revelation of what may be the inner spirit!

On one cross was the man who had no other impulse but to curse his fate. According to early Christian tradition his name was Gestas. He may have been, as his type has been imagined and described, one "who would adorn a Hogarth print of a Tyburn hanging . . . plain brute, foul-mouthed, vindictive." [2] In the tragedy of human life, with its long entail of evil inherited and then accepted, there can be men like that. The Gestas on Golgotha was side by side with Jesus, but Jesus made no impression on him. The only thing that filled his heart was hatred: hatred for everybody who had had any part in bringing him where he was, and savage contempt for anybody who would be thinking of anything but vengeance. This Jesus, talking of forgiveness! Who wanted to listen to that? What Gestas wanted was to get loose from the law that had caught him, go back to being a criminal, and to hell with those who would make him different! If Jesus amounted to anything, let him smash this whole machinery of crucifixion. "Get me down off this cross. That's the kind of salvation I want!" Gestas was not interested in anything else. If he had a soul, he did not think of it. Jesus might have reached it, but all Gestas did was to rave at Jesus.

The other criminal, whom tradition has named Dysmas, was of a different sort. His record may have been as bad as his partner's, but he had a conscience. He had the decency to recognize that he and Gestas deserved what they had got, and that there was no use cursing the consequences which had caught up with them for what they had chosen to do. Moreover, in spite of everything, he could feel the pull of goodness when he saw it. Nobody like Jesus had come into his life before, but now the greatness of this man crucified beside him broke open deep desires in him which he never knew he had. For the moment he could forget the torture of his body and feel the reality of something beyond his pain. There on his cross, with fever racking him, he could have only spasms of clear awareness; and he had to grope for meanings. How could Jesus really help him? He did not know; but somehow he saw a kingliness in Jesus. Maybe Jesus *would* have power somehow, somewhere. Maybe he would come into a kingdom greater than anything Dysmas could understand. Maybe Jesus would remember Dysmas then.

The third figure in that meeting of souls was Jesus himself. It was altogether in character that one man at least from among those whom the world counted as the lost should know instinctively that he could reach out to Jesus and find a compassion which was already reaching out to him. For Jesus, who knew what was in man, had a perception more inclusive than that which contemporary Christians have. With his unclouded realism he knew the weaknesses and sins in human nature, but he did not stop with these. He saw, and brought into expression, the little glimmerings of goodness which may exist under the surface of a life that looks unpromising. His sympathy was like a divining rod which made him know where the answering waters were. In the world of today there may too often be cynical disparagement of human possibilities. What is needed instead is the power of the larger expectation that was always the mark of Christ.

THE DEATHLESS MEANING OF THE CROSS

It was now about the sixth hour, and there was darkness over the whole land until the ninth hour, while the sun's light failed; and the curtain of the temple was torn in two. Then Jesus, crying with a loud voice, said, "Father, into thy hands I commit my spirit!" And having said this he breathed his last. Now when the centurion saw what had taken place, he praised God, and said, "Certainly this man was innocent!" And all the multitudes who assembled to see the sight, when they saw what had taken place, returned home beating their breasts. And all his acquaintances and the women who had followed him from Galilee stood at a distance and saw these things. (Luke 23:44-49.)

In this one paragraph of the Gospel both the dreadful tragedy and the heroic hope of human life are symbolized.

Darkness over the whole land: darkness which at that moment seemed to be the ultimate eclipse of all life's possibilities. Jesus crucified, the redeeming love of God which he had brought to men rejected: no wonder that dazed people returned home, beating their breasts as the sun's light failed. It appeared then that the cross, standing stark upon the shadowed hill, could have no other meaning than defeat and desolation.

But in the words of Luke there was another symbol. The curtain of the Temple was torn in two. The curtain which he meant was that which veiled the Holy of Holies, the inmost sanctuary of the presence of God, into which only the high priest might dare to enter—and he only on the Day of Atonement. But now through Jesus—put to death by the sins of men, but even in his crucifixion bringing the divine forgiveness—the curtain between the needs of human souls and the answer of God had been taken away. Jesus crucified was the answer. Henceforth the cross would be the sign that in every circumstance, including darkness and suffering and death, the way was open to the redeeming strength of God.

The great assurances of the spirit are those which are felt in the deep experiences of actual living, although they may not be analyzed. As Henry Sloane Coffin has written:

We have no explanations to offer perplexed souls in many of the circumstances which raise the insistent, Why? But we have a figure to set before them, a Fellow-sufferer, who dies with an unanswered question on His lips, yet dies placing

301

Himself in a Father's hands. That Figure throughout the Christian centuries has riveted the attention of men in their most tragic experiences. They look at Him and find sympathy, and through Him they regain faith.[3]

In a little village in northern France in the First World War a chaplain who chanced to come that way saw a poignant, simple thing that said more to him than he could say in many sermons. The village, including its church, had been shattered by German shells, and most of it was only rubble. But among the ruins of the church was the cross that had fallen from its tower. Some of the villagers had set it upright, and round its foot they had planted flowers. Here was the instinctive recognition of the eternal truth: wherever in the midst of tragedy men remember the cross, all that is lovely and worshipful can begin to grow there again.

FAILURE, AND FORGIVENESS

Now there was a man named Joseph from the Jewish town of Arimathea. He was a member of the council, a good and righteous man, who had not consented to their purpose and deed, and he was looking for the kingdom of God. This man went to Pilate and asked for the body of Jesus. Then he took it down and wrapped it in a linen shroud, and laid him in a rock-hewn tomb, where no one had ever yet been laid. It was the day of Preparation, and the sabbath was beginning. The women who had come with him from Galilee followed, and saw the tomb, and how his body was laid; then they returned, and prepared spices and ointments.

On the sabbath they rested according to the commandment.

(Luke 23:50-56.)

To speak the name of Joseph of Arimathea is to be conscious of an undertone of sadness. For here is the man who may have been a disciple of Jesus, but was not such in a way that might have counted greatly. The Gospel of Mark says that he was "a respected member of the council, who was also himself looking for the kingdom of God." Luke says also that he was "a good and righteous man," and that he "had not consented to their purpose and deed." But the Gospel of John says that he was a disciple, "but secretly, for fear of the Jews."

If this last statement reflects the truth, then the earlier statement that he had not consented to the vote of the Sanhedrin condemning Jesus would mean no more than that in the crucial moment he kept still. In that case he was the kind of man who knows what is right and wants it, but not at

[3] Henry Sloane Coffin, *The Meaning of the Cross* (New York: Charles Scribner's Sons, 1931), p. 95.

too much risk. In his own mind he could separate himself from Caiaphas and the other priests who were dishonoring their trust, but he would not let himself look too separate when the council was watching what each member did. If he had come out boldly on the side of Jesus, that would have been real discipleship. But it could have been easier just to feel sorry, to say to himself that the tide was running too strong the other way, and that there was nothing effective he could do.

It may have been the shock of Jesus' crucifixion that broke the shell of ignoble caution which Joseph had built for his self-protection. When he went to Pilate and asked for Jesus' body, he showed his colors, and he would have to face the consequences. He would be known now as Jesus' disciple; but how empty that would be compared with what an earlier discipleship might have been! He could offer now a tomb for Jesus' body. But how could he hope to give to the heart of Jesus a knowledge of the loyalty he had not expressed?

Joseph of Arimathea lives again in every time. Who has not known in some moment of self-reproach the same poignant sorrow that Joseph must have felt? A great bereavement comes: one dies who is precious to us above all others. Then with a great rush of emotion we remember all that we might have given to that other life and failed to give: the neglected opportunities, the lack of thought, the love that was let burn down to casualness. If only we could live the years again! But of all the words our language holds none have a more bitter sound than these: *too late.*

Yet, by God's mercy, what has been said about Joseph of Arimathea, and all the others like him, may not be the final truth. The man who looks at his life and sees where he has been recreant may find himself laid hold upon by a love that will not let him go. There is a beautiful legend concerning Joseph of Arimathea. In the middle of the first century he went to Britain, carrying with him the cup which Jesus had used at the Last Supper in the Upper Room. There he founded the ancient church at Glastonbury; and the cup he brought, when it had vanished, became the Holy Grail which King Arthur's knights rode out from Camelot into all their world to seek. It is a legend only, but in it there is a great reality. The life which is remorseful for its partial failure may be purified by sorrow, and may become the carrier of the cup of a new communion of the love of Christ.

chapter 24

THE GOSPEL OF THE RESURRECTION

But on the first day of the week, at early dawn, they went to the tomb, taking the spices which they had prepared. And they found the stone rolled away from the tomb, but when they went in they did not find the body. While they were perplexed about this, behold, two men stood by them in dazzling apparel; and as they were frightened and bowed their faces to the ground, the men said to them, "Why do you seek the living among the dead? Remember how he told you, while he was still in Galilee, that the Son of man must be delivered into the hands of sinful men, and be crucified, and on the third day rise." And they remembered his words, and returning from the tomb they told all this to the eleven and to all the rest. Now it was Mary Magdalene and Joanna and Mary the mother of James and the other women with them who told this to the apostles; but these words seemed to them an idle tale, and they did not believe them. (Luke 24:1-11.)

Some ancient authorities add verse 12, *But Peter rose and ran to the tomb; stooping and looking in, he saw the linen cloths by themselves; and he went home wondering at what had happened.*

The tomb of Joseph of Arimathea had been hewn within the slope of a hill, and it was closed by a great round stone, rolled in a groove across the entrance. This was the barrier which the women feared might keep them out when they came early in the morning of the first day of the week to bring their spices for the body of Jesus. Well might they have asked each other—as the words stand in the narrative of Mark—"Who will roll away the stone for us from the door of the tomb?"

They were thinking, of course, of the material stone; but in addition there was something heavier and more dreadful. It was the stone of desolation that lay upon their hearts. They had seen Jesus crucified, and his scarred body taken down from the cross and buried even before they could anoint it, because the sabbath had begun. Now, the sabbath over, they were coming to do what little their devotion could. But nothing in their power could change the awful facts of Friday which seemed to bury all their hope and faith in the same grave with Jesus. The beauty of life lay dead for them behind the stone of doubt and near-despair. And who could ever roll away *that* stone?

Then the ineffable message of Easter begins in one single sentence which is like the prelude to triumphant music. *They found the stone rolled away*. They could not have moved it, nor can human hearts by themselves roll away the stones of their imprisonment. But there at the tomb of Joseph of Arimathea—and in spiritual fact in all the centuries since—the power of God opened the door, and the Christ whom men tried to crucify came forth alive.

There can be no loud assertions about the details of the Easter gospel. One stands hushed before the mystery of what happened. The accounts of the several Evangelists differ. How many women came to the tomb, and what were their names? What did they see? A young man dressed in a white robe? An angel of the Lord? Or two men in dazzling apparel? To how many did Jesus himself appear? What became of the body that was in the tomb, and what was the risen Jesus like when he came again to his disciples? We cannot surely know the answers to these questions. The disciples could not sit down and write a prose analysis. They could only try to tell the experiences that had come to this one and that one in different moments—experiences so full of more than earthly meaning that the expression of them would inevitably be in eager but stumbling words. If in the Resurrection of Jesus the world of reality that is beyond our world broke in upon our mortal facts with overwhelming wonder, then neither his disciples nor the writers of the Gospels could have painted in any exactitude the glory of that heavenly sunrise. The best they could do was to turn with illumined faces and say, "The sun is risen, and we have seen an immortal day begin!"

So the living witness to the Resurrection is not chiefly in the written narratives. It is in the fact of what happened in the disciples and in what has been happening since. Power was let loose such as could have come only from the experienced certainty that the Lord was alive again. Changes took place which only the Resurrection gospel could account for.

From time immemorial the seventh day was the Jewish holy day; but within a little while the disciples had done that which before would have been inconceivable to their Jewish loyalty: they had changed their day of worship from the seventh day to the first day of the week, because it was on the first day that they had seen the risen Lord.

The Last Supper might have been repeated as a sacrament of memory and mourning for a Master crucified and dead. Instead, it became the Eucharist, the sacrament of thanksgiving for the one whom Peter would proclaim at Pentecost as "loosed [from] the pangs of death, because it was not possible for him to be held by it."

And most important was the change made in Peter himself and in the other disciples: a change from cowardice to courage, and from weakness to such strength that startled communities would presently be saying of them, "These men who have turned the world upside down have come here."

In John Masefield's *The Trial of Jesus*, there is an imagined conversation between the centurion who was at the cross and the wife of Pilate, the Lady Claudia Procula.

Pilate's wife asks the centurion concerning Jesus. "Do you think he is dead?"

"No, lady, I don't."

"Then where is he?"

"Let loose in the world, lady, where neither Roman nor Jew can stop his truth." [1]

HOW CHRIST MAY COME

That very day two of them were going to a village named Emmaus, about seven miles from Jerusalem, and talking with each other about all these things that had happened. While they were talking and discussing together, Jesus himself drew near and went with them. But their eyes were kept from recognizing him. And he said to them, "What is this conversation which you are holding with each other as you walk?" And they stood still, looking sad. Then one of them, named Cleopas, answered him, "Are you the only visitor to Jerusalem who does not know the things that have happened there in these days?" And he said to them, "What things?" And they said to him, "Concerning Jesus of Nazareth, who was a prophet mighty in deed and word before God and all the people, and how our chief priests and rulers delivered him up to be condemned to death, and crucified him. But we had hoped that he was the one to redeem Israel. Yes, and besides all this, it is now the third day since this happened. Moreover, some women of our company amazed us. They were at the tomb early in the morning and did not find his body; and they came back saying that they had even seen a vision of angels, who said that he was alive. Some of those who were with us went to the tomb, and found it just as the women had said; but him they did not see." And he said to them, "O foolish men, and slow of heart to believe all that the prophets have spoken! Was it not necessary that the Christ should suffer these things and enter into his glory?" And beginning with Moses and all the prophets, he interpreted to them in all the scriptures the things concerning himself.   (Luke 24:13-27.)

[1] John Masefield, *The Trial of Jesus* (New York: The Macmillan Company, 1925), p. 111.

When what happened on Easter morning was fully realized, it brought a transfiguring joy. But Luke has remembered how hard it was at first for even those who were closest to Jesus to believe that the report of the women was anything but an idle tale. The instinct of sorrow was to look for the living among the dead. It was out of shadows that the light came; and in this final chapter of the Gospel, Luke draws another picture of men for whom this was so.

Two of Jesus disciples—like so many of us, relatively obscure and unimportant—were walking on the road that led from Jerusalem to the little village outside the city where they lived. It was evening on the day of the Resurrection. They had loved Jesus, pinned all their hopes of life upon his triumph, and now he had been put to death by his enemies. They had felt the darkness of soul of knowing that he was gone. Then later they had heard the news that he was risen and had come back to reveal himself to the fellowship of those who had loved him; but this they hardly dared to believe. It was too wonderful to be true; and with a dim hope, but with a more overpowering sadness, they were talking together of the things which had come to pass.

Then at their side as they walked, there appeared someone else. It was growing dark, and they did not see him well. Moreover, the last thing they had really expected was to see Jesus. So they did not recognize this figure who went with them along the road. In the long-familiar words of the King James Version, "Their eyes were holden that they should not know him."

How rich the significance of this scene becomes! It was possible, then, for Jesus to be very near to men and for them to be quite unaware that he had been beside them until afterwards. If it *was* possible, also it *is* possible. We who think we do not see him, we who say that we no longer hear his voice, we who walk upon our plodding and dispirited roads, supposing that the days of inspiration have gone by—we too may be in the midst of experiences which, if only we can understand them, can be full of the presence of Christ.

Go back to the story of the Emmaus road and see the circumstances under which Jesus came.

To begin with, he listened to all that the two disciples were saying. He did not interrupt or divert their thoughts. He let them talk together as they had been talking before. He drew them out and led them on. They poured out instinctively their fears, their doubts, their discouragements. They revealed to him and to one another how empty and meaningless life seemed to have become.

Then when they were through, in that moment of quiet and at least relative relief which comes to even the most perturbed spirits when they have unburdened themselves of their troubled thoughts, Jesus spoke. Beginning with Moses and all the prophets, he interpreted to them in all the scriptures the things concerning himself. He reviewed for them the hopes and longings of the prophets. He also revealed for them the strange, shadowed ways along which God's deliverance sometimes comes. He lifted their thoughts out of their narrow individualism. He connected them with the great sweep of spiritual hope, faith, and fulfillment through the years. He showed them that nothing is to be judged by the mere moment of its happening, that everything is to be interpreted in its relationship to the whole of life.

This is exactly what we need something or someone to do for us. In mind and heart we may be like the two disciples. There are things we cannot understand. There are contradictions in life which baffle our best faith. Our world has lost its meaning. The sun has gone down, and we walk on a dark road.

Then what happens? You know what happens for you sometimes—sometimes, and often enough for you to know that it can happen again. Some unexpected influence comes and walks at your side. Some voice speaks to you and others who have been feeling as you did. It may be in church, where you have come with no special expectation, but for a dozen obscure reasons which you have not made articulate to yourself. Then an influence sings itself into your soul from the words of a long-familiar hymn. Old associations come back in a flood of memories. Or there is a voice speaking from the pulpit in which today you catch something greater than the human accents, because a man is there who for a moment at least has become an interpreter of his Master—no longer bound by the individualism of his own utterance, but surrendered to a truth of God so urgent that it masters him and makes its way through him. Then in such an hour you have felt your life lifted to a new level. You have known that the outer circumstances of it have not changed. The former problems and difficulties were still there, but suddenly they have been set in a new perspective—your remembrance that for Christ it was necessary that he should suffer before he could enter into glory. You have seen yourself and your life as part of the grandeur of that long destiny which can belong to human souls. You have seen that the things which seemed so poignant and peculiar to you are not peculiar. They are part of an experience which men have always faced—the experience of hardships which are meant to make something heroic, the experience of shadows through which we press forward to the light, the experience of heavinesses which are meant not to bow us down but to make us strong enough to bear them up. An echo of the voice that spoke to the two disciples on the way to Emmaus is opening the Scriptures for you, showing that all the formidable things which trouble and disturb you and might have made your spirit cowardly are written into the ageless reality of all human life which is growing up toward God.

Nor is it only in church or in some other special place that there may be the presence which at first you do not recognize. You come home tired at the end of the day, perhaps discouraged with the confusion of your world. You have been frustrated in some work you wanted to accomplish, and because of that you feel almost as though the fight were no longer worth waging. But love is there with its welcome and its understanding. The voice that is most precious to you is quick with its encouragement. Only a human voice? No, not that only. For wherever love speaks, something infinite is breaking through. Unless our eyes are holden, we can know that again, as on the Emmaus road, Christ is drawing near.

WHEN THE NEARNESS OF CHRIST IS KNOWN

So they drew near to the village to which they were going; and he made as though he would go further, but they constrained him, saying, "Stay with us, for it is toward evening and the day is now far spent." So he went in to stay with them. When he was at table with them, he took the bread and blessed, and broke it, and gave it to them. And their eyes were opened and they recognized him; and he vanished out of their sight. They said to each other, "Did not our hearts burn within us while he talked to us on the road, while he opened to us the scriptures?"   (Luke 24:28-32.)

When Christ has drawn near, then what? Turn and look at the climax of the Emmaus story. There is a beautiful suggestion in the fact that the one whom at first the two disciples had not recognized was known to them only when he had answered their invitation to come into their house. "Stay with us," they begged, and so he came in and sat down at the supper table with them. It was when he took the bread and blessed and broke it that their eyes were opened, and they knew that they were in the presence of the risen Christ. So can it be again. In the ordinary place and at the ordinary moment, if hearts desire to welcome him, the humblest house can become a heavenly place through the sudden awareness that he is there.

"Did not our hearts burn within us while he talked to us?" So the disciples at Emmaus said to one another; and out of their experience the word which comes to us is this: Remember the times when your hearts have burned in you. Cherish above all other things those occasions and influences which do make your hearts burn. You may not be able to analyze all your faith. There may be much that you do not understand. The convictions which you could put into a creed may seem very fragmentary. So be it. The thing which matters is not that. What matters is the aspect of life which shames your hardness, melts your indifference, and makes your emotions glow, and leads you therefore to be more kind, more generous, more consecrated than now you are. Trust those moments, and thank God for them. For when your heart thus burns within you, it is a sign that Christ has come.

JESUS APPEARS TO THE ELEVEN

> And they rose that same hour and returned to Jerusalem; and they found the eleven gathered together and those who were with them, who said, "The Lord has risen indeed, and has appeared to Simon!" Then they told what had happened on the road, and how he was known to them in the breaking of the bread.
>
> As they were saying this, Jesus himself stood among them. But they were startled and frightened, and supposed that they saw a spirit. And he said to them, "Why are you troubled, and why do questionings rise in your hearts? See my hands and my feet, that it is I myself; handle me, and see; for a spirit has not flesh and bones as you see that I have." And while they still disbelieved for joy, and wondered, he said to them, "Have you anything here to eat?" They gave him a piece of broiled fish, and he took it and ate before them. (Luke 24:33-43.)

Filled with the wonder of their experience, the two disciples went back to Jerusalem, where the eleven—now that Judas was gone—were met together. They told of what had happened to them at Emmaus, and they listened to the exultant witness of the eleven: "The Lord has risen indeed, and has appeared to Simon!"

Out of that appearance would come one of the great evidences of the reality of the Resurrection: the transformation that was wrought in Simon. That was his old name, the name that belonged to him before Jesus gave him the new name, Peter, which meant *the rock*. It had seemed that the old name was the only name he deserved to be called by, the name of his poor, instinctive self. Notwithstanding his bravado in the Upper Room he had denied his Master in the court of Caiaphas, kept out of sight when Jesus went to his crucifixion; and that night he had been in hiding in Jerusalem. Where was the Rock man in this shamed and despairing Simon? Then he saw Christ. The Gospels do not tell us how or where he saw him, but from that moment he was a transformed man. There came to him the strength that Jesus had promised when he called him Peter. In a little while he would be preaching in Jerusalem of his living Master, "Let all the house of Israel know assuredly that God has made him both Lord and Christ." And, arrested with John and brought before the Sanhedrin, he had a boldness which astonished these threatening authorities who recognized that he had been with Jesus.

But the report of the appearance of Christ to Simon was not the climax of what Luke reports as having happened that evening when the disciples were gathered together. Suddenly Jesus himself was there. The fact of his coming can be separated from the literal details of Luke's description. Jesus in an entrance so startling that at first the disciples were frightened as though they had seen a ghost, yet Jesus in a form so like the body they had known that he could bid them touch his hands and feet and invite them to give him food to eat—this is a picture of such unusual contrasts that our would-be understanding falters. It is to be remembered that Luke was not there, and that the memories of that evening had come to him through long transmission. The one certain central thing was that the disciples had an experience which to them was utterly convincing: an experience of life from the other side of death made manifest to mortal sensibilities. Who could put into sure frame of speech the incomparable wonder of this? When Luke came to write his Gospel, his supreme purpose was to reflect what to the disciples had been made indubitable: that Jesus, the real Jesus, the Jesus they had known and loved, was alive again. And so he described the scene in colors that seemed to him most vividly to represent this completeness of contact between the disciples and their Lord who had come back.

CHRIST THE SAVIOR

Then he said to them, "These are my words which I spoke to you, while I was still with you, that everything written about me in the law of Moses and the prophets and the psalms must be fulfilled." Then he opened their minds to understand the scriptures, and said to them, "Thus it is written, that the Christ should suffer and on the third day rise from the dead, and that repentance and forgiveness of sins should be preached in his name to all nations, beginning from Jerusalem. You are witnesses of these things. And behold, I send the promise of my Father upon you; but stay in the city, until you are clothed with power from on high." (Luke 24:44-49.)

There in Jerusalem where the eleven were gathered Jesus said to them again what he had said to the disciples on the Emmaus road. He would

have them understand the meaning of his life and his crucifixion in relation to the loving purposes of God. In the law of Moses, there had been
given to the people of Israel the Ten Commandments and all the related
standards for righteous living. Men could know what they ought to do, and
understand the direction in which their moral obedience must continually
try to move. But against that possibility there had been the long record of
human failure. Out of the psalms there came the everlasting echo of
the struggle that can be in every soul: conscience reaching upward, and
old sins holding back; momentary awareness of a heavenly meaning
smothered in forgetfulness, the wings of aspiration lamed and broken. The
prophets, like the psalmists, knew this tragic inability of men to move
toward God. And so they had seen that there would have to be a heavenly
love that would come to men's unworthiness, bear the brunt of the world's
evil, and by the power of its complete self-giving create in men repentance
and bring forgiveness for their sins.

We cannot know the words that Jesus spoke to the disciples as he interpreted the crucifixion, and opened their minds to understand. But even
to our imperfect thought there are some facts about it which are certain.

For the disciples, and for sensitive consciences in every time, the cross
meant, first—*condemnation*. Not condemnation by Jesus, but self-con-
demnation in every man's own soul. We each one are part of such a world
that the spirit of Jesus will be rejected in it. There are sins in us which
compel us to answer "yes" to the haunting question of the Negro spiritual,
"Were you there when they crucified my Lord?"

Studdert-Kennedy, the preacher with the burning heart whom the common people of England listened to and the padre whom the crudest
soldiers in the trenches understood, knew the hidden realities which may
break out into confession in the human heart. In his *Rough Rhymes* he
imagines one of the men in the mud and muck of Flanders thinking about
his life and the people he had sinned against, and the ugly half-forgotten
things that stood up now in accusing recollection. Then suddenly there
breaks in upon him an idea of the crucified Christ: Christ and the cross,
not as an indifferent Sunday school tale, but as a living fact that lays hold
of him. It was as though he saw what seemed to be—

> All men's face yet no man's face,
>   And a face no man can see,
> And it seemed to say in silent speech,
>   "Ye did 'em all to me.
> "The dirty things ye did to them,
>   "The filth ye thought was fine,

"Ye did 'em all to me," it said,
"For all their souls were mine."

And then? Listen to the stabbing truth of what comes next:

And then at last 'E said one word,
'E said just one word, "Well?"
And I said in a funny voice,
"Please can I go to 'ell?"

Such was the condemnation, coming not from without but from within, and having in it therefore the promise of redemption.

And 'E stood there and looked at me,
And 'E kind o' seemed to grow,
Till 'E shone like the sun above my 'ead,
And then he answered, "No
"You can't, that 'ell is for the blind,
"And not for those that see.
"You know that you 'ave earned it, lad,
"So you must follow me.
"Follow me on by the paths o' pain,
"Seeking what you 'ave seen,
"Until at last you can build the 'Is,'
"Wi' the bricks o' the 'Might 'ave been.' " [2]

Along with condemnation, there is *adoration*. If the disciples had loved Jesus before, they must have loved him with a new and passionate devotion as he stood in Pilate's court, and as he went to his cross to win a kingdom greater than the kingdoms of this earth. Somehow they knew that though they had failed him, he would not let them go.

During the First World War there appeared a volume of essays, the opening chapter of which was entitled, "The Beloved Captain." It told of a leader whose courage and self-forgetfulness won the utter loyalty of his men. Their whole morale was lifted when he was near. "We loved him," they said. "And there isn't anything stronger than love, when all's said and done." When he was killed, as he went to the rescue of some who had been wounded, to the spirit of his company he was still alive. "We feel his eyes on us. We still work for that wonderful smile of his." [3] And although any comparison of our life falls short of the infinite reality of Christ,

[2] G. A. Studdert-Kennedy, *Rough Rhymes of a Padre* (London: Hodder and Stoughton, 1918), pp. 14, 15. Used by permission of the publishers.
[3] Donald Hankey, *A Student in Arms* (New York: E. P. Dutton & Company, 1917), pp. 61, 68.

that illustration at least suggests the transfiguring influence of his spiritual presence. He, the crucified and risen, can be to us the incomparable "Beloved Captain."

And if the cross meant condemnation and adoration, so in waking both of those it brings *salvation:* salvation because the crucified Lord

makes us know the shame of what we are,

and the sins we need to be saved from;

feel the strength of the sacrificial

love we are saved by;

and trust the life redeemed which we can

be saved into.

The disciples were to carry this redeeming gospel to the world. Power would come upon them from on high. From nowhere else can the ultimate power come: not from human self-sufficiency, but only through the breaking in upon our little selves of One who would give himself to us.

THE CONTINUING PRESENCE

> Then he led them out as far as Bethany, and lifting up his hands he blessed them. While he blessed them, he parted from them. And they returned to Jerusalem with great joy, and were continually in the temple blessing God. (Luke 24:50-53.)

The climax of Luke's Gospel seems strangely brief, and almost abrupt. Is this all that is to be said of Jesus at the end: "He parted from them"? The answer is that this was not the end, but only the open door into a continuing reality that would be infinite. Jesus as a physical presence would be no more seen. But Jesus as an indwelling inspiration would be with those who love him, always and everywhere. The first disciples learned how that could be, and so have others who have sought to be his disciples all down the years since those first appearances of the living Lord of which the Gospels tell.

Charles E. Raven, Canon of Liverpool Cathedral and Vice-Chancellor of Cambridge University, entitled his autobiography *A Wanderer's Way.* In it he recounts the influences which most powerfully shaped his own convictions and answered for him the question, "Is Jesus alive now?"—alive, that is to say, not in ways that can be communicated only to "abnormal sensibilities or an over-active imagination," but manifest to an awareness that is in every sense normal and complete. Charles Raven had been brought up in the church, and he knew what the Gospels said about Christ and the Resurrection; but he "had no actual first-hand experience of Him as a living and present reality." Then he went to meet a friend whom he had known at Cambridge, who had taken orders and was a curate at Stoke-on-Trent, one of the most grim and depressing towns in England.

He had loved the country, and music, and all beautiful things: and he was living in this hell. I found him, and behold he was not alone. No other phrase will express it. Here walking with him in the midst of the furnace was Jesus: and its flames were an aureole. He had found that which together we had sought. . . .

Since I had seen him, he had found Jesus, and the effect of the discovery was manifest. His whole direction and outlook were altered under the new influence: there was joy and quiet confidence in his face, purpose in his life, sympathy and strength in all his actions. Jesus was alive and present to my friend as he had been to the eleven in the upper room. He was alive and present to me.[4]

And lest this might seem to have been only a fantasy, Charles Raven goes on to analyze the profundity of this experience which was a turning-point in his own life:

I went to see my friend in an entirely normal state of mental and bodily health. . . . He was a man that I knew intimately: . . . his every mood and tone of voice were familiar. He said nothing about religion or the intimate side of his present work. . . . But it was evident that a third person was there: I do not know how else to express it. You have probably had experience of meeting a friend after an interval and discovering that a new and dominating influence has come into his life. . . . Here was my friend, whose way of life I knew as accurately as an astronomer knows the path of Saturn; I could have forecast his every reaction to circumstance and foretold exactly how he would behave; and now the pull of a fresh and mighty attraction had deflected his whole orbit. . . . I could not be ten minutes in his company without perceiving what had happened. It was his comrade, not a projection of my own, that I encountered.[5]

Jesus had become "his comrade," and the inspiration at his side by which all life had been made new. In the light of that, one can understand the reality in another Christian's words: "I know that when I am helpless and feel that the things I have to do I cannot do, there is Someone greater than I who helps me. In ways I cannot predict and sometimes do not recognize the help comes. I know what St. Paul meant when he wrote: "I can do all things through him who strengtheneth me." [6]

[4] Charles E. Raven, *A Wanderer's Way* (New York: Henry Holt and Company, 1929), pp. 108-9, 119. Used by permission of George Allen & Unwin Ltd.

[5] *Ibid.*, pp. 122-23.

[6] Theodore P. Ferris, *What Jesus Did* (New York: Oxford University Press, 1963), p. 104.

And Phillips Brooks, one of the greatest souls of the last century, wrote not long before he died to a young friend who had asked him the secret of his life:

I am sure you will not think that I dream that I have any secret to tell. I have only the testimony to bear which any friend may fully bear to his friend when he is cordially asked for it, as you have asked me. . . . The more I have thought it over . . . the more sure it has seemed to me that these last years have had a peace and fulness which there did not use to be. . . . I am sure that it is a deeper knowledge and truer love of Christ. . . . I cannot tell you how personal this grows to me. He is here. He knows me and I know Him. It is the reallest thing in the world. And every day makes it realler. And one wonders with delight what it will grow to as the years go on.[7]

So for Christians in each new generation the gospel can become not a story belonging to yesterday, but the continuing fact of life enlarged and glorified through the power of the living Christ.

---

[7] Alexander V. G. Allen, *Life and Letters of Phillips Brooks* (New York: E. P. Dutton & Company, 1900), III, 454-55.

index of
references and quotations